P9-ARS-164

CUNA

CUNA

by

Joanne M. Kelly

South Brunswick
New York: A. S. Barnes and Co., Inc.
London: Thomas Yoseloff Ltd

Library of Congress Catalogue Card Number: 66-14601

A. S. Barnes and Co., Inc.
South Brunswick, New Jersey

Thomas Yoseloff Ltd
18 Charing Cross Road
London W. C. 2, England

6385
Printed in the United States of America

To Hal Hennesey
In Memory
of Agoutis, Taboga,
the Isle of Flowers,
and the Zoo in 2 F.

FOREWORD

The moon, yellow-orange in color, is shining full, big, and bright through the high green jungle trees on both banks of the Cangandi River. Off once again in the deep forest there are male howler monkeys screeching belligerently at a dark moving shadow, or hunting jungle cat. Behind me in the "chicha" hut all the Indians are drinking their homemade liquor after which the hut is named. They are laughing. They laugh big, full, not fearful of laughing too loud or too long or even falling down and laughing. They will laugh if they like, until they cry or their stomachs hurt.

And me? Well, I'm standing here looking out over a yellow path spread upon the swift river by the moon because its pretty awe-inspiring. I can smell the night smells now. They are sweet, sometimes of decay, and other times, but not very often, of Picariae or jungle cat or some other inhabitant of the bush. I've been drinking chicha too. That's the reason why I can smell better at this moment and why I can really see this moon that rises like no moon can in the northern forest. There's no moon like a full moon in San Blas, and that, incidentally, is where I am. San Blas, to answer any questions, is in the northeastern jungles of the Republic of Panama. The night breeze feels cool on my somewhat sunburnt skin.

And back there in the chicha hut is the reason why I am here—I should qualify that statement—the main reason among many reasons. The Cuna back in there are celebrating, with all of this drinking, laughter, song, dancing, and playing of river reed flutes, the birth into their society of another woman. Too bad that we've lost the capacity to celebrate like that in our own society; I think they call the process by which we have lost many of the qualities that these Indians possess "Civilization," or something of the sort, although I cannot quite see how that particular word happens to describe the process by which and how my civilization has evolved. In my own estimation, these "primitive" Indians back there in the chicha hut are far more civilized than any peoples I have ever known or met. That, of course, is one woman's opinion and it is subject matter for a debate which could last for days and I have neither the inclination nor the strength on this joyful night to argue the fact with anybody. I'm rather happy to say that there's no one within four days of traveling in any direction to argue that point *with.* I'm just going to go back to my hut, three huts down from this chicha house behind me and I'll listen to the music and merry making from my hammock and enjoy this sense of peace, contentment and this being here, being young, being alive, and knowing it in my own quiet way.

I have a mother in there, or rather she has an adopted daughter out here, outside of this chicha house she's drinking in. She's absolutely loaded by your standards and mine. Her name is Wardada and . . . how can I describe her? Ever see a four-masted windjammer under full sail come through the front door, or anything that would match it in impact? Well, that's Wardada. No doubt I'll be getting to her later, in this (I expect) lengthy history of a bit more than a year and a half's worth of simply being here. She's quite drunk. That may cause many of you to snort your indignation into the air about you, but nevertheless she *is* drunk and she's happy being drunk. By the standards of her people, it wouldn't quite do if she were not drunk, seeing that this is a Chicha feast night. And these Indians, these Cuna Indians, believe that if you *don't* get drunk at a Chicha feast, you won't go to heaven. That's a switch, humph?

By local standards, I should get to heaven judging from the amount of chicha I've consumed during the last two days and nights.

"No Lady," you say? *Two* days and nights? Don't go away yet. This feasting is going to go on all day *tomorrow* too. This is a feast of usual length, three days or so. No doubt I'll be back with all the fine young Indians in the afternoon drinking and singing, and that just happens to be exactly what each and every lady in this district will be doing, from the chief's wife on down. Each and every one of these women conducts herself and carries herself like a queen. Then again, each one is a queen according to any grandfather, husband, or son in the region.

"Ta-*dum*-te-*dum*-ta-*dum-dum-dum* . . . ta-*dum*-te-*dum*-ta-*dum dum-dum*." If you heard what those syllables stand for, the song of the river reed flutes, you'd love the melody. It's pure jungle mixed with many nights of looking at the big full moon in the sky. A rattle punctuates each italicized beat of the song and serves as the drum hereabouts. Fairly tame by most and African standards, but you should hear it for a couple of hours. Puts you into a trance. Your body may start to move in tune to the beat, as most bodies do around here. Sensual? Absolutely, but in a pure way. The body moves because it loves the song, loves what the song stands for, loves the way another body's mind has gathered up the whole forest, the whole moon into itself and compressed it into a study for flute—jungle flute. The nearest comparison I can make to it, by our standards, is applause at the end of a particularly well-acted and beautifully orchestrated performance of *Carmen*.

I'm home in my hut now and grateful that my hammock is already down. I don't have to get it out of the rafters and tie it up. That would upset Junior who generally sleeps on it . . . oh . . . he's a part of all of this too . . . even more so than I. He's a very lovable, loving bird—a cassanga parrot to be exact. I rescued him from Chief Themosthenes' cooking fire some weeks ago. You will, no doubt, hear more about him later.

It's late, and I'm tired—not in a bad way, in a very good, relaxed, sleepy way. It's the result of an individual's having expended physical or mental energy and thought the expenditure all to the good. I'll get up in the morning and I'll go for a swim in the cool clear river, or maybe I'll go hunting or to another village an hour's walk through the jungle downstream for a visit with friends, Indian friends, there. Who knows? I may even loaf. I do know that at one point tomorrow I'll wind my way to the chicha hut and have a drink or two. It is my sincere wish that anyone reading these words could join me in that drink, but that's impossible since I'll probably be back there with all of you by the time you are reading these words.

For all of you who cannot join me in that drink of chicha tomorrow, I offer you the next best thing. I will give you some idea, through these pages, of what it's like to be here, and what it's like to live with the Cuna. I'll tell you all I learned about them. When you close this book, if I have been able to impart something of what the Cuna are and stand for, some part of their joy in living, some part of their wisdom, some part of the jungle to you—minus your having to deal directly with sharks, barracuda, jiggers, snakes, exhaustion, disease, jaguars, and the absence of jelly donuts—then the effort I am making now to keep my eyes open, my candle lit, and this pencil in my hand will be worthwhile. If I impart these things to you, then I am rewarded once again for the rare privilege of being able to live with them. What more can I say, except good night back there in civilized civilization. May your night's sleep be peaceful and your morning's awakening, one of joy.

Joanne M. Kelly
Cangandi Village
Mandinga Region
San Blas,
Republic of Panama
December 5, 1963

CONTENTS

CUNA

1
THE LAUGHING MOLA

I was tired. It was spring. It had been the umptiumph night in as many weeks that I'd been working overtime at the office at my usual secretarial duties. My mind was in a vacuum, unable to focus. I would probably, as usual, make a quick supper and go straight to bed with a book. I knew that I'd only get about five pages of it read before I drifted off into oblivion from sheer exhaustion.

I switched on the living room lights, put my sweater on a chair and my pocketbook on the coffee table. It came to rest, I noticed, on top of a Cuna Indian mola I used as a cover for the table. This mola was a square piece of very colorful appliqued cloth worn by the female members of the Cuna tribe of Panama as a blouse. I had been in Panama on a holiday and stayed with friends from Boston out at Chepo near the edge of the jungle and at the end of the Pan American Highway there. The mola was bright, having many reds, oranges, bright blues, greens, and yellows. I had picked it up some eight months ago when I visited an Indian village near Chepo. I looked at the mola. Suddenly, leaping from the seemingly meaningless pattern of colors came a face I hadn't noticed before. It was the face of some ridiculous primitive clown and it was laughing. I smiled at finding it and at my own inability to notice it before. I remembered the woman I'd purchased it from. She was an elderly grandmother of the tribe who still wore the nose ring and mola dress of her people. We had talked through a translator for an hour or so. She told me of her way of life and I told her a little of mine. When I finished talking, she shook her head back and forth, then spoke:

"That's not the way life should be lived. You have not yet found what is valuable to you and what is not. But I think you will someday. . . ." This, of course, was jibberish to me at the time.

I was suddenly more tired than I had ever been, not only in body, but also in mind and most important of all, in my way of life. I couldn't stand the thought of getting up in the morning and going back to an office world, that world of people trapped in modern glass mortuaries.

I remembered the promise I had made to myself before I left the old woman's village at the Bayano River. I would return someday and spend some time, a good deal of time, with these Indians. They were a laughing and happy people, completely at peace with the world and the beautiful green jungle around them. They had intrigued and fascinated me. I spent three days in one of their villages once, a village not too primitive but still retaining many of the features of Indian life, including the thatched huts. The chief, when I left, had spoken to me saying:

"You will come back and you will go deep into the land of our people because your mind is curious about us."

I sat in the living room of my upper West Side apartment and thought on his words. If I could have left the following morning for the Republic of Panama, I would have. But that was clearly impossible. I had my work, my life here and . . ."

"Why is it impossible?" I suddenly asked myself. I had no husband, no responsibilities, other than myself. I could find no reason, other than working as a secretary as many other young girls in the city were doing and liking it, to stay. But I didn't like it. I didn't like it at all.

I had one life, one entire life to spend in whatever way I thought it best. I went to bed and slept uneasily, knowing what I would do, wanting it and fearing it at the same time.

The next day, right after a typical, cut-short lunch hour, I went into my boss' office.

"May I have a word with you, sir?" I asked.

"Of course, Joanne, come right in." I sat down. "What can I do for you?"

"Well, I'd like to give you my two weeks notice. I'm going to be out of the country on an extended vacation and I have no idea when I'm coming back."

"Is there something that's bothering you regarding your job? Maybe if you got a raise, or perhaps you should take a short vacation. You've been knocking your brains out lately. . . . Are you getting married?"

I laughed and told him that I wasn't. I was simply leaving the country and would be away for awhile.

"Why?"

"I'm going to be spending a bit of time with a tribe of Indians in Panama."

Needless to say, he didn't know what to make of this statement. He thought I was joking and said as much. I told him I wasn't. I'd never been so serious in my whole twenty-one years of life.

"In a jungle?" he asked, his eyes wide with disbelief.

"Well, that's where they live," I answered.

I was enjoying this little scene. I didn't like the man. For months when the going got a bit rough in the office, he'd come out of his office and ask me to take over for awhile. He was going to his analyst's. Most of the time he wouldn't come back, but would call in instructions on what I was to do, I being left to handle his job and write his letters, actually handling his job at one-third the salary. He'd come in the next morning, and even before I could down my coffee, we'd be at it again, full speed ahead. Then he'd tell me what his analyst thought about the whole situation of work, et. al., and I'd nod my head knowingly and in sympathy and then hurry out of his office after dictation to handle the enormous amount of work left over from the day before.

"What are you going to eat? Where are you going to live? You don't even know their language!" he stated.

"I'll learn," I replied.

Before the day was out, the entire office was abuzz with rumors that I had lost my mind, was getting married, and in one instance, and I must say it amused me, was now being kept by a rather wealthy gentleman and was accompanying him to the Bahamas to live there at his lovely winter home.

I walked out into the cool fresh spring air at 5:30 sharp for the first time in months. I felt elated at finding myself on the street while some sunlight was still in evidence. I went home and wrote to the Panamanian government requesting permission to go into the jungle area to study the Cuna Indians for a lengthy period of time. A week later I received my reply. I would be only too welcome. When would I be expected? I told my boss that I had official government permission for the trip now, and he promptly grabbed his hat and made for his analyst's office.

A week after I resigned and started making preparations for my trip, I picked up a copy of a newspaper and saw a short article there on an American girl named Jean Liedloff, who had lived for some time with a tribe of primitive Indians in the Venezuelan jungles. I thought a moment, then picked up the phone; through friends I found out her number. I dialed it and she answered. I introduced myself, apologizing for not having had a formal introduction, and told her what I was planning to do. I thought that since she had just done all of this she could be invaluable to me if she would spare me an hour's worth of her time in helping me plan my trip. She then asked one question:

"Why do you want to go and live with these Indians?"

"Because I think they have something to offer me and teach me," I stated.

"Are you in the city?" she asked.

I replied that I was.

"Come on over now. I'll help you as much as I possibly can," she answered.

I left the house and went over to her apartment.

Jean proved to be a valuable aid in helping me with preparations for the trip. She called the Charles Pfizer drug company and had me adequately supplied with all kinds of medicines I would need for myself and to treat any Indians in the villages in which I would be staying. I could learn how to use them quickly and efficiently. I would have to bring beads, cloth, needles, thread, hunting knives, and all sorts of things for trade. She gave me invaluable hints from the storehouse of knowledge she had acquired on three jungle expeditions. Jean fast became a good friend to me as well as helper.

I went home and for the next month gathered the necessary equipment I'd need for jungle living, acquired two sponsors for my trip, and studied books on Panama's zoology and ecology. I also made a careful study of the anthropological background of the tribe, and read everything I could find about them. They were even more fascinating to me after finishing my studies.

The day before I left was filled with odd jobs and a few minor crises, which are to be expected before leaving on a trip of this sort. The final crisis concerned my film, supplied to me by the Agfa Company. It had been sent by mail and hadn't yet arrived. I was scheduled to leave Newark Airport at 6:30 a.m. Thursday morning, which was just 15 hours away.

A quick call to the company brought a young German secretary and myself to the entrance of the 8th Avenue subway at 125th Street. She delivered the film into my somewhat nervous hands and I returned to my apartment. That action completed all the preparations for the trip. I had beads, mosquito netting, one machete, cloth, tape recorder, camera, poncho (which converted into a tent) for rainy weather, hunting knives for trade, clothes, medicines, and all kinds of odds and ends that I thought might be of value to me.

With several friends I went down to a jazz concert at St. Marks Place on the lower East Side, and then they joined me for a drink at my apartment to wish me well on my trip.

We laughingly went over the preparations for the trip. I now had over 500 bead necklaces made and strung for trading purposes. This job had been my friends' contribution toward my trip. Nobody who came in to visit my apartment left without stringing at least one necklace of beads. I had arranged for the use of an Agfa Optima III camera, which was invaluable to me during my stay with the Indians. I had a Norelco "100" tape recorder to record the music of the tribe. I had my antibiotics and medicines delivered by Charles Pfizer and Company. All was ready.

I finished packing with the help of my friends and they left at about 4:30 in the morning to give me some rest before I boarded the plane. But five minutes later, another delegation of well-wishers showed up to keep me company until I left for the airport.

I rode out there at the crack of dawn with another friend of mine and finally arrived at the airport. I got there five minutes before my plane was scheduled to leave due to a monumental traffic jam on the way.

I was 23 kilos overweight and had to pay a small fortune to insure delivery of my equipment to Panama City.

We took off at 7:40 a.m. and I had a very pleasant trip to Miami. We landed there a few minutes before noon. I was somewhat irritated to find out that there would be a five-hour delay in my flight to Panama City, but spent the time fruitfully in Miami Beach shopping for a few odds and ends which I had forgotten. I was still upset by the delay. I had been informed by letter that there would be some Panamanian government officials waiting for me at the airport to help me get my medicines, which were in no little quantity, through customs. I hoped that they had left word with the customs officials that I wasn't operating the biggest antibiotic smuggling ring in the Caribbean.

I finally boarded my flight at 5:45 p.m. and we took off shortly afterwards. The green Caribbean waters have never ceased to thrill me with their serenity, when viewed from the air. The Bahamas and hundreds of tiny atolls lifted their white-beached heads from the aqua water there. Sunset came soon after we got over this area. The sky was colored pink, orange, and hazy purple. Clouds on all levels, with us, below us, above us, reflected these hues and the entire panorama was awe-inspiring to see. We passed directly over Cuba and the pilot announced it on the loud speaker, thinking his passengers might be interested in viewing the island from the air. Down there, it was already night, but the mountain tops were still in twilight. We could still make out the shape of the island. Several small villages or cities were noticeable in the valleys by their lights.

The gentleman who occupied the seat next to mine on the flight was reading what appeared to be a Bible. I glanced over briefly and ascertained that it was. He was reading Timothy.

Right after passing Cuba, the plane ran into a series of thunderstorms and my traveling companion for the flight appeared to be very nervous because of them. He was occupying the window seat and whenever a particularly bright flash of lightning occurred, he jumped and looked anxiously out of his window. The "Fasten Your Seat Belts" sign flashed on and soon we were hitting air pockets. Up and down we went, the lightning flashing. He turned toward me and spoke with a thick Spanish accent:

"Doesn't the lightning bother you?"

I replied that it didn't particularly upset me.

"Oh," he replied and slipped into silence, looking out of the window.

The storm raged on. Fifteen minutes later, he asked me if I wanted to change seats with him, so that "you can watch the storm better." I knew that he simply wanted to get away from the window and agreed to do as he wished.

He also took this opportunity to introduce himself. His name was Miguel. He offered the following information to me: He didn't like storms at all. He liked white Chilean wine. Wasn't this awful? What will we do if we crash? He also asked where I was going—and told me he was going to Chile, which I had already gathered. I commented on all of his offerings and answered all his questions. He continued to read Timothy, and I continued to read a short story from a collection book I bought in Miami Airport Terminal.

The airline served a very delicious supper, and I found out why Miguel was traveling aboard this particular airline. White Chilean wine was served with supper, and more than one cup was poured for anyone who wanted doubles, triples, and so on. We would be landing in Panama in less than an hour.

For the first time since I began the preparations for my trip I began to panic. I was here—well almost. But what if the Indians didn't like me? What if they didn't let me stay with them? What would I do if I got bitten by a snake or caught malaria out in the middle of nowhere? For the first time I began to realize how much

I would have to depend upon myself and upon the Indians in any emergency. I knew that there were a few mission posts in the area—but there were none in the jungle. The Indians would have to virtually teach me from scratch about the jungle and living there. I knew almost nothing about it except what I had picked up in the books I had studied.

"Eeeeek!" I remember thinking.

But the first hurdle to jump would be getting my drugs and medicines through customs if there were no representatives of the government there to help me. I already knew where I would be staying. My friends from Boston had returned to the States, but the Roosevelt Hotel on Avenida 4 Julio was a favorite haunt of mine and central to most of the areas in the city I would be visiting or doing business in. I looked forward to spending a few days in the city before heading on out to the jungle areas. I also wanted to speak with a man who had spent almost 40 years out in the San Blas and Darien jungle—his name was Mr. Jungle Jim. I had written him of my plans, but received no answer to my letter. I hoped he would be reachable in the city.

We landed at Tocumen Airport, 17 miles outside of Panama City, a little after 11 p.m. Soon the customs officials opened my bags and examined their contents. One moustached, small-built gentleman unzippered my entire bag full of medicines. He stopped moving and stared at the contents. He raised his startled eyes to me and asked:

"You are only allowed to bring in enough medicine for your own personal use. Are you a doctor?"

I replied that I wasn't, but. . . . He stopped me in mid-sentence. "I'm afraid that you're going to have to be detained here until we finish with these people," he said pointing to the rest of the passengers on my flight. I agreed. Once the rush and work of getting them through was completed, I would be better able to explain that I had permission to bring the medicines in. I looked for the letter in my pocketbook, which I had received a week previous to my leaving, and I sat down to wait.

No sooner had I taken a seat than a representative of the tourist office entered the room and spoke hastily with the customs officials who indicated me with waving their hands. Within five minutes, all of my bags and medicines were safely in a cab. I thanked the tourist department official and then got in my cab and drove the 17 miles to Panama City. I told him that I'd be over in the morning to get a bit more information on the area I'd be visiting.

The drive was pleasant and I could smell the sweetness of the bush from the very scanty jungle area in the vicinity. I checked into the Roosevelt* and made myself at home. Music from the "El Rancho" nightclub, a block away, was filling the warm night air. I went out on the balcony. The moon was full and hung low over the Pacific. I could clearly see the beautiful Island of Taboga, where I had spent two very quiet and relaxing weeks a year ago, out over the water by the clear moon light. It was about 12 miles from the city by boat. Crickets from the grassy area in back of the hotel chirped lowly. The drums from the Latin American orchestra at the El Rancho were pulsing, it seemed, in unison with the crickets' song. It felt good to be here, and now the panic I had felt on the plane was gone. I was sure of at least giving the whole thing a try.

I took a shower, then got into bed. It was a long time, even with no sleep for over 48 hours, before I slept. I got to thinking about this place, this San Blas province where I would be going. I knew that the area was a large one. The Indians themselves numbering some 25,000 lived both in the jungle and on some off shore islands in the Caribbean. The islands there supposedly numbered 368. It was said that there was a beautiful island for every day of the week, every day of the month, and year, in the region. They lived as they have lived for hundreds of years—fishing the sea, and hunting the jungle. Their women still wore the nose rings of the tribe and the traditional dress. Their history was a fascinating one. The first contact our civilization had with any member of the tribe was through Columbus; he met the Caribs, the ancestors of the Cuna, on San Salvador when he landed.

Balboa was the next person to have any direct contact with the Cuna. His history is both a fascinating and a ruthless one. It was too bad that the first people whom any of the New World Indians met were savage adventurers in search of gold. These so-called conquerors wrought death and destruction upon millions of help-

* The Hotel Roosevelt has been since converted into an apartment building.

less Indians all over the New World, and destroyed several ancient and invaluable civilizations for all times in the name of the Spanish Crown and the Cross.

Balboa, whose full name was Vasco Nunez de Balboa, first arrived in the New World as a stowaway having secreted himself in an empty cask aboard a ship to the New World from Spain. He reached Santo Domingo in the Caribbean safely enough, but caused so much trouble there that the governor got rid of him by sending him off with a nam named Enciso to the Darien in Panama. Enciso and his men set up the colony of Santa Maria Del Darien on the San Blas coast near what is now Mulatupu Island. But Balboa was a born trouble maker. He immediately organized a revolt against Enciso, planning to unite himself with a Don Nicuesa, when the latter arrived some weeks later. When in fact Nicuesa did arrive, Balboa cast him off in a leaky ship with only 17 crew members. The vessel later sank off of Yucatan, Mexico. Balboa then shipped Enciso off to Santo Domingo under a deportation charge, and proceeded to attack and burn Indian villagers all over the coast. He attacked the villages of the Chief Careta and forced that chief into an alliance with him by kidnapping Careta's daughter and marrying her. He also obtained the friendship of Chief Comagre. Comagre's son, Panquiaco, however, saw Balboa for what he was and convinced his father by telling his father to make Balboa a few gifts of gold figures of the Indian Gods. Comagre saw that Balboa cared nothing about the exquisite workmanship and art, but promptly melted the statues down into bullion for transport back to Santo Domingo.

Panquiaco, wanting to get rid of Balboa from the land of his people, told Balboa that if it was gold he wanted, he could find it in a land further to the south, where even the humblest farmer ate off of gold dishes. After a few futile attempts to locate and get to this land of gold or El Dorado, as Balboa called it, and finding the Pacific Ocean at the same time, Balboa and his men returned to Santa Maria. He did not, however, reckon with the fact that Enciso had reached Santo Domingo and sent a messenger to the king of Spain telling that king what had happened in Panama and of the gold there. The king sent 1,500 men and appointed a governor to Panama, giving orders to sieze, arrest or kill Balboa.

The conqueror, when he returned to Santa Maria, was arrested, stripped of all of his possessions and gold, and sent back to Spain. He did, however, retain the honor of discovering the Pacific, but even at that, he was only the head of the party that reached its shores. A man named Alonso Martin was the first man to actually reach the ocean and see it. Martin was a member of Balboa's party.

After Balboa followed more men like him—adventurers, men who would kill whole villages in the name of God and the Spanish king in order to take the gold from the "infidel" bodies they had slain. The Indians soon grew to hate the Spaniards, through contact with these first few. They went off into the jungle living from the land, establishing no permanent villages, so they could not be found or killed for their gold. They hid all of their gold mines and stripped their own bodies of all but their gold necklaces and nose-rings and hid these in the mountains. Even today, I had learned, the Cuna did not like Spaniards. As recently as 1925 there had been a revolt in the province by the tribe and all white people who were living there were chased out or killed.

It was only through the intercession of an American warship that the Cuna managed to settle their dispute with Panama, and had their jungle lands protected from all outsiders by a law setting aside San Blas as a Reservation. The chief's rule, however, and more often than not Indian law, prevails over any modern law in judging crimes or acts of violence performed on Indian land—even though the acts might have been done by whites or Negroes. Even at this late date, the tribe was still considered quite fierce and independent and somewhat dangerous to outsiders.

I had read, all told, over 12 books on the Cuna tribe. I was somewhat puzzled by several large disagreements on religion, anthropological background, and way of life and was curious to find out who was right and who was wrong. Very few individuals have actually lived with the tribe and taken the trouble to learn their language and their customs from the people themselves. One man, a Mr. Porter, set himself up in the late 1920's as "King of the Darien Jungle," and lived there with the Cuna for a decade or so. It seemed that San Blas had had a more than interesting history. Ever since the first white man set foot on the shores of Panama, the Cuna and their lands have been the scene of almost unbelievable events, some of which figured very highly in the overall history of the New World.

It had only been during the first years of the 1900's that the Cuna decided to come down out of the jungle and populate the off shore islands. The "Mola" tops had been introduced by the Spaniards who didn't like the women walking around with their breasts showing, or their thighs for that matter. The woman only wore a very short skirt called a "pecha" 400 years ago. The man, simply a loin cloth.

I began to tire of thinking and the past two day's events caught up with me. With the music from the El Rancho in my ears, I drifted off to sleep.

2

AROUND PANAMA CITY

The multitudinous chirpings of at least 200 parakeets came drifting across Fourth of July Avenue from Ancon Hill. It was about 7:30 in the morning. They sounded like some kind of a natural, persistent alarm clock.

"I'm up," I whispered and climbed out of bed and got showered and dressed.

I went down to the Napoli Restaurant two blocks from the hotel and beside the university for breakfast. Here I met several Panamanian friends I had made the year before and happily greeted them. I told them of my plans and they were immediately apprehensive about my spending more than one entire day in the area. There had been some trouble on an island named Tigre and several people, Panamanian and Indian, had been hurt. Two people had been killed. This news considerably dampened my spirits, but I decided to talk the situation over with Panamanian authorities and get their opinion on the present state of hostilities, if there were any, and what had caused the trouble, so that I might avoid anything similar. But that would be later, and now was now. I liked the Napoli. It had been my favorite restaurant in the city and still was. Its terrace swarmed with all varieties of well-kept tropical foliage and the food and service were always excellent.

This was one place where a good meal could be enjoyed for any length of time in complete peace and relaxation. My favorite dish here, and I had come often in the evening during my last stay in the city to enjoy it, was Clams Neopolitan.

After breakfast, I went off to the tourist office to see Mr. Dominguez who had assisted me in getting in touch with the various individuals I wanted to talk to in the city, who knew San Blas. I also found out that Mr. Jungle Jim, whose picture I had come upon in a tourist magazine, was at the El Panama Hilton and had an office in the lobby there. A quick call revealed that he was in town and would be free to talk with me if I came on over. I left the tourist office and took a cab to the El Panama.

The hotel, itself, was one of the most beautiful structures in Panama City. I had spent many evenings in its gambling casino on the first floor playing blackjack. The El Bombarde bar was also quite interesting, it having a lovely organ, the parts of which were lighted up and moving behind glass. Whenever the musician played, the mixing of a few brandy alexanders and the soft play of light upon the moving parts of the organ, and the music, put you into an almost trance-like state.

I walked into the lobby and found Mr. Jungle Jim's box-like office right near the El Bombarde bar. It looked as though the man behind the desk might be Mr. Jungle Jim, but I wanted to make sure.

"I'd like to speak to Mr. Jungle Jim," I said.

"I'm Mr. Jungle Jim," he replied. "What can I do for you?"

I told him that the tourist office had called earlier that morning about me.

He immediately eyed me suspiciously with his bright blue eyes and motioned me with a head full of white hair around the counter of his desk to the door on the other side. Before we could get any better acquainted, an American woman came to ask him about tours into the San Blas area. She was nervously twisting a lock of grey hair with her forefinger and thumb while she spoke.

"Are these islands really as they've always been or do the natives dress up just to put on a show for the tourists?" She was standing there, still twisting the lock, looking somewhat like a shark ready to pounce on a little fish.

Mr. Jim brought his palms down full force on the counter. She jumped and looked startled.

"Well now," he drawled in a strong southern accent, "the San Blas have been living the way you'll see them for hundreds of years. There's nobody going to change those people for love or money." He eyed the woman. "Does that answer your question?"

"Oh!" she replied, then wandered off across the lobby twirling a lock of hair on the other side of her head.

"Tourists!" snorted Jungle Jim, under his breath. Then he realized I was there and turned to me.

"Well now, tell me just what you had in mind doing out in San Blas."

I told him.

When I finished he looked fairly upset.

"You know," he bent low and whispered, "the only good Indian is a dead Indian."

"Well, for somebody who does business with them and has been doing business with and by them for four decades, you don't sound too enthusiastic about it," I replied.

"Well, I mean what I say. Why do you want to go down there and LIVE with 'em. I've been down here for 43 years and I know what I'm talking about. You can't trust 'em as far as I can throw a bull."

"Do you have any objection to my going out there?"

"Yes. I sure as hell do. A girl like you can't go running around in the middle of the bush with a bunch of untrustworthy Indians—that's jungle out there! Do you know what I mean?" He looked at me expecting an answer.

"What are they going to do? Carry me off and rape me?" I asked, getting slightly angry with the man. He was obviously not going to help me either understand the lay of the land or to get there. He didn't want me there.

"Now don't go getting all hot under the collar. I'm just telling you what I know about them. No, I don't *think* they'll do that, but they'll rob you blind of everything you got."

"That isn't the impression I've been getting from everybody else. They seem to think these people are pretty nice and hospitable."

"Oh, they are hospitable all right. They'll give you a hammock to sleep in, feed you fish and plantains, boiled incidentally, all the time, every day, and they'll let you stay, BUT, they'll rob you blind the moment you turn your back."

"Why do you bring tourists into the area?" I asked.

"Business," he replied.

"Then, as a matter of business, may I book passage to San Blas on one of your planes."

"I'm warning you. You don't know what you're getting into."

"And I'm asking a chance to find out. I understand that there are some trading boats that visit these islands that go out of Colon. One way or another, I intend to go out there."

"O.K., O.K. I'll book your passage to leave on Monday. Be up at 5:30 a.m. I'll send a car to pick you up and deliver you to the airport. I'm going out there myself on Sunday. Where are you staying?"

I told him.

"Incidentally, young lady, I may as well warn you, it's the rainy season in the jungle. There's malaria mosquitoes all over the place and the traveling is hampered by mud, mud, mud. They got some pretty bad snakes back there, and incidentally, a few minor animals like jaguar, ocelot, tapir, and the rest."

"Yes, the fer-de-lance, bush master, and a few more. I've been studying herpetology books on their habits and the effects of their poison. I've made trips to both the Staten Island and Bronx Zoo to get good close looks at each."

He looked up from his writing pad, on which he had been recording my booking passage to San Blas. He evidently hadn't expected me to take the trouble to study up on a few of the inhabitants of the Panamanian jungles.

"I've also been told that the rainy season starts to slacken off around November. I'm going to be staying in the islands until that time—probably on Ailigandi, Playon Chico, and Mulatupu and Pine Islands. Then I'll go on into the jungle regions."

He was looking at me as though to say "Well, what are you going to say next?"

I was upset. I needed this man's help and his knowledge to

supplement my own. If he'd just settle down and realize that I was going, then he could be invaluable to me as a source of information on the area.

"Do you really think that anybody would be as irresponsible to go charging off into the jungle without any idea of what was there in the way of plants, people, and animals?

"Yes," replied Jim and went back to his writing. "A man went back there three years ago. He was in the jungle for all of three weeks before they carried him out of there more dead than alive with fever."

He put down his pencil, took off his glasses and went over and sat down. He sighed. He examined me, trying to know what to make of me.

"Yep. You're going." He wasn't smiling.

"You sound like the voice of doom," I commented.

"I'm just being fatherly," he replied.

I left and went back to the tourist office, saying goodbye to Jim and receiving a slip of paper telling me what flight I was taking and that the car would meet me at the hotel and take me to the airport. I was still upset in the cab and tried to evaluate or make head or tails of why Jim was trying to keep me as far away from San Blas as he could. He evidently felt guilty about taking some other people in the past, out to San Blas, only to see them hurt or injured in some way or to come down with a tropical disease. If these people, as Jim had said, were totally unprepared, then as far as I was concerned they deserved to come down with something. (This group, did not, of course, include his tourists. He evidently took excellent care of them.) I hoped that the man would come around and at least give me some kind of idea of his own personal experiences with the Cuna and the jungle area.

I spent the afternoon studying magazine articles written on San Blas that were in the tourist office files. I mentioned nothing of my meeting with Mr. Jungle Jim to anyone.

Late that evening after clams at the Napoli, I went up to the National Museum and talked with Professor Reina Torres. She had, I understood, spent a bit of time on Ailigandi as the guest of Chief Ikwaniktipippi. Her attitude on what I'd find was exactly the opposite of Jim's although I didn't discuss that with her. She told me of the people's laws and their way of life as seen first hand by herself.

"They'll hold a council meeting on the island the first night you get there. Don't let this frighten you. It's not held so that the Indians can decide whether you will be permitted to stay or not, as most people think. It is simply so that the islanders and Indians living there can get a chance to know why you are there and how long you plan to stay."

She also informed me that it was against Cuna law to turn a stranger away from their door.

"They believe that God will punish them."

I went home to the hotel that evening feeling much better for having talked to Professor Torres.

Most of the next day was spent wandering around Panama City, visiting the different places that I had particularly enjoyed seeing on my last visit.

I walked from the hotel, down to Avenida Central, then down past Plaza 5 Mayo and the international stores there, and down to the harbor area. I wanted to spend a bit of time on the sea wall at Plaza de Francia near Callé 1. The wall itself had been constructed by Panama City's original inhabitants to protect their city against pirates. The original city had been burned to the ground by Morgan and his gang a few years previous to the founding of the new city. The ruins of Old Panama can still be seen a few miles out of the city and up the Pan American Highway.

I could again see from the sea wall the beautiful Island of Flowers—Taboga, floating like an emerald on the aqua sea. Here. also, can be seen the monument built to the Frenchmen who attempted to build the Panama Canal before the Americans tried. I went back down to Avenida Central, then over to the National Lottery Office and down towards the harbor on that side of town. Here was located the Mercado Publico or public market place. It was my favorite spot in the city for local color and plain enjoyment of people. Inhabitants of every part of Panama showed up here to sell their wares. There were chickens and marmosets, live iguana, all kinds of vegetables, the never-to-be-without National Lottery salesmen and women, the meat market, the pottery section. My walks through this district were always enjoyable. I never saw everything there, but never failed to find something new and interesting each time I turned a corner.

From here I recrossed town again, noting with pleasure the presence of numerous banana boats in the harbor. The entire district I was leaving would be Disneyland to a color photographer.

Next I went in to see the Church of the Golden Altar again. When Morgan's pirates raided Old Panama City, the priests of the church painted this altar black to preserve it from the invaders. After the Church was burned, the priests rescued the altar and brought it to Panama City with them. Today it is quite a famous tourist attraction. I liked the place because of the quiet that generally reigned there and the splendor of its decorations.

Back up on Avenida Central, I spent the afternoon window shopping at the exotic free port market. Many articles here can be bought for a fraction of their United States' retail price.

It was late afternoon by this time, so I ran over to the El Bombarde for a cocktail. I was hoping I wouldn't run into Jungle Jim at that time. I didn't want to speak with him until I was safely in San Blas. I didn't, and thoroughly enjoyed my martini while watching the organ and listening to its music.

I left around six, then went up to the Napoli to gourge myself on probably the last Clams Neopolitan I'd get to see in many months. I was leaving the next morning for San Blas. While I was eating, one of the local girls, a prostitute by trade, came by the Napoli and every kitchen hand came flying to the door to say hello to her. She was a very warm person and conversed with them at great length about the trend of business lately. The local prostitutes, I had observed, were very uninhibited about their trade, and nobody seemed to mind them. All the girls I had noticed were generally quite content and all smiles whenever they appeared anywhere. I much preferred this kind of attitude toward the trade, which, let's face it, it *is*, than one of hiding it under bushels of lies and the "Prostitution here in our fair city? Oh, my God!" attitude I have seen expressed elsewhere. Then, of course, that is only one person's opinion and subject to debate from all sides.

I went home to the hotel and did a bit more reading on materials I had gathered from the tourist office, packed my belongings, and went to bed quite early. I had to be up at five if I were going to catch my ride and plane out of Paitilla Airport to Porvenir Island. I called downstairs to the desk to be awakened at a quarter to five in the morning, turned out the light, and was again lulled to sleep by the marvelous band of the El Rancho.

3

PORVENIR

The persistent ring of the telephone got me on my feet and packing my things. I took my bags downstairs. The car, which Jungle Jim said he'd arrange for me, was nowhere in sight. A quick call to the airport informed me that my plane was now on the runway and ready to take off. I asked the pilot, whom I called to the phone, to hold the plane for a few minutes, and told him that I was on my way.

"How long does it take to get to Paitilla Airport from here?" I asked in Spanish of the night clerk at the desk.

"Ten minutes," he replied.

"Can you hold the plane for 15 minutes?" I asked the pilot.

He replied that he would, but no longer than 15 minutes.

I flagged down an early morning cab and soon was racing toward the airport across the city. We made it in 11 minutes. My bags were loaded onto the plane and a minute later we were in the air. The plane was a small Cesna 182, the type out of which, three years previous to all of this, I used to parachute with my sport parachuting club in Manasas, Virginia. I noted by the compass that we were heading east. Ahead of us were a number of dark rain clouds; the weather didn't look too good at all. There were two other passengers aboard besides the pilot and myself—a young boy named Randy and his father. They were very good friends of Jim's.

We hit a violent rain storm that started to throw us about like a basketball bouncing on a court. We went up, then down, then I noticed that the direcion finder indicated that we were turning back, on a southwesterly course. The weather was a bit too bad and we weren't able to get through.

We circled awhile, then the pilot found a hole in the clouds and went through over the jungle mountains. Not for any amount of money would I have attempted to jump into that tangled green forest. Then I looked out of the window to my left. There was a mountain there. The fact that it was there didn't bother me quite as much as the fact that *it* was higher than *we* were. To my amazement and relief we flew safely over the mountain and headed toward a large bay of water, Mandinga Bay as I later discovered, and into the sparkling sunshine of this Caribbean shore of Panama.

Randy called out to his father: "There it is!"

I looked down into the bay. It was covered with numerous little islands. There was some kind of a small fishing craft under sail down there, but I couldn't make out the craft's occupants. The island that Randy was focusing his attention on, however, was a tiny little spot off toward the end of the bay. As we neared it, I noticed a white strip down the middle of it. It was obviously a landing strip, but it seemed as though a sea gull would have had trouble landing and taking off on it. We circled the island. The landing strip still looked very small to me. I saw only four buildings—three on the northwestern part of the island, and a lone structure on the south side. The entire island, except for the landing strip, was covered with coconut trees. Two large boats, traders I assumed, were tied up at a dock over on the northwestern side of the island and in front of the three buildings. This was Porvenir Island, capital of San Blas. It looked like a small trading post visited infrequently by white men, in the middle of nowhere.

We flew very low and made our approach to the field. The pilot seemed to be playing tag with several coral reefs just under the surface of the water, then we ran on a coral runway and reversed to a stop. When we did finally stop, it seemed as though we had about eight feet worth of runway left. Bush pilots are not unlike God in some ways. I grew to respect the absolute courage and nerve of these men in the months to come. They travelled in the most incredible weather and never had one accident during all of the time I was to spend in San Blas.

We taxied back to the south side of the runway near the lone structure there. It was Jungle Jim's hotel, the Cuna Inn. Jungle Jim himself, wearing the most God-awful pair of loud shorts I've ever set eyes on, came running up to the plane. Then I looked closer. His shorts were actually made in a mola design. He had evidently paid one of the Indians to sew a mola design directly onto them. Somehow I was relieved to find that out.

He called to a small San Blas boy named Machi to grab my bags and then helped all of us out of the plane. He motioned for us to follow Machi, then started some kind of a hassel with the pilot about something which the latter had forgotten to deliver. As I walked away I could hear him bellowing:

"I ordered those things a week ago. Why aren't they here?"

I started to giggle. Of all the people I had ever met he seemed to be the most belligerent of them all, but in a likeable way. He probably hated me by this time, but nevertheless, I thought anybody who would dare to wear shorts in those colors must have *something* to him. I hoped that we wouldn't get into another argument about whether I would stay or go.

He walked back to the hotel muttering to the path he tread upon, then jumped up the steps to the inn. I was introduced to Randy's father, a gentleman named Don, and to Randy himself. The little boy was adorable and I wished I could carry him off and adopt him, but he had a very worthy and good father. He was about eight years old. Black curley hair topped his head and what was underneath was pure boy. He ran off to look into a bit of construction work that was going on near the hotel. It looked as if Jim were adding an additional building, rather than four rooms and baths. Randy picked up a hammer and was about to use it on some newly poured cement when Jim bellowed:

"Get outa' there you lounge lizard before I come over there and skin you alive."

The boy's father simply called: "Randy!"

Randy came bounding up onto the porch laughing and deposited himself in a hammock.

Most of the morning was spent on the porch of the Cuna Inn while all three of us lounged around drinking coffee. I learned that Jungle Jim's true name was James Kyle Price and that he was from West Virginia. He had played football for Auburn in his younger college days, and had first come to South America when he was twenty-two years old. He was now in his sixties.

His first trip into the area had been to Honduras with the United Fruit Company. During this trip, he had acquired the spark of adventure that had sent him off to the jungle again—this time with various scientific expeditions in the same region. He had the distinction of being the first white man to ever cross the mountains from Panama into Colombia. The trip down the San Blas Cordilla took him one month. He had spent several years in the interior of Panama living with the Choco Indians and knew everything there was to know about them, as he is eager to admit.

I made a comment to the effect that for a man who didn't like Indians, he seemed to have gone out of his way to spend quite a lot of time with them.

He looked at me and snorted.

We had a very delicious lunch cooked by Machi, who evidently was the jack of all trades around the hotel. Jim asked around to see if anybody would like to go spear fishing off one of the nearby islands and we all readily replied that we would like to. I'd be seeing the Indians the next day and wanted to relax a bit from the trip itself before I started in on my project.

Machi demonstrated another of his abilities by readying a pontoon style boat and getting a 40 h.p. motor attached to it. Machi seemed to be able to do just about everything. I mentioned the fact to Jim.

"Should," he replied. "Machi's been with me for 23 years. I raised that boy from a baby."

Before I could get into any further details of this fascinating admission, Jim was off giving us another vivid descripton of one of his many adventures in the high jungle.

Then we all settled back to take in the beautiful scenery around us. I was *completely* taken with it. I thought Taboga and that area out in the Pacific beautiful, but this was five times more breathtaking. To the south, high grey-blue mountains mounted out of the jungle and reached to the clouds. In front of these were numerous small islands, each one a lovely gem and topped with coconut trees. To the north was a great reef and the deep open Caribbean Sea. To the west was the high point and some kind of a radar station. I later found out that this point housed a family who cared for the directional radio beam directing all commercial airline traffic to South America. To the southwest, the large ten-mile long Mandinga Bay spread out. In this bay, more than 7,000 Cuna Indians lived on the small off shore islands. In back of us was Porvenir.

The warm breeze felt like a bath to my skin. I closed my eyes and rested my head against the back of my seat.

We arrived at a lovely little island about 12 miles east of Porvenir called Achutupu Island. That meant Dog Island, so Jim informed us. It was an inappropriate name for such a lovely spot. We beached our boat right beside the hull of some kind of sunken craft on the west side of the island. It seemed that this boat, the *Buenaventura* was her name, went down after she had sprung a leak some months previous to this. The Indians had long since stripped her of anything valuable. It had been carrying, among other things, bathroom tile, as I later discovered. Then I remembered the tile in the bathrooms of Jim's hotel and laughed. This is where he had gotten a hold of it—clear salvage. There was still some tile left aboard when I examined her later that afternoon.

Although I had been skin diving before, I had never been skin diving in tropical waters and looked forward to the sights I would see there. Jim had brought face masks and snorkel tubes with him. We went ashore and waded into the water on the west side of the island.

"You can swim?" asked Jim.

I nodded my head. My career navy father had had me in the water ever since I was one and a half. He still made the statement that I could swim a mile before I could walk that length unaided on land. I took a cigarette and broke it, letting the tobacco into my face mask. I mixed saliva with this, then washed the mixture out with salt water. Now my face mask would not cloud under water. I slipped under the surface of the water.

My first view of the Caribbean coral reefs was breathtaking.

Here was another world of color ranging from the dullest brown to the brightest coral and the most delicate blue. Tiny varieties of every color fish darted here and there seeking the protection of the reefs from the large intruders—us. I left the group and went out a bit further. I recognized the shape of the red snapper, but most of the fish were completely unfamiliar to me. This would, however, be excellent spear fishing territory. I was anxious to go back and get a spear gun from shore. I made a semi-turn only to find Jim some ten yards behind me signaling frantically for "stop-retreat." Then he pointed directly out to my left. I caught sight of a long, greenish fish and I caught my breath. He was big and I knew he was deadly, but I couldn't think of its name. I quickly, but with slow and cautious movements, retreated, still facing whatever it was. I kept near the reefs so that I could get up on one if the fish came for me. When I could touch bottom, I lifted my head briefly to ascertain the whereabouts of everybody else. Jim was just wading out of the water, the others were ashore. He called toward them: "Barracuda!"

Back on the beach, Jim cautioned me against leaving the group at any time, just in case something which had just happened, would happen. He also told me that I had done the right thing in moving slowly to get out of its way.

"Damn thing was nearly four feet long." He loaded his spear gun by pulling back the first of two rubber ropes and clicking it into place. He threw on the safety and tested it in the sand. It was alright. "Could have cut you or me right in half with one 'clomp' of those teeth." He turned to face me. "Ever see a barracuda out of water?"

I replied that I hadn't.

"We'll do a bit of fishing on the way back to see if we can find you one to look at. You've never seen a mouth full of teeth like that per square inch of fish in your whole life."

I replied that I hoped I wouldn't get the chance to examine them until I was out of the water. Jim laughed, then conducted us all over to the east side of the island. There was a reef there, he told us, right off shore with plenty of game fish to keep us happy. He was right. I got two fish he called parrot fish right off and later found them to be very good eating. Our catch for the afternoon would be more than sufficient to feed us that night. After spending a good two hours worth of time on Achutupu, we reboarded the boat and got ourselves back to Porvenir in good time.

I saw my first San Blas sunset that night and was silent. There are no words I can use to describe something that turns the sky orange, pink, red, gold, blue, maroon, and violet with one beautiful star shining right on top of the whole scene. It seemed that nobody else paid that much attention to it, but then Jim turned and said: "Pretty, umph?" "Amazingly so," I replied. "That's how it goes down every night," he answered.

"And you were trying to keep me from seeing it?" I asked laughingly.

"That's when I thought you were a damned tourist and one of that rare breed of fools—a New Yorker."

"Oh God. What did we ever do to you?"

"If I could tell you my whole storage house of facts about people from Brooklyn and the Bronx and Manhattan. . . . Listen, I don't even want to go into it."

"I didn't come here as a tourist, Jim."

"I know that now, but I wasn't quite sure at first."

We spent the rest of the trip in silence. Randy was trawling for barracuda off the stern, but had no luck that evening.

When we got back to the inn, I took a quick cool shower and got dressed for dinner. The tide was down, so I walked along the beach all over the island to familiarize myself with the lay of the land there. The three buildings over to the northwest were, I found out, Panamanian government buildings and here the governor, or "entondiente" as he was called by Jim, of San Blas lived. One building was a large residence for the government personnel who numbered some five people. The structure just in back of this was a national guardhouse, housing some four Cuna Indians trained to be policemen. Below that was a jail. The police lived on the second floor. The third building was an office building used by the officials to conduct their work, which consisted for the most part of keeping records pertaining to the coming and going of Cuna from the reservation and trading boats entering and leaving the area.

I went back to the inn and discovered that Machi had supper

ready. It had taken him all of twenty-five minutes. I was amazed. We ate the fish we had caught earlier that afternoon and they were quite good, thanks to Machi's cooking.

Don, Jim, and I took our coffee out to the porch and Randy went down to the beach to see what he could see as only an eight-year-old boy can.

We talked for a few hours out there, enjoying the soft night breezes coming in from the southeast. I liked the quality of peace here very much.

That is, until Jim once again decided that I'd better not go and live with the Indians.

He went into a long speech on the various horrors of disease and sanitary conditions that the Indians lived with.

"And," he continued, "when they have one of these Chicha feasts, you'd better get off the island completely. There's nothing worse on God's green earth than a drunken Indian."

"Listen, Jim," I replied, "I'm not going to live with these people to get an idea of what their sanitary conditions, diseases, or Chicha feasts are or how bad things can get when any of those three happen to fall across my path. I'm going to live with them because I want to learn something from them. From what I have seen personally, they have a wonderful sense of simplicity that I'd like to understand. I'd like to find out why they're so happy and uncomplicated. I've taken precautions against the diseases I could get. My arms have been sore for a month from getting needles shoved in them at least two times a week. I've got more medicines than I could use in a lifetime to treat anything I could possibly catch down here. I know what their sanitary conditions are because I've been talking to some people who have lived among the Cuna. They happen to be relatively clean. Now I don't want to go getting into another argument with you. If I do run into trouble, I'd like to be able to come on back here and not be shot at or thrown off the porch because of a past argument with you. I'm going."

"O.K., redhead," replied Jim. "Get the bee out of your bonnet. I just wanted to tell you about the bad things so that you wouldn't be disillusioned when you met up with them. How about a drink?"

I accepted; the three of us had a scotch and soda and settled ourselves down into some peaceful conversation. I realized what Jim had been trying to do. In some way he wanted to warn me just in case I hadn't planned on any of what he told me. I had, but still appreciated his concern for me and respected his opinions, no matter how they differed from mine. Who knew? Perhaps things would be a bit much for me. Only time would tell.

Jim suggested that I go over and spend a week or so on Wichub-Huala Island, Machi's home island, before I started on down the coast. I thought it would be a good idea. Jim then said:

"Give you a chance to see what you're getting into before you commit yourself to six months worth of it."

"That's the first logical and agreeable thing you've said to me since I met you."

He snorted at me, then went tracking off to his room and bed, along with Don.

I stayed on the porch for awhile reflecting on the loveliness of the region. Tomorrow I'd get to met the people with whom I was to spend a good half year of my life. This first day in San Blas, however, had pretty well cemented my determination to continue along as I had planned. I had never seen such beauty in my life.

"It's like the Tahiti of the Caribbean," I remember thinking. I went off to my own room and sleep.

4
WICHUB-HUALA

The smell of bacon and eggs cooking drifted into my room early the next morning and I got up, showered, and dressed. Machi flashed a smile at me when I got into the dining room and asked if I'd like breakfast now or later. Jim was already up, and I found out he'd eaten an hour ago. He was out supervising the construction of the addition to his hotel with Machi's father-in-law, Alfredo.

I sat down to a very delicious breakfast, and asked Machi if he wouldn't join me for coffee. He did. He told me that he had overheard the conversation of the evening before, and when he had gone home that night, spoke to Wichub-Huala's chief in my name. The elderly chief had stated that I would be welcome on the island. He also told me that his father-in-law, Alfredo, was the second chief of Wichub-Huala. He found out that I didn't have a hammock with me and told me he'd arrange for one for my use during the length of time I'd be remaining on Wichub-Huala. He said that the people were curious to see me. Word had been passed along to them by the chief that I would be coming to live with them. Machi also told me that his wife, Fulvia, and his mother-in-law, Eme, would take very good care of me. When he mentioned Fulvia, Machi's face lighted up in a very special way. He was obviously very much in love with her. I found out later that he had been married for six months and it was still a "honeymoon" as far as he was concerned. Machi then asked me why I wanted to live with his people. I told him about my staying for a few days at the Bayano River with some of his more modern brothers. I also told him of meeting the old woman and my desire to learn a bit more about the Cuna.

He nodded his head, then smiled and asked me if I liked to eat fish. I told him that I did. He asked me what my thoughts were on the Indians. I told him that from what I had seen, I was quite impressed. He smiled again, got up, and told me that he would take me to the village right after breakfast.

At 8:30, Machi got the boat ready and Jim, Don, Randy, and I went over the half-mile to Wichub-Huala Island.

We headed toward two islands. Machi explained to me that the farthest one away from us was called Nalu Nega—that meant red snapper's house. The one nearest to us was his home, Wichub-Huala, and it didn't mean anything in particular. It was just the name of the place.

Nalu Nega had many coconut trees growing between the huts there. Wichub-Huala was a bit more crowded and there were fewer coconut trees in evidence. Thatched huts were all over the place, and in some instances, hanging right over the ocean and held in place by piles there. We curved into the dock at Wichub-Huala Island and soon were walking down what was obviously the main street of a very clean little village. This was generally where Jim took his tourists, both here and over to Nalu Nega. The youngsters were naked for the most part, except for strings of teeth of some animal around their necks. Their bodies were a deep gold color, and they were beautiful. Their faces were smiling, and they had a distinct oriental look to them. Some of the younger boys had sun bleached hair that was red and in some cases even blond in color. All of the adults had straight black hair. The women came immediately up to the group of us and held molas out in front of them at arm's length. The tourists probably bought these from the people when they came. Machi explained that we were not tourists and the people stopped trying to sell us their wares. The women were beautifully dressed. They wore red head scarfs which came down partially covering black bangs across their foreheads. Large globs of circular gold earrings stuck out below this scarf.

"They're pure 11 karat gold," whispered Jim.

Their faces were all smiles and they were quite beautiful even with the gold nose ring that pierced that appendage. Strings and strings of beads hung around their necks. Some of the other women had bars of gold strung on necklaces here. Each woman wore a colorful mola, and each mola was totally different in design and concept from the next. The mola blouse was tucked into a skirt which was wrapped around their waists and hung to just below the knee. On their arms they wore beads in two places—just above their elbows and above their wrists. They also wore beads around their ankles and calves. They chattered to each other in a very strong sounding language, but with smiles all over the place.

One woman was nursing a young boy child from her breast, having lifted her mola up to uncover it. She was completely oblivious to any Western norms on the subject and was interested only in watching the tourists walking along in her village. Another woman cooed to her baby and held the child up in front of her. The baby laughed as she rubbed her nose back and forth along its nose. The younger boys were, for the most part, naked. Others a little bit older in age, around twelve or so, just wore shorts. The younger girls wore their mothers' molas, and these came down in some cases clear to the ground. The children were playing and having a grand old time. Not many men were visible in the village. I later found out that most of these had gone to the jungle to get the day's food. They would be back later in the day. The men that were here, however, wore a strange sort of baggy trousers and brightly colored, obviously homemade shirts. They stayed pretty much in the background, watching us from the sidelines.

Some of the women were pointing at me, then pointing at a young, very pretty girl who was partially hidden by a tree. "That's Fulvia," whispered Machi. "She's my wife—isn't she bonita?" I told him that she was. "She look to see who you are that comes to stay at our house."

The village babies were fat, lovable little things with brilliant, fetching smiles. I noticed, however, that a large percentage of these had something wrong with their eyes. I wondered if the terramycin I had would help this condition.

Machi brought me over to his mother-in-law's house and introduced me to Eme, his mother-in-law, and then to his wife who was about 16. The house was small and compact, and I was shown a small area where my hammock would be slung. Eme was a personality. She looked at me, then came over and pulled a lock of my hair, then burst into laughter.

"She thought that it wasn't real," commented Machi. Evidently these people were not used to redheads.

For a good hour I walked up and down the four streets of the tiny, neat, very clean little village. Everyone was smiling and friendly. I liked them immediately. There was a basic quality of peace and love of life in their faces. Yes, I could and would live with these people.

"Don't let 'em fool you now," whispered Jim.

This time I snorted at him and went on with my walk.

When we got back to Porvenir, a delegation of Indians, Eme, Fulvia, and another girl, along with two children and a tiny white dog, showed up.

Jim came out to the porch laughing.

"They heard you were going to live with 'em and decided to come on over and get a good look at you in your natural environment," he said.

I started to laugh.

I got up from my hammock and went down the steps to sit with this family for awhile. All the women had a long black line painted down their nose. I found out later that that was to protect them from "nia" the devil. As soon as I sat down to talk with these people, or try to, each one hid her face in her red scarf and started to giggle uproariously. Either I was pretty funny looking with my red hair or they were very shy. The dog was eyeing me through the legs of the women with his tail between his legs. He was suspicious of the whole procedure.

"Fire with fire," I thought. I went in and got a table cloth, put it over my head, and started to imitate their laughter while covering my face as they were doing. They roared and bobbed up and down with laughter. The dog went shooting off down the beach, having had enough of whatever it was for the time being.

Eme motioned for me to come. I saw a dug-out waiting up the beach a bit. In it was Alfredo's wife. She wore a continual smile on her face, and her eyes twinkled. She was very small, as were all the women and men I saw earlier. With Machi and Alfredo's help I got a few things, including my tape recorder, into the dug-out and soon we were skimming across the water under the power of large carved paddles. The canoe was very heavily loaded with people and I hoped that it would stay afloat out in the bay. There were six people in all plus the dog and white caps were visible beyond the coral reefs. I pulled out a rain coat I had brought with me and covered my belongings. We were going to get a bit wet, that I could see. I took a spare paddle from the bottom of the dug-out and lent a hand with getting us back to Wichub-Huala. The women were surprised to see that I knew how to use the paddle. Ten seasons at camp in Maine had left me with something of a knowledge of canoes.

A few waves did in fact make it over the side of the dug-out, but we reached Eme's hut safely enough and the women helped me get my belongings into the sleeping hut.

The sleeping hut itself, like all sleeping huts I was to see in the future, was very dark inside and I wondered how these women ever came from bright daylight into the hut and yet were able to see everything. Somewhere in the village a song I was to hear many times in future months drifted to me. It was that of a mother singing a primitive lullaby-chant to her baby to make it sleep.

After I got everything into place I went out to sit in back of the hut on a few chairs and to talk, if I could, with the family. By means of sign language and my limited Spanish we got a few ideas passed between us.

Eme began by pointing to one of my suitcases and asked, "Mesi?"

I replied that I was a Miss. "I don't have a man," I said in Spanish.

I was to find out later that she was asking if I had beads. Machi had evidentally informed the family that I had brought many beads for trade.

One of the many women who then gathered at the hut translated for me. She spoke a bit of Spanish. She told the women that I was single and that I didn't have any children. I then explained to the woman that I was going to take a walk through the village again to see my new home. I walked out of the sleeping hut into the family garden. Alfredo had planted a few banana trees in the back yard along with some yucca plants. The cooking hut was right in back of the sleeping hut and I peeked in here to see what I could see. There was a fire going here and a cauldron full of something or another was cooking. I walked out the front gate and continued walking through the village.

I suddenly looked behind me to find that I had an escort—about 20 women and 30 children. I was naturally surprised and turned to find out why they were following me. My sudden turn frightened the children and they took off in all directions. What had started out to be a simple walk turned out to be somewhat of a social event. The whole entourage was growing in number and I was amused to laughing aloud by the whole thing. Most of the women were stripped down to the waist, it being a hot afternoon, and were walking about "sans" mola but with their skirts in place. Some of them were carrying their lovely children. They came in all shapes and sizes, and each one had a lovely bright-eyed smile—as long as I kept my distance. If I came close to admire these, they would immediately burst into tears.

I took stock of Wichub-Huala. There were about 30 some odd huts on the island and two cement buildings. The cement structures served as trading posts. Three main streets separated the closely placed houses. Coconut trees, banana plants, bread fruit trees, orange trees, and other plants could be seen growing between the huts. Each family had two huts. One served as the sleeping hut, the other as the "kitchen" or cooking hut. There were about ten people to a sleeping hut on the average. The population of the island, therefore, was upward of 300 people. The huts themselves were made from a kind of reed which formed all the walls, and a kind of thatch which formed the roof. There were no windows in any of the huts, and the larger sleeping huts had two doors—one in the front and another in the rear. There was no furniture to speak of in any of these huts. There were, however, small carved seats representing some kind of four legged animal with a head. Small tables were placed, about two to a cooking hut, in that structure. The rafters of the cooking hut served as closets; molas, skirts, and other articles of clothing were hung up there. The average length of the sleeping hut was about 30 feet—its width about 15 feet. The cooking hut was about ten feet long by seven wide.

The younger girls in the village had long, straight black hair. The older girls and women had hair about ear length. I remembered that each of the girls, upon maturity, went through a hair cutting ceremony that left them completely bald. When their hair grew back to ear length, they were considered ready to marry and have children. Some of the young married girls were about fourteen or fifteen years of age. I must have seemed like quite an old maid to these young wives.

The men were now in considerable number. Most of these that I saw were sharpening machetes, or repairing fishing equipment and nets outside of their huts. The others were playing with their small sons and daughters outside of the huts. Others were just coming in from the beach with fish in baskets. They were the hunters and farmers of the tribe. The women tended to the home. A great number of the rest of the women were sewing the mola dress tops they wore. This was evidently their answer to knitting.

I was asked to sit down and have a cup of cocoa drink by the mother of a large brood of children. Then all the rest of the women came to sit down and examine me. I was still wearing dungarees and a light blue blouse. I had two strings of my own beads around my neck, wanting to see how the women liked them before I tried to do any trading with them. They evidently liked them very much because several came over to finger the beads and mutter "Mmmmmm" in approval, as though to say, "They're nice." An older woman in the group instigated the first trade. She took a string of beads from her own neck, made with some kind of seeds and teeth, and offered them to me in exchange for one of mine. I accepted the trade, and put her string of beads around my neck as she did with mine.

My other necklace was promptly traded off with another local woman for a string of beads that had several large teeth of some kind of jungle animal on them. I later found out that these were tapir teeth or as the Indians put it, "nugar moli."

After drinking the cocoa drink I went back to Eme's hut with the whole entourage following. I wanted to get better acquainted with my family, and if possible, start to learn a bit of the dialect. Now was as good a time as any. I wanted to start speaking with these people as soon as possible.

Eme was in the back yard cleaning fish. She had several coconuts along side her. I sat down and she eyed me from on top of the long black line down her nose. I pointed to the coconut at her feet, then looked helpless and tried to find out what the word was for it.

She lifted the coconut and said "Ocop." That was the word for coconut.

The fish turned out to be "uwa," the table, "cana," and so on. The dug-out canoe was "ulu," the house "nega," and last but not least "weni" or "mesi" meant beads. Eme took it upon herself to fill the rest of her afternoon with teaching me different words I would be using in the months to come. She became excited with each new word I'd learn and promptly go on to the next she thought I should know. Here was a woman hundreds of years behind my civilization, patiently teaching me her language and I was her student. The tribe was to teach me more than their language in the months to follow.

I was also shown where the local family out-house was—out over the ocean in the backyard. It was good that these edifices were built there. The salt water would prevent disease and other unsanitary conditions.

Getting to it, though, would be a bit of a problem. I had to balance on boards about six inches wide to get out there. That I'd get to learn later, I knew.

Several other women with their beautiful lovely babies came out to join the seaside classroom. They were chatting happily and asking Eme all kinds of questions about me. The most common questions seemed to be in this order:

"What is her name?"

"Where does she come from?"

"How many girl babies does she have?"

"What is her husband's name?"

"What is her mother's name?"

"What is her father's name?"

I decided that now would be a good time to make a few preliminary recordings with my tape recorder. I wondered how the people would react to it. I went into the hut and got the recorder and brought it out.

Eme promptly declared "radio" and proceeded to explain it to the other women present. I switched the recorder on to *record* and let it run. If they thought this was a radio, then this was going to be very funny when I played back Eme's voice. I let it run for fifteen minutes, recording conversations of the women, dogs barking, the sea lapping gently against the island, and babies crying. Then, in the midst of a very animated conversation, I rewound the tape and pressed "play."

After the first few words were spoken from the tape recorder, the group was dead-silent. All faces turned to face my radio and each one registered disbelief. They listened in silence to Eme's explanation about the radio, then went off into uncontrolled laughter. They couldn't believe it. Several ran out of the hut, being frightened by the whole thing, but returned later with their husbands, grandfathers, children, and relatives. After each person who had spoken while I was recording was again heard, the member of the group would point to the speaker and the speaker would inevitably bolt for the door or cover her face with her red scarf. The tape finished, and I had another idea. I proceeded to record their reaction to the tape recorder, for now everyone was talking excitedly about it. They had no idea that I was again recording their words. When I played that section of the tape back, there was again the disbelief and the laughter. Soon, every person on Wichub-Huala Island was either hanging over the fence in the back yard or in the back yard of Alfredo's hut. Eme left the group and went out through the sleeping hut door into the back yard.

Fifteen minutes later, she came back into the yard holding a plateful of fish—scales, eyes, fins and all. Dinner was evidently on so I put the tape recorder back in the hut and sat down to eat.

I picked up a biteful of fish with my fingers, and then remembered, after it was in my mouth, that the scales were still on it. I had been served in the sleeping hut and couldn't quite make out the form of the fish on the plate. I was not only going to have to get used to this particular food of the Indians—I was also going to have to learn *how* to eat it. After I dislodged the scales from my palate, I scraped off the scales from the rest of the fish with my nails. Once I got the hang of the thing, the fish was quite good. Eme came in again with a plate full of bananas which had also been boiled and a cup of coffee drink. I didn't particularly like the bananas, but the coffee wasn't bad at all.

After supper, I returned to the yard with the tape recorder and played with my neighbors with it until it was dark. When it was still twilight, Eme told us to go into the sleeping hut with the "radio" because now "nia" was about—that was the devil.

Eme sang for me with her rattle and I recorded her song. Many people were all over the sleeping hut. Two kerosene lamps gave us enough light to see each other by. It was lighter in here now than it had been when the sun was shining.

Soon it was time to go to bed. Machi came in from Porvenir and had supper with Fulvia while the rest of us climbed into our respective hammocks for the night. Each person was fully clothed, so I decided to go to bed in my dungarees and blue shirt. I did, however, want to go out back to the outhouse and wash up with a gourd of water. I did, but the trip there and back was a bit of a balancing feat and I almost fell into the Caribbean at one point.

I settled into my hammock in the large sleeping room that was not divided into any sections, but open to all, and made myself comfortable. I had yet to sleep in a hammock, but thought it wouldn't be too uncomfortable.

My thoughts were vivid. In less than a week, I had transgressed a mark in time by being here. I had not only traveled a great distance to get here, I had actually traveled back hundreds of years in the process. The lullaby that drifted to me from the village wasn't jazz at St. Mark's Place, but the two had a lot in common in coming from the heart of the singer and the hands of a guitarist.

The first thing I heard the next morning was a rooster crowing. I listened to it through a heavy veil of sleep before I realized that it *was* a rooster and I was here on Wichub-Huala. I could hear the splashing of water from somewhere close by and the smell of cocoa drink was in the air. I had slept soundly and peacefully in my hammock that night. The hammock had rocked gently back and forth, and I was asleep before I knew it. I was fully rested.

I got up and poked my head out of the front door of the sleeping hut. Evidently everybody was up. All the hammocks were empty. I went into the back yard and Fulvia was there showering by pouring a gourd of water over her head. These gourds were a kind of shell fruit that grew in the jungle. When they dried, they were very hard and it was easy to store and carry water in them. Fulvia handed me a gourd of water and indicated that I was to shower also. I was only too happy to accept, but wondered if it would be right for me to strip down to the waist and wash there in the open as she was doing. She wasn't wearing a skirt, but some kind of a small grey colored slip coming to the middle of her thighs. She pointed to it and added another word to my vocabulary, "pecha." She went into the hut and returned, handing me an Indian skirt. She motioned that I was to put this around my waist and wash up. The skirt, I was informed, was a "saburet." I undressed and wrapped the skirt around my waist then proceeded to pour the gourd of water over my head. It was cold and it felt very good. The dirt under my feet was warm and the sky over my head was light blue and very beautiful. I felt no immodesty in being there, in a half-dressed state. Only an exhilaration from the shower, and an enjoyment in my surroundings. There were a few men out on the sea in dug-outs, but none of them even turned to look at me. As far as they were concerned, I was modestly dressed in my saburet.

"Marvelous," I thought and poured another gourd of water over my head.

When I got dressed, I went out to the cooking hut and Eme handed me a cup of cocoa drink along with a half a loaf of what looked like bread. I bit into it—it was bread and it was still warm and very good. I was overjoyed to find bread here. Evidently the Indians made it right here on the island.

After breakfast, I went out of the yard with ten strings of beads and every intention of doing business with the local population. I barely got out of the yard before Fulvia came running after me. She liked the red beads. She ran into the house and emerged with a mola dress top. She held it out to me and indicated that I could trade five strings of beads for it. I did. Pretty soon, I was trading beads for all the articles of dress the Indian women wear. I acquired several molas, three skirts, a red scarf, arm and leg beads, and myriads of Indian necklaces. I spent the whole morning trading, and I must say that I hadn't had as much fun in months with the barter system. Finally, I called a close to business for the day, then got an idea. I went into the hut and changed into the Indian clothes I had acquired. When I emerged into the yard, all my family stopped dead and stared at me, muttering something about "sepugwa." I didn't know what that meant. They were delighted with the fact that I liked their garb. I looked at the results of my actions in a small hand mirror and suddenly knew why they had stared. With the red scarf covering my hair, I looked exactly like one of the albino Indians among the Cuna peoples. There are many of these albinos here because of inter-marriage between relatives, and some of them, having tinges of European blood in them from the Spanish era, had blue eyes. I looked shockingly like one.

I decided to go visiting again and left the yard in my Indian dress. I left the yard and pulled my scarf down so that it would cover my hair, wanting to find out exactly how much I looked like an albino. I walked down the street and not one woman, man, or child lifted their heads to look at me. It was as though I were just part of the scenery and invisible to them. I passed a group of women who were sitting in a sewing circle. Then I passed them again. They didn't recognize me. Then I took my scarf off.

All of the women looked at me, then started to laugh and talk among themselves.

"Be Tule be," indicated one. I later found out that this meant, "You're Indian you."

"Be nuga Sipu!" commented another one. Soon, all the women were calling me by this name and the children picked it up and ran singing it through the streets.

"Your name is Sipu." It meant the white one, or the Cuna name for an albino Indian.

The name stayed with me during all the time I was to spend in San Blas, and was later to be prefixed with "Puna" or sister in the jungle areas.

I was still getting over the shock of fooling the Indians by passing for an albino, when Eme came running out to get me. She had another mola she wanted to trade. Did I have any more beads? I went home to get them.

Later that morning Jungle Jim showed up with a group of tourists and I succeeded in fooling all of them, including Jim who was walking around trying to find me. Nobody would tell him where I was; for one hour before he tried to find out who the new albino was on the island. Fulvia had painted a long black line down my nose and although I was three inches taller than most of the women, I looked like any normal self-respecting albino would have looked. When I couldn't laugh internally anymore, I took off my scarf and called out to him. He stopped walking and his mouth fell open.

"Jesus God!" he said.

He had a heck of a time trying to explain that I wasn't an Indian, but an American girl, to the tourists who were with him. It had been a fun morning.

I spent the rest of the day learning how to sew molas with the village woman. One of the young mothers in my "sewing circle" had a baby whose eye was quite infected. I indicated that I had strong "ina" or medicine and would put some on the infection if she would like. She indicated that she would and I went home and got the terramycin salve. Two days later the eye was fine.

Little did I know that that action would launch my career as a tribal medicine woman. In the week that followed, everybody, including the village medicine man who had stubbed his toe, beat a path to Eme's front door to get medicine for their various hurts and scratches. I spent half of my day treating infected eyes, bruises, cuts, and insect bites.

In all, I spent a good week and a half on Wichub-Huala Island. My schedule assumed a clock-like pace. At dawn we got up, at sunset, or soon thereafter, we went to bed. In the morning I'd eat breakfast with the family, then help paddle our "ulu" over to Porvenir to get water from a fresh-water well there. I treated the local collection of infections, helped cook dinner, studied the language, traded, and generally got the feel of living with these warm lovely people. I might also add that nothing of mine was ever touched or disturbed in any way. Even Eme, who was as regal and proud as a queen, looked out for me and for my needs like a mother hen. She was a wonderful person, and Alfredo, her husband, and myself got along very well. Machi was my favorite though. He was a warm, wonderful person and a pleasure to talk with. I found out a bit about Machi's life history during this week. Jim had taken him from his Indian mother when Machi, which incidentally meant Boy, was about a year old. The woman had offered Jim her son and he had accepted. Jim raised Machi, sent him to school, and all the rest with his own son James who was now in college back in the States. Machi had been with Jim all of these years and was something of a son to him. He now employed Machi at the hotel and gave him a salary for the support of his family and employed Machi's father-in-law at the hotel also. Their relationship when tourists were about was one of employee-employer, when they were alone—as friends. Machi was supporting a cousin, a young girl, in the city with monthly contributions, so that she could get an education and become a nurse. All in all, he had a marvelous love of life, no little love of drink, which occasionally got him into trouble with Jim, and a great love for his wife Fulvia. One day as I sat peeling plantains, a kind of green banana, in the kitchen I saw Fulvia standing by the front gate in the yard. Machi came up behind her and she wasn't aware of his presence. He took a blade of grass and ran it along her neck. She brushed it away thinking it was a fly. Then he ran the blade of grass along her cheek. She turned and laughed when she saw who had been making her think a fly was on her person. Machi couldn't wait until he got home at night to see Fulvia—oftentimes he'd run over in a boat in the middle of the day to spend a few minutes with his wife. Their whole relationship was a very touching, wonderful thing to behold. Alfredo and Eme were also close. Husbands and wives here generally played together as children, and then were married. They knew each other very well, and the closeness I observed in the families was one of great interest to me. Men adored their children and spent as much time playing with them as possible when they got back from the jungle in the afternoon. They loved their wives and deeply respected them. The children were raised with much love and in ideal surroundings.

One night while a few of the villagers and myself were playing with the tape recorder, the village historian or "Kantule," also known as the singer of songs, came by for a while to sing for us. Machi translated his songs. One song was about the bird's love for the sun and another was about a cockroach and rat who were friendly. One day the rat threw the cockroach into the cooking fire and was sorry for ever after. His voice chanted on, in an almost hypnotic way. The third song he sang sent the group into laughter.

"What did he sing about, Machi?" I asked.

"He says," started Machi, then he laughed and continued, "that pretty soon you'll be a Cuna Indian girl and we'll have to cut your hair and find a nice strong husband for you. He'll make you happy and keep you well fed and buy you much gold so that you can stay on Wichub-Huala and be our medicine woman and raise many good girl children."

I started to laugh uproariously and soon everyone was laughing along with me. I told Machi to tell the Kantule that if I stayed in San Blas much longer, I just might do that. This evoked more laughter from the group.

The next morning Jim came over to the island without tourists.

"Boy, you've sure made my week." he commented. "What are you going to do for an encore?" he asked.

"Think I'll go on down to Ailigandi," I told him.

"You're going Indian young lady, by the time you get back here, they'll have you married off to the chief of someplace or another. To tell you the truth, I didn't think you'd last a day out here. You sure fooled me."

"Well, tra-la, tra-la," I laughed. I told Jim I'd be leaving in the morning for Ailigandi. I found out through the Indians that there would be a trading boat by in the morning. He wished me luck and asked when I'd be coming back. I told him that I didn't know, but that it wouldn't be in less than two or three months. He shook his head and went back to Porvenir.

My small taste of Indian life of Wichub-Huala was most enjoyable to me. I'd definitely be back, but I had no idea when at that point. There was so much to see.

The next morning I left Wichub-Huala for Porvenir. Eme and Fulvia and Machi brought me over in their dug-out. The trader *Muara* was waiting at the dock. I talked briefly with the captain, a Mr. Lam, and made arrangements to take the boat up to Ailigandi. Machi put my bags aboard and we quickly pulled out from the dock.

I looked east to the beautiful jungle mountains there. I was anxious to find out what life was all about to the Cuna of Ailigandi.

5
MUARA

I'm here at Ailigandi and all I can say is the whole place is unbelievable in sheer beauty and events which have occurred.

But first of all, in order to appreciate the task of getting to Ailigandi, it will be necessary for me to recount the trip on the *Muara* from Porvenir Island. It was full of many interesting events, sights, and circumstances, many of which were totally new to me.

Mr. Lamb, the vessel's owner, is one of the men who does a great deal of trading with the Cuna all along the coast of San Blas. His ship, the *Muara,* was about 50 feet long and under engine power instead of sail as some of the other vessels are in the area. The latter are smuggling boats from Colombia and do a whopping trade in the illegal importation into their country of, of all things, coconuts.

The first stop we made that day, after being accompanied to the island by a school of playful porpoise, was at Ecotupu, or Needle Island. Mr. Lam had some rice to be delivered here and also wanted to check and see if anyone had any tortoise shell. He was buying tortoise shell this trip around to be resold at Colon to makers of tortoise shell jewelry. We waited for a good hour at the dock while Mr. Lam conducted his business on shore. I was sitting under the cover of the cabin on a deck chair. It seemed strange for me to find one on the boat, for she was a coconut trader and a sort of freighter and didn't ordinarily carry passengers. This trip around she was carrying lumber for some missionaries on Mulatupu Island and the lumber was on both sides of the deck, blocking passage by anyone except a very agile climber to the rear of the vessel. While business was being conducted ashore, I spent my time observing a flock of pelicans who were amusing themselves with fishing off the shores of the island. They have remarkable powers of mobility and gracefulness, although one could never tell so from the way they squatted on top of coconut trees onshore. I laughed outright when one bird underestimated the height of a wave as he skimmed the water, inches from its surface. He toppled head over tail, then hastily took off into the air again.

When we were again underway and heading east along the coast, Mr. Lam spoke to me of his route along the San Blas Coast.

"I never tire of coming here. It's beautiful," he said.

I found out that he had been a piano player and had had his own band 20 years ago, before he decided to go into the trading business. The trips that he took into the area generally lasted from two to three weeks. Some of the other boats spent a month and sometimes two in San Blas before they went back to Colon.

"You know," he continued, "when I first started coming to San Blas I brought all kinds of goods—combs, cloth, dungarees, beads, knives, cooking utensils, machetes, and all other quick sale items like that. Now other traders are selling those items and I concentrate on copra and tortoise shell." Copra, I discovered, was the dried meat of the coconut. It was shipped back to the States to be used in such things as soap, hand creams, and hair shampoo.

The trip itself was leisurely and enjoyable. I noted with great interest the endless growth of coconut trees seeming to line the entire jungle coast of San Blas.

There was another passenger aboard besides myself, a tall mulatto wearing a baseball cap. He noted my inspection of the coastline and offered an explanation for its being that way:

"They say that 20,000,000 coconuts a year are grown there. The San Blas have cultivated most of the coast line. They use the coconuts as money, one coconut equalling five cents. A coconut is legal tender for buying anything from a comb to an entire dug-out canoe."

I thanked the stranger for his information and he introduced himself. His name was Lipton Archibald and he was on his way to Narkana Island to join his own trading boat, the *Melda,* captained by a man named Milton.

Archibald described Narkana as the unofficial capital city of San Blas. It was a thriving metropolis because of the two missions, Catholic and Baptist, that were there. They even had a junior high school, cement sidewalks on one of the streets and street lights, composed of lightbulbs strung on wire along one main street. The total population of Narkana and the area was about 7,000. I was curious to see this boom town, since it evidently displayed the most advanced renovations yet introduced into the area.

Archibald proceeded to fill me in on the various facts about Narkana. It was right across the "bridge" from Corazon de Jesus. The bridge being newly constructed and wide enough to let two people cross at the same time. I found out that the area was shark-infested. A small boy had been killed just four weeks ago and had been attacked only feet from the shore itself. Nature evidently still ruled civilized Narkana.

We arrived at Narkana Island just as the sun was turning everything in sight a rich gold-red color. Sunset hadn't disappointed me, as usual, but began to take on a sort of "event of the day" status to me. I spotted the streets immediately. They lined only part of one street right next to the Catholic church there which was a good three stories high, and also had bell towers. I went ashore to have a good look at the town.

A bit further down from the church was a plaza named Claudio Iglesias Plaza and there was even an outdoor soda fountain there—at least they served fruit juices, although actually an authentic vanilla ice cream soda couldn't be had. I wondered who Claudio Iglesias was, although the name did sound familiar. I had come across it some place. I continued walking down the main street which ended at a long airstrip. The island was very large and could be comfortably inhabited by several thousand people.

I struck up a trade for a pineapple and went back to the *Muara* to snack upon it. Another vessel had come into the dock while I was away. It was the *Melda* and I saw Archibald talking with a young Negro man aboard. He must have been the owner-captain of the vessel, Milton.

Since it was late in the afternoon, I knew that we would be spending the night at dock on the island and wondered where I'd sleep. There was clearly no room on the *Muara*. I would have to curl up in some corner and make myself comfortable for the night.

Mr. Lam was buying copra, receiving it from the Indians, weighing it, and giving each person his due in cash money instead of goods. I settled back to eat my pineapple and watch the procedure. There was nothing terribly civilized about Narkana. A few innovations had been introduced, such as the street lights, but the Indians were for the most part still dressed in their mola dresses and still had their nose rings—and everybody knows that a mission post does not indicate that the territory in which it is placed is totally civilized. As far as I was concerned this was still bush country.

I noticed a tall blond man walking toward the dock area and looking around. He didn't look Spanish. He definitely wasn't Indian. I wondered a moment and came to the conclusion that he was American, and not a member of any missionary post from his garb, which looked very sporty. He was carrying goggles. "He looks like a pilot," I thought. I hadn't noticed any planes on the strip when I had gone down there and none had come in in the interim.

His eyes caught me, sitting on top of a coil of rope on the *Muara* and he examined me at length before coming up onto the dock and to the boat.

"Are you American?" he asked.

I nodded my head.

"Where are you headed?"

"Ailigandi," I replied.

"Who are you going to see?"

"I'm going to be living in the village there with the Cuna."

"Well, Claudio Iglesias, the head of the Mulatupu Island mission, is here on the island. He flew in with a Dr. Kingsley from the Zone and myself about an hour ago. His sister is pretty sick. Would you like to come over and talk with him?"

I replied that I'd like to very much, but considering the circumstances of why he was here and all, he probably had enough worries about his sister at the present time and I preferred not to intrude upon them.

"No," the blond American said carefully, "I know he'd want to talk with you. Come with me."

I went ashore. He introduced himself. His name was Mike and he was the vice-president of a large American bank near the El Panama Hilton in Panama City. He was married and he had a little girl. His wife was back in the States waiting for the birth of her second child, due shortly. He flew the doctor in, as he generally did, on request from Claudio. Claudio was an Indian and was pretty well liked by the people.

"The plaza is named after him?"

"Oh that—no. That's named after an older brother who was killed by his own people during the revolt out here in 1925."

"What's wrong with Mr. Iglesias' sister?" I asked.

"Cancer," he stated walking toward the southwest corner of the island. "She's dying."

I stopped in my tracks.

"Now listen, now I know he wouldn't want to see anybody. I don't think I'd better intrude."

Mike replied that he was certain the elder Iglesias would be upset if he knew that I had been here and had left without saying hello.

I knew I could always leave if I saw things were in sad condition.

We came upon a two story wooden structure and Mike pointed out Dr. Kingsley and Claudio Iglesias standing outside of the house.

I waited with Mike. The conversation broke up and Claudio came over to speak with Mike.

"You must be Joanne Kelly," he stated.

I laughed. No one knew that I was coming down this way. Then I remembered the jungle "grapevine."

"I was told that a young red-haired American girl was on her way to talk with Chief Ikwaniktipippi at Ailigandi. It was said that you had medicine and many beads to trade."

I laughed at this description and acknowledged that it was true.

I apologized for appearing on the scene at such an inopportune moment for the family, and suggested that we talk another time. Claudio would have none of it and promptly carried me off to the soda fountain for a can of apricot juice.

"You aren't interrupting anything," he started. "She's been sick now for some time. There is nothing anybody can do for her now except to make her as comfortable as possible in these last few months."

I found out from Claudio that there wasn't a single resident doctor in all of San Blas.* A Doctor Arias, a wonderful Panamanian physician, flew in as much as he could and Mike brought other doctors in from Gorgas Hospital, but that was the extent of the medical help the people had. We both thought this to be a heck of a situation indeed.

Claudio was married to an American woman named Marguerita. They had three children ages five to fifteen and lived on Mulatupu Island, 27 miles from the Colombian border. Marguerita had some nurses' training.

I asked Claudio if he could use some medicines at his mission and his reply was that he'd be elated to have some, but didn't know where to get any. I replied that I had brought quite a supply with me and offered to split what I had with him. He turned to me and was obviously surprised. He had heard that I had medicine, but not in any great quantity. I took him back to the *Muara* and Claudio and another relative helped carry back the medicines. We placed them in Mike's plane, which had taxied off the air strip onto a point of land near the Iglesias home here on Narkana. Claudio was very happy to get the medicines and thanked me warmly for them. They were needed badly in his area. I replied that I felt grateful for the opportunity to be of some assistance.

Mike, Dr. Kingsley, and Claudio took off a half an hour later for

* An Italian doctor is now in residence on Narkana Island—August 20, 1964.

Mulatupu to deliver Claudio safely to his wife and then they would fly back to Païtilla Airport to deliver themselves up to their homes in the city.

I went back to the *Muara*. The crew was now engaged in playing dominoes on the front hatch cover. They had set up a card table there. On the *Melda,* right across the 20 foot wide dock, a crewman was playing a horn. . . . The song sounded familiar and I realized with a start that the song was "Jingle Bells."

Archibald came over from the *Melda* and told me that arrangements had been made for me to have the captain's cabin all to myself that night. I was grateful, but didn't want to put anybody out of their cot. He said that it was no trouble whatsoever. Mr. Lam was going to spend the night comfortably on the *Melda.* I accepted, but decided to stay up for a bit and write a few letters which I had neglected for two weeks, letting my friends know that I had arrived safely and was in San Blas.

The men were enthusiastically enjoying their domino game and I must say I've never observed a group of men enjoying a game as much as they did. They were warm and interesting people and I envied their easy going life in the beauty and serenity of this coast.

The horn player broke into a Panamanian bolero. Organ music was coming from church. Of course, this was Sunday. I wrote my envelopes, inserted their cargo of written letters, sealed them, then went back to the captain's quarters. Soon the easy swaying movement of the *Muara,* which reminded me of a hammock, put me to sleep. But not before another chorus of "Jingle Bells" was again offered by the musical crew member of the *Melda.*

I woke up and wondered how many thousands of them there were flying right over the boat—parakeets, I mean. I've never heard such a racket in my whole life. I began to regard these birds as the self-appointed disciplinarians of jungle life. No man or animal would ever dare to over-sleep with them around. If some poor soul did, I half believe the parakeets would swoop in the unfortunate's window and peck at him until he was up and screaming for mercy. But I'm being too harsh with them, I'd rather have them singing in my ear than hear an alarm clock any day of the week.

I got up, washed in the stern with fresh water from several

drums of it aboard, dressed, and had breakfast which consisted of coffee and quite good cornbread. Breakfast was eaten on the dock watching the sun come up.

The village was alive with the smell of many cooking fires and the scent of coffee and cocoa. I looked across the bridge to Corazon de Jesus and decided it was time to explore that town. I crossed the bridge and went over. This town also had its own dock. There was a strange looking craft tied up there—it looked like something straight out of history and at least 400 years old in design. She was a sail craft and very sleek in design and line. This must have been one of the smuggling craft that Archibald had been telling me about the day before. The craft was a Colombian boat and she had numbers over her name that began with a 0 which was followed by a dot and the rest of her number. For purposes of illustrating this chapter, and these are not her real numbers, the identification symbol ran 0.432. These crafts were called "canoas" by the local Indians and the Panamanian traders along the coast. This vessel's crewmen were a rough looking lot. Most of them were stripped to the waist and again most of them were wearing knives or machetes in plain sight on their persons—generally on their belt or around their waist. When one of them saw me, he called out for his companions to look. The examination I got can only be compared to a doctor's looking at an uncontrollable outbreak of the bubonic plague. I quickly went on into town and left the Colombian craft to herself.

I did, however, want to get a look at one of these crafts on the open sea. They must have been beautiful under full sail. Corazon de Jesus looked exactly like Nargana, mission and all. There was nothing of great interest here in the way of sights. I walked back over the bridge to the *Muara*. I looked behind me on the way and was startled to see a group of uniformed school children walking two by two across the bridge toward Narkana behind me. They were led by a white-cassocked priest.

At 7 a.m. the *Muara* left her berth at Narkana and chugged slowly out past the reefs to open water. Fifteen minutes later we were again cutting the waves and heading east along the coast. The sea, however, was not in good temper this morning. The waves were bad and they tossed us about soundly.

I had gotten badly burned the day before and this time I crawled up under the protruding cover of the captain's bridge to get myself away from the sun. I promptly tripped over a piece of lumber that was sticking out from under the piles at both sides of the deck and acquired a rather nasty cut on the leg. I was also beginning to feel somewhat queasy from the roughness of the water and hoped I wasn't going to be sea sick. Fifteen minutes later I was miserable. I decided to go back over the pile of lumber and pay a visit to the head. I started across the lumber on my hands and knees, as anybody who was going there had to. I got about three quarters of the way across when a king-sized wave hit us and I lost my balance and started to go over the side of the vessel. I grabbd desperately at a piece of rope hanging from the side so that I wouldn't be lost in the water. I had just gone under when the next swell, a pretty close cousin of the first, brought me up to the level of the railing again and I hung onto it and scampered aboard the pile of lumber. I was panting and shaking. I had come close to getting myself lost in the Caribbean. I sat on top of the pile of lumber to calm myself and rest a minute. I felt sick.

"Are you alright?" I turned to find the startled eyes of the cook examining me from his window, which was level with the lumber pile on the port side of the *Muara*.

"Si," I replied and continued to make my way back to the head. When I returned to my bow seat on a coil of rope, I sat down to try to keep my stomach calm. I had changed clothes, but my hair was still soaking wet. Nobody noticed as the shower I had taken that morning had left my hair wet and it hadn't dried yet.

I started to think about what had happened and a discomforting thought presented itself. If I had gone over the side as I did but didn't hang on to the rope, I would have been in quite a predicament. First of all, the cook hadn't noticed me going over. He stuck his head out only after I regained the pile of lumber. Second of all, nobody would have missed me for a good half an hour and my knee was still bleeding a bit from my earlier fall. It would have taken the boat, and that's *if* somebody had found me missing in half an hour, a good hour to retrace their course and search for me. Unless I had been charmed, the sharks would have been at me before the *Muara* could find me. I was bleeding from the leg, and it was feeding time at the old ranch for the sharks, who generally do most of their hunting in the early morning and late afternoon.

I felt sicker. I went and got some gauze and antiseptic and dressed my leg over. The bleeding stopped once again and I again seated myself on the coil of rope. I finally discovered that if I kept my eyes glued to the coast line, or at anything that was steady, I didn't feel half as bad. I spent the next couple of hours examining every coconut tree the Cuna had planted on the San Blas coast, or as though I were watching for a Mau-Mau invasion to come after the Cuna in dug-out canoes.

Mr. Lam stuck his head out of the window of his cabin.

"Pretty, eh?"

I replied, "Mmmmmmmmmmmmm," not taking my eyes from shoreline.

About ten minutes from the island of Playon Chico, we entered a break in the reef and calmer water. I gratefully offered thanks to the thousands of years of natural development which had put the reef there. It was about four miles out from the coast line proper and huge white breakers were hitting it. The bases of the waves were a lovely green color.

We didn't stay long at Playon Chico, but did pick up a few passengers there who were heading up the coast toward Colombia. One was a Panamanian boy from the bush and he had a guitar case with him. He had one outstanding feature and that was his eyes. They were blue and the right one was crossed.

He at once took a more than just curious interest in my blue overnight case which was placed beside me under the cover of the captain's roof. He fingered it delicately and then turned to smile at me. He liked the thing.

He asked in Spanish how much it had cost and I gave him a rough estimate. He said that he thought it was very nice. He then opened his guitar case and took that instrument from it. I noticed a two foot-long machete in the rear of the case.

He sat down in the shade of the cabin roof and played some marvelous music on that instrument. He sang the bush songs of the Chriqui Province to the west and we enjoyed his music tremendously. The boy didn't have much about him in the way of looks, but he could sing like I have never heard a Panamanian sing, before or since. He loved music and his love of the songs he offered us came through. Everyone on board joined him in a few of them. Soon we had a band going back there complete with maracas from the Lord only knows where and a tin wash basin for a drum. The crewmen and the boy harmonized like professionals. Mr. Lam commented, and he should know, that if he still had his band he would have hired the boy after hearing one song. He took a great interest in the music, closed his eyes, and smiled as his hands beat out the accompaniment to the drum on the wheel of the *Muara*.

When the boy finished his songs, he shyly put the guitar back in the case and sat down at the bow alone. I wondered where he was from, what his life was like, what his thoughts were, but now was not the time to ask or find out. In the east, Ailigandi rose from the sea and was growing bigger as we chug-chugged toward her.

6

AN AILIGANDI JOURNAL

It's early morning and I'm here on Ailigandi Island sitting on the second floor of one of the two concrete buildings on the island. This particular structure is the mission house built by Marvel and Lonnie Iglesias, both Baptist missionaries who were here for 30 years. Lonnie, incidentally, is Claudio's brother. It seems that the whole family is going through some kind of reigning dynasty in San Blas. Marvel was an American woman Lonnie fell in love with and married some 35 years ago. When they retired, they left this building, formerly their home, to the Ailigandi Baptist Mission, to be used in any way the mission desired. This second floor consists of three bedrooms, one of which I'm occupying at the moment, a spacious living room, a sort of an anteroom, and a front door. The steps outside lead to ground level.

The downstairs part of the building serves as a classroom for a kindergarten class which incidentally is now in session. Ever hear "Twinkle, Twinkle Little Star" in Cuna Indian dialect? Not one of those children is off key, either. There's a kitchen off to the seaward-side of the building downstairs, but nobody makes much use of that except Artilio. He's the head pastor of the mission here and a San Blas Indian by birth. He stores his cheese in the refrigerator in the kitchen.

Outside, and visible from where I am sitting here at the living-room desk, are the grey-blue mountains hugging white clouds to their green bosom. On the other side, the Caribbean is lapping almost right under the window itself. The island is colorful, and it's situated in one of the most beautiful spots on the face of the earth—really lovely.

I arrived here yesterday afternoon. I found that all the chiefs were off the island at an inter-island congress meeting on Mulatupu Island near the Colombian border. That's Claudio's home ground. Since they were gone, I asked for the Millers. Claudio had told me to get in touch with them the moment I landed and they'd make me comfortable. Mr. Miller, Sr. was away to the States, but his 28 year old son Peter, Jr. greeted me and brought me over to these luxury quarters. And I thought I was going to have to sling my newly-bought hammock from the rafters of the council hall.

Pete was educated in the States, in a college in Texas. He's a full-blooded San Blas Indian and has been, to me, a storehouse of information on his people.

Last night was a bit of an experience. Here I am in a concrete structure, the height of luxury hereabouts, and I still had to sleep with a machete in one hand and a flashlight in the other. I no sooner climbed into bed last night than several dog-sized rats began scampering about—then came the bats. They are called "muercelas" and the translation of that would be vampires. The things actually live on blood and they aren't fussy where they get it—dogs, babies, mothers, adults, or redheads. The reason for the machete was that I found one perched on my big toe when I woke up feeling uneasy about something. They have needle sharp fangs and don't particularly hurt when they bite. Most of the time, I understand from Peter, you don't know it until the next morning. They generally go for toes, necks, arms, or elbows, prefering those parts to any others for some odd reason known only to the bats themselves. They are not to be confused with their close cousins, the fruit bats. These latter are larger and do not require blood for food, but prefer a nice yellow banana.

One had come after me one night on Wichub-Huala Island, but I hadn't paid too much attention to it because the bats out in the middle of Mandinga Bay weren't as numerous as those here at Ailigandi—the same is true of the rats. I had been sleeping in my hammock there and I woke up in the middle of the night not knowing why. Then I noticed a small mouse climbing down the ropes of my hammock, but there was something strange about the mouse. Then it occurred to me that the mouse would have had to climb a perpendicular wall and crawl down my hammock rope to get where he was. No self-respecting mouse would ever do a thing like that unless the darn thing could fly. Then I had it; maybe it did fly. I reached for a machete, which I always kept beside me with its blade stuck in the dirt on the floor. I hit the "mouse" sideways and it fell to the floor stunned. I saw it was a bat before it regained consciousness but it flew away before I could kill it.

Peter informed me this morning that if a Kerosene lamp is kept on low all night long, the bats generally don't give people too much trouble. Nevertheless, they're here, and that's all I needed or need to know. The machete comes to bed with me tonight too, and I've got to get a supply of batteries for my flashlight. I wouldn't be without either now until I get used to the things.

There seem to be many rats here on Ailigandi. I wonder why so many more here than on the other islands. Perhaps they come in on the Colombian trading boats.

So much for the local village fauna except for one minor news item of the morning. I heard a commotion shortly after dawn and looked out of my window to see a delegation of men, one with a spear and what looked like a five foot long snake on the end of it. I found out later that it was not only a snake, but a poisonous and deadly fer-de-lance. The village men thought that it must have crawled into someone's canoe while the man was over in the jungle river across the channel. It then slipped out onto the island while the canoe was sitting on land, probably in an armfull of firewood. No harm done, however. It didn't bite anybody, although it scared the heck out of an old grandmother who went to light her fire in the morning and found the snake coiled up on top of the still warm cinders.

The sense of peace and love of life is strong among these people. They're completely real and so much a part of the earth that it's difficult to believe they didn't spring out of the ground with the rest of the trees in the jungle. There is no rush to do anything. They are secure in the land because they are Indians. They know that food, shelter, drink and all things needed to sustain their life are in the jungle mainland. As long as the jungle lives, the people do. If it were to die, they would have to move or would not survive.

They have several interesting rules for leading a happy life. They never, for one thing, speak about any person who is gone from their midst, dead or otherwise. There is a mourning period, but if a child's father dies and a week later the child asks if his father isn't coming home that night, his mother will tell him, or for that matter anyone of the adults who is near, that the child must not now speak of one who lives in the house of the Great Father, or "Tiolele." A man gone from the island either into Panama proper or to another island is not spoken of until he returns. A second rule is that one must not rush; regardless of what the subject matter is that must be discussed immediately, or acted upon at once, they don't rush. A council meeting of the chiefs on a pressing matter will sometimes drag on into days or a week or more. A third rule is that of not disciplining the children. The children are the treasure of the adults in the village, and the adults' example of how things should be done. And the Kantule, or singer of songs, gives lessons on how to lead a good Indian life. The songs sung in the council hall serve to teach the child what his duties will be when he grows older. The parents have nothing to do with telling the child what he should and shouldn't do. Their duty is to give the child love and I've never seen children loved as much as these. No wonder there isn't any insanity or aren't any angry young Indians running about. They are the most mentally healthy people I have ever run into. A fourth rule for staying happy is to enjoy each and everything as it happens. There is no past now; there is no future now; there is simply and only *now.* A fifth rule is one dealing with married life. A girl and boy marry very young. They have no doubt played on the village streets when they were children and have known each other all of their lives. They marry when both are old enough to enjoy a happy sexual life and then they grow up together.

The community itself is set up for the protection of any man, woman, and child fortunate enough to have been born on the island. From the moment a child is born, the community is helping him. It teaches him, it protects him, it feeds him, it gives him joy and life, it gives him a wife and it will even build a new home for him if he wants one. Take the last point, for instance. Say a boy marries and within the four following years of marriage his wife presents him with three children. Now when he married, he, as every male Cuna, moved into his mother-in-law's house. The tribal society is matriarchal in this regard. Now the hut was small, and it's getting a bit crowded. The man can go to the council hall and during a meeting request permission of the chief to speak. He is, of course, granted that permission. He tells his tribal leaders and his fellow villagers that he married (as they all know), and that he now has three children (this they also know). Then he tells them that his mother-in-law's hut is very small and that his children do not have sufficient place to sleep in. Then he requests the chief to appoint 12 men to help him build his new house. The chief will do this and within a month the man will have his own hut built by his village on the island.

The same thing is true of a man whose house is in need of repair. He will go to the council hall and request help in repairing it.

Both of these men, on entering the council hall with their request, tell the chief how much thatch they will need, how many poles and how tall they should be, how much behuco vine for rope, and how much reed for the walls.

The communal living even stretches to guests that appear on the island. Anyone passing through their village is treated royally and given the best that the village can supply. He is offered food, drink, and a place to rest. He is treated courteously and with respect and can count on the Indians to help him if it is at all within their power. This marvelous rule of hospitality stretches even further than this. I was in the council hall listening to a meeting last night—one in which the Kantule was singing about the duties of a chief. I found out that if a man is greatly troubled by anything when he arrives on an island, be he Cuna or purple in color and three feet tall, the chief is bound by law to talk with the stranger and help him come to a rational solution to his problems. If the man requires much time, the chief will talk to him every night for six months to help the stranger get things settled.

This to me is noteworthy and does the laws of the tribe honor. What a wonderful, warm, human wish to love his brother, to have as an actual law for a race of people.

I must further mention that I'm very highly impressed with the chiefs of the people that I have met so far. Each one has been elected by his village for his wisdom and knowledge of the Cuna law. Each one is a fair minded, gentle, and a wonderful person. The wisdom of at least one chief I have already met and spoken with down in the Mandinga Bay region would put half the diplomats at the U.N. to shame. I almost wish they'd send him up there and let him spend a week talking with everybody about the world's problems. I have a feeling that he'd offer some of the most constructive ideas on how to live in peace ever spoken on the floor of the General Assembly.

Another thing I've noticed about these people is that they are physically cleaner than we are, bathing four and five times a day, and changing clothes at least two times. Fresh water is brought over by dug-out from the river some 100 yards across a small channel on the jungle mainland. It takes 15 minutes to get there via dug-out.

This scene from my window is intriguing me. The sea surrounding the island is a very light shade of green and is crystal clear. I can see fish moving in it from up here. I could throw a line into the sea from here and I'd probably catch something. The color of the sea out near the surrounding reefs of the island is a deep aqua. The barrier reef, out about three miles from the island, stretches for miles along the coast out there and keeps the sea within it calm. The mountains themselves have changed color three times today. Early this morning, clouds hung low over them and they were grey in color. Later in the morning they turned green-blue, and now they are higher and a sharp, lush green.

Tuesday, July 24, 1963

It's been a quiet, peaceful day on Ailigandi, but somehow the bats are bothering the life or rather sleep out of my nights. I got bitten last night. I woke up to find myself the frightened owner of a bloody elbow. The thought of another night spent chasing them away is upsetting me. I suppose I'll eventually get used to it. The Indians don't even think about them. Actually, it would take an explosion or a jaguar loose on the island to upset them at all. Nothing seems to perturb them to any great degree. Their patience is amazing.

I went into the village to the huts of a few new acquaintances this morning. I traded more beads for mola dress tops. The value of my beads is constant here in San Blas. I got the molas for four strings of beads, a pocket knife, a small tube of lipstick (which the woman used to promptly redden her cheeks) and a tiny post-card of New York. That's about par for the course.

After bringing the molas back to the mission house, I went on my usual morning walk through the village. I space these walks far apart because I'm generally ready to burst from being over-fed when I get back to the mission house. The people can't just let me go undisturbed down their streets. I'm bigger than most of them are and they must think I'll starve to death if I don't get something to eat or drink in every other hut on Ailigandi Island. They generally carry me bodily into their huts. They indicate that I am to sit down, then all the neighbors come in to have a good look at me. I found out I have the same color hair as their great teacher Ibeorgan. He was evidently a redhead. I keep wondering about that man. I tend to think that Ibeorgan was a white man who somehow found his way into the jungle 300 years ago and loved what he found so much, that he instructed the Cuna on how to keep themselves apart from anyone who would hurt them. His teachings seem to indicate this fact to me. From translations of Ibeorgan's teachings to the Cuna, as per the Kantule of Ailigandi Island, I have deduced the following:

All of his teachings are strictly for the protection of the Cuna from outside influences. He taught the people to greet strangers hospitably, but at the first sign that the outsiders were after gold or were evil, to order them away. If they didn't go—then it was alright to make them "disappear" into the jungle. He taught the people better ways to trap food. He told them about the house of the Great Father and that everybody would go there when they died.

From just this scanty information, I should have guessed that in order to warn—he must have known about the outside world and that he was from it at one time. He knew about the Great Father, or the one God, and taught the people about him. He taught the Cuna that the Great Father was a benevolent God and there is no mention of a hell or the possibility of anyone's going there in his teachings. He must have spent a great deal of time with the Cuna people and he must have loved their simplicity and child-like ways.

I visited the medicine man's hut today and picked up a very small, very old medicine doll in his collection and asked him about it. He mentioned something about Ibeorgan's looking something like the doll. The doll was named Ibeorgan. The doll was wearing a kind of helmet and a skirt, which looked vaguely like a kilt. As far as I have ascertained, at no time in the history of the Cunas did the men wear skirts. They wore loin cloths, then went to pants of sorts. If the doll represented Ibeorgan, I think Ibeorgan to be a Scotchman and the fact that it is said he had red hair ties in very well with that theory. Whoever he was, he loved the Cuna people and his teachings are gentle teachings and wise teachings. He was a good man. It is said that Ibeorgan went to the land of the Great Father and lives there with him. When a Cuna dies, he will rejoin this great teacher in the "land beyond life."

I traded the medicine man for the Ibeorgan medicine doll with a small fortune in trade goods and money. I gave him eight yards of red cloth and four dollars for it because he was so reluctant to part with it. I convinced him that I was without one single medicine doll to protect my spirit and a medicine woman without a medicine doll to protect her spirit is like a president without a country or a chief without a village. I still have the Ibeorgan doll and it occupies a prominent place in my New York apartment and in my Cuna Indian collection.

But back to the food situation. I really don't know quite what to do about it and it is getting to be a problem. If food is offered to me, I must drink or eat at least a little bit of it or the family who offers it will be offended. I can't leave the house and walk around the village without being offered (without exaggeration) at least 20 feedings from the families there. Even if I just eat one mouthful of the food from each offering I'm stuffed before I get back to the mission house. I'm holding up marvelously against the bats, rats and other difficulties here, but I'm not so sure my stomach is going to be able to make it.

I'm going to have to speak to Peter about the situation and find out what to do.

While walking this morning I came across an interesting sight. It was a kind of sugar cane press that was being operated by several of the Indians of the village. Sugar cane was being pressed between two logs, the ends of which had been inserted into a tree stump. The juice was being collected to make one of the morning drinks served at dawn by mothers to their families. I understand from Peter that this same sugar cane juice is used in the making of Indian liquor drunk during the puberty or Chicha feast hereabouts. I hope I get to see one of these celebrations before I leave Ailigandi.

Wednesday

Lord, did we have a storm here this morning. It was raining so heavily that I thought Ailigandi would be washed right back into the sea. The wind was so strong that it blew in two of the windows in the mission house and broke the latches on every one of the windward house windows.

It struck at dawn and I first became aware that something was wrong because the rats were in a panic. Two of them jumped right up on top of my bed and frightened the heart out of me—the rest of them were scampering about hysterically in the rafters. I looked out the window and at first thought a hurricane was going to hit us. The entire sky in the east was as black as night and the storm stretched endlessly east and west. It hit us fifteen minutes later with a force that is unequaled to anything I have seen yet in this area. I was running about trying to keep the windows secured, but to no avail. I ran to each window and the rats ran about under my feet; the wind howled and the rain was blinding and whew!

After a half an hour's worth of this storm, I became alarmed about the village and the people there. The streets were flooded and in some places the sea was up on the island to a depth of at least a half a foot. The people inside of those huts must have been soaked and some of the huts would be considerably damaged by the force of the wind and rain.

After an hour's worth of this howling, raging torrent, the wind subsided and the rain stopped. The village looked like what the earth must have looked like after the flood.

Then amazingly, the people came out of their huts laughing. The children emerged onto the streets with tiny carved boats and were having themselves a marvelous time pushing the boats down the flooded streets. The storm didn't seem to upset them in the least. Women ran over to the dug-out canoes pulled high up on the beach and dipped half gourds into the fresh water collected there and poured it over their heads. Everyone was having a grand old time with fresh water everywhere where it had collected.

Peter's mother, Mrs. Miller, came over from her house to fetch me to breakfast. I peeked inside of several huts on the way over there. The floors were dry and it was then that I noticed that the floors of the huts are raised a good six inches above ground level. The quality of the thatch roofs was evidently very good also, because the huts seemed dry and fires still burned merrily.

Mrs. Miller is one of those people you meet every once in a while who is a mark in time. She never frowned—never. It was as though a plastic surgeon had permanently put a smile on her face. She was motherly and laughing and took excellent care of me during my stay on Ailigandi. She was Indian, as was her husband. The latter was back in a hospital in Texas having a skin infection treated. She had long black hair and wore western dress.

After breakfast I went for a walk in the village again, wishing I could have done it invisibly. However this one morning I found the solution to my problems—make a quick bee-line for a hut and get there fast. Then I'd only have to drink maybe two cups of sugar cane or cocoa drink all over the village.

Once I got there the curious would come and ask questions, and anyone who spoke any Spanish would translate for me if Peter were not around.

Last night's happenings were fun. I walked about the village talking with new friends with Peter and stopped in several huts to spend a little time.

One woman, eyeing my New York slim figure, asked this question:

"Your father doesn't have many coconuts and can't feed you well?"

Peter immediately laughed loudly. I didn't know what the woman had said. He translated, then I laughed. Evidently that was why I was being fed so much. Everybody thought I was too skinny. The Indian women are not fat but are well-padded. The happy solution to the "feeding" problem was then to continue eating until I was bulging at the seams. When I was fat enough to please everyone, then I'd presumably be left in peace.

Visiting at night is a very pleasant, relaxing occupation. As soon as a friend or visitor entered a hut, he was offered a hammock in which he could lie. The entire conversation and question and answer period which followed was conducted Roman style from a reclining position. Sometimes there were two dozen people involved in a conversation and each one was in a hammock by him or herself enjoying the talk. It beats sitting up on their carved wooden stools any day.

A drink was generally offered the visitors. There were a variety of these. There was "obdudu" or soft boiled corn drink. There was cocoa or coffee drink sweetened with a bit of sugar cane juice, or if there was any around, sugar. There was "masi" drink, made from crushed boiled plantains, or one was offered a combination of any of the above. They were all quite good and after a while I began to like all of them, although I didn't care for them at first.

This visiting at night was restricted to young unmarried boys, married men, and women who were married. The "yargwas" or unmarried girls never walked the village streets after dark. Boys who were interested in a particular girl dropped by her house to talk with her. The girls were never allowed to visit the boy's house. When the courting became serious, the youngsters were allowed, only under the supervision of an old grandmother of the house, to lie down in the same hammock together and talk, but just talk. The grandmother enforced herself quite strictly on the youngsters if anything else were experimented with. There was an interesting side-light to this custom, not unlike our own early American custom of bundling. It was said that if a mother wanted her daughter to marry a particularly rich boy, meaning that either he or his father had many, many coconuts and therefore money and could buy the girl much gold, she sometimes called the grandmother outside of the hut while the youngsters were in a hammock. The young people were left alone for very short periods of time, and they no doubt took advantage of these few minutes to experiment a bit. The boy would become a bit more interested in the girl, and in many cases would marry her. If this didn't work, the children were left alone for longer periods of time, and if that didn't work, the mother took her daughter aside and spoke to her using something of this sort of language:

"You like that boy?" asks Mother.

"He is a good hunter," answers Daughter.

"His father has many coconuts," says Mother.

"Mmmmmmmmmm," replies Daughter.

"I see him play with his younger brothers and sisters. He likes babies very much."

"Mmmmmmmmmm," replies Daughter.

"He will buy you much gold if he likes you."

"Mmmmmmmmm."

"I think he'll make a good husband."

"Mmmmmmmmm."

"Maybe I should call out old "moo" (grandmother) when he comes to visit you tonight so that you can find out if you like each other?"

"Mmmmmmmmmmmm."

The children are left alone and if two months later Daughter finds out that she's having a baby, the two are swiftly joined in marriage by the village elders.

This kind of drastic action is not done all the time, but nevertheless it is done.

During a visit to one of the houses on the east side of the island last night, one of Peter's friends, a young Indian boy, gave me a present. He said that he had heard that I was having trouble with bats. He handed me a long reed and smiled, obviously assuming I knew what to do with the thing. I looked at Peter for help. He gave me a blank stare. He didn't know what to do with the thing either. It was some kind of a bat chaser awayer and the boy decided that he'd better demonstrate. All I'd have to do is stand in the middle of a room that had a bat flying around and wave the thing quickly back and forth swiftly until it "hummed." It seemed that the bats hated this sound and quickly fled from it. I thanked the boy and dubiously accepted his bat stick.

Peter and I walked down to the other end of Ailigandi Island to see how work was coming on the clinic that the Baptists are building on Ailigandi. It will be a blessing to the people when it is built and hopefully manned. The Baptists didn't know if they'd be able to get personnel for it even at this late date. The Cuna of Ailigandi Island, under the supervision of Artilio's brother who is an engineer of sorts, are constructing this clinic with village men. Their tools are the crudest possible, but the thing is going up by leaps and bounds and will probably be finished in the fall of 1964.

When we approached the clinic, a round of female cheers went up from the area and we found that the wives and children of the men who were working on the clinic were out cheering their men on with their work from the sidelines. None of the men were paid for their work, but contributed it to the future medical health of the island. The chief made up lists of who was to work when and the men were only too happy to contribute this little bit for their island.

When Peter and I left the clinic, I was surprised to see the *Muara* chug-chugging toward the dock in the darkness. The *Muara* had completed her rounds to the border at a town called Puerto O'Baldia and was now on her way back.

I took Peter and my bat club over to visit Ricardo, the Kantule, and Maria, his wife. They are fast becoming my favorite family in San Blas. I had promised Maria that I'd visit this night for a drink and sit and talk with them. It was now dark, but there was enough light from the full moon for anybody to walk around without a flashlight. The stars in the sky here, out in the middle of nowhere, are like no other stars I've ever seen. They are all colors, reds and yellows and blues, and can be clearly seen in the sky. The whole sky is magnificent in its brilliance.

Maria was a jovial, warm person. She was Indian, regardless of the fact of her name, an introduction by the Spaniards. She sat in her hammock smiling at the world in general and her nose ring flashed in the fire light. Her husband Ricardo was a bit of a fireball and a fun loving character. I enjoyed visiting this couple tremendously. They had two children, both boys—one was named Ricardido and he was three years old. The other's name was Leopoldo and he was about twelve.

Ricardo is one of those savants in the history of the tribe. He is a Kantule and a much respected member of the tribal council. It has taken him years to learn the songs passed down by mouth from Kantule to Kantule comprising the history and religious beliefs of the Carib Cuna Tribe. He knows exactly what Balboa did when he landed and the names of all the people and chiefs who were dignitaries of the tribe at that time. He knows of the massacre of almost 700,000 Choco and Cuna Indians in the Darien Jungle that took place as a result of the Spaniard's vicious lust for gold—all of this without a written language. Ricardo knew the duties of children to their village, chief, mother, father, brothers, sisters, and younger babies in the family. He knew the law. He knew the religion. He was a Kantule.

Some of his duties were to sing with the medicine man during the "Great Devil Chasing Out" ceremony which took place about every seven years on each of the islands in San Blas. He sang with the medicine man to help him get back the soul of a fellow villager unfortunate enough to have come down sick because some devil in the underworld ran off with his "purba" or soul. He sang joyfully during the puberty rites; sadly during a burial ceremony, the songs of which last for 24 hours without interruption. It had taken him half a lifetime to learn this particular series of chants describing the trip and trials and tribulations that a soul must go through before it reaches the house of the Great Father in the land of Ibeorgan.

Peter and I made ourselves comfortable in hammocks in Maria's sleeping hut which also doubled as a kitchen at the far end and since there was a cooking fire there. Ricardido, already my favorite child in the village, climbed up onto my lap and started to play with me. He was a beautiful, warm child and I loved him.

I wanted to talk with Ikwaniktipippi, the second chief of Ailigandi Village, to hear his own words of his people, their history, and their way of life. I asked Ricardo to talk with the elderly chief. He said that he would speak with Ikwanik, as he was called for short, the next day.

Peter and I went back to the mission house to talk awhile. We no sooner sat down than a fairly large bat flew in the window.

"Ha, Ha!" I cried, "Now's my chance." I grabbed the bat stick and started to beat the air feverishly with it. I remembered Ricardo's singing a little chant for me in his hut and asked Peter if there was a chant that went with the excorcism of bats. I started to dance around the room chanting in a mumbling voice "Bat be gone. . . ."

My stick hit what I thought was the rafters.

"Aiiiiiie," cried Pete, "you got 'em!"

I stood there looking around the floor and my surprised eyes found the grey form of the bat. It was crawling there, obviously stunned, and unable to rise. It looked small and totally helpless.

Before I could utter another word, Peter had taken my machete from a corner in the living room and he dealt the bat a side way blow. Dead, it didn't look half as terrible as it had flying around my room. It looked tiny and I was almost sorry that Peter had done away with it. He lifted the bat to my writing table for inspection. We studiously examined its teeth and found them to be needle sharp. I could see why victims rarely woke up when they were being bitten. Pete took it downstairs and threw it into the ocean.

"Sharks will eat it up," he stated.

"Must you feed them?" I asked. He laughed.

I went to sleep that night feeling much less jumpy about the bat population than I had in the past.

Tuesday

I'm still upset from yesterday. What a day! No sooner did I come back from breakfast at the Millers' than Artilio came running into the mission house all upset about something. He asked me if I knew anything about taking fish hooks out of people. I said that it was necessary to push the hook through the skin, then take a pair of pliers and cut the barb off, then pull the hook out through the original cut. He looked flustered and in a bit of panic, so I offered to take a look at the fish hook wound in whoever it was—probably some village man who had the thing enter his finger while he was fishing off the reefs. He thanked me, grabbed my wrist before I could get away, and took off down the stairs with me in tow. We entered his house and I noticed that there was a crowd of people standing around and looking in the windows. I thought that this was a bit unusual for a fish hook, but let the thing go—probably the only exciting thing that had happened in days or something like that.

I saw him first. He was about nine years old and in the back of his thigh was a shark hook as big as my clenched fist. He was stomach down on a bench.

"Good grief Artilio!" I exclaimed.

"We don't have pliers," he added, smiling shyly. "My wife's away and she's the only one who knows anything about medicine on the whole island." He looked at me hopefully.

"Artilio, now wait one minute," I said getting a bit panicky myself, "I'm not a doctor, nor am I a nurse. The only kind of medical training I have is from watching *Doctor Kildare* on television."

"But my wife's away—I don't know how to take it out! The boy's from Mamitupu and his family brought him over here reluctantly. The island is very primitive. They allow me on it only because I can occasionally bring them medicine and because my wife Felicia has nurses' training and can help them. This is the first patient they've ever brought over from the island. If we can't help the boy we may lose a year's worth of working on the island to try to get a mission station and a school set up there."

"Oh joy," I whispered despondently.

"Do you think you can get the hook out?" he asked, eyeing me like a big beagle whose master indicates that he can't come hunting with him today.

"I'll look at it, Artilio, I'll *look,* but that's all I'm going to do."

He smiled and then told the people in Cuna that the American *doctor* was going to look at the boy's leg and help him. I caught the "doctor" and "help" and became angry with Artilio.

The boy's mother immediately set to objecting, telling the whole crowd that I was about to do away with junior, that I was not Indian, and that I was therefore a bad person. She and Artilio had a huge argument, but the islanders of Ailigandi were on Artilio's side and he won. The mother lapsed into silence and sat down at one side of the room on a small wooden bench there.

I was upset, she was in a quiet rage, Artilio was nervous. The only person who was calm was the boy himself who eyed me from big wide curious eyes. Obviously he was not in much pain.

I poured some antiseptic over the wound and over my hands after I washed them. No use getting an infection started from just *looking*. The hook was a huge thing and had penetrated the boy's flesh to a depth of at least two inches, probably a bit more. I wondered what blood vessels were in the area, and feared anyone's pushing the hook through. If there were a large vein in the area the hook could pierce the vein or artery and we'd have ourselves a bit of a problem.

I also knew we didn't have pliers. Pushing the hook through without pliers would be ridiculous unless we would bend the barb back so that it could be pulled through easily. I didn't think this would be a good idea. The only thing to do, if the hook was to come out without too much injury, was to cut down into the wound, locate the barb and extract it. I told Artilio so. I also asked him when he was doing all of this, to give the boy some anesthetic, a local variety, or a good dose of liquor.

Artilio asked me if I knew any local anesthetics. I looked at him blankly. I had no idea in the world what they were called or what the bottles would have looked like. I told him to feed the child alcohol if there was any straight liquor on the island. Artilio said that there was just beer, but that there was a medicine cabinet in the mission house, just maybe. . . .

We went to have a look. I found some xylocaine. I remembered that my own dentist used this on my gums before the drilling began. Perhaps. . . . We went back to Artilio's house with the xylocaine. I put the bottle down on the table and asked Artilio to put a little on the boy's leg. He handed me a hypodermic needle and walked out the door. I hollered for him to come back. He did.

"Artilio, I can't accept responsibility for getting that thing out of that boy. This is absurd. What if some doctor comes through here and hears about this. They'll throw me out of the country."

"There is no doctor on the island," he repeated. "Juanita," he started using my Spanish name on Ailigandi, "would you please TRY. Do your best. If something happens, I'll assume responsibility."

"Damn!" I said at nobody in particular. I wished I were on another island. I looked at the boy, he was grinning at me.

"O.K. Artilio, O.K. But if they decide to cut me into little pieces when he starts to holler," I said, indicating the child "you'd better be standing at the door with a shotgun."

I washed up again and poured more antiseptic on the boy's leg. His mother immediately started into some kind of tirade and I told Artilio to get her out of the room and keep her out of it until after whatever I was going to do was done. He did. She left angrily, and poked her head in through a window. The child was frightened now and he looked it. I smiled at him and told Artilio to tell the boy what I intended to do and that it might hurt, but that he was a man and men could stand the litle pain he would feel. He nodded his head and turned it away from me. I filled the hypodermic needle with xylocaine and not wanting to inject it into the boy directly, went down the side of the wound very very carefully and squeezed a bit of xylocaine into the wound with the plunger. I took it out and waited for a minute to see if the boy would react in any way to it. He didn't. I re-inserted the needle amid much moaning from the crowd and let the rest of the 2 c.c.'s worth of xylocaine run into the wound. I waited for three minutes, then started to probe around the hook with my fingers. I asked Artilio to ask the child if it hurt. The youngster replied that it didn't.

Artilio handed me a surgical knife from a basin of alchohol we had prepared and I started to cut, slowly and carefully, watching for any blue colored veins or what have you. Two minutes later I was halfway down to the wound, but blood was blocking my view. The boy was starting to feel the pain. I sponged the wound out with a piece of surgical gauze then gave the boy another dose of xylocaine. I reached the tip of the barb and found that it had indeed pierced a vein there. I had to get the barb out of the vein very carefully, then I eased the hook out of the boy's leg, holding the wound open with my left hand. When the hook was out the crowd cheered, but I was still uneasy about the vein.

I poured more antiseptic into the wound, then pressed the edges of it together and then pressed down with the palm of my hand to stop the bleeding. It was under control shortly thereafter and Artilio handed me a small plastic bag with a watery solution and some kind of needle and thread inside of it. It was a suture. I took it from its case and sewed the wound up as best I could, then covered it with gauze smeared with terramycin, then covered all of this with tape.

By this time my blouse was dripping with sweat about my waist, back, armpits, and chest. The child, accompanied by a good dozen relatives, set off in a dug-out for Mamitupu Island four miles east. Nobody had so much as uttered a "Mmmmmmm" as a thank you. Not that I expected it, but I thought that somebody would have been happy to see the hook out of the boy. His mother gave me one long aristocratic look and departed.

I helped Artilio, who was beaming happily, clean up his kitchen. I went back to the mission house and tried to calm my nerves and stomach which were relatively upset. I couldn't calm down up there so I went out back and sat on the sea wall. The breeze there soon had me dry and I felt much better.

"Juanita!" It was Artilio's voice. I turned around to find him with one of the elder council members of the village. "This man says that his son is running a very hot fever and is very sick. He asks that you come and look at him." He emphasized "look." I told Artilio to go to hell bluntly—missionary or no missionary. Then the council member looked very hurt and dejected and started to walk away. I called after him and went back in the house to get some antibiotics. He smiled and we went to see his son. The boy had a fever, but this morning he's cool and smiling. I think he's going to be alright—I hope.

Friday morning

I don't even know if I can record what has happened today. I feel sick, shocked, and frightened. I remember five things most vividly. I remember the grey fin shooting across the water. I remember the small Achutupuan boy playing there. I remember his scream. I remember the pink color of the water. And I remember his mother, who stood on shore and watched the whole bloody, sickening horror.

I could no more forget what has happened than forget where San Blas is located.

Artilio and I went to Achutupu this morning on a sort of medical jaunt. This week has been pretty well filled with looking at everybody within a ten mile area who has anything from t.b. to malaria. My treating of the lad from Mamitupu won me the official title of "medicine woman." A delegate from Ailigandi's council offered me a seat in council (a medicine man or woman has the right to speak in council in the Cuna government) calling me "ome nele sepugwa" or white medicine woman. I refused, but felt a bit elated, for it was a great honor. The man had been sent by Ikwanik. His brother's son was the boy I had treated for fever. He's running around and well now, thank the gods. But this morning, oh God. I don't want to think about it but it happened and I feel like the earth's biggest coward. I was 15 feet from the boy when he was attacked. I keep thinking that maybe I could have done something—anything, but I was paralyzed, I think, for the first time in my life. No, I can't think about it today. I'm shaking just remembering it.

Saturday morning

The funeral services have been begun on Achutupu Island and the whole island is in deep mourning. Men have been fishing the channel off the island trying to catch the shark, hoping that he'll return to where he attacked the boy yesterday to look again for food. They have to catch him to get the parts of the boy's body to bury or he'll go to the house of the Great Father without his leg and arm.

Today, I feel much better, although I did have a few nightmares about the affair iast night.

As I said yesterday, Artilio and I had gone to Achutupu Island three miles from Ailigandi on a medical jaunt. I was received with Artilio by the chief of the island who offered us hammocks in his house and sat to talk with us awhile. We then went over to Mamitupu. I had to take the stitches out of the child's leg. The leg was in perfect condition—no infection visible. I felt elated and proud. The child beamed happily at me and called me his "ei nuadi" which is friend and gave me three eggs. This was an offering of friendship to me, Artilio explained. I gave the boy a necklace of beads I had around my neck to seal the friendship. Artilio lifted his eyes to the roof of the hut as if thanking heaven. When we left the island, it was about eleven o'clock, and we went over to Achutupu again. The chief told us that a "moli" or tapir had been killed by one of the village men and that he would give us lunch in his hut with real meat. I was beginning to miss meat. I hadn't seen any in weeks so I accepted readily as did Artilio. When we reached Achutupu Island, I noted that a trading sloop had pulled up at the dock. She was a Colombian vessel and I noticed that she had quite a bit of sugar aboard. I wanted to purchase a 25-pound bag for the Miller family to say thanks for the marvelous hospitality I was receiving in their home and I went over to talk with the captain. Artilio went on to the chief's hut for lunch. I told him I'd join him in a few minutes. The captain of the vessel and one of his crew members were standing on the dock with me as we discussed the price of the sugar when the crewman suddenly cried out "Madre Mio!" He was looking with a horrified expression at the water. We all turned to see a fin coming in a straight line for two small boys playing in the water at a depth of about three feet. One boy was in a six foot long dug-out and the other was in the water.

The fin headed straight for the boy in the water. I screamed "Look out!" The captain cried something in Spanish and his crewman ran back at a dead run for the trading boat. I watched horrified as the child screamed, the fin turned sideways in the water and disappeared, leaving the child with his arms flung pleadingly in the air. Nobody watching moved. The second child sat hypotnized in his fragile craft his arms gripping the sides of his dug-out. Then he started to scream; he screamed and kept screaming until everyone on the island was running toward the dock. I watched in poignant horror because the sun was at an angle which permitted anyone on the dock to see exactly what was going on under the water. The water was crystal clear—at first. The captain was gripping my shoulder. I didn't realize later that he had gripped it so hard. I have black and blue finger marks there. The shark had the boy by the left leg and was shaking him mercilessly from side to side trying to rip that appendage from the child's body. Then the shark let go for an instant—the child surfaced in a growing circle of red, then started swimming toward shore; it was like watching a horror movie. He swam lazily and slowly, as though he were just taking a dip in the ocean. Everyone was screaming for him to swim fast, fast or "quai, quai!"

The crewman returned with a shotgun, hastily loaded it, and shot at the shark. He hit him, but the shark wasn't deterred—it circled the boy twice—no more than seven yards from shore, then in the midst of his second circle lunged for the child's body once again. The gun went off again. It didn't stop the grey, seven-foot monster. The crewman dropped his gun and ran back to the trading boat. By this time several men were in dug-out canoes trying to get to the boy. The shark was dragging him out into deeper water, the water was pink all the way to shore. For the second time the shark let go—then I saw that he didn't—he had what he came for, the child's leg. I almost fainted. By all reasoning, the child should have been dead, but he *again* surfaced and headed for shore, again swimming lazily, leaving a trail of red behind him. The shark was circling again. I picked up the shotgun, loaded it, and waited until the shark passed about four feet from the dock. Then I fired at his head. I hit him, but he kept going. He finished the boy by taking his arm. Now a dug-out was beside the child and pulled him hastily and with much screaming into the dug-out. There were three men in the canoe—two hit the shark, which was actually trying to tip the canoe over, with spears. The shark darted out toward the reefs with the spears still in his head and the men took their charge to shore. Then I saw a woman who was screaming hysterically on the shore. She was being supported by two other Indian women. She was about 30.

The child was brought to shore and a woman hastily took off

her saburet skirt and laid it on the sand. The men sadly put the boy on the skirt and the child's mother, as I found out, took her boy's head into her lap. He was trying to say something to her and he was smiling. We ran down from the dock to the beach. The child spoke with her for about a minute, then suddenly, as though on signal when he finished a sentence, his eyes lost their luster and remained open, expressionless, blank, dead.

Immediately, every woman in the group pulled the red scarf they wore down over their faces and broke into a high-pitched chant. They sat right down there on the beach rocking back and forth, and singing their cry-chant. A man was running up the beach, two companions behind him. He stopped when he saw the circle of islanders around the boy's body, then cried out and ran to the boy's mother. He looked down briefly at the child, then lifted his wife from the sand. He had been out fishing on the other side of the island when it happened. His wife had been on the beach, watching the whole death from beginning to end. He started to sob, his shoulders shaking, then he looked out at the water and pushed his wife from him. He ran still sobbing to a dug-out canoe, picked up two of the numerous spears lying on the beach, and put out from shore in the dug-out—the other men went after him. They pulled him back on shore and had to pin him to the sand to keep him there. When he quieted down, they walked him back to his hut. That afternoon all the men of Achutupu Island were in the channel looking for the shark. They were there this morning too.

I went back to Ailigandi with Artilio. We were both silent during the trip. We haven't discussed it, and we don't want to. He saw it too from shore.

I'd been skin diving a bit in these waters. Today I'm frightened to death to even put my toe in the water. This shark did not even give the child the benefit of circling several times, as the books say, before he attacked.

Artilio has asked me to go swimming with him and the Baptist mission teachers out in the reefs this afternoon. I don't want to, but I know that nobody can live on an island and be afraid of the water around him. I also know that if you fall off a horse, you have to pick yourself right up and remount. So does Artilio—that is, so does Artilio know that if he doesn't get me into the water today, I'm not going in again—ever. I'll fear these waters for a long, long time.

When we got back from a couple hours' worth of skin diving this morning after church services, I learned two more things and news items which have made me uneasy once again. A small boy has been attacked and killed by a shark off Mamitupu Island. Everybody thinks it was the same one who killed the other boy two days ago. Secondly, Ikwanik has spoken in the council hall that none of the people of the island can go swimming at the mouth of the river. A large shark and also some kind of monstrous alligator have been seen right at the mouth of the river. The alligator went after one of his daughters earlier this morning and Ricardo, who was the first man in the river, saw the shark in just a few feet of water inside of the river's mouth. Ikwanik seems to think that God is terribly angry with the whole Ailigandi area for some huge lapse in tribal law. He's vastly agitated and refuses to talk to anyone. He's in his hut now pondering what grave thing the Cuna could have done to God to cause all of this mass uprising of the creatures of the river and the sea. Both seemed to have developed an overpowering taste for human flesh.

Also, last night, when I went to the town council meeting there was a bit of excitement. We heard all kinds of screaming going on outside and everybody ran to see what was happening. Somehow, a cayman had swum right from the river, through the salt water, and up onto land in back of the medicine man's hut. It was shot and its head was cut off on the spot.

Hurray for Archibald! He brought the *Melda* into the dock early this afternoon, heard the shark attacks in the area, and put out a shark line with a fat piece of pork on the hook right in Ailigandi Channel. He caught a seven foot long grey shark and we think he's the one that attacked the two children. He has two spear marks in his head and they're down towing him over to the mainland now so that they can cut him open and find out what they can.

Two hours later

Two spear heads were still in "her" head and she had two babies inside of her body. They were both promptly killed and the shark's head was cut off and brought back to Ailigandi. The shark will be buried near the graveyard so that both boys' souls can join whatever parts of their bodies are still left in the shark's stomach. Everyone has been to see the shark's head at least twice this afternoon. They look and cry "Hoooooophaaaaa!" at the thing.

I have been asking around about the unusually large number of sharks in the area lately and they seem to think that the sharks came in to avoid the series of early morning storms we've been having lately. They say that the bad weather brings them close to land. I don't know how accurate of an idea that is, but it is their opinion on the subject. Anyway, they say that when the water is rough the sharks come in and feed off of the garbage thrown from the island. When they find they can eat well near the islands, they stay close by and, consequently, that's why the attacks have been occurring. Once a shark attacks man he knows that it is a simple matter to get another, and another—these fish must be hunted and killed or the waters around the island can never be safe.

They have the most phenomenal noses for blood. The slightest bit of it in the water seems to attract them for a mile around and once there is a great amount of it in the water you can even have a frenzy, each shark eating the shark next to him. Cannibalistic b's!

This afternoon I accompanied Artilio and his helpers on their rounds to Achutupu and Mamitupu. On Achutupu a young husband had succeeded in cutting off his little finger with a machete while stripping sugar cane. We managed to stop the bleeding and then treated an older man who had also cut his hand. The wound was greatly infected and swollen. He had split his right index finger down the center two days ago and didn't go to anyone for treatment. I hope that he doesn't loose the finger. Artilio is taking him back with us to Ailigandi and we're going to keep a fairly close watch on him and keep the wound as clean as we can. I made a poultice for it out of plantain—it seems to have a drawing action on infections—hope it works. It's in pretty much of a mess.

We went on over to Mamitupu and there I encountered a child who was to become very special to me in the weeks to come. I was brought into a hut where the villagers told me was a young boy who was shortly going to the house of the Great Father. I felt an immediate revulsion when I saw the child in his hammock. Large fungus-like growths covered his neck, throat, arms, and totally disfigured his left foot. He first attracted me, though, when he turned his eyes on me from the hammock. He seemed to be asking if I too would run away because his body was covered with sores and ugly. I did feel an aversion for the physical condition he was in. He looked as though he had leprosy, but he was lonely and he was sick so I smiled at him and went over and playfully tossled his hair. He broke into one of the most beautiful smiles I'll ever see anywhere. His face was very sensitive and yes, the correct word is beautiful. After he found out that I wasn't going to run away because he was dying, which he was, he settled back to win his name, the Philosopher-Poet, as I called him, by talking to me and telling me his thoughts on life through Artilio. He talked about the sun and peoples' souls and good things and bad things, birds and what the birds said to each other in the morning, late afternoon, and again in the evening. His language, which Artilio translated exactly, was colorful and beautiful. When he spoke, something totally true, totally arresting and interesting came forth. If anyone deserved to live, this beautiful child who loved life did. I could do nothing for him except to leave his mother some antiseptic to wash and clean his wounds with. I promised the family that I would contact an American doctor and have him come down to look at the child. I thought that he had t.b. from the looks of the scars and from his emaciated condition. I did write a letter that afternoon and it was off on a plane the next morning.

There was much sickness on primitive Mamitupu—t.b., malaria, skin diseases, and fevers. These people needed a qualified medical doctor badly and I hope someday soon, when the clinic is finished, they'll get one who will truly care what happens to them.

Unlike Ailigandi, both Achutupu and Mamitupu Islands are relatively untouched by civilization. The population of Achutupu is somewhere in the area of 1,000 and Mamitupu's population is something like 700 judging from the total number of huts on the island.

Achutupu particularly interests me because of the tame birds there. On the west side of the island, where I was drinking a cup of coffee one day, I was amazed when a large macaw came diving down from a coconut tree to alight in front of me. I froze, not wanting to frighten it away, loving its bright colors and rare beauty. Then I heard a young girl laughing behind me. I turned to see her dragging her skirt across the ground and it looked as though she were teasing the bird in somewhat the same manner as a young boy would tease a puppy. Sure enough the macaw took off in a run, its wings outspread after her skirt. The bird was completely tame, yet could fly. It choose, therefore, to stay on Achutupu with its young mistress who obviously loved and took good care of the exotic bird.

All over Achutupu there were tame birds—parakeets, toucons, turkeys (the wild black variety), even roosters and several large sea pelicans and more common sea gulls. I found that if you sat on the west side of the island long enough, all the birds there eventually came by to examine you at length and gave you a chance to look them over at close range. They were lovely and the peace that seemed to reign here on this lovely west beach was superb and refreshed my soul. It was a totally new experience to me to see that nowhere on the island were any of the monkeys or birds caged. They had the run of the place and were well fed and loved. What gentle people these Indians are.

The island itself is shaped like a horse shoe. Numerous coconut trees grow all over the island and at the two ends of the horse shoe, the middle land is the land of the village. There is a native woman here who wears western dress. She is the representative of modern medicine on the island, having had a few months of nurses training in Panama City. She is the island doctor, surgeon, nurse, midwife, and the moral support for the relatives of any sick or dying or dead person there. An amazing woman, she is. Her name is Aleta, and like Artilio she is a full blooded Cuna Indian. Her husband is also Indian. They have a lovely two year old daughter who is as enchanting in personality and innocence as she is in her radiant, child beauty.

Manitupu is not pretty. It is a living island and it serves as such. However, if anyone wanted to find a classic labyrinth—lo and behold here it is. Drop your unsuspecting victim in the middle of the village and tell him to make his way to the shore or beach. It may be days before he finally makes it. There are no streets on Mamitupu—just a random arrangement of huts here and there. In some instances, it was necessary for me to go right through two sleeping huts and one cooking hut to find my way to the "street" again. The huts were closely placed in many cases, and anyone who tended to be the least bit obese couldn't possibly make it without knocking down the walls of two sleeping huts. I had trouble enough getting by as it was.

Here was the most primitive of all the islands I had yet seen. Most of the men were not even wearing long pants, but simply trader-boat bought shorts. The children were all naked, and I noted with laughter that when we arrived by boat a good half dozen little boys were on the dock urinating into the water with nonchalant calmness. One youngster was urinating into the water and, with the free hand, waving hello to Artilio, the Baptist mission boys, and myself.

Another interesting thing about Mamitupu is their "new" dock. It had just been erected when we came and somebody forgot that a dock goes "down" when it reaches the beach and left the structure hanging there, nine feet in the air. Boards had been placed haphazardly on the dock structure itself and there was a long log from the top of the dock to the sand beach. Getting down this ramp was not unlike a contest of physical balance and endurance, and of course speed counted also. It's a wonder half the island boys hadn't broken a leg by this time. Then again, it has been my observation that most of these Indians have uncanny balancing powers and grace.

Everywhere Artilio and I went we were served drink and food. I've gained about five pounds since I set foot on the island of Ailigandi. I'll be fat before I leave, that the Indians have decided, and when an Indian decides (finally) to do something, he usually does it. I'm going to gain at least another ten to fifteen pounds if I don't stop accepting most of the food and drink offered me.

I'm really fortunate as it is, not to have come down with anything from eating all over the place. I fully expected at least one minor case of dysentery, but I've never been so healthy in all my life. I feel fine.

Mamitupu's history has been a fascinating one. There have been very few white people ever allowed near here. During World War II there was a radar station on top of a hill near Ailigandi, but that's rusted away to ruins now and all the U.S. servicemen who were stationed there are gone. They did leave their mark, however: a pool table which I have been using as a minor operating table in the mission house. But they were not allowed on Mamitupu. No one but a person in some kind of dire emergency has been allowed to remain on the island for a few days. Even the boat captains who dock here are not allowed ashore after the sun goes down, unless they are requested to come to a council meeting and discuss prices for goods traded or bought. If a boat arrived on the island after dark, the crew members were required, unofficially of course, to stay on board their boat until the morning.

Mamitupu was one of the few islands which did not join in the 1925 revolt against Panama—mainly because they had never had Panamanians visiting their island.

One wild tale of World War II, however, did have its beginnings and endings in the channel between Mamitupu and Achutupu. It has been authenticated by several people so I believe it to be true. It seems that in 1942 the islanders of Achutupu became very angry at those from Mamitupu because the latter villagers had taken over a very good fishing channel near the two islands. Unfortunately the argument came to blows and the Achutupans put out one morning in their dug-out canoes to raid Mamitupu carrying their flag, made during the 1925 revolt. It was a red and yellow flag—having red borders and a central panel of yellow upon which an inverted swastika, the symbol of life to the Cuna, was sewn.

The Achutupan men set out with this banner flying from the lead dug-out canoe just at the time when an American reconnaisance plane was surveying the area. The pilot spotted the flag and radioed back immediately to the Canal Zone a message that the Nazis had landed and were doing battle in dug-out canoes with the Indians in the area of Ailigandi. Immediately, an entire squadron of planes was sent out to confirm the report and attack the Nazis.

Now while all of the planes were on their way, the Mamitupans and Achutupans had their clash and were engaged in a pitched battle. The planes swooped down on their frightened heads and the cry went up that the Americans were trying to break up the fight between Achutupu and Mamitupu. They heard that the Americans were fighting a big battle across the water because somebody attacked the land of somebody else and thought that the U.S. was angry because both islands were at war with each other and were fighting. The U.S. was interceding.

Well the planes swooped and fired, the Indians raced back to their respective islands, and it was months before the truth was really found out. An entire detachment of soldiers was sent into the jungle areas to ferret and search out the guerilla Nazis. The islanders were frightened to death of the soldiers, thinking they were there to keep the peace. The whole thing was hilariously funny.

When the Americans finally found out what happened they apologized, and had a council meeting with the chiefs to tell them of the fight between the Nazis and the U.S. The Cuna Indian tribe promptly declared war on Germany and swore that if they ever landed in San Blas, the tribe would fight to the death against them.

Thursday

This morning Maria, Ricardo, Ricardido and I went over to the Tiwar. That's the river—the Ailigandi River. I thoroughly enjoyed myself there as I generally do. The forest holds a great fascination for me with its high jungle trees, vines, animals, and birds. The vividness of so many different color plants and the multiplicity of beautiful looking and sounding birds would be a constant source of pleasure to any beholder.

The jungle is not all exotic and the luxurious green covers earth of high trees and fierce jaguars where hunters and explorers live dangerously. Granted, it is a beautiful cathedral like place, but you have to watch your step, literally, to make sure that you aren't treading upon a snake or some other jungle inhabitant who may resent your inability to spot his dark or in some cases bright form on the forest floor. There are, of course, the jiggers, which penetrate your skin leaving their red tails on the surface to let you know they're there. Squeezing them out to try to make them stop itching is virtually impossible. They are stubborn and strong and once they find flesh they don't let go. The only thing I've found that seems to loosen them a bit is gasoline. A thin solution of gasoline over a jigger infested area of skin will considerably loosen the parasites and make it easier to either squeeze them out or scratch them out.

Then there's the mud, and the mud, and the mud. It's exhausting just walking on flat land with it under foot, but when you start climbing hills or, even worse, going down them, it can give an awful lot of trouble to anyone's balancing ability. Maria went charging to and fro like some kind of mountain deer, balancing Ricardido who was chattering gaily away on her hip with all the grace of a queen. I fell at least a half a dozen times until I learned never to fight the force of the mud, but to go *with* it. If you're slipping, you must slip or perhaps break your neck trying not to. I have also learned that shoes get me nowhere in the rain forest. Shod feet don't have the gripping ability of the feet and toes. The first time I came to the river, I wore sneakers for the first time in weeks. I never wear them on the island. Nobody does. But the sneakers that morning were absurdly slipping on every minute piece of mud in the area. I finally took them off and tied the laces together, hanging a sneaker over each side of my shoulder, back and front. There's a special way of walking that one eventually learns when one goes barefoot. The entire sole of the foot is put flat on the ground. If there is a stone there, you learn to subconsciously distribute the weight of the body to spots on the feet where the stone is not touching. It takes a bit of practice and a few minor battle wounds, but it's much more comfortable on the feet than shoes in the jungle.

There are animals here, but not in such profusion as one would imagine from seeing jungle film after jungle film. They are there, but it's rare that you see them or are able to differentiate between them and the foliage which very amply blends in with their various body colorations. On no occasion would any inhabitant of the jungle come right out and attack someone without provocation. Perhaps if it is being hunted or is trapped it will attack, but most jungle animals will go miles out of their way to avoid even smelling or seeing a man. Even the poisonous snakes will not come after you—given half a chance if spotted, each will run in the opposite direction from where you are standing or walking. Even the notorious boa constrictor will turn tail and run if he and a human meet. I saw one last week that rather frightened me, it being one of the largest snakes I have seen anywhere. I would estimate its length at approximately 17 feet. Most of the small boas I have seen in the Ailigandi area are relatively small, measuring on the average eight to 12 feet, and these are not very many. The particular boa that I saw was a brownish-grey in color and he was half in a tree and half out of it on a stream bank on the upper Ailigandi River. His reaction when he did see me was to *flow* foot by foot directly into a pool of water near the stream. It seems that I watched him disappear for minutes before I realized I was watching him and wondered where he was going. As I was standing on the opposite bank of the river and he was now in it, I had the sudden impression that he might be flowing *toward* me, as I was downstream from him. My reaction was to turn tail and run straight back down the river bank toward my dug-out about a mile away. That was even knowing that the snake wasn't after a meal—namely me. His size just surprized me. I hadn't expected to see anything quite that large in the jungle. My first thought had been that the snake was an Anaconda, but there are no Anaconda in the Republic of Panama, and they are more yellow in color than brown.

This particular stretch of jungle along the San Blas coast is very hilly. It seems that anywhere you want to go is separated from where you are by at least eight small hills. That means walking up and down almost vertical rises at times. An hour's worth of this kind of travelling can be physically exhausting with every muscle in the body and some you never knew you had before crying "stop" at the top of their nerve-ending voices. There are certain plants you can't touch, others that are edible, and others that you cannot stand under during even a light rain, such as the star apple, because the water hits the leaves and drops down on you and the result is a stinging pain where the water has fallen. There are mosquitoes in the jungle, blood suckers in the streams, and caymans on the river banks in early morning and late evening. The bush is so thick in certain places that you can't see a companion standing five feet away and he can't see you even though you may be facing each other. The jungle is sometimes very dry, sometimes wet, sometimes dark, and sometimes bright. It's a totally fascinating world in itself.

Jungles can also be mentally trying—especially when it rains. I remember vividly one session with my friends, the Dickens' at Chepo the year before. The three of us were in the house for four days because torrential rains flooded the October forest around us. At the end of a day we were irritated. At the end of two we were restless and ready to climb the walls—the room was hot and humid, cigarettes fell apart and out of their paper. Books began to feel slimy. We sweated. The third day it rained; we were touchy and a little remark would be blown all out of proportion. The fourth day, we were ready to kill each other. The sun came out on the fifth day and all was well and forgotten.

Any animal, including the human variety, rejoices when the sun comes out after a long, heavy rain.

Maria and I started out via dug-out canoe from Ailigandi, with me convinced that we weren't going to make it no how, no place. We were going to sink. It was as though I had said that within the next week we'd see the sun come up seven times and day would come. I *knew* it. But I went—always do. There's something inevitable about knowing catastrophe is about to descend upon oneself and yet going with the anvil on the thread right over one's head.

To begin with, Maria's household dug-out is a tiny little thing about eight feet long that would ordinarily safely support only herself and Ricardido *if* it didn't have a crack in the side and *if* it didn't have a hole in the bottom. The presence of those two obstacles made it a bit tricky with Ricardido. One had to bail constantly, which Ricardido had learned from his first reasoning moments. Secondly, it was necessary to keep the old rag of saburet stuffed in the crack—it needed restuffing about every ten minutes.

Well, this morning as usual Maria called me under the mission house window and said that we were going to the river to get water. I went down feeling happy that maybe I'd get a chance to do a bit of crab hunting on the riverbanks, and took a spear which Artilio made for me with an iron barbed top and reed body.

I took one look at the boat and started off in a tirade of Cuna mixed with Spanish, which became my own special form of dialect in this area, and generally understood by all, on how ridiculous it was to even set foot in a vessel like that. Maria laughed. I should have expected it. She just laughed and pushed off from shore signaling me to follow.

"She *must know* what she's doing with sharks and alligators and all that," I remember thinking.

I pulled the blunder of the day by bringing my Agfa Optima III camera along with me to take pictures. I sat down in the dug-out, right in the water. There was nowhere else to sit except in water. I crossed my legs and sat on the bottom balancing very carefully. The rim of the boat, piled high with empty water gourds, was two inches from the water. Every time a wave came along, it washed over the side requiring that I bail frantically to keep us afloat. Fortunately, I had the camera in a plastic bag just in case.

As the inevitable will happen, we were out in the channel between Ailigandi Island and the jungle mainland when we sank. As I say, I knew we would. We sank unceremoniously. A wave just came over the side that was bigger than all the others and "plomp blub" we were under. I had a spear in one hand and my camera in the other and was hollering for help while we treaded water. Maria was still laughing. Since there were many canoes in the area, we were hauled out in minutes and my camera didn't get wet at all since I held it over my head as we sank. Our dug-out was floating overturned on the surface. It was righted by some of the men and our gourds, which were floating on the channel water, were retrieved and given back to us. I rode to the mouth of the river in another canoe and later transferred to Maria's dug-out once again. She was still laughing. Well that was Maria. The world could have turned upside down and somersaulted and Maria would still be smiling. I had to laugh in spite of myself.

We went up past the "laundry" areas of the river. Here the Ailigandi women did their wash and took their baths. Further upstream, they got their good water to be used for drinking water and for showering back on the island. Here all the women were, for the most part, just wearing their pechas in the water. The dug-out itself was used as a scrub-board, the women rubbing their soapy clothes (they had soap from the traders) on the wood in the inside of the boat to get them clean. They'd scrub for a few moments, then take the whole skirt and beat it against the boat, then they'd rinse it and start the same operation over again.

Children were swimming about playing water games among themselves. When they finished the wash they would hang it on the bushes and trees about the river, then play in the water themselves until the laundry dried. Mothers with young children took to washing the children after the laundry was done and hung up to dry.

Maria started to eye the riverbank intently at one point, then she went over near it and picked up a whole bunch of debris and dumped it into our dug-out. There were carp there and they made good eating. She sorted these from the debris, then dumped the unneeded garbage back into the water.

Ricardido and his father were already in the jungle, having gone there earlier. We were to meet them with their big dug-out a bit further upstream. We reached their dug-out as Ricardo and his son were coming down a jungle path to their canoe to deposit bananas and thatch for a new addition to the house he planned to build.

I noticed with joy that there were quite a few crabs out of their holes this morning and went off to do a bit of hunting of my own. They made delicious eating.

Hunting crabs isn't as easy as it may seem. Some of these nine inch delicacies were as cautious of the approach of any living thing as a man would be of any large fish in the water. Actually, the trick was to hunt them by night with a flashlight. Shining the beam down into any of these holes made them come out to look and they could be easily speared at close range. Hunting them fairly on their own ground during the day was another matter entirely. It was necessary to be either deadly accurate with a spear or a genius at sneaky camouflage and silent tracking. I possess neither of these shining qualities.

The usual tactic for a person of my calibre was to run down the river bank full speed and *surprise* the crabs before they could know anything was wrong and go back in their holes. A quick jab with a spear *could* get a good sized crab lodged on the end of it. I would like to have been a disinterested observer sitting in a tree that morning. I must have been a hell of a sight, running full speed bare-footed, wearing dungarees and a loose blue long sleeved shirt, my pigtails flying in the breeze and a spear raised in my right arm, my beads jingling and jangling. I probably frightened to death any crab I got that afternoon before I speared the thing. The birds on the banks of the Ailigandi River had a show that morning.

Another tactic that I tried out briefly and with some success was that of the "casual passer-by" technique. I walked casually along the riverbanks as though I were just an innocuous sight-seer. I whistled and just walked by several crab holes in time to see the occupants half in and half out of the hole trying to figure out whether I was hunting or not. It was then necessary to be very quick. The spear was then thrown quickly into the *hole,* literally letting down the iron gate so that the crab couldn't get in his hole, and nobody else was going to let him in *their* hole once that happened. Then a quick hit over the head with the flattened side of a machete stunned the crab enough for me to get him into my woven crab basket which Artilio's father made for me.

Another technique and one which requires patience is the "tree" technique. It requires that you walk right into the middle of an area simply crawling with crabs and turn into a tree—that is stay absolutely still. This can be a bit tiresome as your spear arm is up in the air when you begin and by the time the crabs are convinced that you're gone, it can go completely dead. However, it does work.

Another tactic is the "attack from the west" method. This requires that you go into the jungle and sneak up on the riverbank. The crabs' holes are usually built so that most of the dirt is thrown to the west of the hole. It has been my observation that most crab holes face east. It is then necessary to sneak up on a crab hole and peer very carefully inside of it from the rear, spear first. Many an unwary crab has met his end on my crab spear with this fierce tactic.

In the midst of my experimenting with all of these various tactics for the successful hunting of the jungle river crab—somebody hit me on the back of the head with an orange. I picked up the orange. It was half eaten. I knew it just didn't fall, particularly if it was half eaten. Somebody had deliberately thrown it at me. "Game time at the old ranch," I thought and inspected the area. "Unprovoked attack," I thought again. "Maybe it's one of the crabs retaliating?" I couldn't see any irregular movement of the trees because a light breeze was blowing. The orange had come from above, that I was sure of. I decided to let the incident pass and was employing the casual passer-by technique when another orange came cascading through the trees, landing on my back.

"Deadly accurate," I thought as I inspected the landscape again. I found the branches of a particular tree moving when there was no breeze.

"Your days are numbered," I thought and set off as silently as I could in a full wide circle keeping a good distance and much foliage between myself and the tree from whence came the orange.

There it was on a lower branch of the tree. It was a beautiful little black and white marmoset with a branch of oranges in his hands. I stood watching him for some time. He couldn't see me and was facing the other way. He would walk up and down his tree branch looking off in the direction in which I had disappeared. At one point the little beauty jumped up and down holding an orange in his hand, screaming his rage at the whole forest world. He had lost me. I found this too much and started to laugh aloud. The sound of my laughter may as well have been the "Call to Arms" of a British regiment to the tiny furry creature because he dropped the whole branch of oranges and the one he had in his hand and went climbing feverishly to the top of the tree screeching as though I'd wounded him, his brothers and sisters, and slaughtered his mother and father in cold blood. When he attained the highest height he clung there by one arm and cried out at me. To me it sounded like:

"You tricked me! You tricked me!"

I laughed for a long time—between the marmoset and the crabs I'd had a marvelous afternoon. Just at that moment, two beautifully colored macaws flew into the tree occupied by the marmoset. He angrily chased them off with his screams and they went on to another part of the forest.

I went on with my hunting. I came upon the straight path of the large sail ants in the jungle undergrowth and sat down to have a look at them. They carried leaves, sometimes four times their size, to their home somewhere up from the river. Their paths through the jungle were cut straight and I knew they could strip a tree in a matter of hours. I could have found their mound if I so chose, but I also knew that "guard ants" had been placed around it and I was an intruder, a bare-foot intruder at that. I decided that it wouldn't be worth it. I found the orange tree my tiny playful marmoset had evidently snacked on and picked myself a few oranges. It is not easy to starve in the jungle if one knows what to eat. Water can be had from any of the great liana vines—it doesn't even have to be boiled, but can be drunk straight from the root. A thick liana vine is cut about three feet from the ground, then at ground height—a good gallon's worth of *water* can be had this way. It is somewhat bitter tasting, but it nonetheless quenches thirst.

I went back to the river and found Maria and the family swimming there. I dove headfirst fully clothed into the pool. I was hot and sticky and the water felt deliciously cool to me.

After our swim, we all went back to Ailigandi.

I was good and tired by this time so Mrs. Miller gave me an early supper and I went upstairs to sleep. My crabs were now being devoured by Ricardido. The knowledge of being able to provide actual hunted food is a very gratifying feeling to any human being. I slept well that night.

Saturday

Last night I accompanied Maria and her husband Ricardo to the Kantules' song rehearsal. There's going to be a Chicha or puberty feast in the village soon and they all want to be in their best voice for the occasion—hence, choir practice.

The practice of the puberty rite chants took place in the hut of the chief Kantule at about seven this evening and Maria's two children, Ricardido and Leopoldo, were with us. We were ushered into the hut and shown low-lying hand carved seats placed in a semi-circle around a small table on which stood a kerosene lamp.

A young Kantule performed the first act of the evening by passing among everyone present with a long roll of tobacco, the lighted end of which was in his mouth. He blew through the "cigar" and smoke came out the wrong end as we know it, into the faces of anyone at the other end. The smoke had a relaxing effect on all of us, and was given to all to keep "nia," or the devils away from the Kantule's hut and the people there during the practice ceremony.

As far as the Cuna are concerned, there are devils all over the place just waiting to pounce on any unsuspecting Indian who happens to be around when a particular devil gets the urge to be naughty and carry off somebody's soul to the underworld. When that happens the person's body immediately gets horribly sick with fever or some other deadly disease and a medicine man is summoned to come and sit with the Indian whose soul or "purba" has been stolen and sing. The purpose of his chants and great use of medicine dolls is to instill life into the dolls themselves. Then the dolls' souls go down into the underworld and talk things over with the devil and barter for the return of the soul to the world of the living. The doll's soul may fight, be diplomatic and talk, be sneaky and steal back the soul, or simply threaten to beat the devil within an inch of his life. Any way of fighting devils is fair.

Sometimes these devils take on a very definite form and can be seen in the most common art work of the Cuna—the women's mola blouses. Here, in dark destructive horror, the imaginary devils take on the form of sharks, sea snakes, land snakes, stingrays, and other nameless horrors which go about eating people, poisoning them, or simply swallowing boats whole.

One of the most commonly portrayed devils, and one of the fiercest and most feared is the dog—bull—jaguar combination, which no man may look upon without falling dead in his tracks. This particular devil lives in the high jungle regions.

A common devil on the island may take the form of an "usir" or vampire bat who goes around at night looking for young unmarried girls to bite.

Naturally, with so many fierce horrors lurking at every turn and in every aqua wave, the Cuna have had to devise numerous protective devices to save them from this host of unmentionables.

The best protection for any of the above named is a small carved medicine doll hung about the neck by a piece of string or twine. This doll holds a special place of respect in the house and if a man is fishing in heavy shark waters, the night before he leaves on his venture he will sing to the medicine doll to awaken it to be watchful and protect him the next day. An unsung-to medicine doll soon falls asleep and doesn't do its job.

Each household has its own retinue of medicine dolls especially for protecting the hut itself. An offering of a banana or perhaps an orange every once in a while keeps these medicine dolls on their toes and watchful for nias.

But these are strictly for the protection of the household itself. If an unusually strong devil descends upon the village with a bunch of his friends, the result is dreadful indeed. A huge sickness may hit the village and cause a dozen people at the same time to fall ill. Then it is necessary to join forces at this time and make a combined effort to rid the village of the host of devils.

A general council meeting is called and the head medicine man describes what everybody knows is taking place in the village. A strong devil is there. He must be chased out and everyone must help. A general smoking of tobacco, a hated scent to any devil anywhere, must be made immediately. Giant medicine dolls must be carved, so that when they are chanted to life, they will be able to deal effectively with the strong devil. Men go off into the jungle and bring back balsa logs and carve furiously and feverishly for two days. The dolls are supposed to represent the strongest men the Cuna can think of. I found a John F. Kennedy medicine doll and a General MacArthur medicine doll on Ailigandi Island, sitting outside of the council hall when I got there.

When all of these dolls, numbering anywhere from two to 20, are finished, they are brought with all haste into the chicha hut. They are set up along side the walls and immediately the medicine men and Kantules start their chants and everybody else smokes themselves blind. All the men of the village congregate in the chicha hut in the morning and smoke until night fall. No one may leave or enter the village for seven days and nights. Walking on the very streets is permitted only in an emergency. All the women generally stay indoors and wait until their men chase the devil away.

At the end of the seven days' smoking ceremony and the huge pitched battle between the medicine dolls' souls and the souls of the strong devil, the men go home and recuperate. Their island is saved. All is well, hopefully.

Cuna women are especially afraid of the devil. They paint a black line down their long noses to prevent him from nearing them. The seed of a pine plant is cut open and the sticky sap applied to the bridge of the nose with a small stick. Then black coal dust is applied to this with the small stick to make the black line. Such protection generally lasts from two to three days.

When all the smoke had been dispersed around the chief Kantule's hut, and in all of our respective faces, the practice session was ready to begin.

Each Kantule had a rattle made out of the same kind of gourd we used for carrying water from the river, but smaller in size. It had been filled with hardened flower seeds and a handle was affixed at the opening so that no seeds could escape.

The hundreds of years old chants commenced and I sat back to listen to them. They were sung in minor scale and in 4/4 time. Ricardo didn't join in right away, but sat beside me and translated some of the songs.

One song dealt with the duties of a young, mature, but unmarried boy toward his family:

> A grown boy who has no wife
> and lives in the house of his parents
> must listen to their words and gain wisdom.
>
> He must think to go out and get fish for them
> He must think of growing plantains and food
> so that his house will have enough to eat.
>
> When he sees that the thatch on the roof lets
> in rain,
> He must think to gather new palms for a good roof.

If a boy's father is very old, the boy must
think to do the hardest work for him because
a boy's body is young and strong.

A boy must think ahead to when he gets a wife
and must grow more than enough to eat in the
'Sapuro' or jungle so that he can feed her well.

A good boy must think to bring home good firewood for the cooking, so that the fire burns
always in the cooking hut.

Another chant described the duties of a father to his children:

A good father must think to plant more bananas,
corn, fruit, sugar cane when a good baby is
with his mother's body and growing strong.

A father when he gets a new baby girl must think
to save coconuts to get her a good nose ring.

When the new baby is a boy, the
good father thinks to plant coconut
trees for him so that when he is seven
orange seasons old, he will have money.

A good father thinks to clear good land
when his son is seven seasons old, so that
his son can begin to learn how to grow food
to keep his family well and fed.

A good father thinks of buying a new hammock
for a baby who is no longer drinking from
its mother's breasts.

A good father must think to catch more fish
to feed his good babies.

A good father thinks to talk to his good
children to teach them the ways of our
people and to be a good person.

There are also chants describing the duties of a young girl to her house and to her mother:

A good daughter must think of building
the fire for her mother when the sun is
still peeking from the sea.

She must think to help her mother
crush corn for the morning drink.

She must think to fetch water from the
river and help nana with the family
washing.

A good girl helps nana with her babies
and takes good care of them, teaching
them what she has taught her.

A good girl must think to sweep the
cooking hut floor with pepper tree
branches, and she must think to
do the same to the sleeping hut floor.

A good girl must think of taking the
cachi (hammocks) out into the sun
so that any devils will be heated out
of them.

A good girl thinks to peel plantains for
the family meals.

A young girl who has no husband
must not have her man to visit
too long in the hut with her at night.

A good girl knows not to leave the hut
when the sun goes into the sea in the
west because devils will come and steal
her soul or beat her.

A young unmarried good girl must guard
her pecha (slip) well and not lose
her honor until she is in her marriage
hammock.

Other duties of a wife and mother were sung:

A good wife must think of her
family and keep them well fed.

A good wife must have good girl
babies and not look at the moon
too long when the baby is growing
or a moon child (Albino) will be
born to her husband.

A good wife must bear her children
well, and when they are born,
deliver them with pride and strength.

A good mother watches out well for
the purbas of her children and lets
nia never close to them.

A good wife and mother must think
to get up early and with her daughters
prepare the morning drink for her sons
and her husband and grandfather.

If a stranger comes from another land
a good mother will give him food to eat,
a cup of good drink and a place to sleep
and rest in.

A good mother must think that when her
daughter becomes a woman, she must think
of a good man for her daughter that works
hard and can feed her well.

These chants are sung in the council hall at least twice a week and all the villagers attend and the mothers with even their youngest children. The children listen to the songs as soon as they can reason and learn from them what their duty is at any particular age in life. I am truly sorry that there is not space here to list the songs in their entirety, but the short examples here will give an ample idea of what is taught to the respective age groups and sexes.

This system of teaching works very well, for in more than a half year's worth of time I was to spend in the area, I never found an evil or delinquent child.

The hierarchy in the set-up of a house is interesting. The eldest woman is the head of the household and that is usually the old grandmother. She is responsible for seeing that the household functions smoothly. She is the ultimate arbitrator in a dispute that may arise. She is a young mother's advisor and helps her care for her children. She is respected and loved by all, down to the youngest newly arrived baby. If the old grandmother is sick or bedridden, her eldest daughter takes over her duties, but still consults her before making any decision affecting the household.

The Cuna men know from the time that they are babies what their responsibilities are to their women and village. They are in charge of building huts and keeping them repaired. They are in charge of feeding their family and protecting them from any danger. They are in charge of fishing and hunting and all farm work.

The women are taught to cook, sew, take care of babies, care for their men, wash, sew, and perform their duties without a word being passed between them such as "it's your turn to sweep the floor this morning." Each person knows what he has to do in order to keep the household functioning properly and goes about his duty. There is never never any talk of "Darling, please bring back an extra hand of plantains this evening from the river—a guest is coming." The man realizes that he must always bring a little bit more than necessary to feed one and all and does it.

Consequently, because of all this automatic knowledge, there is rarely any domestic friction in an Indian household or community.

The practice session was soon over and Maria and the children and I walked back to her hut. On the way my eye fell on a rather large tarantula sitting in the middle of the path, and Leopoldo immediately dashed to our rescue grabbing a piece of a branch and beating it to death.

After a cup of sugar cane drink at Maria's I went back to the mission house and slept peacefully.

7

CHICHA

One morning when the sun found Ailigandi, eleven-year-old Tuhele awoke and got up from her hammock to discover that she was no longer a child, but a woman by tribal law. She took steps to conceal the evidence of her maturity from any eyes in the household, then went over and whispered the news to her grandmother. The old woman nodded her head unexcitedly, then removed the pipe on which she had been chewing from her mouth. She whispered something back to the girl who shyly returned to her hammock.

"Why do you return to your hammock?" asked the girl's father Ipilele who was preparing his hooks and lines for a day of fishing off the great reef.

"You are more than a little bit lazy today," he commented.

The girl did not answer, but blushed.

"Tuhele is now a woman and soon will be ready to take a husband into our house. She will give forth many good girl babies," her grandmother said.

Ipilele, hearing such happy news smiled, then quietly gathered his sons and the husbands of his other two daughters. A small hut must be constructed immediately within the large sleeping hut of his family for Tuhele's first puberty rites. Even before any of the men had any cocoa or coffee drink, they were swiftly off in dug-out canoes across the channel toward the jungle mainland and Ailigandi River. The sun had not been visible an hour before they returned with banana leaves and several small newly made posts. Four posts were placed within Ipilele's sleeping hut to form a small square. Small supporting posts were tied horizontally over these with behuco vines. Tuhele herself, was brought into the miniature roofless, wall-less hut and made to sit on a small carved seat within this enclosure. The family men handed her old grandmother the slender long banana leaves which were fitted into place between the behuco vines, forming walls for the enclosure.

While this was going on, several neighbors came in and out of Ipilele's hut, each being served a cup of cocoa drink, according to hospitality customs, and observing the ceremony in progress. Soon news of Tuhele's coming of age was all over the village. According to Indian law, no one spoke a word or discussed the event. The villagers looked and could see that a normal social event had taken place, and seemed to keep the information for themselves. It was nonetheless known by one and all in Ailigandi.

All day long, Tuhele was confined during daylight hours within the small hut. During this time, young married girls of the village, who had themselves recently become mature, carried gourds full of salt water from the ocean to pour over Tuhele's body in order to keep her "purified" and to keep the devil away. At night, Tuhele was bathed by the same girls with fresh water from the Ailigandi River, carried over to the island by dug-out canoe, and finally allowed to return to her hammock for the night. This same washing ceremony was repeated for four days. On the fifth morning after she had become mature, Tuhele's father and several of his friends again made their way to the Ailigandi River.

What took place there is generally a most secret ceremony and as a rule, non-Indians are not allowed to view the event. I was allowed, by virtue of the fact that Tuhele was one of my favorite friends in the village, to accompany the men, provided I didn't participate directly in the ceremony that ensued and that I keep my distance. I was not allowed to bring my camera with me.

I was in a separate canoe paddled by myself and Ricardo, following Ipilele and his friends in their's up the river when darkness was still covering the mountains to the south. One-half mile up the river, all the men stopped talking to one another and two, Ipilele and his friend, crept onto the river bank with tiny trading boat-bought flashlights. These they flashed into crab holes in evidence along the high sand banks until an occupant stuck his blue body out of his hole to find out why the sun had come up so quickly. He was forcibly snatched and put into a straw basket uninjured by Ipilele. A hoot went up from the men. Such ease in catching the crab meant that Tuhele would deliver her first child with ease. If they had had a difficult time catching this crab, it would have meant that Tuhele would experience difficulty with her first baby. A further search was made for a white female crab. After several blues appeared in the openings of their holes, a large white female was finally caught—just as easily as the blue male had been. The men cheered again. Tuhele's marriage and child-bearing would go exceptionally well according to all these good omens.

The dug-outs continued up river and were finally tied beside a large stand of plantain and banana trees on the south riverbank. Here ensued the secret fertility ceremony of the Cuna peoples taught to them by Ibeorgan, their great golden-haired teacher.

The men went to a special plantain tree which had been marked the day before in red with a cross made with the juice of a flower. A cross and inverted swastika are ancient symbols of life in many primitive tribes. Ipilele then chopped down this plant with his machete and let the entire growth slowly tumble to the ground. From the stem of green plantains that were attached to the plant, he chose the largest plantain and picked it. He then signaled that his friend who had helped him in catching the crabs was to have the rest of the plantains for his family. The group followed by Ricardo and myself, then proceeded to walk down a long river path that cut away from the waterway and into the jungle. After a half an hour we came upon a clearing with a small star apple tree in the center. Dawn was starting to come, turning the jungle grey.

The men circled the tree and Tuhele's father walked around it seven times. He climbed up the tree to the place where two main branches of the trunk grew apart and placed his plantain there.

He then continued up the tree, to sit on a branch and shake it, making three dozen or so fruits fall to the ground. These were quickly gathered by the remaining men on the ground who put them all into another waiting straw basket. We all went back to the dug-outs and then continued on to Ailigandi Island.

I thought a moment about the significance of what had just taken place—the fruit—obviously representing a man—had been placed at the break of the trunk of a tree—a woman. The ceremony had insured that Tuhele would accept her husband into her hammock readily.

When we reached Ailigandi, Ipilele's friend then took the basket of fruit from the canoe and ran through the village streets until he reached the house of Tuhele. Ricardo and I also ran so that I might see what happened next. The "fruit" man ran in and out of Ipilele's hut making sure that several fruits dropped in the vicinity of the small hut in which Tuhele and her grandmother were waiting. The grandmother reached out of the enclosure and chose one of these fruits. I was allowed to sit with the female friends of the family on the side of the sleeping hut itself. We were waiting the results of the cutting of this piece of fruit that would determine the whole course of the girl's future wedded bliss. The fruit was duly cut and the old grandmother called forth the results. No one but the girl and her grandmother were allowed to see the ceremony. If, when the fruit was cut, there were more seeds in the right hand piece of fruit, the girl's husband would be unfaithful to her. If there were more seeds on the left than on the right, then the girl would be unfaithful to her husband at some point during their married life. If an equal number of seeds were in each half of the fruit, then the girl would live in marital bliss until the end of her days. Tuhele's fruit foretold that she would be unfaithful to her husband. This news evoked a good hearty laugh from all the women in the room. No men were allowed to be present in the hut, but many children were at the outside wall. The news would soon be all over the village.

After this ceremony, Tuhele's grandmother gathered the rest of the fruits, cut them open, and coated Tuhele from head to foot with the juice—which turned her golden skin black. This was to protect her from any attack by devils from the underworld who seeing that Tuhele was now mature, would try to steal her "purba" or soul and take it down to their world with them. This would result in Tuhele's becoming gravely ill and possibly dying. No devil would now come near her, as the juice from this fruit made any person using it invisible to the devil.

It was so that Tuhele appeared in public the next morning—very shy and totally invisible to devils, but totally spottable in a crowd of hundreds because of the color of her dyed skin.

The next step in Tuhele's preparation in becoming a wife and mother was the great "Ina" or medicine feast in which the entire village would participate. Anywhere from a month to a year after coming of age, a young Cuna girl goes through the sacred hair cutting ceremony accompanied by a feast of two or three days duration in her home village.

In Tuhele's case, two weeks after she was mature, her father, having many coconuts and being therefore wealthy, decided to have her "coming out" party. The coconuts were needed to pay medicine men, singers, dancers, and dignitaries for their services at the Ina, which was also known in general as the "Chicha" feast. This was the name of the homemade Indian liquor served during the ceremonies.

Ipilele requested that a general council meeting of the village elders and chiefs be held. Here he announced the already well-known fact that his daughter was now a woman and had gone through the primary puberty rite. He requested that the village work together to give her a feast within the month.

Chief Ikwaniktipippi then made the announcement official and asked for a feast to take place. He appointed several young men to gather sugar cane from the jungle mainland. Another dozen or so would help bring the stalks to Ailigandi to be crushed by the women for the chicha drink. "Ikwanik," as I called him for short, further decreed that each man in Ailigandi Village must bring 12 big fish (measured to be as big as the distance from finger tips to elbow of the first chief's left arm), to the chicha house "kitchen" or cooking hut for meals that would be served for all the people of Ailigandi and guests during the three-day feasting that was to be held for Tuhele.

When all of these preparations had been called for, the village men went to the jungle mainland after the needed sugar cane. It was brought to the village and the families of each of these men took turns in operating the sugar cane press to extract the juice from the cane. The press in which this was performed was made from two logs placed in a stationary tree trunk one on top of the other. A woman or young boy got on top of the uppermost log at the opposite end from where it was lodged in the tree trunk and jumped up and down. The cane was placed between the logs on the "up" jump, when the logs were parted, and on the "down" jump, the cane was crushed and juice flowed out. It was caught in containers right under the press. The juice was then carried to the big chicha house cooking hut and placed in large iron cauldrons to boil. These were tended by one of the most interesting Indians or people I ever met in my travels. He was about 25 years old and a deaf-mute. His eyes were the happiest eyes I have ever seen anywhere. I was invited into his kitchen one day with myriads of sweeping gestures and sign language. I was offered a log seat on the side of the hut while the boy tended his cauldrons, much in the same manner as a lovable witch would have tended hers. The boy was very gracious, offering me tastes of the heated sugar cane to drink and demonstrating exactly what process the cane juice would take before it became "chicha." I was completely fascinated with the preparations, but more so with the boy's child-like gesturing, whistling, and sign-language. At one point in his work, he danced clear around several of the cauldrons then jumped clear over a rather large one, laughing at his own fun-making, as I did. He had a marvelous sense of humor and a sensitivity to people that was rare in a world like his, or mine for that matter. I should have imagined that he had never left Ailigandi, except to go to the jungle, but he was completely content and happy with his island and his life. When the cane had reached the boiling point, he poured into it a mixture of herbs and corn. This mixture was let boil for a good hour. The fire was then extinguished and by means of a large half-gourd joined to a stick, much in the same design as soup ladles, he transferred the liquid into very large waist-high earthen jugs lined up against one wall of the cooking hut. When the jug was completely full, he took banana leaves and wrapped them with behuco vine around the mouth of the large jug. He repeated this process until each jug had been sealed tightly.

These jugs were then carried, with the help of three men, into the chicha hut, four huts down. They were placed beside ten other identical jugs. The drink would ferment for a period of from 11 to 13 days at the end of which time, the great Chicha feast would begin.

This boy, whose name I later learned was Machi Pepe, or Little Boy, a fond nickname, given to him by the villagers, was very proud of his proficiency and usefulness on this important occasion. I also heard that Machi Pepe was not allowed to marry. The chiefs were afraid that some of the boy's offspring might carry his same physical defects. I wondered how he had survived as long as he did. Deformed children have been often times known to disappear soon after birth. It is generally believed that the children were left to die on the jungle mainland, the father and mother believing that the child would not be happy if it grew up with a deformity or was unhealthy. I figured that since Machi Pepe's deafness or muteness could not be detected at birth, the mother and child had been attached when the child's defect was finally uncovered. By then, nothing could be done to take the child from its mother.

If a defect were found later in life, then for the greatest good, the deformed individual was not allowed to marry. The same was true of the "Moon Children," who are so much in evidence in these islands. An albino "Moon Child" did not, unless unusual circumstances prevailed, marry. The exceptions to this rule were few. I met a perfectly healthy San Blas woman of normal coloring married to the albino chief of one of the small islands not far from Ailigandi. In this case, the male Moon Child had proved himself superior in many ways and was granted a normal wife. He had two light haired albino boys, and three normal girls by this woman. It is my opinion from observation of the albino Moon Children, that they are generally possessed of more than average intelligence and more often than not were chiefs, Kantules or medicine men in their home villages. They were treated with great respect by the rest of their village because it was believed that if one treated a Moon Child well, one would share in the much bigger happiness the Moon Children would have in the land of Ibeorgan and the Great Father after death.

Since Machi Pepe was neither a Moon Child, nor particularly intelligent, the village had decided that he should remain celibate. I was pleased to see that this didn't lessen his enjoyment of people, his work, or his life one single bit. He was a beautiful person.

While all of these "Chicha" preparations were going on, the village men were catching their allotted number of fish and the women were cleaning and smoking them over fires in the cooking hut. The fish would keep well this way until the time of the great feast. The Kantules were consulted by Tuhele's father and a certain number of coconuts, plaintains and fish were agreed upon as payment for their singing services during the feast. One chicken was bought and set aside in an enclosure near the chicha hut for the first-day ceremonies. All the village women and young girls were busily sewing new mola dress tops so that they would look their best on that great day.

The village medicine man was busily manufacturing long cigar-like rolls of tobacco that would be smoked by the Kantules during the feast. These were symbolic of the birth umbilical cord. The cord, an item of superstitition to the Cuna, was buried under a mother's hammock soon after she gave birth. The reason for its use during puberty rites was that it is also a symbol of life to the Cuna—and the reason for the feast was the birth of a new woman into tribal society. This same medicine man was daily visiting Tuhele's hut, spending at least an hour with her chanting the songs teaching the duties, sexually and otherwise, of a woman to her husband, family, mother-in-law, other women and so on. He also sang off any devils who might have been lurking in the area waiting for a chance to carry off Tuhele's "purba" before the Chicha feast. She was no longer painted black and consequently was quite vulnerable and visible to devils. Pots of green pepper incense were prepared and set aside for burning each day in Tuhele's hut. This smell more than any other single thing was detestable to devils and I might add, to any other human being in the area. I got a lungfull of it walking by the house one afternoon and found myself totally incapacitated for 15 minutes, coughing and having my eyes water their irises out. I was a bit more cautious to check which way the breeze was blowing when I walked past her hut for the next few days.

At night, all the local Kantules gathered to practice their songs in the hut of the chief Kantule of Ailigandi. They all wanted to be in good voice for the up-and-coming feast. Judging from the sounds coming from that hut, I decided that this was going to be a fascinating ceremony to listen to as well as watch. I distinctly remember one medicine man's voice which sounded completely hypnotic and nasal. I later found out that this Kantule was a visiting dignitary from Narkana Island who had been invited to take part in the feast by Tuhele's father. He was well regarded all over San Blas for his singing powers, although for the life of me, I couldn't tell just why. Of all the men singing in that hut, he was the worst by my own Western standards of judging singing ability.

Relatives of Tuhele's from all over the vast area that was San Blas gathered a few days in advance of the first day of the feast to help with preparations. Everywhere on Ailigandi activity was in evidence, preparatory to the feast. Excitement was high. News, though not by any official means of communication, had gone out over the "jungle grapevine" and there were sure to be hundreds of people from the surrounding islands present for the feast.

A further situation developed. Tuhele's father had been contacted by another father in the village whose daughter had recently matured. It seemed that he was not as wealthy in coconuts as Ipilele, and wanted to make use of Tuhele's puberty hut to have the hair-cutting ceremony performed on his daughter. This was an accepted custom in the village and Ipilele readily agreed on a normal price for the use of the hut—200 coconuts. The hair-cutting ceremony must be performed as soon after a girl becomes mature as possible if the girl is to marry a year after that, which is the custom among the Cuna. Also, those girls who had gone through this ceremony already, during the last two years, were told by their parents to be watchful because they might find themselves married before the feast was over with.

At last the final preparations were completed. Two days before the feast would begin, the chiefs, medicine men and Kantules gathered in the chicha house for the tasting ceremony. The hut had been guarded now for 11 days and nights by three men who ate and slept there so that no one could get in and disturb the chicha or taste it before the appointed time. I went into the hut to watch this activity.

Machi Pepe opened one jug of chicha, filled a gourd with the reddish-colored liquid and handed it to Cerefino Colman, the first chief of Ailigandi. Cerefino nodded, muttered "Mmmmmmmmm," then handed the empty gourd back to Machi Pepe. The latter refilled the gourd and handed it to Ikwanik, then in turn to all the other village dignitaries in order of their rank. It was generally agreed that this was a very good batch of chicha and that the feast would take place as planned in two days. Machi Pepe smiled proudly at this news. It was the greatest compliment he could have received.

Tuhele, upon reception of this news, was taken into conference by her grandmother who told her in those two days all the things the medicine man couldn't describe to her about a woman's knowledge of sex, child-bearing, and generally how to keep her man happy and children healthy.

A small hut was constructed outside of the chicha hut door. It was about 12 feet long and ten feet wide. This was covered all over and roofed with banana leaves brought from the jungle mainland by Tuhele's father and friends. A hole was dug at the far end of the hut to a depth of about two feet, and two carved seats placed behind the hole for the girl's grandmothers to sit on. Board seats were placed on both sides of the hut for visitors, and incense pots set up for later lighting when the feast got under way. That completed most of the preparations for the feast.

The night before the first day, the chief medicine man sang in council at the council hut of the events which had taken place concerning the "ina," and their meaning to the Cuna tribe.

Soon, everyone went home and to bed to rest up before beginning the three-day feasting. I went back to the mission house to spend a peaceful night with the bats and rats there.

Somewhere in the village I could hear a mother singing her baby to sleep with the music of a "narsis" or rattle. Then I thought for a few moments before sleep came of all I had observed that week. I was looking forward to the events of the morrow.

With the sound of tiny rat feet running along the rafters, as usual (I would have thought something drastically wrong if I didn't hear them) I drifted off to sleep.

Monday—the first day of the Chicha feast

Well, my only comment about today is that it was worth waiting two weeks for. As a matter of fact, I would have waited months to witness and partake in what I have seen today. More of the same is in store for tomorrow and I'm looking forward to that too, provided no more accidents manage to occur on the island.

I was up at dawn this morning so that I'd be able to drift here and there looking at everything that was happening in preparation for 11 o'clock and the opening ceremony of the Chicha feast. In the cooking hut, fires were started before dawn. These would be kept alive for three days. In the cooking hut, piles of logs, brought by the men from the jungle mainland, would be used as fuel. Great iron cauldrons of plantains cooked in the juice of grated coconut meat and water started to warm over the heat of the fires. Other cauldrons full of cocoa drink and coffee drink were also heating here. Bowls and cups full of these drinks would be given to guests who arrived from other nearby islands to join in the feast. These cauldrons would be empty by the end of the day and the patient old grandmothers who tended to the stomachs of thousands would be up into the night preparing more coffee and cocoa beans for the next day's drink. Another great pot was full of rice. If a visitor was hungry when he arrived he would be fed the rice to "keep his stomach from dying" as the Cuna say. No Cuna Indian would ever let a visitor be hungry while visiting the villages of the tribe. The Cuna believe that if a person departs hungry, unrested, or sad from one of their villages, that the Great Father who lives with Ibeorgan, would be more than a little bit angry with them. He would send sickness and possibly death to the village for such unhospitable acts.

Racks full of smoked fish received a fresh envelope of the smoke from the burning "nalup" or black palm logs. This tree makes the best fire wood since it burns longer and with cleaner ash than any other wood in the jungle. The five elder women tended to their cooking and by the time the sun was an hour in the sky everything was well on its way to being ready for the first visitors to arrive on

Ailigandi Island. In the east, the sun turned the sky gold once again. It rose from the green sea, as I had seen it rise for weeks. This was a special time of day for me. I went to the sea wall to watch the event as faithfully as a "Mets" fan would have gone to one of their ball games, win or, as the case generally is, lose. It was a wonderful thing that people could watch a sun rise like this on almost any morning. Living in San Blas was like living in the place that was shown on Tahitian travel posters. The Cuna had the benefit of the rugged beauty of the high jungle at their island finger tips, and the beauty of the Caribbean Sea at their front door. The life here was full of peace lived in almost constant marriage with nature's beauty. No wonder the Cuna were so wonderfully happy.

I walked back to the chicha hut to see what preparations had been made there for the day. The hut had been sectioned off into three parts and hammocks were hung in all three sections. The chicha guards were still faithfully present and explained to me where everybody would sit once the ceremony got under way. I noted with amusement the large supply of hammocks near the two doors which had been placed there for the convenience of merrymakers who passed out or were tired from too much chicha. The central five hammocks were to be used by the Kantules once the feasting got under way. From the preparations that I saw, there was no need to leave this hut at anytime during the three days of partying, except to answer the call of nature. Food was to be served here twice a day—hammocks had been provided for those who had too much—liquor would flow in unlimited supply for three days. This, I was sure, would rival a Roman feast or jet set affair.

I walked back to the mission house to change into Indian dress for the feast. I still had my Wichub-Huala trade items which included among other things, a complete set of Indian skirts and molas, with plenty of beads. After changing I had breakfast with the Miller family at the Baptist mission, then went back to the chicha hut. The reception to my putting on Cuna Indian dress was amazing. I seemed to be accepted more by the people who gave me several very nice comments on the beauty of my clothes. The mola blouse I wore this day had ten different colors in it on a black pattern. It depicted two devils fighting over who was going to eat a smaller, less-potent devil.

When I returned to the area of the chicha hut, I entered the small puberty hut for the hair cutting ceremony outside the main south door. There were now two holes in the ground and two young girls swinging somewhat uneasily in their hammocks. Both of the girl's faces were covered with thin blue veils of flimsy material, tied around their heads with pieces of string. I gave each of the girls several small gifts including cloth, beads, hunting knives, and combs. The latter gift was in anticipation of the time when their hair would grow back again. Within six hours, both girls would be minus their waist-long tresses and be completely bald. When their hair grew back to ear length they would be ready to marry. Both girls seemed delighted with the gifts and invited me back later that morning for the actual hair-cutting ceremony, an invitation which I quickly and happily accepted.

At 11 a.m. the opening ceremony of the Chicha feast began. The live white chicken which had been tied up outside of the chicha hut was killed with a bow and arrow by the chief medicine man of Ailigandi. Its blood was collected into a small wooden bowl and the bowl placed at the door of the puberty hut. The door itself had been covered with a large cloth so that no one could see what was taking place inside.

In the big chicha house, several Kantules, along with Ricardo, Maria's husband, were chanting. Each seemed to be singing a different song than the other but that made no difference to the Kantules. Each man wore a necklace that came all the way down to the wearer's waist. The necklace was made of pelican bones. This was a musical instrument in the tribe, played by Kantules, but there were few men left who knew how to blow the tricky songs on the bones. The bones seemed to ring out in song with each dancing two-step the Kantules took. Red "rouge" adorned the cheeks of these officials, and each also had a long black line painted down the bridge of his nose to protect him from the devil. The chief Kantule's nose line was partitioned into three equal parts by horizontal lines across the vertical main line he had painted on. The Kantules continued to dance and sing about the chicha hut, two beats on one foot and two on the other. Ricardo started to do a particularly interesting step. With each two beats he would toss his head proudly, causing the pelican bone necklace to bounce up and down. The bones coming together sharply created a drum-like rhythm and the musical accompaniment for the dance he did. The other Kantules soon picked up Ricardo's step.

The dance got wilder, the chanting too, then finally the chief Kantule picked up a rattle from a seat. A piece of behuco vine had been attached to the handle. He held his vine and swung the instrument around his head several times, then all of the Kantules ran from the chicha hut toward the puberty hut. Beginning with the chief Kantule, each one emersed his rattle in the chicken's blood (representing the proof by which the young girl had become a woman) and ran back into the chicha hut for another half hour's worth of wild singing and dancing with the blood market rattles. More and more of the villagers were assembling in the chicha hut. Soon the chanting stopped and the chicha drink was ready to be given in ceremony to the Kantules. The banana leaf tops were removed from two of the large clay jugs. Four gourds were filled by Machi Pepe with the red liquid and handed to the chief and four assistant Kantules in the order of their rank. The hut, which had been buzzing, quieted.

A square was formed in the center of the hut by the men. They walked around seven times, slowly, keeping the form of the square. Then they broke into a circular run.

"Whooopa! Whoooooopa! Whoopa!" they called, then lifted the gourds to their lips. When the gourds had been drained they were handed to Machi Pepe. After this, and while Machi Pepe refilled the gourds, the Kantules who had drunk of the chicha started to dance, sing, and jump about the central area as though each had just inherited a large coconut plantation from a distant cousin.

The newly filled gourds were then handed back to the same Kantules who in turn presented these to four other Kantule companions. They repeated the same ceremony complete with hooting and dancing, then handed their gourds back to Machi Pepe. More gourds and more "bartenders" were added to these and everyone present was served with at least one cup of chicha within a ten minute period of time.

Then it was every man for himself, and everybody within hearing range was getting inebriated. During the handing out ceremony, I was also given a gourd of chicha which I drank and found to be not at all unpleasant. It had the consistency of very sweet wine and tasted very much like a red wine. The drinking went on, and on, and on. . . .

By noon, nearly 75 per cent of those in the chicha house were good and drunk—that included everyone over age 14. The children had also tasted the drink and a few of the younger spirited boys looked as though they had had enough for the present time. The Kantules were by now all in their various hammocks in the center of the room and chanting as though, if they stopped, at the first suggestion of silence the sun would fall from the sky right on top of Ailigandi. I was feeling none too sober myself and wondered what the alcholic content of chicha was. Everybody was weaving this way and that and the large room was full of the sound of laughing, singing, and dancing. Smiles were in effervescent plenitude. Never have I observed a happier group of people anywhere. I never saw a drunker group either. Unlike some of the guests at our own New York gatherings, no one here became belligerent or moody when drunk. Every person in sight was as happy as a black bear with a bee-deserted giant honey comb.

I was thoroughly enjoying such simple, absolute child-like joy as I found in every direction I looked. Maria came skipping over from the woman's side of the hut to my doorside seat. She took me by the hand and transported me bodily to the chicha jugs. The way she ordered another cup of chicha for me reminded me of a medic calling for blood plasma on the battlefield. I downed the large gourd of chicha, then returned with her to the women's section of the hut in the north end of the hut. We sat and joked with those women there. We spoke by means of a few basic Indian words which I had picked up, and the rest was in sign language—very few Indian women spoke Spanish. In the midst of this flowering conversation, every woman present got up and headed for the door. Somewhat startled, I looked blankly at Maria who gestured that they were going for a community walk to "Nature's Cove." I was fascinated with the unity of this action. Some of the women couldn't even walk and were carried, chanting, from the chicha hut by companions a bit more sober than they. Some of the women danced all the way to the ocean and back again. Lost, detoured, weaving their way, finding their way, losing their way, they all arrived back in the chicha hut again. When the women had returned, the men performed similar rites. Most of them were much worse off than the women were.

Some merrymakers were going about the chicha hut hugging and bubbling over this and that particular friend, relation, or acquaintance much in the manner of an inebriated rooster after hens. The men, after they returned from the oceanside, started to chant, and dance singly, in groups, in pairs, in threes. The women chanted, breast-fed their babies, and cooed to each other in the familiar language of the Carib-Cuna dialect. Every once in a while someone would hoot or cry at the rafters just to let Ipilele know that they felt pretty good about the get together and that he had organized a marvelous Chicha party. The party swung with high spirits into the afternoon.

I grabbed a quick lunch at the Millers' and returned to the chicha hut. I was informed by Maria that the ceremonies in the puberty hut were underway and quickly accompanied her to that place. I noticed that all of the hammocks on either side of the hut were now full. There was a group of women all gathered about one paricular hammock occupied by one delirious female. She was chanting in a high-pitched broken tone and tossing and turning about furiously. Several times, it was necessary for two or three women to hold her down or she would have tunbled from the hammock onto the ground. I joined the crowd and found out that she was evidently in one of those prophetic trances which the Cuna women go into when drunk. It is said that they can see both into the underworld of the devils and into the house of the Great Father in the land beyond life and can converse with both world's inhabitants to find out what is going to happen in the future.

Maria and I continued out the hut into the sunny afternoon and went the ten feet to the puberty hut. I requested formal permission of Tuhele's aunt who was guarding the door of that place against all men, to enter. It was granted to me. There were about 15 older women sitting along the seats on the side of the hut. At the far end, the two girls were buried waist deep in the holes and their grandmothers sat on stools behind them. The reason for the girls being buried was told in one of the formal chants about the ceremony. "Another woman has been born of the earth." I could see that it was meant as it was said. Boards were placed in front of the girl and incense pots were placed on the boards. The fragrance in the hut was one of lilac, not green-pepper I am happy to say. The room was full of smoke. I examined the girls. Their faces were still covered with veils. They seemed to be in some kind of trance or dead-drunk. They just sat there in their dirt filled holes neither speaking nor raising their heads from their chests. One of the girls was sobbing quietly. I couldn't tell which girl it was— I couldn't even see the faces of the grandmothers, since both women covered their faces with the red veils all mature women wear on their heads.

Then one of the grandmothers pushed aside the head veil of her grandaughter and I caught sight of Tuhele, who was now half bald. The elder women took a lock of Tuhele's hair in her hand and snipped it with a pair of small scissors, further contributing to the girl's progressing baldness.

One of the girl's relatives was passing among all present with a long tobacco roll the lighted end of which was in her mouth. By blowing through the cigar, the smoke came forth from the wrong end, as we know it, into the faces of each person present. We inhaled the smoke from the air, never touching the cigar with our lips. It seemed to give an exhilarating feeling and I thought at first the tobacco to be some form of marijuana. I later examined the cigar and found it to be just ordinary tobacco grown in the mountains by the Cuna men. It was evidently the mixture of chicha and smoke that was beginning to make itself felt in my brain. At one point I became so dizzy that I had to leave the hut, much against Maria's wishes, to get some fresh air. If I didn't and continued to drink chicha as I had been doing every since I entered the small puberty hut (two jugs of chicha had been set aside here for guests) the women would be carrying me to the ocean on their next trip while I chanted "Jingle Bells."

I passed the hut of Artilio's mother on the walk I took. She was quite a striking woman, being both tall, dark-skinned and, blue-eyed—very unusual for a Cuna woman. She still wore the nose ring and mola of the Cuna even though her son was the pastor of Ailigandi Baptist mission. As I passed by, I was invited into her hut for cocoa drink which I gladly accepted, hoping it would right me in somewhat the same manner as coffee did back home. I did want to observe the rest of the day's activities from a sober vantage point, It had the desired effect along with the fresh air on my chicha-tinged brain and I returned to the puberty hut to join Maria. The pary was going as strong as ever and I was becoming more and more fascinated with it.

I no sooner sat down in the puberty hut than Mrs. Miller came running into the chicha hut, evidently quite upset about something. She found me. There had been an accident, a bad one, would I come and see if I could help.

"Oh, good grief," I thought, not knowing what this one might be. I was beginning to be very sorry about helping remove the shark hook from the twelve-year-old boy's thigh. I was neither a doctor nor nurse. I couldn't handle these things, yet, if I didn't there was only the local medicine man who could. I agreed to go and take a look, but further explained to Mrs. Miller that this really wasn't my field at all. She didn't reply, but eyed me angrily and lead the way, knowing I'd follow.

She made her way toward the mission house. There was a crowd of people outside the front door and the first thing I noticed was a trail of blood outside the door leading from a motor boat, a strange one, tied up at the dock.

"Oh, no," I remember thinking.

I entered to find Artilio bent over a twenty-two-year-old boy whose thigh was bleeding badly. I was quickly told what had happened. The boy had shot himself in the thigh with a heavy spear gun. It had gone in very deeply. The accident had taken place three quarters of an hour away on the island of Tupili. While I listened to the details I tied a tourniquet around the boy's thigh and tightened it with a piece of wood. The boy was barely conscious but made an effort to stop me from touching the obvious place. I told Artilio to tell the boy to get his hand out of the way and keep it out of the way; then I continued my work with the tourniquet. When this was done I put a few pieces of gauze right over the wound and pressed down on it with my hand, alternating every two minutes with the other hand and loosening the tourniquet every ten minutes. I thought that the bleeding would never stop. In all, it took us 35 minutes to control it. The boy, by the looks of him, had lost quite a bit of blood. I found suture in the medicine cabinet and proceeded to sew up the wound, leaving a small area at the base through which it could drain in case it became infected as most wounds out here do. I drenched the wound with peroxide, and hoped for the best. At that point I didn't know whether he'd live or die. There was no way we could radio for help or blood; we only knew that we had done our best. I didn't want the boy moved under any circumstances and told Artilio to announce that fact to his relatives. My statement upset his old grandmother to no end. She couldn't understand what I was doing around there in the first place, then to have me order her not to take her grandson home was too much for her. I told Artilio to explain that the boy was very sick and that it would be good for him to stay here on Ailigandi for a few days. She could stay with him if she liked. She said that she certainly would. Artilio told the woman that she and her grandson could stay in his mother's hut and she accepted.

It seemed that the boy had been spear fishing off the reefs near St. Ignasius Tupili Island. A shark had snuck up on him and he turned to find the animal reaching for his body. He shot, but in shooting knocked his arm against an outcropping of coral. The spear entered his thigh. His friends who were right in the water with him, all shot at the shark, chasing him off briefly. They pulled their wounded companion into their boat and got him back to the island. Their medicine man told them that there was an American medicine woman at Ailigandi and that it would be good to get the boy to her. They used the island-owned outboard to make time and arrived here as I was just returning to the chicha hut.

When the boy was finally carried off to Artilio's mother's hut, I was soaking wet with sweat and relatively upset by the incident. One of these days they were going to drop somebody into my lap and he was going to die there and then what would happen. The local medicine man, already upset that I was taking business away from him, was going to have my head on a stake for the life of an Indian who died while I was trying to help him or her. But there was nothing I could do for the present time except hope that such an incident would not occur. If they did eventually bring someone more dead than alive—I would have to refuse to help in order to protect my own life. These Indians were my friends now—but if it were found that someone died under my needle or thread or what have you, that friendship would go up in thin air and I would be somewhat in danger from the incident. Motor boats and transistor radios did not make primitive Indians civilized, in the sense that they would understand that I did try to help if a "patient" died.

I went out in back of the mission house and poured a gourd of water over my head, clothes and all, then went to the sea wall to sit and wait until the water dried and I cooled off. What if the boy didn't pull through or the leg became infected. His grandmother would murder me in my sleep herself.

"Be nuadi nele." I turned to find Maria standing behind me smiling. "You're a good medicine woman," she had said. Not if that boy doesn't get up and walk in a week, I thought.

"Takwele." "Come," she said. I got up and followed her back to the chicha hut. I needed a cup of chicha at that particular moment. Soon I had two and was back enjoying the feast once again—my fears put aside for the time being.

By sunset that Monday night, both girls were absolutely bald, more than five hundred men, women and budding adults were drunk, and one man's arm was cut when he fell on a machete (guess who to the rescue). The boy from St. Ignasius Tupili was resting quietly in Artilio's mother's hut; Ricardo had knocked himself out cold having run into a supporting beam of the chicha hut, then come back strong as ever singing and dancing the rest of the day; two meals had been served for 1,500 people and the party went on, and on, and on. It would continue for two more days. Chief Ikwaniktipippi, whom I meant to speak to later on that afternoon about the meaning of the Chicha feast to his people, fainted dead away when I greeted him and had to be carried home by his wife and two daughters.

I went home and got into bed. No thought of rats, vampire bats or waring Indians entered my mind that night and I was asleep as my head touched the pillow.

"Juanita, Juanita, takwele." I knew whose voice it was, but I couldn't understand what Maria was doing, nose ring and all, in my New York apartment where I was serving brunch for four friends. I shook my somewhat throbbing head and called out "Aye," or "Yes," from the bed. The next time I opened my eyes, Maria was bent over me and my nose was itching from her playful and not appreciated wielding of a chicken feather on it. I bellowed at her to let me die in peace. It was the morning after the night before in Ailigandi. I could hear flutes being played somewhere in the village and the sun was high in the sky—nine-ish by the looks of it. I had never slept this late since I arrived in San Blas.

Maria pulled a pillow out from under my head, ran across the room and threw it at me. I was angrily up and after her, but she was faster than I was and got downstairs before I could hit her back with a book. Maria told me that Ricardo was nowhere on the island. Would I help her find him? (They think I'm clairvoyant too, I thought.) I had momentary visions of Ricardo's being caught red-cheeked in the bed of somebody's wife, but gave him the benefit of a doubt and thought perhaps he might have fallen into the ocean and drowned. The way my head felt, I wished the whole island had sunk. I'd know better the next time. Chicha was potent. I felt every drop of what I had consumed the day before in the front of my skull and behind my eyes.

I walked out into the strong morning sunlight, but had to return to the mission house to get my dark glasses, then I continued on with Maria to her hut. I was given rice and coffee drink here, both of which tasted very good to me at that point. The rice was native Indian rice, red in color and delicious. Since we were only four huts away from the chicha hut, I could hear the party STILL going on, stronger if anything than ever. "How can they do it?" I thought. I wondered what was going on now—soon my curiosity got the best of me and within the hour Maria and I were back in the chicha hut again drinking chicha.

Events in brief for the day:

Everyone again dressed in finery from large gold earrings and necklaces to coins—twenty-five cent pieces, ten cent peices and five cent pieces all jangling and gleaming in the sunlight. Each and every person once again red-eyed and drunk. All the hammocks were again occupied.

Noon: Tuhele slipped in her kitchen hut, having been released from the puberty hut; she broke her big toe. I set it as well as I could.

The Kantules are hoarse, but still singing with as much vigor as ever. They sing the simple facts of life and procreation which are sacred to the Cuna, but highly pornographic when printed. I found the songs fascinating in their candor and simplicity.

The chief Kantule handed me a roll of tobacco, already lighted and indicated that it was my turn to blow smoke into peoples' faces. I couldn't refuse as he had done it seriously, not in a joking manner. It seemed that I was becoming more and more one of the fine young Indians and therefore was no exception when duties were performed. I took the roll of tobacco and put the lighted end in my mouth, keeping my tongue well down and wet, away from the heat. I then blew smoke into the first Kantule's face. He nodded his appreciation with a short inclination of his head and "Mmmmmm," and I continued in ceremonial fashion and order of rank until I had performed similar services for the Kantules and medicine men. As I approached Ikwaniktipippi, he looked up at me, smiled, and for the second day in a row, passed dead out on the dirt floor of the chicha hut. I couldn't help laughing and had to take the cigar from my mouth to do so. Maria, who had watched as I tried to greet the elderly chief the day before also found the re-occurrence of his action very funny and soon both of us were beside ourselves. I handed the tobacco roll to an old grandmother nearby and she continued to smoke to all the women on my side of the hut.

This second day of the Chicha feasting was almost unbelievable. One couldn't walk down a street without tripping over somebody's body. I found Ricardo. He had passed out the night before in a dug-out canoe on the east side of the island and had been out cold until two p.m. Maria was grateful for the return of her man. She had been thinking that he had gone out to fish and drowned.

Nobody was speaking coherently anymore and several times I was very exasperated trying to understand what was either being said to me or asked of me by several boys who insisted on punctuating each and every point wtih a none too gentle poke in the stomach. I did lose my temper nicely once. I poked one man back with a bit more force than necessary smiling like a chimpanzee, and he went back over an incense pot landing in the chief Kantule's hammock. The chief Kantule, I might add, was in it at the time. The man got up muttering something about a machete and left the chicha hut. Maria and I had to laugh—I hadn't pushed the man that hard, but with a little chicha in one's blood, one doesn't stand very well. The man came back—with a machete—and I almost dropped my gourd of chicha. Maria took it away from him with a slight twisting movement of her wrist and said wryly: "Be dodoay Pepe Soule." (You're playing more than a little bit.) The man burst into tears and left the hut. I was standing where Maria left me, the cup of chicha half way to my lips amazed. Would he really have tried to hack a piece of me from my body for the incident? I truthfully couldn't answer. He probably wouldn't remember the incident on the morrow, but I vowed to be a bit more careful with anyone else in the hut or village sober or full of chicha in the future. No one else had even noticed the movement—except, and I didn't like it, the island's medicine man. When he noted that I had observed his observation, he pretended to sway a little bit as though he too were drunk. The man obviously neither liked me nor my antibiotics. I also made a mental note to keep my eye on him for the duration of the feast.

He reminded me of the boy at Artilio's mother's house and I left the chicha hut to go take a look at him. He was awake—he hadn't been earlier that morning when I went to see him. I decided that sleep would do more good for him at that time than my changing his bandages and left. His eyes were alive and he smiled as I entered the large sleeping hut. His grandmother even smiled. I feel very good knowing that now he was obviously much better. I changed his bandages and had a cup of cocoa drink with him. The wound was in excellent condition—no infection visible. I redressed it, first putting a small butterfly bandage on the still open base of the wound. I'd get the boy on his feet the next day. I wondered if the medicine man knew that the boy was much better. I went back to the mission house, feeling suddenly very tired, and went to sleep for the next 14 hours.

The next day it was more of the same. The ending ceremony at night was very interesting to me.

Everyone left the chicha hut at five p.m., went home, took a bath with gourds of water carried over from the river, ate, and returned to the chicha hut. The chief Kantule, still going strong (that was probably why he was chief Kantule) was emceeing the ceremony. A huge dance was performed. Several different variations were presented, the first of which interested me very much because the women's coin necklaces were clanging like hundreds of tiny bells on a Siamese temple, in tune to the rattles that each shook. Two circles were formed. In the center stood the form of the chief Kantule in all his glory with red cheeks, his nose lines, pelican bone necklaces, purple shirt, and red pants. On his left stood Ricardo, just as colorfully garbed, and at his right, Manitule another Kantule, who held the big ceremonial rattle. The Kantules sang and the women danced to a 4/4 beat sounding their rattles loudly on every other beat. Intermittent beats got a soft shake of the rattle. The ground literally shook with the force of their feet hitting it. I could feel the vibrations even where I stood. Gold nose and earrings flashed in the bright firelight as round and round they danced until the chief Kantule called out and the women broke into pairs and continued their mambo-like beat. The dance got wilder and wilder until at one point they were joined by a third circle of men who danced with as much vigor as the women. Flutes joined in the music of the rattles and soon nobody was standing still, including the Kantules or flute players who reminded me of the legendary Pan figure of the forest. I was hypnotized by the beat, and at one point felt my own body start to move with the beat of the rattles and flutes, almost of itself. I decided to go for a walk, then returned to watch the next offering of the evening. This second dance was a strictly male dance, during which time young men of the village strutted about and danced, imitating jungle animals. I was fascinated by the dignity yet earthy quality which the dance possessed.

I noticed Peter, Jr. at the opposite end of the chicha hut. He was looking in the door at the people, his own people, but refused to enter. The Baptists generally didn't attend the Chicha feast in order to register their disapproval of the drunkenness and dancing that went on at this time. I wondered about Peter. He was Indian, even with his American college education. The difference between him and me, even though he understood much more of the relation of the two worlds than I, was great. I felt that if left with his people back in the jungle he would probably join in the Chicha feasting—but here on the island with his mother—who incidentally still had the hole in her nostrils where she had worn a nose ring in her younger days—he was obliged to honor the beliefs of his parents. My relationship with Peter was good. He appreciated someone who could understand his life at college and to whom he could speak as he had spoken when in Texas. He did his best to explain rituals of the tribe and unwritten law to me, so that I might live among the people in peace and in strict obedience to their law, which I respected. He generally accompanied me on walks around the village right after supper, at which time we'd visit his friends and sit down with cups of cocoa or coffee drink and talk. Yet, there was that gap—I felt that he was in many ways further from his people than I, a stranger, was. His future was decided. He was the son of Peter Miller. He would take his father's place in the respected Baptist society. He was a teacher at the school. He was single—a fact not one unmarried young lady in the village didn't know. He would eventually marry. Then his children would follow him in leading the Cuna people of Ailigandi or San Blas to education and eventual civilization of themselves and their children. Within two generations, what I was seeing now would be for the most part a written history, no longer practiced by the Cuna race. Their dances, their beautiful jungle music would die and in the place of the Indians who hunted the high jungle there would come men with scientific raising of coconuts. The Indians would mine their own land, rich in minerals—there is gold in most of the rivers of the San Blas coast. The women would let their hair grow long and put on Western dresses, as was the case already starting at the unofficial capital of San Blas, Narkana. Somehow, knowing these facts and realizing that they would come, I felt a great sense of loss inside of me—a form of regret—my grandchildren would never know this world that I walked in. Most of my own generation would never know the richness in human wisdom and understanding that this "primitive" tribe possessed. Oh it would be good for many of the Indians. Those who would have died before will have the benefit of modern medicine and doctors, I hoped. They would raise their standard of living and who knows —within ten years maybe someone will be building a huge resort hotel down at this end of the San Blas coast and the Indians will find themselves hurtling ahead down the road to modernization at break-neck speed. Even so, there would be those, the children who stood about wide-eyed and watching, who would remember this night—remember their mother and father dancing at the fire, the gleam of gold earrings, the taste of chicha, the sound of the flutes, the beautiful Pan-flutes. I wondered if "Junior," as Peter was called, remembered his mother in a mola dress and his people's song. I would have liked to think that those were his thoughts as he watched from the door of the chicha hut.

If the Chicha feast and the hair-cutting ceremony were to disappear in the next generation, the loss to the Cuna people of this beautiful part of their heritage would indeed be great.

Several other dances were performed, ending up with the traditional dance by the villagers with their rattles and flutes—not unlike our own American barn dances. The partners faced each other, the men with flutes on one side and the women with rattles on the other. With that the similarity ended—the rest of the dance looked like an untamed mambo. The last dance ended and a short song from the Kantule followed. The villagers left the chicha hut and went home to recover as I did.

Thus did the Chicha feast, celebrating Tuhele's coming of age, begin and end in the age-old traditions of the Cuna tribe.

8
LIFE IN AILIGANDI

I have been neglecting my journal outrageously for the past week due to the occurance of yet another Chicha feast in the village. I tried to speak with Ikwanik again, but had no luck as he repeated his performance of the last Chicha feast and passed out as I was asking him my first question. I'm going to have to catch him when he's sober.

The usual run of accidents have occurred and Artilio and I do the best we can with them. This morning it was a small boy who cut his hand open when he ran and tripped carrying a machete. We put it together under the usual surveillance of villagers and the boy's relatives each claiming that the child was being murdered before their very eyes.

Ricardo is working on the new addition to his hut and the construction of it is interesting to watch. He hasn't used one nail yet and the house will stand for a good 50 years with occasional repair.

He already has the frame up. This "frame" is made from the wood of black palm trees, a very durable jungle wood. Three large central posts were put up first, then followed the perimeter posts which were placed in a square. All of this framework was then joined by horizontal beams and "voila," and the frame is ready for a roof. Branches of trees are joined to the central posts and the roof is ready for thatching and the structure ready for habitation. Reed walls are then added for privacy and another hut will be ready for the family's use. This construction work on such a small structure as Ricardo is making will take only about a month.

Behuco vine is used to hold all of the construction of the house together and is so strong that it will last longer than nails will in most cases.

Life here on Ailigandi Island runs in a well-ordered pattern which I shall convey to you from my standpoint. The actual day begins at dawn. The women of the house immediately set about getting the fire roaring, grind corn or prepare the material for the morning drink and get water from the village mainland by paddling over with their gourds and filling them, then paddling back over via dug-out to the island. The men, in the interim, sharpen their machetes, check their fishing lines, guns and spears, and generally prepare themselves for hunting, fishing or farming on the jungle mainland and in the sea. It has been my observation that they will spend about four to five hours a day working. The rest of the time will be spent with their family and children.

The children get up at dawn, too, and begin their day's play. They play until the morning drink is almost ready, then they take their first shower of the day with gourds of water which "Nana" has brought over from the river. The men also shower at this time.

The morning drink is first served to all the men who are leaving to go fishing or to the mainland, then to all the young adults in the house, then to the children. Meals are always served in this manner.

When a young girl is about eight or nine she begins to take an active interest in Nana's work and generally gives her a hand with a little something. As the girl grows older she assumes more and more responsibility for house-hold duties. Young boys generally start accompanying their fathers out fishing or to the jungle mainland when they are about ten or eleven. Their fathers begin teaching them how to farm and fish and care for a family at this time.

By the time a girl is thirteen or fourteen she knows all there is to know about keeping house, cooking, and caring for babies and children. She can do the laundry, cook any dish the Indians eat. She knows how to care for her future husband in all ways, and is ready for marriage and motherhood.

A boy progresses less hastily. By the time he is sixteen or seventeen he is considered a man and should have all kinds of food growing on the jungle mainland. He can fish well, hunt well, and has proved himself worthy of a wife. He then marries and settles back to enjoy the fruits of his many earlier years of work to raise and get food, by enjoying his wife and children.

It has been my observation that a young girl of six years is well capable of taking care of any and all younger brothers and sisters. She has been caring for younger children since she's been able to lift one in her arms. The young girl children are instinctively motherly from an early age on.

It is interesting to note that an Indian mother will never let any member of her family know what the word *hunger* means. I can truthfully say that since I have set foot in San Blas my stomach has never growled or felt any sensation other than that of being full. It is so with all the fine young Indians.

The first actual meal of the Indian day is served around 11 o'clock in the morning. Of course, if anyone is famished before that time, there are bananas always at hand in the kitchen for nibbling material, as well as sugar cane, oranges (when in season), and what have you. This meal is attended by most of the family—the young adults and women and children. The men of the family, if they got a late start, may still be over in the jungle mainland or fishing, in which case they will have brought along some of the morning drink in gourds in their dug-out canoes. If they are in the jungle mainland and are hungry, they don't deserve to be called Indian. They know where to find food and it can be obtained readily.

When the men do return in early afternoon, they may spend anywhere from an hour to four just simply playing with their children. I've never observed such closeness between father and child as I see here. The closeness betwen brother and sister is equally touching. They truly love each other and watch out for each other. Families are closer here than I have ever observed in any society before. It is a joy for me to just walk by a hut or two and see the fathers throwing the children over their heads and listen to the children scream with laughter and happiness.

Brothers call their sisters "Punolo Pepe" meaning little golden ones. Sisters call their brothers "Urba" or my big brother.

By four in the afternoon, after the women have spent some time at the river bathing and doing laundry and getting water for the evening meal, they return to the island to prepare dinner, usually plantains and fish. This meal is eaten and neighbors visit each other. Evening comes on slowly and the day's events are discussed in each household. There may be a council meeting in which case all the men and women and children attend. Life is slow, unhurried, healthy, good to these people.

If a family has children attending the school run by the Baptist mission then the children do their day's work for the house after classes.

After the boys finish their daily work for the household, they many times engage in the principal sport of San Blas—basketball. This activity has taken the fancy of the young Indian boys as no other sport ever has. When these teen-age boys gather at the basketball court outside of the trading stores, they will sometimes play three games straight through without taking breaks. They go through some of the most physically exerting contortions I have ever witnessed without seeming tired at all after they are through.

I was watching a game yesterday afternoon. The players themselves are graceful as forest deer and their beautiful young golden bodies danced around the court. One play I watched required reception of the ball in mid-air by a center forward. He caught the ball in mid-air, avoided his guard, turned, and threw for a perfect basket from almost the center line, then came down to touch the ground. His coordination was beautiful to watch and I held my breath while the action took place.

I've been watching these practice sessions every night now and am never bored with them because the boys are enjoying themselves so much.

When it begins to get dark, kerosene lamps, a fairly new introduction into the area, are lit and friends visit each other.

By nine or ten, all is quiet in the village except perhaps for the song of a mother singing her baby to sleep or the sounds of howler monkeys screeching in the jungle across the channel.

It is a good life for these people and they thoroughly enjoy every minute of it.

The sun rose, Sunday services were held, and 11 a.m. came around slowly and lazily in the village. Artilio asked me to join him and some of his friends in a bit of skin diving off the reefs and soon we were off in his large dug-out canoe zooming across the calm water pushed by a 28 hp. motor owned by Artilio. We stopped about 20 minutes later near a lovely island off Achutupu. This island was named Pun Tupu or Twin Island—its counterpart being right across a small 40-feet wide channel to the east. Both of these islands are used for the growing of coconuts by an Ailigandite and a man from Achutupu. I was wearing my bathing suit and wondered why everybody else was climbing into shirts, trousers, and putting on shoes. Evidently, they planned to swim that way and I wondered if there were a reason for it, but didn't question it.

Artilio and Fernando, the latter being one of the teachers at the Ailigandi Baptist mission school, went over the side first. I was just about to join them, having prepared my mask and spear gun, when Artilio's head popped out of the water near the boat. He shouted something in Cuna to the younger boys still in the boat and they replied by shouting:

"Aaaahoooooooooohhhaaaa!" Then Artilio proceeded to climb back into the boat, which rocked at the shift of weight.

I wondered why he was back so soon. Then I saw that he pulled his gun over the side after him and that it had been fired—the rope from it was still in the water. Perhaps he'd seen a shark—and if so, where was Fernando? Then Artilio solved the mystery:

"Got 'em!" he said grinning happily.

"Got what?" I asked apprehensively. He had just gone over the side and he had something?

"Barracuda!"

"A what?"

"Barracuda," he repeated looking at me for a reaction.

I gulped then asked "How big is he?"

"Oh about this big." He stretched his hands as far as they would go in either direction. I felt weak.

"But you just went into the water!"

"He was right under the boat," replied Artilio, still grinning.

I sat down.

One of the younger boys was pulling in the line attached to Artilio's spear. There was something on the end and it was doing feverish battle with the forces outside of its water world. After five minutes we had him alongside. It was a three foot barracuda with a good eight inches worth of mouth and the sharpest teeth in the entire under-water world. The boy started to pull the fish up over the side with the aid of another boy.

"Good Lord in Heaven!" I said. "You're not going to bring it in the *boat,* are you?" I was by now on my feet and ready to go over the side if anyone gave the slightest indication that they intended to do that.

"Where else shall we put it?" asked Artilio.

"But it's dangerous and it's still alive!" I reasoned.

"He won't hurt you," said Artilio and helped the boys bring the 'cuda into the bottom of the dug-out. I was by this time balancing on the bow of the dug-out. The fish thrashed wildly opening and closing its gigantic mouth with every sideways turn of its body. He managed by some system to get his body headed toward the bow, and in no little time, had found his way there. I grabbed a crab spear that I used for jungle hunting and put it between his teeth. I could feel the ensuing "clomp" all the way up to my shoulder bone.

"Artilio!" I shouted.

He hit the big fish on the back of the head with a strong downward swing of my machete, almost cutting that member from his body. The barracuda started to madly put up a final fight for its life, then was quiet. I was by this time in no mood to stick my baby toe in the water.

Artilio grinned briefly, then went back into the water. He came up and looked questioningly at me from his face mask like some kind of prehistoric creature of the deep. I answered his eyes by grinning weakly and donning my face mask and rechecking my spear. Evidently there was nothing in the area. Artilio was absolutely still in the water. I went in. When I reached the bottom of the sandy channel, which was about ten feet under the boat, I made a complete 360 degree circle and surveyed everything in sight. Nothing but some relatively good game fish were in sight and I felt relieved. No sooner did I complete this careful scrutiny of everything in sight, then Artilio, who was leaning over a coral reef about 25 feet away, motioned me to come. I paddled my way over there with my one free arm and two legs, since I held my spear gun very tightly in the other, and looked over the reef. There was a sand shark eyeing Artilio with a curiously frightened look on its large brownish face. Upon the appearance of this additional apparition of some kind of redheaded fish wearing blue and white skin, it turned tail and quickly scurried away. We both looked after it for a good two minutes to make sure it had indeed scurried far away and had not snuck back to find out if we might make good eating, then went about our business of the morning—spearing fish.

I left Artilio and went on the other side of a stand of coral. The inside of this coral reef formed a circle and as far as I could see, it was completely protected from big fish all around, although within it abounded in red snapper. I watched them for awhile, they not knowing that I was there yet. The water out in this area was absolutely crystal clear with the faintest tinge of green. The reefs were in their usual multicolored glory and the whole scene was its usual breath-taking self.

Then I went after the snappers with a vengeance. I stopped after making a half-hearted attempt to spear one and found myself sightseeing more than desiring to hunt that day. The entire place had an air of sacredness about it, and if I could have talked with the snorkel in my mouth, I would have whispered any conversations I cared to have. It was like being in a cathedral.

Inside of the ring of coral, I found some kind of wreckage from what appeared to be a very old ship about 70 feet long—its beams were made of wood, I discovered when I scrapped off some of the crusty coral from one. It was lying about 25 feet under the surface of the water and therefore I couldn't examine it for a very long period of time. I did, however, ascertain that its anchor, a three pronged affair with balls at the end of each prong, was intact and I therefore assumed the wreck to be recent. I made a note to come back and check her over someday with a metal detector and appropriate equipment.

Right behind the wreck was another wall of coral. I swam there and entered another pool of water about 30 yards long. The coral formation turned sharply right at a corner and I couldn't see beyond that, but after a careful check of the area, I decided it was as safe as my last sight-seeing stopover point. I entered the pool. There were numerous red snapper about and some were quite large so I decided to bring back at least one so that Artilio wouldn't think he was wasting his time by bringing me out here. I aimed at one large snapper about 30 pounds in weight who stood belligerently in his pool watching me and ready to fight if necessary. I was about to fire when I had a feeling something was not quite right and again turned toward the sharp turn in the coral to check the deep water there just to be sure. My red snapper wasn't going anywhere. All was clear—for about a fraction of a second. Before I could so much as blink my eyes, my heart jumped up into my throat and I screamed into the snorkel tube. I couldn't have fainted if I wanted to, I was too frightened to pass out. There was a barracuda sitting on the surface of the water right at the turn in the coral and he was five to six feet long. I had understood them to be at most—four feet long. This was a monster or else the grandfather of every barracuda I had ever heard of in the area.

"What am I going to do?" I asked myself backing off toward the red snapper who had taken cover the moment the barracuda appeared in the coral reef. I was some 50 yards from our boat and there was coral on three sides of me. As I backed off, I then realized that my secure little pool had an opening some eight yards wide at the deep "sea" end of the reef. That's how it got in. It was not a reef fish—it was a sea Cuda—the largest there are.

As I backed off into the reef, the barracuda slowly advanced, keeping no more than 20 feet between itself and me. I remember that I was trying to think straight into the barracuda's eyes and reason with him. "Now listen fish, I'm not going to hurt you—how could I possibly hurt you (oh God)! Now look me over very well. Take your time. I'd taste horrible. I wouldn't even give you a good battle for your trouble. I'll fight all of one second before my soul goes to the house of the Great Father. They'll never find enough to bury me! Alright fish, I'm going to back right down this stretch of water until I get into a nice shallow area. Then I'm going to climb straight up the wall of coral and go home and leave this castle to you. (Nothing but a killer whale could have taken it from him.) I'll go home to my island and you'll stay in your water and maybe I'll visit you every once in a while."

I stayed absolutely still, breathing quickly and heavily next to the coral reef. The pool was absolutely deserted of all other fish life. It seemed as though I'd been there for a half an hour.

"Maybe he's just trying to figure out what kind of fish I am," I thought. I only hoped that his curiosity didn't go as far as finding out how the strange fish *tasted*. Barracuda are very curious fish.

With this in mind I slowly raised my spear gun (it would have been like hitting an elephant with a pin) and started to push off from the reef toward the shallow area, slowly and quietly. The spear gun was out in front of me.

I didn't even see the next movement except for a flash of green. My spear gun went floating to an outcrop of coral ten feet below me. Well that settled that. The barracuda had attacked and was now sitting out in front of me in his same spot waiting to see what I'd do next.

I felt weak. One flick of its head and no spear gun. Nothing but an explosion was going to stop it from having me for a first course at lunch.

I decided to make it as difficult as possible. I wished someone would come. I wished someone would figure out that I was in trouble. No one did.

"O.K.," I thought, "try and get me off this coral in one piece, because if you can't you're going to break some of your pretty white teeth on it."

I found a crevice that somehow seemed to fit my body. A mousehole would have done at that point.

I suddenly decided that if the barracuda were going to come after me, which was the most probable course of action, he was going to have a spear gun for an appetizer. I dove straight down inhaling a deep breath of air before I did and picked up my gun. I shot right from there hoping that I'd at least hit a sensitive part of his skin and scare him off briefly. I aimed right behind his throat and fired. The gun slit the entire side of the barracuda open, but didn't stick in him. It just cut open his skin.

"O.K.," I said, "here he comes." I let the air out of my lungs slowly and braced for what I knew would be the only counter-attack I'd ever see it make.

He glided slowly toward the opening of the reef with his cut skin drifting beside him in the green water.

I didn't wait to ask him if he were serious or not. I raced for the coral wall opposite me and literally jumped-swam over it. I reached the surface and climbed up on top of the reef, which was out of the water. I looked at the sun, the islands, and Artilio's dug-out canoe as it seemed, for the first time in my life. I was alright, breathing, and standing safely on a coral reef in the Caribbean Sea. I thought I was going to cry.

I shouted for the boys in the dug-out to get the boat over to me because I wasn't about to swim to it. They came. When I climbed ino the dug-out I was shaking as though in the hold of a huge chill. I shook for five full minutes before I started to calm down somewhat. Artilio was summoned and he climbed aboard and looked at me questioningly. Then he smiled and I noticed for the first time that he had dimples—a full-blooded San Blas Indian with dimples—I started to laugh.

I stopped a little while later and told Artilio what had happened. Just telling it seemed to calm me somewhat.

"It didn't eat you alive?" he asked.

"No."

"You're not hurt?"

"No."

"Then what are you all upset about?"

I looked at him as though he'd lost his mind.

"You should have brought it back with you. He would have made good eating." With that last statement, the great optimist hopped over the side and splashed into the water. With one last wave of his arm, he was below the surface and hunting the reefs again. I stayed in the boat for half an hour, then went over the side right near the boat for five minutes, just to get used to the fact that I was going over the side again, sometime, somewhere.

Nevertheless "King Cuda" did manage to plague my memory for weeks to come.

Wednesday

Well today I have received nothing less than the best rat keeper awayer in all of San Blas as a house guest. His name is Snoopy and I think that it's the only domestic tiger cat in all of San Blas. It belongs to Marina Iglesias, Claudio's youngest daughter. The whole family arrived this morning via Claudio's dug-out canoe from Mulatupu Island on their way to Narkana Island in the middle of a choco sano storm, which was the only reason they put into Ailigandi at all. I was standing talking to Claudio when suddenly, some kind of animal laid its body across my feet. My reaction was to scream wildly as though an anaconda had been there. Claudio's laughter reverberated throughout Ailgandi Island and the poor cat took to a coconut tree eyeing me as though I were a maniac. When it saw that Claudio, who was evidently fine because he fed him, was talking to me, he assumed that I had temporarily lost my mind and that it was alright to come down now. He did and cautiously tried again to lay itself across my feet. This time I not only let the beautiful animal stay, I picked him up and petted him. He was a marvelous tomcat of a specimen, but obviously didn't like being picked up by anyone or didn't trust me as yet. His ears went back and his muscles tensed and a "fizzzzzzzzt!" which sounded like "Look lady, the ground please!" and I deposited him there. He went back to my bare feet and with a final sigh of contentment collapsed into a tiny tiger colored ball of fur there.

Claudio had brought his younger daughter Marina with him. She was a lovely quiet child who seemed to stay in the background and look at everything. She didn't miss anything either and by the looks of her, she was highly intelligent.

It was Marina who later that evening said that she'd heard that I was having some difficulty with the mission house rats and thought that a loan of Snoopy for a few days would do some good. It had been her idea to bring the cat. She was going to have it flown in from Narkana to Ailigandi the next morning, but this was more convenient seeing that the storm had chased them here anyway.

She was about 12 and spoke perfect English and Cuna dialect as well as Spanish. Her mother, she said, was now in Panama City, but would be flying to Narkana in the morning and then they'd take her home. The family, with two guests, stayed in the other bedrooms of the mission house that night, and left early the next morning for Narkana minus Snoopy who was following me around like a tiny puppy for the rest of the day.

That night I was calmly reading a book by kerosene lamp light in my bed at the mission house when Snoopy, whom I had forgotten completely about, leapt up to my bed with a "Pprrrrruuufft!" to announce his arrival and I almost cut him in two with a machete, thinking the rats were getting pretty brazen in their attempts to climb up onto my bed in the lighted room. He collapsed at the foot of my bed, paying me no heed and went to sleep, wrapping himself with his tail in a half moon.

I didn't hear the patter patter of little rat feet that night at all and felt elated at the pleasure of Snoopy's company and thankful to Marina for her courtesy in loaning her pet to me.

Right now, I'm again sitting with my notebook in the mission house and we're having another storm outside. I'm used to them now and have devised a method for keeping the east windows well closed from the torrent and wind.

In the west I can see a small dug-out coming from the sea. There is a man, stripped to the waist, paddling slowly towards the island. Now a woman, barebreasted and wearing just a grey pecha, is running out toward the logs where the boats are kept right under the mission house window. Her left breast is hanging lower than her right one. She has evidently been nursing her children more from that one than the other. The boat is coming in. She waits. Now the boat is there and she's helping her husband to lift the bow from the water to a log on shore. He bails the boat out with a half a gourd, then they both lift the boat to the logs, using the logs to roll the boat ashore.

The woman lifts a large hand of plantains to her shoulder and now a tiny naked boy runs and jumps into his father's arms. Then he is on the ground and dancing with glee either because his father is home or because he has brought supper. The man is taking the plantains from his wife's shoulder and she smiles at him and lets him have them. The child dances a wild, childish dance around his mother and father and they are out of sight.

I'm beginning to love these gentle, loving, beautiful, and kind people.

Saturday afternoon

It was back to the reefs today for more spear fishing. Artilio asked me to join his group after breakfast.

"Fine," I replied, but knowing that a ridiculously large barracuda was filling my mind with all kinds of warning buzzings.

One thing about my last trip, and a footnote I forgot to tell about. When I did go back into the coral reef from the barracuda, I got a back and leg-full of sea spines. It took three people to get them out of me when I got back to Ailigandi. In all the excitement, I hadn't even felt the pain.

Soon we were in the dug-out and heading for the sea. I noticed that Artilio, who was in the stern, was heading his dug-out straight for the great reef on the horizon.

"Good grief," I thought, "we're not going to fish the great reef!" I decided that the pastor couldn't possibly, wouldn't even think, wouldn't dare spear fish the great reef. Waves broke a good three feet over the reef and the fish out there were a lot bigger than the ones within. Sharks especially loved this outer perimeter and it was considered insane to go there by all the islanders.

Artilio turned to me from his examination of the wake behind us and smiled shyly at me.

"Oh no!" I thought and lapsed into a mental blank. Now I knew we were going to fish it. Maybe he wanted all of us dead, maybe he wanted to tell an exciting story on the radio tonight. Anyway, we were going to be in the reef waters in less than a half an hour.

Somewhere within me a serpentlike nobility reared its head and I accepted the challenge. No one was going to say that American girls were afraid of the big reef, or the big bad wolf or what have you. I felt that the very honor of American womanhood was on my shoulders. It was my duty to protect the female American race from disgrace.

If trumpets had blown at that moment, I wouldn't have thought it strange. I wondered if American womanhood had a banner or flag.

I was boiling angry at Artilio. I knew why he was doing this. He wanted to shock me into forgetting "King Cuda" which now dominated my brain like a submarine must an angel fish's consciousness.

Regardless of the fact that I was frightened, I'd go into the water after Artilio. After all, American womanhood and all that.

Oh well, I could see that I was doomed never to speak to Ikwaniktipippi. Artilio tossed out a trawling line for barracuda from the stern. After all, this was excellent barracuda water—even I, inexperienced as I was, knew that. The lesser reef inside of the great reef was full of them. They stayed right off the reef in the grassy water there and waited for things like Artilio's trawling lines and redheaded fish—then CRUNCH. The ten years they waited for me would have not been in vain.

A small boned, white skinned, blue-eyed albino boy stood squinting at the bow of the dug-out to watch for any hidden outcroppings or uncroppings of coral in our path which could foul our motor and leave us to the mercy of the reef and the waves. Green-bottomed white caps broke on them 20 feet away. They were a bit more violent than they seemed from the mission house window.

We pulled into a shallow stretch of water and lowered anchor. Artilio was, as usual, the first over the side. I went through the identical procedure a moment later and was soon paddling on the surface looking at the unbelievable landscape or rather seascape below me. The first thing I learned that day was to balance in the force of the waves. If I were thrown off balance, I would be heaved by the swells into the reefs and there were numerous black spines there that wouldn't be easy to extract.

The moment before I went over the side, the mission boys were laughing—I had taken to dungarees, socks, sneakers and a long sleeved brown shirt to fish in. This garb would give me some protection from the spines and poison coral if I hit any.

But all of these precautions melted away when I saw the great reef from the water. Walt Disney would have patented the scenery around me. If anyone wanted to build something of beauty and awe-inspiring majesty to match this, he would have to spend millions of dollars. The beauty of the reef was beyond description. Coral giants in tree form leapt 60 feet from the bottom depths into the warm sunlight, sending their uppermost branches, just a few inchs past the surface. Quiet, hidden fantasy land that it was, buried beneath tons of water—full of fans, color, fish, tiny swaying organisms here and there—red, orange, green, purple, blue, yellow, maroon, aqua, colors that were muted, bright, vibrant, shaded, colors that barely reached the name of blue, and others that exceeded it beyond the color of any birds in the jungle. I raised my head out of the water—up here was just a thin cover of green and a dug-out canoe and waves. I put my head back into the water—the other beautiful world of the sea. How many people, I wondered, had ever seen such a sight. All at once I felt grateful to Artilio. How many people would have shunned the place because of fear. I would have if I had not known what was here. Now, all I felt was a child's delight at being back in the water and seeing what was before me stretching endlessly from the deepest depths to all sides.

I wished I could have gone below, but that was clearly impossible with my snorkel tube. I felt the pressure when I was just down 20 feet. If I went deeper, my ears would clog and I'd feel the force of the water.

I spotted a good sized red snapper, 40 pounds or more, and went after him with an elated feeling of the hunt. This time I didn't miss and towed it back after a good ten minute battle to the dugout. Artilio was startled. It was the biggest game fish caught that day. No sooner had I delivered my catch and been rewarded by Artilio's surprise, was I off again to the sea world.

I wondered if anyone knew how much delight ten dollars worth of snorkel and false mask could provide. The cost of a small dinner and a movie could buy a sight more thrilling than any epic film ever made. I thanked the inventor of the face mask and snorkel whereever he was.

Red snapper again, and big ones. I got a small five pound specimen and brought it back to the dug-out—that would be Snoopy's food for at least three days.

Going back, and leaning over the great reef, I caught sight of a huge sting ray with great globs of comic strip eyes affixed in his triangular body, his great waving sting tail trailing behind him in the water. From my safe vantage point he was beautifully graceful and looked relatively friendly. I knew he wasn't and would use that tail if he felt threatened by the presence of man fish in his water. I stayed on my reef until he was well gone.

Going home, I felt marvelous and elated about the afternoon. In all we had five dozen good sized fish in the boat and I was responsible for eight of them. It had been a good day. Artilio was beaming proudly, having brought in a tasty moray eel, and another small barracuda for his day's efforts.

When we put into the dock, Snoopy was waiting there for me and I tossed him a good sized chunk of snapper. He caught it in mid-air and ran off gratefully to the backyard of the mission house to chew on it in peace.

Tuesday

It's dawn and the sun has just crept over the line marking the separation of light green, orange tinted sky, and deep aqua water. A chorus of howlers are crying in the forest and can be heard plainly right here on the island. In the village, the men are coming toward their dug-outs to begin their day's work or just plain walking about. The sea is absolutely calm and there's not a ripple on the surface of the water. Coming from the west is a dug-out canoe, orange sails to the wind. The regular dipping and pulling out of the paddle by the man seated in the stern is the only trace of movement on the water. Roosters are crowing. Today I leave for a few days visit with Mamitupu Island to the east.

Saturday

The only reason I'm sitting at this typewriter is because now it's the only thing that makes sense to me. I'm nauseous and the heat of the fever that's crowding my body is intense. I'm running 103.5°. It has climbed there in only four hours. This is the morning. It will rise before tonight. Mamitupu and the jungle river are running through my brain along with sharks and cudas. I think

I'm starting to get delirious. Must be malaria. Can't think. The effort to sit is too much. I've got to go to bed. Think I'm going to black out.

Fever over 104°. Hot, sick. Don't know what it is. Not having chills. Not malaria. Can't remember getting up from bed to get this notebook and pencil. I'm the only source of help I've got. Got to get fever down. Maybe if I go and sit in the cool sea. Drugs not working. If I don't break it, it will break me. No possibility of help until the morning. Too sick to go to window and call for Artilio or Mrs. Miller. I've got to sweat—only way—heat will fight heat.

Monday

I'm still in bed, and very weak. Artilio and Mrs. Miller found me out of my mind with fever two nights ago, and managed to keep me under covers and full of terramycin until the fever broke in the early morning Sunday, leaving me soaking with sweat and exhausted. We have no idea what it could have been.

Anyway, I suspect that I picked up a bug at the river when I went in during my trip to Mamitupu.

The first night I was on the island there was a council meeting going on and everybody was there. A young boy, the brother of the Philosopher-Poet, who had been to the Canal Zone and therefore picked up a smattering of English, translated for me.

"A white snake will come," said the medicine man in the dim light of the council hall on that island. The air was stuffy and the smoke from an ill-burning kerosene lamp filled the air.

"I have seen a great tree split in the mountains and a white snake crawl from it." He looked about the room to let the full impact to the statement strike home.

"The snake was as big as four men and had two heads. From each head there came the smell of two great sicknesses. It is coming to the island the day after tomorrow. My spirits have told me that it comes to bring the sickness."

"When will it come?" demanded a village elder, "and when will we see the sickness in our people?"

"In two or three weeks time—the old people will suffer first, then it will sweep through the whole village and not a hut will remain without at least one down with fever. The young and the strong will fall before it."

"Why will the illness come?" demanded the second chief.

"The spirits of our fathers and our father's fathers and the earth itself have been wronged. Why has there been no rain in three days? Surely the river will dry up and our food plants will die."

"It is because the season which is dry is coming. This is the way things have always been. On what do you blame these things? I think you speak unwisely." The chief Kantule looked about the room for support for his words.

The first chief, who had been silent up until this time, spoke:

"What are these angry words you speak to us? What is their meaning, medicine man?" His eyes flashed in the light.

"We have broken a rule," answered the "nele" or medicine man.

"Oh, oh," I thought. I knew there was and had been some difficulty about having me stay on the island. It was clear what the medicine man was saying—even José, my young eighteen-year-old translator, looked at me to see if I caught the meaning. It was more than evident to me.

I had the permission of the chief, but the medicine man wanted no part of my being on the island.

The council meeting ended by the chief's telling everyone present that I was his guest and that if any harm came to me, he would hold whoever it was responsible. José did not translate this, but I understood it, having by this time picked up quite a bit of the dialect.

The council meeting broke up and I went back to my hut with my beautiful Philosopher-Poet child and spoke with him for an hour or so through José. He finished the evenings conversation by saying:

"Sipu, it would be well to avoid the poison of a snake in the jungle—is this not so?"

I replied that it was.

"Then avoid making friends with a snake who thinks and hates." He looked intently at me to make sure I understood his words. I did. I slept well that night.

It was obvious that the child meant I was to avoid the medicine man. It was more obvious to me, the next day, that I didn't pay too much attention to his words.

I went into the jungle river wih José and another brother of his. We were going to visit a family of mountain Cuna who lived half a day from the river.

We paddled two hours the next morning to get to the river, then rode the huge breakers, splashing white, right into the mouth of the river. There were still waves a quarter of a mile up the river from the ocean. When we reached the first rapids they stopped.

The Mamitupu graveyard was right inside the river, but there seemed to be quite a bit of activity on the banks. I found out from José that there was a village right beside the graveyard and we stopped for cocoa drink there. The usual occurrences happened. Children ran screaming to their mothers—everybody came around for a look at me and I was introduced to the chief. Then we continued our journey to the first rapids, tied up our dug-out there and proceeded on foot into the jungle and up into the mountains. Before we reached the foothills we crossed the Mamitupu River nine times, having to swim the river on two occasions. I was carrying my camera and it was no easy feat for the current was strong and swept me off balance a dozen times. My camera, however, was safe in its plastic case. After an excruciatingly exhausting trip of five hours duration, we reached the village at noon—for it was a village and there were some eight families living up there. They wore the traditional Cuna dress, nose ring and mola, and the men were in loin cloths. I talked with them for only a half an hour before it was necessary to go back down the foothills to get our canoe back to Mamitupu. It would be about eight p.m. when we would finally get there. I did, however, like these jungle Indians. They were an unaffected and natural people and I wished I could have spent more time with them. However, walking at night in the jungle becomes dangerous and it is wise to either be in a hut or set up a camp and stay there until the sun comes in the morning.

José and I did a bit of spear fishing for crabs at the riverbanks and returned to the island with coconuts, plantains (given to us by the jungle Indians) and two dozen crabs.

When I reached the island that night, I was tired and sweaty from the day long trip through the jungle. A woman came and offered me something to drink at her house and I decided to accept it whatever it was.

I was offered the cup and was about to drink whatever it was, a darkish concoction, when José appeared and ordered me in English not to drink from the cup. I asked why. He told me that the woman was the medicine man's wife and there was talk on the island that he wanted to get rid of me.

I paled and told José to go back to the hut. I wouldn't drink any, but wanted to put a plan into effect which just popped in my mind. I raised the cup to my lips and keeping them shut pretended to drink some of the liquid. José's mouth fell open, but the tall, stately medicine woman's wife gave him one long hard look and he backed off and went home. I pretended to have another sip, and then wiped my mouth on the sleeve of my mola blouse, for I was dressed Indian here, and thanked the woman in her dialect.

"You've had enough?" she asked. I replied that I had, thanked her again and handed the cup back to her. She handed it back to me and told me that the liquid would give me strength. I took the cup, not knowing what to do, then thought of something. "Masi?" I asked—did she have any plantains? She immediately went into the cooking hut to get some for me. I dumped the cup of liquid in the grass and when she returned, said that the drink was delicious and asked what it was made out of. She laughed. I ate two plantains and went on my way. As I left the yard of her house I bumped right into her medicine man husband who looked at me and laughed, then entered his hut. I went home.

When I got into my guest hut, Talilu, my child philosopher, called me.

"You do not listen well. I have told my mother to make you a drink to fight the one you have just had. You are going to be very sick tonight."

I told Talilu what I had done. He looked at me in surprise then burst into merry laughter. He was still laughing when his mother entered and forced a miserable tasting concoction into my hands and mouth. I drank a little, then took her into my confidence. She laughed as fully as her son had and vowed she wouldn't say a word to anyone in the village. We slept well that night.

The secret was well-kept by my house. The next morning when I went walking in the village all smiles and evidently in perfect health, I visited the medicine man's hut and asked his wife if she didn't have anymore of that wonderful tasting drink she gave me the night before. When she saw me, she stopped where she was standing and spilled over a gourd of shower water. Her husband was also obviously shocked to find me on my feet. When they heard I wanted more, they looked at each other and said that they didn't have anymore. I left the yard and went back to the house. I hoped that would teach them that white people, especially American womanhood and all that, are not affected by poison. They probably think so to this day and are trying to figure out some dire potion to affect the next one they catch on the island, or better still, have decided that since I committed no horrors or crimes on the island, that we were best left alone.

The medicne man avoided me for the remainder of my stay on the island and no more was heard from him in the council hall regarding my visit.

I returned to Ailigandi that night in Artilio's dug-out canoe. I didn't tell him what happened, he'd no doubt hear about it after I was gone.

It was in the reefs Saturday morning, while again spear fishing with Artilio, that I began to feel sick, but attributed it to seasickness, although I hadn't felt any in weeks. When we got back to the island, I began to feel the fever and knew that I wasn't sea sick. That night I passed the crisis and am in fairly good shape today, although I think I'll spend the day in bed just to make sure. The fever, however, cannot be attributed to any of the medicine man's concoctions or chants—I no doubt caught it in the river during my trip up to the mountains. Hopefully, it will stay away now.

Tuesday, Wednesday and Thursday were spent celebrating yet another Chicha feast and, wonder of wonders, I talked with Ikwanik for an entire half an hour before he passed out.

While Maria and I were sitting in the puberty hut in our usual places, an impromptu dance broke out directly outside of the door and Maria threw herself into it with a passion. Soon, river reed pipes and rattles joined in and the party was growing.

I went outside to watch, feeling myself a bit under the chicha and needing the fresh air. They were beautiful, these jungle people. They looked for all the world like Pan escaped from the forest and gone primitive. Maria came dancing by at one point, caught my arm, and the next thing I knew, I was part of the long red-yellow-green-black-blue-orange-brown-and purple hopping, skipping, sweating line, I began to whistle their chant.

"Namake Juanita!" cried an old grandmother "Sing!" I did, chanting slowly to their music the Cuna words for the "Forest Gives Life," that went with the song. I sang, danced, floating with the people and feeling joyous with my friends. The music picked up more speed, more river pipes started, then Maria and I and ten other women sat down on the ground laughing, exhausted and sweating. We had all been children, playing as children and enjoying our marvelous game. In the midst of the laughter I heard a voice from far away.

"Venga Juanita—comida!" It was Mrs. Miller and I looked up to see her eyeing me sternly. I knew she didn't like my fraternizing with the Indians during the Chicha celebrations.

I made my way to my feet and left the group still laughing and followed Mrs. Miller.

The pipes started up again and the people continued their dance that they and their forefathers had done since and before Columbus had ever laid eyes on the rain forest of the San Blas coast.

Today is a very sad day for me. An American doctor arrived this morning with Mike via plane to Ailigandi Island after I sent word to them that Talilu was dying. They couldn't get into the island because there was a seven days' smoking going on. Talilu died today at ten a.m. this morning. We got word via the jungle grapevine.

"My people were born of the Earth Mother and came down to the mountain of Tarcarcuna to the east," said Ikwaniktipippi through my translator Au Savio. "Even in the time when much water came and covered the earth, during the time of a whole moon, Tarcarcuna was the sanctuary of the Cuna. The water did not cover the top of the mountain and the people lived. But still, many of the race died, the Olowaipepelili, our Great God, gave these who survived babies, the Golden Ones. There were nine of them. These were of good heads and became the medicine men of the tribe. They taught our people how to take the fish from the sea, and how to build houses in the jungle and keep our people strong and good. When the water went away, the earth grew again and our people multiplied and went all over the jungle. We built a great city near Tarcarcuna and we had much gold, but when the Spanish came, they burned our city and took our gold and killed many, many of us. We thought Ibeorgan had sent the great boat with the men with hair on their faces, but we were wrong, they only wanted our gold. We left the city and our villages and went into the jungle. We buried our gold and hid the places where we got it. We stayed many, many years in the jungle until the evil men went away, then we came down to the islands. Now my people have forgotten and don't remember what happened."

With these few words Ikwaniktipippi brought me up to date on the history of the Cuna peoples.

He was referring with his last statement to the troubles at Tigre Island—and the gun battle there between the Panamanians and the Cuna. I'll go into this in more detail later, but it must be said that one teacher at Ailigandi school told me that if the Guardia from Panama had hurt anyone on Tigre Island after the fight and ensuing capture of hostages, that every island in San Blas was armed and would have gone to Tigre's aid. As it was, war was narrowly avoided.

As it is, I can truly understand and sympathize with the distrust expressed by the Indians for outsiders. Ever since the first white man set foot in San Blas, the story of the Cuna has been the story of a constant battle for survival. Even today, if anyone comes into the area looking for gold, he is asked to leave in no uncertain terms. The Indians remember that 750,000 of their ancestors were slaughtered for gold and they want no more of greed in their lands. If any gold seeker does not leave, he just might be "missing" in the jungle mainland in the area. Now, although gold is still worn in some quantity by the Indian women in the form of necklaces and gold nose rings, it is not traded and is never passed on from generation to generation, but buried with its owner. Any theft of gold from a graveyard is punishable by death according to Cuna law and that death is not an easy one—burial alive fits the crime and it is still carried out in some spots in San Blas.

On an island which shall be unnamed, I was allowed to sit in on a theft case from a graveyard. Two Colombians, dark-skinned and frightened, had been caught coming out of the river earlier that morning with gold they had taken from graves at the riverbank. Unfortunately for them they were too late in getting out and were caught by the Indian men at the mouth of the river. They were taken to the mainland and an immediate council meeting took place. The Colombians were known to the Indians and therefore the crime was considered more heinous. The chief said:

"If you were new to the laws of our people and didn't know that our law says you must not steal from the dead, then we would have held you here and frightened you, then let you go. But for 15 years now you have traded with us. You know the law as the people of the village do. You know the punishment for your dishonor to the graves of our mothers. Therefore, you must die."

The Colombians begging for clemency were tied in behuco vine and taken to the jungle mainland. I never heard of them again and the affair was nevermore mentioned in the village. I didn't like to see what happened happen, yet what the chief said was true. I had been only five months in San Blas and I knew the laws by heart. I would never have stolen gold from a graveyard under any circumstances, out of respect for the hospitality of the people I lived with.

Ikwaniktipippi proceeded to tell me a bit about his religion. It seems that at first there was nothing but Olowaipepelili, or the Great God sleeping in the sky—then the God had a dream and with it came a nocturnal emission. Since God was God, this emission turned into an earth that was barren.

This earth was shaped as a woman, and when God awoke and saw it he loved it and said (quote Ikwanik) "Ha, ha! That looks like a good idea!" and made love to it. From this union came three forms of life: devils, turtles, and the first Golden Ones—a man and a woman. God liked the earth woman so much that he made love to her and produced a sun, fish of the sea, stars, plants, and all kinds of birds and wild life.

It is interesting to note that the Cuna still call disease "kilu" or uncle when the medicine man chants to his dolls for a sick person. This is logical since the devils which cause sickness were born at the same time as the first Golden Ones. This fact makes the devils uncles of the children of the Golden Ones. The name is still used today and nobody seemed to know why. I found out because while listening to a council meeting one night, I caught the Chant of Creation. It was obvious to me that the "relation of uncle" to disease by the Cuna race came from this song.

The Cuna venerate the earth as the giver of all life and there are many ways they respect it. They take only what they need for food and shelter and clothing from the jungle. They do not kill or destroy anything they do not need. They do this so that the earth mother will not have to work too hard to keep up with their greed. If that happened, then the earth would get angry and a famine or flood would ensue and the Golden Ones would starve and go homeless.

Ikwaniktipippi was a marvelous old man. During our talk his mind would sometimes wander, but he spoke poetically, as had Talilu, sincerely and lyrically. Every once in a while he would turn to spit on the ground, as that was the custom. Au Savio, my translator, would always look at me sharply to see if I'd say or indicate anything to embarrass the old man about his spitting. Evidently someone had at some time or another. I didn't mind it for it was his way and he was unconscious in this action. Ikwanik signaled to Au Savio that the conference was over, and with this the wonderfully wise old man and gentle Chief of Ailigandi rose and went into the warm sunlight outside of the mission house and over to his dug-out. He was going fishing.

Saturday, August 31st, 1963

Time, time, time, you fly so fast in days and weeks, yet slow in hours and minutes. Where has the time gone. It seemed to slip through the streets and into the sea. I've been here for years in mind, and only a bit more than a month in time.

I'll be leaving here tomorrow morning on the *Melda* when she comes to port, but I think I'll be leaving a huge chunk of myself in the streets of Ailigandi.

I must pack and get ready for the trip.

I'll be going to the Mulatupu mission to the east to spend a few weeks with the Iglesias family there and to view the village first hand. I'm anxious to talk with Marguerita, Claudio's wife, and to visit the surrounding islands in that area. I'm curious to see if life is any different there than it is here on Ailigandi Island.

The moment I set foot on the *Melda* this morning, Maria started to wail as though she'd lost Ricardo. It took me all of a half an hour to convince her that it wasn't as though I were going back to New York. I'd be back in Ailigandi within three weeks. That seemed to calm her somewhat and I left Ailigandi on the *Melda*. I had said good-bye to everybody earlier that morning. Most of the village turned out to see the boat until it was out of sight. I felt kind of silly at all of that show of affection, but I felt as much for these people. I loved them.

I went to bed early last night. The sounds of Ailigandi reached me in my room. In the rafters, two rats played tag, and the song of the sea, ever constant, ever beautiful, continued its undulating beat outside the window. In the sky, the big full San Blas moon lit the way I would follow in the morning. I knew that regardless of where I went and for how many years I would be away, this place, this room, these people, the tiger cat now in the rafters and giving the rat population a run for its money, would always be with me. There would be parts of me in the coral reefs, on the island, in the green jungle. There would be nights back in civilization when I'd look up at a moon something like this one and remember how it looked over the sea and lighting the streets of the village.

I remembered the Chicha feasts, the crabs, a marmoset, a barracuda, shark hooks and spear guns, medicine men and girls turned women. I remember dug-outs sinking and babies laughing. No, I wasn't leaving Ailigandi, I was taking it with me, the whole village, the river, the jungle, the sea, and most of all, her people, in my heart.

9

MULATUPU ISLAND

It's Tuesday, September 3, 1963, and it's a big holiday here in San Blas this being the date the Indians celebrate Nele Kantule's death. He was one of the well-known and respected chiefs who headed the revolution in 1925. Nele Kantule, or translated "the medicine man-singer of songs," is somewhat of a national hero to the Indians. Today his home island of Ustupu-Conception, which I passed on the way here to Mulatupu, is having a big celebration to honor him.

There were a few men, all chiefs of their tribe and one American, who were involved in the revolt. Nele Kantule was one, another was "General" Colman from Ailigandi (chief of that island in 1925) and a Mr. Porter, an American whose history is fascinating—he later set himself up as emperor of the Darien Jungle and lived with the Cuna on and off for ten years. But it was Nele Kantule who was the undisputed leader of the affair. His wisdom and logical demands from the newly formed Republic of Panama when the revolt was brought to the conference table spelled a new life for his people and their survival on their own ancestral lands. He demanded schools and medical help, trade with both Panama and Colombia, and "hands off" policy from Panama in tribal affairs. He was granted his wishes, which were the wishes of his people, and now the Republic of Panama and the San Blas Province are the better for it. The treaty does credit to Panama and to the wisdom of Nele Kantule.

I have spent some time discussing the revolution with many of the Indians, some of whom still remember it vividly. Panama, then rapidly modernizing herself because of the presence of the new canal, became a leader in South American affairs. She naturally wanted all of her citizens to enjoy the fruits of the new prosperity and modernization. Schools and health agencies spread their arms even to the most outlying provinces, including San Blas. Some of the means that the new republic took to enforce modernization on some of her Indian peoples were well-meant, but a bit hasty. Indians who had for years lived primitive lives could not understand the new ways and thought their own good enough—for them. It had been only a quarter of a century since the Indians came down out of the mountains to populate the off-shore islands. They were still leary of outsiders regardless of good intentions.

When the officials of the new republic of Panama saw that they were making no headway with the Indians, they decided, unwisely, to increase the restrictions and rules on the people to see if that would get better results. It only served to anger the Indians against their new "oppressors."

Men going into the jungle or to a nearby island to gather coconuts were required to carry passes signed by government officials. No one could leave an island without one. Those who did were arrested and they often did not know why. Islanders were told to be in a certain place at a certain time for a meeting and didn't even know how to read a clock. Women were told to take off their silly mola dresses and nose rings and put on Western dress. Rules and regulations increased—understanding of "why" to the Cuna peoples did not. They had no idea why all at once everybody wanted them to dress differently and be in certain places at certain times, and as for leaving the island to go to the jungle—they had to have food for their families as their fathers, grandfathers, and all of their ancestors before them did.

If tact and a bit of patience were used at first, the story might have been different. One of the greatest modernizers of the Cuna people was a Cuna boy named Claudio Iglesias who was working with the Panamanian government officials to help his people. His intentions were none but the best. He wanted the best for his people. But he forgot that it is hard for peoples to understand and accept a new way of life—time, lots of it, was needed.

Consequently, the Indians grew restless in their anger. Arrests increased. Rules and regulations still increased. Finally the entire affair came to a head one night at the mouth of the Sugar River, Rio Azucar near Narkana Island. Claudio accompanied several National Guardsmen there to arrest a man who was evidently in the wrong about something. On arrival at the mainland village, he and all of his Guardia companions were macheted to death on the beach. With these deaths, an island-wide revolt began. There was an American man named Marsh at Ailigandi at the time. It has been said by four different people that he organized that island and the surrounding ones for defense of their land. He has been accused by several Panamanian history books of having "instigated" the affair, but this is purely a misunderstanding. I have spoken with several Indians who remember 1925, including Ikwaniktipippi, and they tell me he had nothing to do with starting the revolution at all. It started and was caused by the points outlined above.

As I say, it was no one's fault, but the fault of a vast amount of misunderstanding between two otherwise wonderful peoples. Both sides meant well, but unfortunately the affair did not occur and the people of San Blas still talk of it occasionally, in not too happy terms. In the years to come, both peoples will realize that the main instigator of the revolt of 1925 was purely misunderstanding of each other's motivations and ways—nothing more than ignorance on the part of both good peoples.

When the revolt got under way, any white people caught in San Blas were told either to leave or were killed. The exception to this was the Baptist missionary of Narkana Island. She was helped to escape by several of her students to Porvenir. Their arrival marked the first word of trouble that that governing island had concerning the revolt. When the revolt reached a head, the Americans, fearing that the two sides would slaughter each other, sent in the battleship *Cleveland* to Porvenir Bay and had the two sides settle their dispute then and there to avoid any further bloodshed. They feared an Indian war in such close proximity to such an expensive project as the Panama Canal and hastily took the matter in hand and got it under control.

So much for that bit of history. I'm presently swinging in a hammock in the downstairs portion of the home of Claudio and Marguerita Iglesias on Mulatupu Island. Claudio is presently in Panama City, but his lovely and gracious wife Marguerita is here and has made me at home. Her eldest daughter is in the city, but Marina, the owner of Snoopy, and her young son David are here with me.

It's ten a.m. on a lovely sun-shiny morning and Marguerita is presently teaching a kindergarten class on the front porch upstairs.

I had a brief opportunity to talk with Marguerita before classes began. We had a cup of honest to goodness coffee upstairs with milk and sugar, a beverage I haven't seen in months—the Indians serve their coffee black and may add sugar or sugar cane juice to sweeten it. I found out that Marguerita met Claudio at college in the States. They fell quickly in love and after a two-week honeymoon in New York 15 years ago, the couple joined Claudio's brother Lonnie and his wife Marvel at the mission in Ailigandi. They stayed here learning about the work they would be doing for two years, then came to Mulatupu at the request of a delegation sent by that island to ask them to come and teach their children and help them with their medical problems.

Already Marguerita has struck me as a most unusual person. She is a strong person in body and mind and has a spiritual quality about her which has so far and in just such a short time, amazed me. Anyone who can spend 12 years in the middle of a bush area such as Mulatupu, which is as far away from civilization as one can possibly get in the San Blas Islands, has to be a mental giant. She finds her strength in her religion and in the work she does. Last but not least, her strength and full support is in and with her husband Claudio.

Malatupu Island itself is situated 27 miles from the Colombian border west and approximately 100 miles from Porvenir Island. It is close to the mainland, there being about a half mile separation between island and jungle. The mountains in this part of the jungle are higher than any others along the coast and there are several passes located there including the famous Passo Sarsardi, where Balboa, along with his Spanish crewmen, carried ships over the mountains to be re-assembled on the other side for exploring the Pacific. Pizarro followed and went on into the land of the Inca. Choco Indians, the golden-skinned lords of the Darien Jungle, come down here often, their villages being just on the other side of the high mountains in the jungle. The name Mulatupu means vulture, hence this place is named Vulture Island, but it is not an ugly place at all, but rather quite charming in many ways.

When I got off the *Melda* this morning (the events of our trip I will talk about later) I was immediatley attacked by a small jaguar kitten who frightened the heart out of me. I was carrying a bag of my belongings on my shoulder, when suddenly I thought Snoopy was after me once again. I looked down at my foot to see the small jaguar wrapped around my dungaree leg and dropped everything and performed a minor act of levitation. My first act on the island of Mulatupu vastly amused the local population. Later on that morning, around nine, I played with the kitten; he was adorable and belligerent. Afterwards I wandered through the village trying to locate the kitten again, and all at once it demonstrated the same affection Snoopy has for my feet and flung itself there in a very narrow alley. I tried to buy the kitten from the family, liking it tremendously and thinking it might be salable back in the States to a zoo, but the family wanted 60 dollars American for it and such an expenditure was clearly not for my limited budget.

I was very amused when I found out how and where the kitten was sleeping at night. The family that owns it has constructed a small hammock within a sort of corral. The jaguar kitten sleeps very comfortably in the hammock at night. I couldn't quite bring myself to believe such a statement and asked that it be demonstrated. The Indians who owned the kitten immediately looked indignant, grabbed the kitten by the scuff of its neck and brought it into the hut, motioning for me to follow. It was deposited within its corral and sure enough it hopped right into its hammock, curled up, and went to sleep. I laughed heartily and apologized to the kitten's owner for my Doubting Thomas qualities.

I arrived on Mulatupu Island Wednesday last, aboard the *Melda* after a somewhat eventful and fascinating voyage.

The *Melda,* the crew of which I first met at Narkana and two of whom were very good friends of mine—Milton the owner-captain, and Archibald, his co-captain—is one of those rare traders which carries radios, batteries, flashlights, soap, dishes, foods, salt, sugar, coffee, clothes, and what have you on the San Blas coast.

After leaving Ailigandi, we put in briefly to Achutupu Island to engage in a bit of buying and selling and I went over to say hello to the nurse. I got to her house and there wasn't any—house that is—not a post was standing and I feared something dreadful had happened to her and her family. A quick frantic conversation with a young Indian girl and sending her off brought the nurse to me. A new house was being constructed on the sight of the old one today, and that was why the old one was no longer in existence. I felt considerably relieved and sat down for a drink of lemon and sugar with her while the trading was being conducted aboard the *Melda.* When I started back to the *Melda,* I passed the chicha house and remembered the sorrow which had happened and permeated the entire island just a few days ago. Two men had had a violent argument on the island and both had gone for guns. They shot each other right in the chicha house in front of the whole village. There was quite a bit of mystery attached to the double death. It seemed that the two men just returned from Colombia. Why they were there nobody seemed to know. Both were unmarried, both had fathered no children that anybody knew of on the island. I pitied the girl whose feast it had been. To have a death occur during a Chicha feast was a very bad omen. It will be hard for her to find a husband now.

When I returned to the *Melda* we were soon under way and by-passed Mamitupu, as the "smoking" was still in progress here and no one was allowed in or out of the island for another three days.

Once past Mamitupu we headed outside the great reef and into the rougher waters. The sun was hot and the reflection of its light on the water, blinding. I took to sitting on the back "storecounter" which doubled as an engine hatch, bed, and dinner table when the appropriate times came around to use this waist high wooden platform for such purposes. I spotted several dozen sharks out here, one of which was 15 feet long. This was non-reef water and one would expect to see these garbage collectors in abundance here.

The coast of San Blas was its usual coconut-profused self, shortly followed by and in this order, high river trees, then high jungle, then the foothills, then mountains and the Darien Jungle. Also as usual, it was beautiful. If I ever saw an ugly spot I would have gazed upon it in wonder as I would have a beautiful spot anywhere else. Amazing place, this coast of San Blas.

After two hours worth of graceful sailing, we re-entered the reefs and I examined a sort of indentation in the coast, which turned out to be a rather large bay, more long than wide. At the entrance to this bay were three islands. Archibald, who had been busy with Milton discussing sales, came back to tell me that we were now going to put in to Ustupu-Conception Island. I was pleased, as I'd never been here before and there were two Baptist missionaries here that I wanted to talk with—Mr. and Mrs. Milton Morris. She was from America—he from San Blas. It seems that the biggest status symbol in San Blas, and I say this uncattily, is an American wife. If I had a coconut for every proposal I've had since I set foot in the area, I'd be very rich by local standards. The two American women I met did honor to their country. I've never met two more dedicated and marvelous women in all of my life than Elizabeth Morris and Marguerita Iglesias. They served in these bush areas with all the dedication of saints, to the cause of educating and giving medical help and assistance to those who needed it. They never expected a thank you, never expected anything but a heavenly reward for their Goliath-like efforts. If they were not there, many lives would have been lost including mothers and children in childbirth; youngsters would have gone uneducated, and much less would have been accomplished than has been done. For both of these women and for their efforts to help the Cuna peoples I say *"BRAVO!"*

The largest of the islands in the bay looked as though it were a coconut island, those trees dominating and filling the entire island in vast profusion. The second island was a rather lovely and well kept little graveyard off the southeast corner of the actual living island of Ustupu-Conception.

We pulled into a dock at the Conception end of the island and soon Mr. Milton Morris and I were having a conversation Romeo and Juliet style from ground and balcony. I was immediately dispatched home to his wife, while he continued his classes. I hadn't wanted to interrupt, but my arrival was announced before the boat was docked and Mr. Morris, summoned hence by the village children, had taken the matter out of my hands. They even knew my Indian name and Spanish name and went singing it through the streets. I didn't know quite how to take this and felt rather uneasy about a tribe of children singing "Sipu-Juanita" through the streets of a town I'd never been in before, but I could no more have gone to the Morris house in peace and quiet than MacArthur could have re-entered the Phillipines secretly after the war.

A safari line of children picked up my baggage and all 13 of us headed off toward the other end of the island, where Milton's home was. Elizabeth made me immediately at home and I sat sipping a glass of chocolate drink while she conducted a third grade arithmetic class to some young children on the front porch.

On the way to Ustupu, I had come across some kind of line marked by logs across the entire length of the island, and after Elizabeth finished with her class I asked her about them.

"We call that the Mason-Dixon Line," she commented laughingly and informed me that one side of the island was Catholic and the other Protestant. I was immediately outraged that such a border line should be marked because of religion and told her so. She informed me that Ustupu had nothing to do with it, and that the distinction had been the idea of the Conception side of the island. This was the first indication I had of any strife between the two religions in San Blas and I resented the whole thing. Why two peoples couldn't get along who had the same God and almost the same form of religion was beyond me and beyond my power to comprehend. That an actual demarcation line of who was to be Catholic and who was to be Protestant on which side of the island, was in existence was to me an absurd policy. I thought about it for weeks afterwards. The logical thing for the two missions to do, was to not vie with each other for converts, but to join hands in helping the people for the betterment of the people themselves—not for figures on pieces of paper testifying to someone's ability to speak from the pulpit.

I should think that the policy as it stood, Mason-Dixon Line and all, did far more harm than good, showing the Indians, who had never thought to segregate themselves in anyway before the arrival of any missionaries, what kind of hostilities can arise from such a situation.

I left the subject and went on to life on Ustupu-Conception from Elizabeth's point of view. We immediately got onto the subject of chickens, since I noted with some amazement the presence of white Rhode Islands all about the house. Elizabeth had imported these chickens, hoping to get better egg results with them than with the local scrawny looking Indian chickens.

"But their egg output has gone way down. Eggs are like gold out here at this time of year. No one seems to know why this happens, but they just seem to lay less."

She looked at me hopefully. I nodded my head in sympathy, not knowing too much about chickens and certainly not being able to help with the problem. The numerous clucking subjects under discussion were flapping about merrily on the porch railing, under the benches in the classroom and on into the kitchen. An angered cry of outrage emitted from the kitchen startling Elizabeth and myself. This was followed by a squawk in *haute voix* and from the kitchen door, two large white hens and one rooster exited hastily with wings outspread followed by a young San Blas girl whose nostrils fairly twittered in her nose from her dark-eyed anger. She spotted me, shot a look of fright to Elizabeth, and backed off into her kitchen once again.

"I employ two of the village girls to help me with the housework and the children," explained Elizabeth.

The house itself was a rather large white affair having two stories. I should have imagined it to be at least a four bedroom home. I later discoverd this to be so. It was situated at a point of land that jutted into a small peninsula to the north and toward the sea. Milton often caught supper right out in the back yard, there being numerous and varied shapes of coral visible from the porch.

Milton came in the door of the porch along with eight Rhode Island chickens. The former stayed and the young cook in the kitchen chased the remaining eight white feathered tenacious chickens from the area with a cooking spoon and much gesturing of arms and body.

We listened *en groupe* to the broadcast from Mulatupu, Ailigandi, Narkana, and Balboa in the Zone. It was announced among the daily passage of news that I was heading for Mulatupu and would probably spend the night on Ustupu.

After the radio broadcast, Milton and I found ourselves engaged in a fascinating conversation of life along the San Blas coast. He spoke with vividness and love of life and I sat totally silent and intent listening to his tales of San Blas. Soon I knew quite a bit about the goings on in Ustupu-Conception without even leaving Milton's house. Both towns had separate council halls because of the two-religion standard; both had separate chiefs, meeting places, and chicha houses. It was as though the two islands were not joined together at all.

The Conception side of the island was the more progressive of the two separate towns. Here there were five concrete buildings and one trading shop selling among other things, a kerosene stove. It looked as though it had been there for a long long time. I never saw one of these in an Indian home, just the regular cooking fires made on the ground with wood. The Usutupu side of the island was more primitive by choice. The people there wanted none of the "new fangled ways."

I was also informed by Milton that he was attempting to get an Alliance for Progress school built on the large coconut island beside Ustupu-Conception. He hoped to get Peace Corps vocational workers in carpentry, electricity, and machinery to teach there. During our talk Mrs. Morris, who had left earlier in the direction of the kitchen, came back and announced that dinner was ready.

I followed Mr. Morris into the kitchen and was pleasantly surprised to find that it had been decorated in Early American style. I thought I was having hallucinations when I saw a side of roast beef on the table—something like finding caviar at 11 dollars a spoonful on your home breakfast plate back in New York.

Mrs. Morris noted my amazement with the dish, laughed, and told me she'd been in Panama City the week before and had purchased it at that time. I thanked her profusely for sharing this treat with me and we said grace and commenced eating.

Our dinner was saturated with more magnificent conversation from Milton.

"Do you remember when we had that unusually high tide about a month ago?"

I replied that I did.

"Well, there is a middle-aged grandmother here in the village. On the night when the tide was highest, she ran through the village streets dressed in only her nose ring, screaming at the top of her lungs. The people thought that some kind of devil had possessed her. Well, we're watching the family and the woman closely now because there have been attempts to kill her. Two of the women of the village claim to have had dreams that the soul of this insane woman would, at the time of the next full moon, which is now, enter a well a few feet below the ground under her hammock and her soul would join with the sea. They claim the sea will then come up and flood the entire island and kill many people. Of course, when the council meeting heard this, they were thrown into a panic. An attempt was made to kill the woman and chase the devil spirit from the island by poisoning her. It didn't work and she got very sick, but lived. During the height of the high tide, another attempt was made—also a failure. The people were angry with the medicine man because he didn't use enough poison. He claimed that the devil within the woman was strong and it would take more than the average dose to kill a person to get rid of it. Right at this moment the woman is locked up in a hut and being guarded there by her family. Before the full moon is over, she would no doubt 'disappear' as we say. Any insane person 'disappears.' The Indians do not allow insane people to live on the island for fear that the possessed person will infect others."

He also filled me in on some interesting facts concerning the albino "Moon Children." There were mixed feelings about the Moon Children. The people realized that it was some kind of a defect, but it had its advantages. The albinos made the best night hunters and night fishermen, for they could see in the dark better than anyone else on the island. In daylight though, they squinted and had to stay out of the sun because they burned quite easily. But if, God forbid, a moon eclipse should occur, the entire island is at the mercy of the Achu Sapuro or the Great Tiger who is eating the moon—if he fully succeeds, then the very earth will crumble and fall away beneath their feet. The Moon Children are responsible for the salvation of their island in a time of crisis such as this. Everyone else, as soon as it is known that the moon is being eaten, runs in doors cowering with fear. The Moon Children rush out into the night armed with bows and arrows to shoot the "spirit" of the arrows straight up at the Great Tiger in the sky who is perpetrating such a heinous act as eating the moon. When the eclipse is over they get credit for having saved the day and are feted as heroes.

But still, the Moon Children have a stigma attached to them. They can generally only marry among themselves, and sometimes, if an albino girl is born to a normally colored family, its mother is degraded for having "looked at the full moon too long" when she was carrying the baby. In times past and in a few instances in modern times these children "disappeared" into the jungle mainland. It is difficult to find a husband for an albino girl, and since she spends her life just eating and not hunting or fishing, they believe it is better to let her "disappear." In a boy's case, it is different. He can hunt, fish, and raise food. He is of value to the family. Generally, these boys live.

I delved a bit into the reasons for the killing of insane persons. The reason is a simple one. A devil, instead of simply stealing the individual's soul, has taken the soul, killed it and taken possession of the body by entering it. That means that a living devil is among them—the worst possible form of devil. It is believed that the original person was dead the moment the body became insane, for in order to enter the body the devil had to break off its ties with its soul. Now all that remains is to kill the devil and chase him from the village. Then they bury the person's body with full honors and ceremony, knowing that the original person died sometime before the devil got into the body. They do not think of this form of killing as a mercy killing, but as an exorcism.

After supper I walked back to the *Melda* to sit and talk with Milton and Archibald. Milton was a jovial creature of the sea who loved his work, his wife, his children, and life in general. He had been trading on the San Blas coast for 15 years and his Panamanian wife lived on Narkana Island. There was a certain down to earth, common sense quality about everything he did, which did not lessen his love of even the simplest things to any degree. Archibald on the other hand was more serious. He was tall, being about six foot four, and *cafe-con-leché* in color. He had bright blue eyes and had very few real loves in life. He loved fishing, hunting, and boats. It was he who caught the shark off of Ailigandi during the week of the invasion from the sea, when the young boys from Achutupu and Mamitupu were killed by sharks. He offered to be my guide, when I finally went back into the mountains, on a bit of a jaguar hunt. I thanked him for his offer, but thought it best to depend on the Indians up there for their help.

When I walked back across the Mason-Dixon Line and down to the dock area I found Archibald contemplating the cement walk in front of Nele Kantule's statue. Here, a monument was constructed for the wise old revolutionary leader, a full bust on a pedestal. Archibald was as usual wearing his baseball cap. He hardly ever took it off. This was because his hair was thinning out beneath the cap and he didn't want too many people to know about this—not for a few years anyhow.

Before I reached him to say hello, I stopped startled in my tracks. At that moment a cry of rage and anger emitted from at least 200 throats within the huge council hall in front of the square dedicated to Nele Kantule.

"Jesus God!" I thought picturing another revolution or the trial of grave robbers or a murderer.

Archibald looked up from the cement walk and came over to me.

"Hi!" he called.

"What in heaven is going on in there?" I asked.

"Congress meeting," he mumbled, looking at me shyly. "A girl from this island is in a family way by a public school teacher from Narkana, who is Indian, and who works here. I think they're going to make him marry the girl before this meeting is over."

The place was beginning to look more like a New Jersey suburb every day. This I wanted to see to find out exactly how they would go about affixing legal responsibility for the boy and getting him to marry the girl. I decided to go and have a look at the situation and goings-on.

"The whole thing is," stated Archibald as we walked toward the congress hall, "that he's engaged to a girl from his home island, Narkana, and I don't think he's going to agree. The chief put him under arrest in the congress hall now for three days and they're going to keep him here on the island until they decide the case." He looked at me studiously then regarded the ground again, "I think they're going to decide in the girl's favor if it can be proved that she ah, well, didn't go with any other men."

A young man's voice drifted out into the square. An uneasy mumble followed his words.

Archibald translated for me.

"That's the boy. He says that he doesn't want to marry the girl. He'll take care of the baby after it's born with money and all that, but he won't marry the girl."

Another voice shot out into the twilight. It sounded like what the Archangel Gabriel's must have sounded like when he told Lucifer to go you know where.

"That's the father," said Archibald. "He says if it isn't taken care of in the right way, then he'll take care of it in the wrong way."

A cheer was still penetrating the air. The villagers were obviously on the side of the girl's father.

"What's the right and wrong way?" I asked. I pictured machetes flashing in the kerosene lamp light and the immediate death of the boy.

"He'll give the boy medicine to make him stay at home with his daughter."

"He'll give him WHAT?" I asked completely baffled. "Medicine? What kind of medicine?"

Another roar filled the air. This time it was outright anger.

"He says that many men have slept with the girl."

The father's voice pierced the air again.

"He wants to know who and when and where."

The boy's voice answered. By this time I was trying to get on my toes to look over the crowd at the door to the participants in the wordy battle.

"The boy says that he can't say a thing like that in public. He says that the men are right in this room and it would embarrass them and they probably wouldn't admit it."

The crowd answered with a roar shortly followed by the father's voice.

"The father says that he will give 1,000 coconuts to any man in the room who would testify that his daughter has slept with another man. The man need not be named. He will merely state that he has knowledge that the girl has been with other men."

The hall was silent. Then the father's triumphant voice pierced the air with a cry of triumph.

This I didn't want to miss. I nosed my way through an almost all male crowd. I caught sight of the central portion of the hall. An exceptionally beautiful girl was seated alongside who I thought was her mother. The latter was calmly smoking a pipe. The girl was in tears. The boy was a handsome lad but plainly uneasy and frightened at the mess he'd gotten himself into. The father was angrily pacing about the center of the room glaring like a fighting bull at the boy and gesturing to the council members with his arms. He wanted action.

"Archibald," I whispered, "what in the devil is this medicine?"

Roaring again.

This time the crowd got to its feet and kept roaring happily.

Archibald put his head to my ear and whispered:

"The chief just said that he's going to marry them."

"When?" I asked.

"Right this minute," replied Archibald peering down on the affair since he was shoulders high over any Indian in the place.

The boy was pushed forward unceremoniously by two council

members and the girl's mother pushed forward her daughter who was by now almost hysterical with tears.

The chief council member got to his feet and stood in front of them.

"He's asking the boy again if he'll marry the girl willingly."

The boy spoke vehemently and angrily.

"You're forcing me to do what I do not want to do," he said.

The council member gave a short huffy laugh and turned to address the packed to capacity hall.

"He says that since the boy has warned all of us ahead of time, the council and chiefs will instruct the planes and boats not to take him aboard. That means he's a prisoner on the island and that the father will give him medicine," commented Archibald.

"What in God's name is the medicine?" I asked for the third time.

The crowd surged forward taking Archibald and me with it.

The two were married by being taken bodily by members of the village and dumped into a hammock.

"How long will the marriage last?" I asked.

"Maybe three or four months. Then I think he'll run away. I saw the girl he loves on Narkana. She is even more beautiful than this one.

"Can they go after him and bring him back?"

"Not unless the chief of Narkana says so. He's responsible for the boy and he's not represented here. This decision may not be valid on Narkana Island."

"If he leaves the hammock of the girl, though, isn't that an automatic divorce hereabouts?"

"Yes, all they have to do to divorce each other is for him to take his hammock out of her hut for a few days, then they're divorced."

The young people were taken from the hall amid much joyous cries from the crowd and home to their hammock. They would sleep with each other this night.

The crowd slowly flowed out of the vast council hall and into the streets. Archibald and I went for a soda and some candy at a store nearby. When I walked back to the Milton household, I said goodnight to Mrs. Milton and quietly went to bed in my upstairs room. A thunder storm rumbled in the distance, and the breeze coming through the windows was like soft balm on my extremely burnt skin. The breeze smelled of the sea and the jungle surrounding us. I slept soundly all night long.

I awoke Tuesday with one thought on my mind—what in the world kind of medicine was everybody talking about? I had neglected to ask Archibald during our ensuing stopover at the trading post for cokes.

I got dressed and hurriedly made my way downstairs for breakfast. It was the first question I addressed to Milton after I said good morning. He laughed.

"So you saw the council meeting?"

I nodded my head in the affirmative.

"Well it's a kind of Indian medicine and . . ." He paused and examined me as though wanting to find out how I would take what he was about to say. "Well, they get it from the mountains and if a girl puts a little in a cup of drink she gives to a boy she likes, then he will never leave her. One further thing about the medicine—it works."

I humphed my disbelief.

"I knew you wouldn't believe it, but believe me, I've seen it done time and time again. It works."

"But Milton that's absurd—you're telling me that the medicine is a love potion designed to keep a boy with a girl he'd never look at before."

"It's not only for that—sometimes a boy goes off to Panama and doesn't come back. His father will go and get some of this medicine from the medicine man and bring it to Panama with him. He gives it to the boy and within a few months the boy comes back to his village."

"But Milton," I began again, "you're a missionary with a college education. You can't possibly believe in the potion!"

"And with that education I accept the fact that these people have so much faith in the power of their medicine, that psychologically, there *is* such a thing as a love potion. To their minds it works. To them it does in fact work. Now whether this would work for outsiders or not, I have no idea. I doubt it."

I looked at him. He was right, absolutely right; the Indians *did* have a love or rather stay-at-home potion. If a race of people believe they have a purple devil guarding their homes, there is one—such as we in our civilization firmly believe in God and very few, if any, have had any proof of his definite existence.

Before he made this statement I was thinking feverishly about the possibilities of packaging and supply to the United States. I had even wondered what the import laws would be for such a marvel of marvels.

Milton proceeded to give me other examples of the power of the stay-at-home medicine. If a man knows that his wife is not behaving as she should, he will go to the medicine man and ask him for a bit of his concoction to make his wife stay at home. This was given to her without her knowledge, and after she drank it, her husband would laugh and tell her what he had done. The same thing can be done by a wife whose husband is straying.

I went back to the boat at 9:30 and after talking with Milton for another couple of hours, I left with the *Melda* for Ustupu-Conception. We were out to sea once again.

Everything was so calm, so completely serene and utterly peaceful, that I curled up on the back hatch and didn't wake up until two hours later when we reached the mainland village of Napagandi. I sensed some kind of change in the sound of the motor, woke up, and looked around me. I saw that we were pulling into a dock. Then I looked over toward the east and thought I was seeing a mirage. There was an island there shaped like a whale, sprouting a mountain in the middle of it. It was quite large and utterly beautiful, even from this distance. None of the other islands in San Blas were mountainous or even tended toward the hilly side—most of them were flat coral islands. What was this island doing here?

"Isla Pino," offered Archibald. I turned to find him holding a cup of coffee out to me. "She's about 800 feet at the top of that mountain and she's very pretty all over. That's the best island in San Blas. We boat people always like to stop over there, and she's got some of the best fishing right from the dock that you can find out here. If you like, we'll try some tonight. If I can get some sardines in this village, we'll fish and see what we can find."

I thanked Archibald and accepted the coffee, which was perfect and wanted at that moment, and sat up cross legged on the engine hatch to await docking and drink my coffee.

Our stern and bow lines were tossed to the dock and some of the Indian men made us secure. Old tires creaked against the side of the dock. These had been put over the side of the *Melda* by our crew of three to protect her from scraping.

While business was being conducted aboard the *Melda* with the natives of Napagandi, our cook, quite an unusual Chinese gentleman, proceeded to start making lunch. He stripped the skin from some ripe plantains, and put them in strips on the bottom of a frying pan, into which oil had been heated and was sizzling. While the plantains cooked, he spotted a young boy on the dock holding a papaya fruit, quickly handed me a wooden spoon, gestured emphatically that I was to watch the plantains and made a leap from the bow to the dock that would have done credit to an Olympic champion and cornered the lad. There proceeded a lengthy bargaining session and in the end the cook ended up paying the lad ten cents for the papaya fruit. He happily climbed back on board and flashed me a triumphant smile, then, with a clean machete, cut slits along the length of the fruit and put it above his kitchen, or rather galley, cabinet. When the bad juices drained, we would have it—I imagined we'd probably have it for breakfast tomorrow morning. By this time the plantains were done and he took his wooden spoon back from me, saying nary a word and proceeded to get lunch ready for six people in record time. We had heated beef hash and the plantains along with more rich, dark coffee.

The afternoon heat was already with us and there was hardly any breeze on the *Melda,* so I handed in my dishes to the cook and climbed onto the dock and walked to the village. This was my first big mistake of the day.

The moment I climbed off the wood of the dock, bedlam broke out on all sides—children started to cry, frightened villagers ran for their huts. Women who had a few moments before been sewing peacefully in their yards or cleaning fish threw down what they were engaged in and ran for the protection of their yards, peering out at me with astonished eyes for the length of what was obviously the only main street in town. Their reaction was most unusual and I believe I was more astonished than they. I expected the usual retinue of children, and the curious to follow me as they did everywhere I stopped, but certainly not run for their very lives as though I'd break into an Irish jig, throw off every stitch of clothes I had on, and grab a machete and disembowel the first man, woman or child I laid eyes on. By this time, I was more curious than astonished, so continued on down the main village street, my camera swinging from my shoulder, to see if anyone would stop and let me in on the panic, whatever it was. When I got to the middle of the village I turned to find that most of it was trailing me some 20 yards to the rear. As soon as I turned they scattered as though I'd fired a machine gun into their midst. Just for the heck of it, I stood there and said "booooooooo!" The result was, if it were possible, even more disasterous than before. Nevertheless it was funny, and I started to laugh as though I'd seen a dog climb a tree to get away from a cat. Then, as though on signal, the sound of laughter came from all over the village at me. Evidently, the presence of anyone as ridiculous looking as a girl wearing a mola, dungarees, red pigtails, sunglasses, carrying a camera, and barefoot was not the usual thing. I wondered if many white women had ever been here before. Very few I thought. Then finally an Indian man came over and asked who I was and where the devil I was from in Spanish. I told him. He laughed merrily and repeated the information out loud to the gathered villagers. They then went back to their respective houses or seats outside of their doors and continued their work. I found out from the gentleman, whose name sounded something like Malikapi, that the villagers were afraid not of me, but of my camera. I was going around on my usual white person rounds of catching souls. When I took a picture, I had the person's soul and could sell it to devils if I wanted to. He entreated me to take no pictures while I was on the island or another panic would ensue. I promised I wouldn't although I dearly wanted a picture of several of the people there who had fascinating faces.

The village of Napigandi was quite small, comprised of some 50 huts and therefore some 300 to 500 villagers. Their homes were right at the edge of the jungle and this was to cause me no little fright some minutes later. Napigandi was extremely primitive, but had that status symbol of status symbols in San Blas—a village radio, which I was escorted to and shown with much pride by the village chief who came to greet me. I was given the run of the village to peer and flutter about as I wished and I did. As I walked along the back part of the huts facing the jungle, I passed over a stick on the ground which promptly turned itself into a snake, and I promptly turned myself into something which resembled a helicopter. My scream, of course, brought out half the village and the snake was dispatched promptly and with some show of prowess and strength by the village men. It turned out to be a fer-de-lance and why I hadn't been bitten I'll never know, for I did walk directly over its body. I had been looking into a tree at what appeared to be a howler monkey examining the village systematically when the movement on the ground caught my eye. I decided to go back to the *Melda* and collided with the Chinese cook who got himself to his feet, but not without placing his palm backwards on a rather large dog's front paw. His scream and the dog's yelp sounded simultaneously, but I just sat there wondering why an Afgan in full furry glory was in an Indian village. The cook got to his feet, as did I, the dog went bounding off down the street, and I gratefully reached the *Melda* without the dock collapsing under my feet. No doubt the Napidangites had much to talk about for the rest of the week and no doubt hoped that the *Melda* would never again appear in the bay with such a motley crew as the village had played host to that day.

We pulled out at about three that afternoon and went on to Isla Pino, or Pine Island. I was completely captivated by the beauty of the island. Tiny waterfalls coming down from the rainforest mountain were cool and delightful to watch and sit by. The water all around the island was of a very light green color, and lovely. There was a total population of about 200 Indians on the island, which was some five miles long and three wide. I further delighted in the fact that no matter from what angle the island was seen, it resembled a whale. Beautiful birds flew gracefully through the emerald trees. I was told that no poisonous snakes were on the island, although there were a few boa constrictors of small size—certainly not big enough to do any harm whatsoever. The bird's song, the tiny marmosets jumping, chattering in the high forest trees soon won my heart over completely. I wanted to stay there right then, but decided first to continue on to Mulatupu, then return to Isla Pino for a short, and I was sure, delightful stay.

That evening, in keeping with his promise that I'd catch a few big fish from the south dock, Archibald baited a line for me and into the water it splashed. No sooner had I taken the line from Archibald and sat down on the dock to wait patiently for a nibble, than my line pulled taut and something was pulling with all of its strength, fighting admirably. Archibald helped me get it ashore. It was a moray eel and would make delicious eating. The Chinese cook hooted with pleasure and promptly dispatched it with a machete and hauled it off to the galley before I could so much as examine it. The evening passed delightfully with a full dozen five pound beauties of red snappers being in glorious abundance on the dock. I took five of these to a Mr. Davis on the island, who was the second chief. His daughter Marina was a nurse living at Mulatupu in Marguerita's house. Her father was very proud indeed of her vocation. He accepted the fish I offered him with great flourish and invited me to spend a few weeks or months, whichever I preferred, on Isla Pino. I gratefully accepted and told him I'd be back within two weeks.

I went back to the *Melda,* choosing to spend the night aboard on the rear engine hatch on a straw mat that had been set out for me there. Our Chinese cook had a hammock stretched across, barring the way to the galley. I wondered if he thought someone were going to come during the night and steal either our papaya or our moray and fish. He curled up with a sigh and went to sleep. The rest of us curled up on our engine hatch and did likewise. I slept soundly all night long, well almost.

During the night, I was awakened by a sound from the rain forest of Isla Pino. I had only heard the song once, and that was a year ago at Chepo out near the Bayano River on the other side of the mountains. It was the Tinamou bird and its plaintive, train whistle song sang out in lonely beauty from the mountain. The night was warm and comfortable. I fell into a deep undisturbed sleep.

I woke in the morning to the smell of coffee, the sound of

hundreds of birds singing from the island, and the fresh clean smell of the sea in my nostrils. Archibald was up fishing from the dock and no sooner was I awake than I heard him singing a lively Panamanian bolero. Milton was whistling and the cook was doing a "pachanga" while tending to the frying pan. Our moray, by the smell of him, was going to make delicious eating. I got up, climbed into a bathing suit, and went over the side of the boat for a morning swim. The water was marvelous. Since I was on the port side and Archibald was on the other side fishing, I decided that this was a good opportunity for a practical joke. I swam under the boat and through the dock piles and located his line with no difficulty. Red snappers were already in the area. I found a piece of rounded coral on the bottom and carefully put it on his hook then pulled with all of my might, then swam back under the dock and to the other side of the *Melda.* I emerged from the water to hear Archibald announcing to all that he had something on the end of the line which felt like a small whale or a shark. The dock was soon covered with Indians, our Chinese cook looking greedily at the green water and the rest of the crew. He pulled in his line to find the coral and a general laugh went up from the observers. "Some whale!" announced Milton between laughs. Archibald went back to his fishing. During the melee when everybody's attention was focused on the water to the other side, I climbed aboard and took a goodly chunk from the papaya and a cooked piece of moray from a plate and went over the side again. I went back to Archibald's line and, careful not to pull it, impaled the two tid-bits on his hook. Then once again I gave the line a good pull and retreated to the dock piles, and on under the *Melda.* Archibald's cry of surprise was quickly followed by a torrent of angry words at the cook who looked blankly at him. I climbed up onto the *Melda,* via her anchor line and laughed merrily. Archibald shot me a very dark look indeed and then realized that his fanaticism for fishing had been the cause of my play. He turned red and pulled in his lines. Then he thought the whole thing amusing too, as did the entire crew, and he joined us in laughing deeply. It had been a good trick—papaya from the sea indeed!

I went for a shower at a small stream I had spotted the evening before on the west side of the island. It was a perfect place for bathing. There was even a seat made of stone right under the ten-foot waterfall and a deep pool below this. A cave was behind the waterfall itself and one could hide there easily at any time if some-one came along and one was in one's bare skin. Brightly colored and singing macaws flew over my head in the trees there and the whole process of washing the salt water from my body was a rare delight and enjoyed tremendously by me. If an architect had set out to design such a beautiful and useful spot, I don't believe he could have done it. Everything was perfect, even the cool tempera-ture of the water from the fall. I went back to the *Melda* in high spirits and we left some 30 minutes later for Mulatupu Island.

Wednesday

It's a warm and lazy afternoon and outside of my window I can see Devil's Point in back of Claudio's house. The natives of Mula-tupu Island did not want Claudio and Marguerita to build their house on this point because of the presence of a particularly strong devil here, but Claudio, hearing this, decided he would build it nowhere else to prove his superiority and the superiority of his religion over the devil. A man named Ignasio had coconut trees growing here, but let Claudio cut a few of them down to build his house. That was more than just a friendly act; it was the act of a great man for coconut trees are money in San Blas. Consequently, Ignasio and Claudio are the best of friends now.

The point got its name because of the wind howling through some unusual coral formations sticking out of the water off the island here. The Indians, hearing the howling during storms, pre-sumed automatically that the devils were the ones bringing the storm and ran away frightened.

Out there now, however, several men are hacking away at newly purchased dug-out canoes under the coconut trees. These boats, when brought by the Canoas from Colombia are in floating shape, but that's about all. They must be shaped and tared before they can be used.

These dug-outs are made by Indians of Colombia and sold to the Canoa people for very little money. Some of them, the larger, must have been made from trees 20 feet in diameter and it must have been months before a dozen Indians completed their work on the huge trunk and got the dug-out down to the ocean to sell it to the black-skinned traders for resale on the San Blas coast. The Cuna do make their own dug-outs, but find it easier to grow more coconuts and trade these for the dug-outs than work many months to make them for themselves. It costs approximately 1,600 coconuts for a dug-out canoe three feet across and nine feet long. That would be the price at five cents per coconut or approximately 80 dollars worth of coconuts equal that size dug-out.

It is not unusual to see one of these beautiful sailing crafts called "canoas" to be trailing from her stern some dozen dug-out canoes of all shapes and sizes. It is an impressive sight on a calm sea to watch one coming across the bay with the dug-outs in tow.

It's siesta time in Mulatupu—meaning that it's siesta time all over San Blas—and everybody stops dead for a couple of hours right after the first meal of the day and doesn't really start working again until about two or three in the afternoon. School on the island has virtually gone on vacation because of Claudio's absence. Marguerita is not in very good shape today, having come down with some kind of fever and chills. I certainly hope that it's not malaria. It seems that about a fourth of the island is down with it at sometime or another. I've been pretty much in charge of household activities, including cooking meals for the family consisting of David and Marina. The other Marina, Mr. Davis' daughter, is here too. She's a dark-eyed and lovely San Blas girl who dresses and looks more Panamanian than Indian. She has been helping efficiently with the medical assistance the people need and is much respected by all the islanders.

The younger Marina, and the child who lent me Snoopy some weeks ago, is highly unusual and I'm quite amazed at both her knowledge of Indian, American and Spanish ways, and her youthful love of life. It is unusual for such a young girl to have the zest and zip for life that Marina does. She is dark-eyed and very Indian looking, quiet and reserved around the house. When she is in the jungle as we were earlier today, she is Indian and goes into the river, or hunts crabs or gives out information on what tree yields what, when, with absolute intelligence. It is a joy to watch the child in the rain forest, for she is in her element there and knows the forest well. When she is in the house, she is completely American and the absolute image of what a well-mannered, intelligent, quiet American child is supposed to be. When she is talking with Panamanian boat captains she is Spanish, conversing fluently in that language and laughing as a Spanish youngster would laugh at their jokes. All in all, she leads three separate lives and is expert in all of them—a most unusual and lovely child. She intends to study medicine when she is older and will become the first female doctor in San Blas of Indian blood in the history of the area. I think she'll make it.

David, Marguerita's youngest child and Marina's brother, is a playful and quite handsome little boy. He speaks more Indian than anything else and plays with Ignasio's eldest son. They are both the same age.

Ignasio himself lives in a hut right out beside Claudio's house. I understand that he was divorced about a year ago because his first wife insisted on running about the island with every other man there, but Ignasio decided he didn't want her and took his hammock from the hut. He was remarried some weeks later to a young and very beautiful girl and they have a little baby girl who is charming and as lovely as her mother. Ignasio loves his daughter and everytime I see him he is playing with the child happily.

However, of all the people here, it is Marguerita and her daughter Marina who impress me the most. Another few things about the child. She is totally observant, ever watchful and learning, speaking only when she has something to really add to a conversation or a question to ask she considers important. She possesses an amazing amount of maturity and continually has me surprised by the accuracy of her observations and the clarity of her thinking. We have swiftly become friends and swim together in the reefs every afternoon. She is as much at home in water as she is on land and delights in the fish and beauty of the water world.

The floor of my downstairs room is still a bit damp from last night. We had a storm that raged with an unusual violence during the night. The force of the wind sent water under the front door upstairs and down through the ceiling and hence on top of me. Rain was also coming through the back door on the ground floor and into my room. It was also coming through my window. Consequently everything is soaked and it will be a few days before the room dries out to any degree. I've taken everything movable and put it in the sun hoping it will dry this afternoon.

Marguerita added to my wariness of island life this afternoon by telling me a tiny household tale.

It seems that some weeks before I arrived, she was over at her classes in the two story school house the Iglesias' have built to the east of the house, when she sent two small boys to clear out some wood which had been piled in the room I'm in. She was calmly teaching biology to her students when suddenly two earth shattering screams ripped through the air and the youngsters ran from the downstairs of the house screaming "Naipe! Naipe!" or "snake."

Claudio, who was in another classroom at the time, dropped his books and raced down the stairs, picked up a spear on the way and entered the basement. He stabbed the snake in the head before it could escape and go into some Indian's house and kill someone. It was a five and a half foot long bushmaster—one of the deadliest snakes in Panama or the world for that matter. I keep wondering if it were a female.

There is a strange sequence of dangers here. First the bats and rats, then the sharks and barracuda, now poisonous snakes. It seems that the moment I get used to one form of fright or danger, another puts itself in my path. I'm really beginning to wonder what will show up once I get used to the snakes.

Actually, the only thing to do is think like an Indian. If your house is in good shape and keeps out the rain, if the food is good and your stomach is full, and if your body is healthy and you have many friends, you are happy and can't be anything else but happy. Danger is something that is lived with constantly, therefore these people have a sense of humor which far exceeds our own American brand. Most mishappenings are funny to them and they seem funny to you after a while. The dangers are not thought about until they present themselves in full form for action. Otherwise, one can't possibly live around here because you'd live in a constant state of fear.

For instance, if you're afraid of sharks, you can't swim in the sea. If you're afraid of snakes, you can't walk in the jungle without fear. If you are afraid of caymens or alligators, you can't swim in the river and wash there. In other words, you have to stay in your hut on the island all the time, and even then snakes, caymens, rats, and bats are in presence.

The fear around here takes the form of healthy respect for each inhabitant of anywhere the Indian is treading. If a snake is crossing a path, unless he comes directly at you, he is let roam where he will in peace and the Indian waits for the snake to pass in respectful silence and stillness. If a shark is spotted in the water, he has the right of way and let pass and swim without a fight because that is his land. The rats and bats have precautions set out against them, but are generally not attacked unless they violate the Indian's land—the hut and home itself. So the Indians have a healthy outlook at the dangers around them and never watch for dragons where mice abide.

I've picked up a few more facts about the island. Officially in Panama, this island is known as Mulatupu, however here it is two islands—Sarsardi and Mulatupu. I won't go into the distinctions again, since they anger me, but the reason for the separation of the town is again a religious item as in Ustupu-Conception. The towns have separate chiefs and separate council halls, chicha houses and schools. The placement of the huts is similar to that of Mamitupu, or at random, having very few real streets (but I'm finding my way around here easier than I did on Mamitupu). At least I don't have to go through somebody's sleeping hut and kitchen to get to the other side of the island.

Mulatupu is the larger section of the island being on the north, west, and east. Sarsardi comprises the southern tip and is about one half the size of Mulatupu.

The biggest bit of news I have to offer is the fact that I am now at the site of the 1963 Basketball Tournament in San Blas—a fact which most amazed me, after finding out that there *was* such an event in the area. It seems that for the past five years Claudio has sanctioned this event and it is like the World Series around here. Participants come from all over the islands to participate in the tournament and the winning team's island is respected as the island that won the game for the rest of the year—no little honor in

San Blas. The games will begin on the 6th of September. I think I will be over in Isla Pino by then, but will keep myself abreast of news concerning who wins.

Speaking of the future, I'd better go and bake a dessert or two for supper. Marguerita's still not feeling too well this afternoon. After this is done, Marina and I will play at being tropical tramps and lazily swim the reefs in search of the sight of colorful and graceful fish there.

Thursday

The *Melda* is back from Puerto O'Baldia up at the border 27 miles from here. Marguerita, who is feeling much better now, went down to buy a few things from Milton. Claudio came back this morning via plane and landed on "sand flea" island out in the bay two miles from Mulatupu. Ignasio went over in Claudio's boat to pick him up. Louis, Ignasio's son and David, Marguerita's youngest accompanied him.

When Claudio got to the island he told us the news of the coast. That bad storm we had a couple of nights ago hit Narkana very badly, tearing roofs from huts and flattening a public school building. I thought it would do a bit of damage along the coast. It had been the worst storm I saw since I got here.

A little later this morning I was treated to a sight I hope that I will never see again. That of the *Carmen Sita,* a passenger trader pulling into Mulatupu Island. She chug-chugged across the bay and I stopped in my tracks when I saw her cargo. People were on the roof, clinging to the sides, climbing up on the mast. She must have been carrying 100 people and she had room for about 20. They're here for the basketball tournament which begins in a very short time. I'm wondering when Ailigandi's players would arrive. Of course, I'm rooting for them. They are my "home" team.

Claudio presented an interesting fact at the dinner table. He was talking about how difficult it was sometimes to get the Indians to take modern medicine. There will be times when you arrive at a hut. Within is a man dying of malaria fever and you're outside with Quinine or Atabrine—still the mother or father of whoever it was dying wouldn't let you near them. He told us of an old man who had been bitten in the leg by a snake. Claudio had antivenom, but nobody would let him use it. The man died. The next time a man was bitten and taken to the tiny coral island in the south bay, which is incidently where such individuals are taken to keep them away from contact with outsiders and other non-infected Indians, the family asked Claudio to treat him. Claudio agreed, but scolded the family for not calling him earlier. The man had been bitten more than 24 hours previous to this. He died. The *next* time this happened, the stricken man, a young Indian whose wife ran to Claudio's hut and begged him to go out to the snake House on the coral island. The medicine man was summoned and came with all haste to the hut, ordering no one to join him until he signaled that the man was getting better or dying. His young wife ran to Claudio's hut and begged him to go out to the snake bite hut and give her husband some of the medicine. He did and saved the day.

There are many superstitions attached to snake bite by the Cuna. The first thing that happens when the snake bites a man is that a snake devil (all snakes possess many devils) goes into the man's body, steals his soul and lo and behold is off to the underworld again. The man gets deathly ill, of course. It is believed that the man's disease is contagious, this snake devil having the power to infect others, so the man must be isolated. The only person strong enough to fight the snake devil is the medicine man and he is the only person allowed to see the man at all. Generally an old grandfather, who is no longer of any use to the village, is delegated to go out and deliver meals. If he gets sick, then it is no great loss to the village, but no other man or woman or child must look upon the man until he is either better or dead.

Saturday afternoon

I'm sitting on the Iglesias' dock on the northeastern part of the island watching the strangest thing! A flock, no, an entire nation of butterflies is flying by. I didn't know that they traveled in flocks, but as I write, more than two dozen flocks of butterflies, about 30 butterflies to a flock are passing over Mulatupu Island. It all started yesterday, but I didn't much notice it until the same thing occurred again today, only there are thousands of them—thousands upon thousands of butterflies coming from the point of land enclosing the bay to the northeast. I believe them to be swallow tails. They have a tail shaped like that of the swallow bird. Their bodies are black with green markings and sweeping behind them are long tails and their triangular wings. They are truly beautiful creatures. Marguerita says that they migrate south at this time of year. I wonder where they are going. She's just as fascinated by them as I am.

I've never seen so many butterflies in one place in all my life. This whole migration is an incredible sight to watch and truly awesome.

I learned a few more stories from the annals of Mulatupu Island today from Claudio. It seems that some months ago a man was cleaning a pig high up on the beach about 15 feet or so from the water. His small son was playfully running in and out of the water's edge when suddenly, a huge ten-foot hammerhead shark came right out of the water and after the boy. It flopped directly up onto the beach and then went after the pig, 15 feet from the water. The man immediately struck again and again at the shark until he beheaded it with his machete. It seems that the blood from the pig was in the water and the shark thought that here was a feast worth spending a few minutes on land to get. He must have thought the young boy to be the source of the rich taste in the water. Fortunately the young child was left unharmed by the attack.

Oh, oh! The wind is beginning to turn and come from the east and it's darkening up. I think we're in for a "choco sano." What are the butterflies going to do? Here's another interesting fact about living out here. I can see the storm coming across toward us. I can actually see the rain traveling in this direction across the mountains to the east. The wind here is starting to get very strong. I have about five minutes before it hits. The mountains are now misty, turning grey, the first line of mountains are now getting misty—the rain is pussyfooting across the bay. Now the terrain behind the rain is completely invisible. This is going to be a heavy one. Here it comes! It's at the south end of the island. Going to run for the house. . . .

Claudio is an interesting character. He fascinates me. He seems to have combined, as the combination is present in his daughter Marina, the best of Indian with the best of modern culture.

He is as capable of running off into the mountains to hunt deer as he is capable of sitting down to write a study of the anthropological history of the Indian drinking gourd. He has more energy than I have ever seen in two people yet. His sermons in church on Sunday are strong and to the point. He handles his mission capably and I admire the knowledge his students have acquired from him.

During lunch I picked up another tidbit of information from Mulatupu. It seems that last May, three University of Notre Dame students were found wandering around in the Darien Jungle by the Cuna. They were sick with fever and exhausted from having made a trip across the full length of the jungle from Yavisa or El Real without a guide. That was sheer foolishness. They knew nothing about the jungle and had been back there for almost a month before they were found. They were lucky to get out at all. They were taken to the mission, treated, and Marguerita radioed for a plane to come and get them and take them to a hospital. They were in none too good a shape.

Wonder of wonders—a copy of *McCalls* arrived via plane this morning. I spent the afternoon reading "Caravans," by James Mitchener, who is one of my favorite authors. It's the first English language or any language magazine I have seen in months. I enjoyed it tremendously and spent hours reading even the ads. I'm glad to report that Marguerita is back on her feet and going full force again. How she does it I'll never know. The spirit of a missionary is an amazing, resilient, forceful thing! Tomorrow morning I leave for Isla Pino, a trip I'm looking forward to with more than average anticipation.

The trip over here today was not an easy affair as we did it in the open sea in a dug-out canoe run by motor. All of us were soaked and both my belongings and Marina Davis' were dripping wet. I tried to cover what I could with the poncho, but decided that bailing was a much more necessary action than protecting ourselves against the water. If we didn't bail frantically we would have sunk in the open sea. We didn't realize it was so rough out there.

Maria is going to be spending a few days with her father before she leaves for Panama City to take up a position in a hospital there. She intends to come back out here after a year or so to help her people once again. She's an admirable and wonderfully dedicated person and has some of Marguerita's spirit in her.

We arrived at the dock in Isla Pino in good spirits regardless of the rain and salt water which had plagued our voyage. I was escorted to the Davis hut and he showed me my bed for the next week in the (architects forgive me) upstairs of the hut. The upstairs consisted of several boards placed haphazardly on the supporting rafters and it required the agility of a deer to keep from tumbling through them to the bottom "floor." By hit and miss and oh so cautious stepping here and there, I discovered and consequently marked with lipstick, the boards which were safe to walk on. I didn't want to tumble down on top of any downstairs inhabitant peacefully sleeping in his or her hammock.

My own hammock and mosquito net was slung from the roof rafters and I settled myself down to rest for a bit and dry out from my trip. I unpacked my belongings and sorted the wet from the dry. I was particularly fearful for my film. Film and jungle are not very compatible items. It was necessary for me to not only have my exposed or used, and unshot film in metal cannisters, but it was also necessary that I put absorb-moist pellets in each cannister. The "shot" film was sealed into balloons to keep moisture out. Each week it was necessary for me to take out all of my film, open the cannisters, extract the absorb-moist pellets and heat them over a fire to dry out the water that they might have contained. When the pellets were again dry, I would place them once again in the cannisters of my Agfa IF film and wait for another week to come. If I hadn't done this, my film would have been destroyed within two weeks from moisture or sweating within the cannisters. The process of protecting the film took all of a day to accomplish. I had already sent in as many cannisters of film to Panama City as possible, but most of these were destroyed in the shop there, mistaking the color film for black and white. The rest, and I shall go into the details of that trying and frightful adventure later, was destroyed by the rioting in Panama City on January 8th, 9th, and 10th. However, I did rescue the greater part of the film, bringing it back to New York and watching over it like an expectant mother until the wonderful Agfa people in New York developed it beautifully. My efforts to protect the film had been worthwhile and it was with a great deal of grateful relief that I saw my first proofs of the San Blas trip.

Nevertheless, on Isla Pino, I at once took steps to protect my film since it had become wet during the trip over. I again opened the cannisters and carried my absorb-moist to the cooking hut and heated it. I did have one bad moment, when Mrs. Davis, thinking that this was a new kind of food, ate half of my absorb-moist before I could enter the hut and bellow at the top of my rather powerful lungs that the material in the iron pot was not edible. I had a rather frightening hour making Mrs. Davis regurgitate the material, not knowing what effect it was going to have on her. I had the local medicine man mix me a solution of salt and star apple which performed the job in good time. My clothes were the umti-umph time soaked and as usual, before I could say boo, fungus was growing on them. All I could do was set them in salt water and wait for a sunny day to dry them out. The salt water seemed to stop the growth of the fungus, but nevertheless, before I left San Blas, everything I owned in the way of clothes was fungus destroyed, and anything metal had a light film of rust over it with the exception of my machete, since I took extra pains to protect it by filing the blade every night and scraping the sides with a piece of flat coral every time I used it. My camera, which received more care than any other item in my baggage except perhaps my shotgun later on in the jungle, was in perfect shape all during the trip and did the Agfa people credit. It had fallen in the salt water once, destroying some film I had in it at the time, but a thorough washing and later drying in the sun did it no harm, although I feared the worst. It was lost once in the Cangandi River when it fell overboard after my dug-out canoe capsized in the rapids there, but again, it dried out and continued to work in perfect order. It was the single most compatible camera to the jungle and all kinds of miserable weather I have ever owned, and I prized it above all my other possessions. Unfortunately, this camera was later destroyed by a rock that hit it and me while I was taking photographs of the rioting in Plaza 5 Mayo in Panama City during the disturbances there in January. I had all I could do to save myself from physical danger and unfortunately could not rescue the camera. It had been smashed by the rock, so I left it where it was and ran, a group of students screaming for my blood not too many feet behind. I'll get on with that later though.

When I had gotten myself somewhat organized and Mrs. Miller in better shape than she had been after swallowing the absorbmoist, I settled back to rest up and relax. Marina came up and invited me back to the cooking hut for a bit of plantain drink and I finished it in record time. After this I went about an inspection tour of the Isla Pino Village. I crossed over a little stream via a beautifully carved little bridge the villagers had placed there and went over to the western tip of the island. I found myself on the most civilized spot on the entire island, the basketball court, and what to my wondering eyes should appear wrapped up on the center line right in the center forward's spot? A boa constrictor that was no "little" thing. I decided to have a look at the reptile, knowing that I'd probably run into them during a trip I planned to the jungle in a month or so. I took a forked stick from one side of the field and advanced cautiously toward the constrictor. A light drizzle of rain was still falling and the field was deserted. I inched forward, then I charged a full charge that would have done credit to the Light Brigade and pinned the reptile's head into the sand and commenced to holler for all I was worth for assistance in handling the rest of him so that I could examine him. Half the village turned out and we got the snake stretched out to full length. He was ten and a half feet long. His heavily muscled body was trying desperately to get away from all this commotion and he wasn't in the least bit fierce. After I finished examining his mouth and body, poking here and there very unscientifically and feeling pleased with myself, I asked the Indians to let the creature go back to his jungle. They would hear none of it and before I could so much as utter another word, dispatched him to whatever heaven he was destined to abide within, via machete. I felt rather badly about this, but the Indians claimed that the snake would have fed on some chickens or something or another if let go. That was that.

As soon as the rain let up, I was treated to another fleet of swallow-tails, seemingly coming from the the east side of Isla

Pino's shores. Thousands of them again, all flying toward Mulatupu and the jungle.

When I got back to the hut, an hour later, I heard a disturbing piece of news. The island's chief is in danger of dying from snake bite. He was bitten two hours ago at the beach of Napagandi across the bay. He had just stepped out of his dug-out canoe and was pulling it ashore when he stepped backwards and onto the head of a fer-de-lance. It was right on the sand of the beach and therefore, except for his coloration, looked like any other piece of wet, colored wood lying on the beach. I hope he pulls through. We're all going to the council hut tonight to help him fight the devil by drinking some of the snake bite medicine that he has taken to fight the poison. They won't let me near him to help out by either trying to cut his foot and extract the poison by suction, or go for Claudio at Mulatupu. There's nothing I can do. Marina isn't even allowed to go near him. He's been taken to a snake bite island off Isla Pino's shores.

We went to the council hall after the evening meal. When I entered, I was offered the chief's empty chair as a symbol of hospitality, but refused it preferring to sit with the women on their side of the hut. The seat itself was quite unusual. It was carved from a single piece of wood and adorned wih a huge Aztec-like eagle on the top of the back piece. It's quite a beautiful piece of art and I wonder what the eagle signifies, for I haven't run across it in the Indian art as of yet.

The chief is still alive at any rate, but is very sick and it is feared that he will die. If he does, Mr. Davis, who probably picked up that name from an American in the Canal Zone at one time or another, will be chief.

The village Kantules were in their central hammocks ready to begin the evening's "help fight the devil who has the chief's soul" session. They began to chant and we all sat quietly listening while they chanted in mournful voices.

The placement of individuals in the council hut is one of very strict custom. The women were all within the inside square. The council members sat at the south end of the hut, on seats beside the chief's chair. The children sat in back of these, and the rest of the islanders in back of the inner square of women. Most of the women were sewing molas by kerosene lamp light, paying attention to only the chant and their work. The younger children were all well-behaved and silently listening to the Kantule's words as he sang. Every once in a while, one of the men in the back would break into a chant off key from Kantule's. I noted with some amusement that the words meant "Stay awake and listen." My dialect learning was by this time progressing by leaps and bounds and I could understand much of what was being sung and said around me, although I could not answer in the same fluent manner in which they conversed. Young babies were drinking at their mothers' breasts.

Soon the village medicine man appeared. He was a strange one, not greeting anyone or speaking a word. His face was deathly serious. I found out later that he is not permitted to utter a single word until his patient either died or got better. He was carrying a huge gourd full of some kind of brownish liquid, and in his other hands, three tiny miniature half gourd shells which he dipped into the liquid and handed to each and every person within the council hall. The gourd never touched anyone's lips. The liquid was brought to the mouth area, then tossed into the mouth. Most of the women got at least two tiny gourdfuls of the medicine, the children got one, the council members three. Marina and I were made to drink four. Evidently, we were considered powerful aids in helping the chief recover from his snake bite. I wondered how Marina felt about the whole thing. She hadn't made any attempt to dissuade the medicine man from bringing the chief to the snake bite hut or to treat the chief herself. She was respecting the wishes of her own people to do things their own way. I followed her example of non-interference. If we tried to help, our wish to help would be considered an attempt to hinder his recovery and things would not go well for us. We kept our silence and joined into the thousand-year-old ceremony of drinking to let the devil know that the chief's friends were with him and were going to fight him tooth and nail. This was supposed to scare the snake devil into releasing the stricken chief's soul with all haste seeing that there were so many people fighting him. If this were not enough, small carved medicine dolls introduced into the snake bite hut would do their best to fight the devil in his own field, the underworld. There were generally a good baker's dozen of these medicine dolls at work during such a crisis as this one. If all this failed, then the man would die and his spirit would be automatically released from the underworld to return to the village where the body was. It would then accompany its body back to the mainland graveyard and when the body was buried, begin its trip to the house of the Great Father.

When all of us had drunk of the medicine, its distributor then climbed into a dug-out canoe and went back to the snake bite hut off the island. He would not return until the chief died or was better.

The Kantules then began chanting their teaching chants for the duties of young boys to their families. One Kantule would begin the chant in a high pitched minor key in b flat, then go on down the scale until he finished the sentence or was out of breath. Then the second Kantule would hum "Mmmmmmmmmmmmmmmm" until the first one caught his breath and continued. This way, there was never a break in the chanting and it continued for an hour or so. Several of the older men and some of the younger boys were by this time napping in their seats. The "stay awake and listen" interruption in the chanting took care of them. I began to feel somewhat sleepy from listening to the chant. The more I tried to fight it, the more I felt my whole body going into a minor hypnotic state and decided that I'd better not let my consciousness go. Several of the other women looked as though they were in a trance, having stopped their sewing and sitting absolutely still, staring at the floor. It was possible to go into a trance while listening to the chants. Marina touched my elbow and looked at me.

"Passio?" "Shall we pass around?" she asked. I nodded my head in the affirmative and we got up and walked toward the south door of the council hut.

As we walked in back of the huts at the edge of the miniature rain forest of Isla Pino, I spied a tiny moving object on the ground and quickly called for a halt not knowing what it was. I went down on the ground and looked to find a small brown and white bird there. It seemed to be hurt in some way and it couldn't fly.

I picked up the tiny bird and gently cupped it in my hands to show it to Marina. We took it home and I found an old basket in the cooking hut, put the bird carefully in it along with water, corn, and some cane juice and hoped for the best. I would see what was wrong with the bird in the morning. We gave it a tiny bed of banana leaves and I went upstairs to my "cat bird" loft, while Marina went back to the dock to sit awhile and enjoy the night air. I read by candlelight from a collection of short stories I had found among my baggage until I was too sleepy to keep my eyes open. It had been the same book I had been reading from on the plane to Panama City from New York. When I finished reading, I got up and started to get undressed. I could hear the rest of the villagers coming down the street from the council hall. The meeting was over. I no sooner removed the last stitch of my clothes, than a seventeen or eighteen year old boy appeared at the top of the stairs of the perch and proceeded to go over to the other side of Marina's hammock and prepare himself for bed. My first reaction had been to wildly grab for a saburet and wrap it about my torso. He threw me a puzzled look, then sang out "panemalo" or goodnight and climbed into his own hammock. I felt embarrassed. It had been a civilized reaction, and he couldn't understand why I had been so frightened by his arrival. He would no more hurt or come near me than kill his own mother and father. Such was the moral code among the Indians concerning outsiders. Any kind of sexual contact with any outsider was strictly forbidden by Indian law. The only exception I ever met to this rule, was the Baptist Missionaries' American wives, and these were the only other nationality married into the San Blas Cuna race. It is one of the purest races in the world.

I climbed into my own hammock, brought down the sides of my mosquito net, and was soon slumbering peacefully.

The name of this day forever more will be the "day of a million butterflies." Then again, yet another name could be "Ring Around the Rain Forest," for that's exactly what Marina, Lonnie, her father, and her brother, Peti, and I did today. It took us all of five hours to accomplish the trip.

This island is remarkably beautiful and this day I have seen more lovely and unforgettable sights than I believe I have ever seen.

Shortly before dawn this morning a Chichi Coley, or Funny Bird (as I call it, but its name means black and white bird) started to sing on the roof of our hut. Since I was up in the "cat bird" loft, it seemed to be singing right on my hammock strings. I was only a few feet from the strange and beautiful melody of its song. The smell of the jungle hit me just as soon as I pulled away my mosquito net. It was sweet and fresh and I wanted to run out immediately and begin exploring the mountain on the island. It had been considerably warmer inside of the mosquito net than outside and it was actually cool up there. The bird continued to sing and I could trace its hoppings about on the roof. It seemed to be greeting the just rising sun with all of its happiness at the event. It would strike two high and disjoined notes followed by a flat lower one, then it went off into a very cute series of lower notes. It repeated this seemingly disjoined song at its whole world, then flew off for another part of the forest. The pattern of its song and its meaning was known only to itself. I liked to think, since the song sounded somewhat like a comedian's lines, that the Funny Bird was sitting up there in the trees making fun of the whole world around him. He taught anyone listening to him not to take life too seriously. During later jaunts about the island and in the jungle I caught sight of this black and white feathered creature. That little glob of bird was so happy and full of life!

I got up, dressed and went running off down the beach to the east side of the island to my "shower." I spent all of 45 minutes just taking in the early morning splendor of this lovely little spot, then went home for breakfast. I was somewhat disappointed, upon arriving in the cooking hut, to find my little bird of the night before in a very dead state. I took it out to the backyard and buried it, then went in to have breakfast.

The gorgeous sun tinted everything orange when we all set out to walk about the island. Since I wanted to go fishing later that afternoon, Peti and I wandered off and on the path searching for palm tree crabs on the trunks. The snappers especially liked this meat and our fishing would go the better for it. Mr. Davis let loose a rather large black dog he called Nia Chichi, or Black Devil, and got him on a leash of rope for the walk. It had been given to him by a Columbian who had put into Isla Pino some weeks previous and Lonnie was quite attached to the huge furry dog. The dog itself was a happy, lively creature and longed to be off exploring on his own by the looks of him whinning and pulling at the rope collar he wore. We went walking off toward the west side of the island and along the beaches there. They were sandy and white and I wanted to stretch out and chew on a piece of grass and just watch the green water for hours and hours. Sea grape trees were all over the place and by the looks of them the fruit would be ready in another month. The air was rapidly filling with butterflies as we walked and I noted with some enthusiasm that they seemed to be coming from somewhere right on the island, since I could see no strings of them joyfully flapping their wings over the sea at all. As we collected hermit and palm crabs, we all walked up and down the tiny craggy hills at the base of the mountain, looking at the tiny streams winding their way through the jungle and into the sea. Way out, waves broke over the northern barrier reef 200 yards or so from shore. Several times during our walk, the rain forest flowed right down off the mountain and joined with the sea, necessitating our walking up the mountain and down to the next run of beaches. As we walked, we also looked for the tracks of any tortoises. Their meat was tasty and their shell sold for three dollars a pound to the traders. A good-sized shell went for from 12 to 15 dollars.

We did find tracks, but we also found the signs of a struggle—someone had found a tortoise as it came up on the beach to lay eggs. They had gotten it, but not without an almost successful attempt on the part of the tortoise to re-enter the sea. The men turned it over on its back four feet from the edge of the water. There had been two men from the tracks and they were fresh—the affair took place less than an hour previous to our coming upon the obvious markings in the sand.

We climbed up once again to a tiny hill where jungle met sea. I came over the top and stopped. What I saw next was a bit of a shock. The beaches up until now were all pure sparkling white. This one was jet black and glittering in the sun. As our group walked down the hill and onto the beach, I realized that it wasn't black at all. A whole patch of the darkness suddenly took to wing and at least 1,000 butterflies flapped into the air. The whole north beach was covered with more than a million butterflies. It was one of the most moving sights I will ever witness. We walked on and the butterflies detached themselves from the sand and took to the air. I walked on in a daze. The whole air was full of them—thousands and thousands of graceful swallow tails. It was raining, snowing a full blizzard of butterflies. The very sun was clouded over by their shadow in the air. I was afraid to open my mouth fearing I'd swallow a good four of them before I could close it again. People have talked about the dance of the elephants and such of nature's wonders, but I don't think I have ever been quite as awed as I was the day of a million butterflies on Isla Pino's north beach. No one spoke as we walked on. Even the black dog was awed, not running down the beach to scare the winged creatures, but staying close to Lonnie whose eyes were full of joy at the sight. Marina's face was lighted up as if she had seen an apparition from above. I knew I was wearing an expression somewhat similar. We walked on slowly, disturbing as few of the lepidoptera as possible. When we reached the next rise I fully expected to see more of them lining the beach. There wasn't one in sight and the white sand was catching the sun like so many tiny diamonds. We walked on around the island searching for crabs and looking, looking at the beauty of the place. Three hours later we had almost circled the island. We crossed a small red-clay topped hillock overlooking the channel between Isla Pino and the jungle mainland. It was as peaceful a spot as anyone could ever wish for. Here there was a tiny, lovely well-kept little graveyard. A final resting place with such a beautiful view; no one could hope for anything better. It was lovely.

Back in the cooking hut, Marina, Lonnie, and I were fed plantain drink. It was delicious. I sharpened and washed my machete, then went upstairs for a nap. I slept until late afternoon. My day had been full to the brim with pleasures for every sense—smell, sight, sound, touch, taste. My heart was happy and full with contentment at the morning's activities.

10
CANOA

It was late in the afternoon on the day of a million butterflies that I awoke on Isla Pino to hear the "Funny Bird," or Chichi Cole as the Indians call him, singing on the roof of the hut. I got up, went to the tiny shower stream to wash up, then went off walking again on this beautiful island. I felt elated at being here. It was the single most beautiful place I had ever seen or imagined in all my life. No other island in San Blas had the lovely tropical forest or mountain in the middle of it that Isla Pino did. It was here that Balboa and Morgan stopped to rest before heading on into the jungle and across the isthmus and on to be written up in history books—stories of pirate treasure and sunken gold ships were linked with Isla Pino's name. I could see that if I had been a pirate, I would have chosen Isla Pino as my stopping-off point. There were monkeys, beautiful birds, all kinds of wild life on the island—but no poisonous snakes. Nature seemed to save this island from any animal capable of doing harm to human inhabitants.

During my walk, I noticed that a canoa, or Colombian smuggling boat, was tied up about 50 yards off the dock. Since I was hungry by that time, instead of asking about it, I went off to the cooking hut of the Davis family to get some plantains and fish. I had speared the fish the previous afternoon while swimming with Marina, Lonnie's pride and joy of a daughter, and the only native nurse in San Blas. She would be leaving soon to take a job at Gorgas Hospital in the Canal Zone. Marguerita, the wife of Claudio the Baptist Missionary on Mulatupu Island a half hour away, would miss her services tremendously. I found it funny that I was actually beginning to develop a taste for this Indian food "tule masi" or fish and plantains. I began to look forward to eating it at meal time. There was no change in the diet; except for an occasional lobster or piece of meat it was always tule masi, but that was fine with me. I knew that four months ago, if anyone had offered me such a concoction back in New York, I would have tasted it, then begged off quickly enough claiming that I'd eaten earlier and thought how horrible the dish was. Now it was not only acceptable, but good tasting to me.

After dinner I left the family and the Davis cooking hut and took a walk about the village. In turning a corner I managed to literally run right into the captain of the sleek Colombian vessel at anchor in the channel. He stopped and took a good look at me, stunned to find a redhead in the midst of this Indian village and started to question me about what I was doing here. Presently, we got into a lengthy discussion on the dock about smuggling—its good and bad points on the San Blas coast. He proved not only to be most knowledgeable in this area, but also extremely cordial and very funny. I spent two hours close to tears laughing at his tales of San Blas from a smuggler's view point. His name for purposes of this book shall be Valencia. We enjoyed our conversation very much. His boat and crew were well liked by the villagers of Isla Pino.

There were several boats of this type that were lookd upon with a great deal of suspicion by the Cuna. The men were either out and out crooks or the Indians thought them evil in some way, but Valencia's boat, which here shall be called the *Matilda,* was a favorite on this island and many others. Valencia spoke Cuna like a native and knew all there was to know about the Indian customs and laws. These he respected as he would respect his own wife's customs. He was a good man, the Indians said when I later questioned them. I trusted their opinion of a man much more than the opinion one generally has of smugglers. My curiosity had been more than slightly aroused by Valencia's talks about smuggling on the San Blas coast. Just before I left to go back to my hut and hammock for the night, he invited me to accompany the *Matilda* on her trip back down the coast. I was forewarned that if there was any trouble, I would be strictly on my own as would be every crew member. I thought over the offer, checked the man's reputation with the Indians, then made up my mind to board the vessel and see first-hand what smuggling on the San Blas coast was all about.

I had to be aboard before dawn the next morning, so I went back into my hut, climbed the log to my "cat bird" loft near the roof and packed. I was soon asleep. Lonnie woke me up and he and Marina wished me well on my trip and took me out to the *Matilda* in the family dug-out. I trusted Valencia enough to know that just in case anything did happen, he would have the entire village of Isla Pino to answer to if I was lost or hurt in any way. Indeed, news would travel down the jungle grapevine, and Valencia would never be able to take coconuts on the San Blas coast again. I would be safe.

When I climbed aboard the *Matilda,* I felt as though I were carrying the black plague or something equally as drastic. None of the dark-haired, black-eyed Colombian men seemed to be very happy to have me aboard. Evidently they thought that I'd jinx the operation in some way. I silently got my things under a tarpaulin over near the captain's quarters, then settled myself on a pile of coconuts near the bow. These were stopped from tumbling overboard by a corral like fence surrounding the whole upper deck of the craft. The only superstructure on the main deck was a small cabin for the captain. The crew and I would sleep out in the open on grass mats for the remainder of the trip. I sat in silence sipping a cup of hot coffee given to me by a happily smiling Valencia who was now busy getting the vessel ready to leave the channel. Sails were raised, tied into place, the rudder was checked, decks washed off with buckets of salt water, and coconuts fenced in closer so that they wouldn't roll once the boat got under way.

I loved to see the sails above my head. The canoas on the San Blas coast were all under sail with an auxiliary motor helping over the rough places. They were beautiful to see out beyond the reefs or at sunset or sunrise. The sails always turned gold and the very sight of them set me back 400 years in time. On this deck, the entire area of the bow was covered with coconuts. I knew that the hold was also full of them since coconuts were never placed on the deck until the holds were also full. The coconuts stopped at the first mast, then came a small clear area where the stove was, covered by the tarpaulin which also covered the captain's sleeping room. Then the tarpaulin ended. There was another clear space before the second mast, then more coconuts, but a path cleared so whoever was steering the craft would have a clear field to the rudder. The canoas were very fast—especially when running with both motor and under good wind. They have many times had to run for their lives from a patrol craft from either Colombia or Panama. The slower ones didn't make it, but Valencia had told me that the *Matilda* was one of the fastest ships on the San Blas coast. I believed him—she was a beautiful, sleek vessel. Her capacity for coconuts was about 100,000. She was long, about 60 feet, and her sails were high, strong, and full. Her motor was in excellent condition and all in all the boat was in great shape. During my examination of the *Matilda,* a tall Colombian cocked his head to one side, then came over to ask:

"Are you the American nurse from Ailigandi?" he asked in Spanish.

I replied that I supposed that I was since there were no other Americans in that area, but that I was not a nurse, but a free-lance writer of sorts. That didn't seem to matter to him. I was the nurse, he told me, whom he had heard of who had red hair. He told me that I was known in Cartagena, Colombia by the smugglers there by the name of "Juanita." I was beginning to feel as though I was supposed to be some sort of Jane of the jungle and didn't like the idea of my being known and evidently discussed clear over into Colombia. As a matter of fact the whole thing frightened me somewhat. I hoped that anything that was said was at least factual and not exaggerated into wild tales I wouldn't even recognize. I had given Valencia my name as Joanne the evening before, and also my Indian name Sipu. The sailor went over and talked with Valencia and the captain smiled a sort of smile that spread like a bush fire all over his pinkish moustached face then said something like "Chulettas con papas!" meaning pork chops and potatoes. He came over and further invited me, not only on this operation, but clear back to Cartagena where I could stay with his wife and seven and a half children for a few weeks. Since I didn't have a passport with me (I left it on Isla Pino) I didn't want to take the chance of being caught "sans papier" unless there was a pretty good reason for doing so. I told Valencia that after I returned to San Blas, I might take a rain check and go back to Colombia in a month or so with my papers.

The sun was still a red streak on the horizon to the east when we hit the open water. The whole boat turned gold-red when the sun hit us. The color caught the mast first, then quickly climbed down and finally hit the deck and then the sea. Everything for miles, everything in sight in every direction was gold colored. It was a dazzling sight.

Carlos, the name of the sailor who discovered that I was a refugee from Ailigandi, arrived with a slab of fresh bread and another cup of rich Colombian coffee. The coffee here on board, I must say, was some of the best I have ever had anywhere. Carlos kept pointing out the sights along the coast to me and telling me any past history he knew of the places. I was told where pirates used to moor their vessels. I found out which channels in the great reef were certain death and which were navigable. I was told the location of several wrecks in thick shark water that have never been examined by teams of divers. I might add that I later checked out two of these wrecks. Their anchors were still intact and I will eventually go back to have another look at them with metal detectors. In examining one wreck, I almost lost my life to a hammerhead shark who chased me right up on a reef after I had time to ascertain that indeed the odd coral formation was an old wreck and Spanish in orgin. In order to examine any of the wrecks closely and in detail, divers would have to bring cages down with them and aqua-lungs for their own safety. I was told who had been a good chief in the last twenty years and who had been a bad one. I learned stories the Indians would never have told me about incidents on the San Blas coast. One story was particularly interesting to me, as it showed a side of the Indians I didn't know yet.

Ten years ago, there had been a very beautiful girl on the island of Quaitupu. Her brother, who had gone to the American Canal Zone to work there, found himself in love with his own sister. He brought back many gifts for his family—and gold necklaces and earrings for his sister. She was fifteen years of age and was soon to be married to a boy who would one day be chief of his island and who at the present time is chief of his island. The two, being brother and sister, were not suspected when they went together to the river and to the jungle mainland. They were in love for a year after he returned, and consequently, the girl put aside the laws of her people and made love to her brother, who was very handsome. Well, soon it became apparent that she was starting to get fat. The islanders noticed, said nothing, but kept their eyes open. The brother was one of the last to see that his sister was indeed with child, but by this time everyone knew that it could only be the brother who was the father since the two were inseparable. The boy became moody, then very touchy to any joking remarks by his friends who kept their comments far away from the subject. The girl grew bigger and bigger. She began to cry herself to sleep at night.

"The mother," spoke Carlos, "watched them, and she watched them good, but she doesn't say anything. When the girl was just a little fat, the people used to joke and say 'Hey, you better stop eating so much,' now they don't say anything. Nobody says anything, but the chief; he finally calls a council; he says 'I think we got a big problem on the island.' Nobody says what—everybody knows what. He says, 'We must think a lot about what we are going to do about the problem'; everybody knows what he means—sometimes people who do this are there one day and then not there the next—they die. The girl, she's brought into the council hall and she cries a lot. 'Who makes your baby?' The girl she doesn't answer. The chief says to the mother 'You know who makes your daughter's baby?' The mother, she stops chewing on her pipe, then looks at the chief, then looks at the girl, then puts the pipe back in her mouth again. She don't say nothing. The girl she don't say nothing. The chief tells everybody to go home and think. They talk again soon. Then the boy, he gets drunk from liquor bought on trading boats every night. The girl she cries every night. Time's getting close for her. Then one morning, the boy's not on the island. It was said that he goes back to the Americans to earn more money. Nobody saw him leave though. Nobody knows where he is. Then one night, the girl's baby comes. The mother knows it, but nobody else on the island does because the girl is very strong and doesn't cry out, but the mother, she doesn't let the baby come. She jumps up and down on the girl until the girl and the baby die. She gets her husband to take the girl and the baby to the jungle and bury them. The next day—no girl—no brother—no baby. The problem's gone. Everything is back to normal and nobody says nothing, but everybody knows everything."

And so the laws of the people and their execution again become clear to me. The people are strict about their law. I made no comment to Carlos.

We passed by Mulatupu Island, then continued on past the landing strip near the island, called by me "Sand Flea Pass" and rightfully named it is. I noticed Carlos' blue eyes. He had Negro features and was quite dark, unlike Valencia who was light and brown-eyed and Spanish in every way. It is unusual for a Negro to have such coloring, but not unusual for the mountain bandits of Colombia to have blue eyes. I learned this many months before from a friend of mine in New York who had been in a Colombian village when it was hit by a pack of 40 bandits from the hills. I asked Carlos where he was from. "The mountains," he answered laughing, "but I am not like the people there." I knew he wasn't and laughed with him.

Captain Valencia came back to discuss the trip with us. When I last looked at him he was, with as much flair as Maxime of Paris, tossing ripe plantains into the frying pan to be cooked. He was whistling to himself and dancing about the area in a very good pachanga. He was fat and fatherly and jolly—sort of like a Spanish Santa Claus. He didn't look like anybody's idea of a smuggler. He just looked like a happy man going about a small job and making it more interesting for himself by singing. He was content with his entire world and enjoyed his life on his *Matilda*.

He sat down with a "plop," his hands on his knee caps, then examined Carlos and me with his warm brown eyes. We would be bringing coconuts across the border and I could either join the boat for this voyage or remain on a nearby mountain and watch the operation with binoculars. I decided silently to do a little of both, and play it by ear once we neared our destination—which would be somewhere in the area of Puenta Tiburon, Shark Point on the Colombia-Panama border. It would be dangerous for me if I went, but then I would see exactly what was happening from an observer's view-point. I decided to go. I would, we figured out, ride with the *Matilda* over the border, then take a dug-out canoe back to shore, climb the mountain with a look-out who would be Carlos, and watch the mountain and sea for Colombian or Panamanian police with binoculars. I could see the entire operation from a "cat-bird" seat yet be in comparative safety. This seemed acceptable to me.

There would be fifty-thousand coconuts passed this trip. Valencia paid the Cuna six cents apiece to get them (one cent more each than the Panamanians paid). He would pass them along at eight cents apiece giving him 1,000 dollars for his trouble. About 700 dollars of this would be clear profit. In all it was a pretty good salary for five days worth of work which is how long they had been in San Blas. By Colombian standards, Valencia was a very rich man for his trouble. Then again, every time he went into San Blas he risked losing his 10,000 dollar craft to his own country's police or to Panamanian Guardia.

Valencia had collected his coconuts twice as quickly as a Panamanian boat because certain islands in San Blas save coconuts for sale to the Colombians for the higher price they get for them. Valencia had purchased his coconuts along the way to Isla Pino, then stayed in the channel for the night to hide out until he could get under way again. I knew that he bought no coconuts on the island—his holds were already plump although not full.

We passed the villages of Calidonia, Careto, Anachucuna, and Armila and soon we were in Puerto O'Baldia, the Panamanian border town, with an actual bar and concrete streets, for the night. It was the first "town" I had seen in months. All day long a watch had been kept for Guardia boats and we skirted the great reef through a channel and were out on the open sea. It was much rougher out here but I loved the easy rise and fall of the bow in the greenish waves. If we had been found, an order would have been given for us to abandon ship; then our craft would have either been sunk or taken back to the governing island, Porvenir, and the crew arrested. Since I was an observer and not participating or helping in any way, I was not a part of the operation and therefore couldn't be held on a smuggling charge. The Indians and islanders had told me stories of canoas being sunk on the high sea. It was a risky and dangerous business and I could see why few men were involved in it. It is also a well-known fact that if the abandon ship order was not obeyed and the canoa decided to run for it, a gun battle always followed the canoa right back to the border. I certainly hoped nothing of the sort would happen this time.

After a delicious supper of plantains and tortoise meat, we sat around talking for a hour. I noted with relief that the crew accepted me now and no longer eyed me with suspicion thinking I was going to become seasick at any moment. After talking died down we all decided to sleep for the night since the morning would be full of activity and early rising was called for. Sleeping is not as easy as the word may sound aboard a canoa. I was surrounded on three sides by piles of coconuts and was in fear that an avalanche would start in the middle of the night by the up and down, then side way movement of the *Matilda* and they'd come down and bury me. I spread out my straw mat and bravely tried to sleep. Occasionally a coconut did, in fact, dislodge and come down, but I slept fairly well after I got used to the basic fact that I *was* sleeping with coconuts around me and I didn't think they were going to kill me if they fell from such a small height.

I woke up while it was still dark to find preparations underway for getting ourselves moving. The smell of coffee was in the air and it was good. Valencia was busily humming to the cooking fire. At once a cup of hot coffee found its way into my hands. I drank it and immediately felt refreshed and awake. I made my way to the *Matilda*'s stern where a washroom had been improvised to freshen up with water from Isla Pino's streams and a new set of clothes. The crew was again washing down the deck that wasn't covered with coconuts. One tall Colombian crewman started a kind of song as he put up the sails. "Vamos, Vamos" was the name of it so it seemed. It was catchy and like a chant. Soon, two, then three men, then the whole boat reverberated with the song. The sun found us again turning the sea gold and we started to move out under the wind. The whole earth was good and beautiful and peace was in the air.

A large fin broke the surface of the water near the canoa. It cut steadily across the cove not disappearing as the fin of a porpoise would—shark, and a big one. Now I knew why this area had been called Puenta Tiburon or Shark Point. Sharks generally feed in mass at two times during the day, although they will not refuse a tasty snack at any hour, at sixish in the morning and then again just before the sun goes down at night. Before the morning was over I saw a good dozen three to ten foot long grey sharks in the area.

Breakfast was served as we got under way. I had another cup of coffee and a loaf of non-Indian bread—it had been purchased that morning at Puerto O'Baldia by one of the crewmen. The bread was still warm and very very good. Carlos, warming his hands around a cup of coffee, talked about how economically poor the people of his country were. "To us," he said "10 dollars of your money is like 40 dollars to you." We talked on through breakfast.

I was still talking to the crew members when the *Matilda* threw out her anchor from the bow into the waters off D'Armila on the Panamanian side of Pta Tiburon. All was beautiful, very peaceful and quiet—then. I was told that there was a river off to one side of the tiny bay and asked if I would like to go there and swim.

A native dug-out canoe pulled up alongside the *Matilda* and the captain and a dark Negro man who came over in the dug-out talked for five minutes. Valencia then announced that there would be a slight change in plan. His cousin's boat would meet us here on this side of the border instead of our going to the other side. There were Colombian patrol boats uncomfortably close and this way it would be much safer.

I climbed into the dug-out, having been offered a lift ashore to the river, and Carlos joined me. He would go on up the mountain after I went to the river. I took my machete with me since I would now be in the jungle. My wash, with soap and a change of clothes, was handed down to my by Valencia who wished us well, then we were off.

Carlos on the way over, to keep me informed, mentioned that there was a path leading from this side of mountain to the other and to the village of Sapsuro, Colombia, the border town there. He said that if I liked, I could walk right over and have a look at the town itself if I was careful not to get into trouble and attract the town policeman's attention. I thought that I would like to see this town and decided to go.

The climb up the hill was excruciatingly exhausting—we went up over 700 feet in 20 minutes time. There was a marker at the top of the hill that stated Panama on one side and Colombia on the other. I rested a minute here standing up, as did the Indians when they did a great deal of climbing since it doesn't tire the leg muscles as much, then continued on down the other side. The trip down was something like a controlled fall and I wondered how I would ever get back up again, but that I'd worry about when the time came for me to get there. The hill was rather a small mountain. I could see Isla Pino way down the coast from us from the hilltop.

"Whew," I uttered when we finally got down to the base of the hill. Carlos and I were sweating and tired. He returned to his mountain top watch-point and I went on into the Colombian town I found there ten minutes from the base of the mountain. The entire area was covered thick jungle and I'd have to watch for snakes coming back. I still carried my machete in a leather case tied to my dungarees.

The town was very small—having only one main street with buildings on either side. No buildings were made with wood or cement, and none were over two stories high. The windows on each house or store were thickly barred and courts were walled and broken bottles had been set on top of the walls to discourage intruders or thieves. I hoped I wouldn't be questioned by the police as I had not one inch of identification on me at the time. I knew that I couldn't be inconspicuous in this town. I was red-haired, wearing a Cuna Indian mola—not knowing I'd be coming here until I was in the dug-out. The town was mulatto or black. It would be like trying to keep an elephant out of sight in the living-room while the landlord made an inspection tour to see how things were going at the old leased homestead. Nevertheless I decided to play it as though of course I belonged here and walked out of the jungle and straight down the main street of Sapsuro village. Eyes looked surprised and people's mouths dropped. I was promptly signaled into the second building I passed, which was a store and politely asked if I wasn't losing my mind. I was obviously here illegally.

A strikingly beautiful Negro woman named Carmen decided that I needed an escort if I were going to get in and out of Sapsuro and go about my business whatever it was without being jailed. As far as I was concerned, I wasn't about to trust anyone in a border town, but decided that she looked sincere enough and that I would follow her until I sensed something wrong. She led me out of the back door and into an alleyway facing the jungle out back. I was brought into a store some eight buildings down, having expressed my desire to purchase some Colombian perfume, "Narcissa Negro," which I liked very much. I bought my perfume from a surprised storekeeper. Then I turned to leave—walking straight into somebody wearing a grey uniform. "Oh, oh," I thought, "here's where I end up in the local jail if I can't give any good answers."

The man excused himself profusely, while I examined him at length and came to the conclusion I already had; the local law was here. I countered with apologies, then turned to go. He called out for me to stop. I stopped, then turned and looked innocently in his direction smiling like a Russian diplomat in Havana.

"Where are you from?" he asked in Spanish displaying a moustached smile.

"New York," I answered.

"Why do we have the pleasure of your company here in Sapsuro?" he asked indicating the whole town with a sweep of his hands. Carmen had disappeared and the store keeper was busily occupying himself with re-arranging bottles on his shelves. "This better be good," I thought.

I made my face very sad and spoke softly.

"I have just come from Carthegena," I replied. "I'm on my way to Panama City. I got a letter saying that my mother is very sick in New York (forgive me mother) and I must go to her at once." I looked as helpless as I possibly could.

"Ahhhhh, pauvre sito," he exclaimed, then motioned me to follow him back to what I could only suppose was the jail. I was trying to remember what city the American Embassy was in—Bagota I supposed. Still, there was a chance that he believed me. I cemented a smile on my face. On the way to his office he asked if I had a way of getting to Panama and then to New York. I said that I had my airplane ticket to New York from Panama City, but that I would have to get from here to Colon. I had heard that it was possible to walk over the mountain a little way and get a Panamanian boat to Colon. From there I would take a train to Panama City, Non? "MMMMMmmmmmm, si," he replied very nonchalantly.

"Do you have a Panamanian visa?"

"But of course," I replied hoping he wouldn't ask to see it.

Out in the harbor a canoa was at anchor, legally here.

He motioned from the steps of his office toward the mountain in back of us.

"You may have to walk over the mountain back there. It is a very hard task for a delicate girl such as yourself." He stopped and eyed me again. My sneakers were covered with mud from the mountain and I knew he was thinking that maybe I got the mud there crossing the mountain. I also knew that he knew about the Cuna, but I also knew that there were several villages on the Colombian side of the border.

"That's a nice top you have there. Where did you buy it."

"Acala," I replied naming a village on the Colombian side of the border.

"Ahhhhh," he replied opening the door and motioning me to a seat near his desk. He asked if I wanted some coffee. I nodded. He made two cups.

He sat down, then back in his chair, touched his finger tips, then asked:

"Now, young lady, just how did you get here?"

I pointed to the lone canoa out in the harbor and took a long hard swallow of my coffee.

"Oh, the *Carmen Nita?*" he replied. "She's a good coconut boat. I know her captain well, but he's sometimes mixed up in some bad business dealings." I grinned weakly. That was the name of the boat we were going to pass our coconuts to. The policeman then pushed himself forward in his chair. He whispered, his eyes big and expressive:

"You don't know it, but I think I can get you over the border on the same boat you arrived on. She's going over to the other side this afternoon to get some coconuts from the *Matilda*. I'm sure Valencia, her captain, can help you find passage on a boat to Colon. You have money?"

"Of course," I replied laughing. "Exactly 23 cents," I thought in silence.

"That captain of the *Carmen Nita,* Rodriguez, he owes me many favors," said the policeman in much the tone an avenging angel would have declared the world was ending.

I gulped down my coffee still smiling, then said that since I still had my suitcases aboard, when I went out to pick them up I'd speak to the captain myself.

The Guardia man held up his arms in disagreement, then with his index finger of the right hand circling in the air declared that as long as he was there, there would be no need to find a dug-out to go out there, besides which, Rodriguez might refuse if he, the policeman, didn't accompany me. He had a motorboat and we'd get all this over with quickly and I'd be on my way.

"Oh Good Grief," I thought seeing how the net was quickly closing around me. The policeman might have let me off if I had told him the truth, but his pride would be hurt if he knew I lied to him. I politely tried to refuse his offer, but the more I tried to get out of it, the more he insisted on bringing me to the *Carmen Nita* personally.

Five minutes later we were on our way to the *Carmen Nita* across the green waters of Sapsuro Bay. "In five minutes they'll throw me to the sharks or into the Sapsuro jail," I thought grimly.

We pulled up alongside the craft. One of the crew men called out "Juanita." I looked up quickly and recognized the boy whose hand I had sewn back together again in Ailigandi when he had cut it trying to open a coconut shell with a machete.

"Maybe I've still got a chance if . . ."

I dropped my bag of perfume into the water, calling out to the policeman to help me retrieve it. He bent over the side to get the bag and I quickly got helped aboard the *Carmen Nita* by the boy.

"No time to explain," I spoke hurriedly in Spanish. "Ask the captain to tell the policeman that I've been on this boat since Cartagena. Remember, Cartagena."

The boy nodded his head slightly then returned to the captain's quarters just as the policeman climbed aboard rather clumsily.

The captain stepped out of his quarters and called:

"Juanita! Back so soon?"

I breathed a silent thank you to my former patient then answered that I had been kindly offered a ride by the policeman and I couldn't and wasn't allowed to refuse his generosity. The policeman then took the captain aside to arrange my passage to the Panamanian side of the border while I hurriedly explained to Martino, my former patient, what had happened. He stifled a laugh just as the conversation between his father (as I discovered) and the local law was breaking up.

Rodriguez came over bubbling effervescently. He reminded me of Valencia because of his plumpness and cheery voice—then of course, they were cousins.

"You should have let me know!" he spoke to me directly chiding me with his eyes.

"I didn't want to worry you with a family illness," I replied.

"Ayiiiiiiieee," he bellowed once over all of Colombia in general.

"What are we going to do with you?" He eyed me sternly waiting for an answer. "We'll get you safely to Colon. Don't worry. Now go back and sit with your cargo and bags for punishment." I laughed and as I passed Rodriguez, he gave me a none too gentle pat on the behind, to scoot me on my way.

The local law got in his boat and left after wishing me and my mother well. Martino explained the goings on to his father and the crew and they laughed loudly over the incident.

Arthuro, which was Rodriquez's first name, soon had the *Carmen Nita* under way and heading out to the open sea to turn the bend of Puenta Tiburon and go into Panamanian waters. As we left, the policeman waved farewell from shore and I caught sight of a bewildered Carmen standing in the door of the perfume store on the main street. Actually, the whole thing turned out for the best—I didn't have to go back over the mountain again.

In 45 minutes we pulled up alongside the *Matilda* and dropped anchor of the bow. Needless to say, Valencia was duly surprised to find me aboard his cousin's canoa. When all was explained he laughed louder than anyone and ended up by announcing that someone should give me my own canoa.

"We'd all be rich!" he commented.

The unloading process of the coconuts from the *Matilda* to the *Carmen Nita* began with all haste. This was the most dangerous part of the whole operation since we were right here in the open in a cove and trapped if any Guardia boats showed up. Both vessels, representing a considerable investment of 20,000 dollars, would be lost and both crews in danger of losing their lives.

The counting and exchanging process was done in a ritual form that in itself was very interesting. One man from the *Nita* and one from the *Matilda* were used as counters as is the case in all operations of this type. Four men would be used for the actual transferring operation from the *Matilda* to the *Nita*. One man would pick up four coconuts with his two hands and throw them into a special straw basket used for transferring coconuts. "Uno," he would call. The next man picked up four coconuts and put them in the basket, "Dos," he called and so on until the basket was full. The baskets were then passed to the *Nita* "chain" style and dropped into the waiting hands of two men in the hold who threw up the empty baskets to the men on the deck after depositing the coconuts safely in the hold. This process was repeated until the count reached 25. Instead of calling out 25, whichever man put the last four coconuts in called "tale" and both counters simultaneously marked a line on their papers. That meant that 100 coconuts had now been passed. When all the coconuts were passed, then the counters would tally up their sheets which should match. When these were added up, each would hand his chart to his captain and the men would figure out how much was due the seller.

There were only four marks down on the sheets when I got tired and hot and decided that I would like to go to the river and finish my laundry which was waiting for me on the riverbank. The sun was already noon high and I was hot and sticky.

I got a ride to shore with a man who came in a dug-out to sell

Valencia some bananas. I first made a return trip uphill to let Carlos know what had happened and so that he wouldn't worry knowing that I had been gone a very long time. He was indeed glad to see me and I told him of the events of the morning. He shook his head and chuckled to himself. I then left the look-out post and went down to the river. Carlos must now concentrate if the canoas were going to be safe.

The water was delightful, cool and clean—it was entirely deserted of all human beings, although a shy agouti did poke his head out of a clump of bushes to take a look at what was so avidly splashing about in the river. I did most of my wash in the shallows of the upper stream, then soaped my entire self and dove into a quiet pool of water shaded by a large leafy tree. My clothes, in the meantime, were drying on bushes on the riverbank. The heat of the hot sun would dry most of them by the time I finished swimming.

I didn't bring a towel with me on this trip, nor did I have one aboard, so I stretched out in the heavy grass riverbank to dry in the sun, hoping my hair would be pretty well dry by the time I got ready to leave. I heard a far away voice call, but didn't pay too much attention to it. Then I opened my eyes briefly, feeling that something was not quite right. I decided it was all my imagination and closed them again. I was almost asleep when Carlos came splashing across the river bellowing at the height of his vocal powers:

"Pronto, Guardia venga, JUANITA!"

"I'm not dressed," I gasped hiding myself in the grass.

"Ayiiieee!" he cried gesturing pleading signs to sun. "This is no time to be modest. Quick, the Guardia are coming, get your things and come quick."

He turned and ran towards the beach where a dug-out was waiting for us that the plantain boy had moored there. I hopped into my dungarees, quickly grabbed my drying clothes, and started to button up my blouse as I ran after Carlos.

I reached the beach just behind him. Our canoe had come untied and was drifting out 20 yards from shore.

"Sharks," I called

"Guardia," he replied.

We both went into the water at the same time and swam, I with my belongings in a satchel formed by wrapping a blouse around them, tied to my back and Carlos fully clothed and minus his shirt, but with shoes, etc. We reached the dug-out safely enough, Carlos getting there before I did and helping me aboard. We started to paddle for all we were worth, seeing both of our crafts raising sail and wild activity aboard each. We reached the *Matilda* as the *Nita* was pulling away from her. Carlos threw a rope to the stern of the *Matilda* and a crew member tied us up. We pulled ourselves as close as we could then were helped aboard by the men. The *Matilda* was already under way—one more minute and we would have been stranded for perhaps days on the jungle coast of San Blas.

I threw my clothes and things on a pile of coconuts and went up to the bow. The Guardia boat, a fast motor craft about 30 feet long, was in sight and closing fast. Valencia was bellowing orders right and left. I went to the tarpaulin to get out of everybody's way and load my camera with film. Just as I snapped the first picture, the Guardia boat opened fire across our bow. A sound not unlike a bee buzzing went by me and a bullet lodged in the front mast. I dropped out of view and behind a pile of coconuts up there.

"Aiieee, Madre mio, get down, you crazy gringo," shouted Carlos.

I didn't need to have his sentence finished before I was flat on the deck. All I knew was that somebody had just fired a bullet in my very near vicinity and I was scared. Actually, I reasoned, if that shot had been across our bow, as somebody once told me "First they fire across your bow," then it was pretty lousy shooting. That frightened me more. Those were the shots that killed people. "Jesus God," I thought for the hundredth time since I first landed in San Blas, "What am I doing here?" I wish we had not made it in time to catch the boat. I could have lived off the jungle for a few days—the Indians had taught me a lot since I lived with them.

Somebody was talking over a megaphone ordering all of us over the side. They said that they'd picked us up after we abandoned our *Matilda,* but that if we didn't then they would open fire.

"The hell with him!" I whispered thinking of Puenta Tiburon's sharks. I'd fight my own U.S. Navy before I went over any side of any boat in this area.

"Vamooooooos!" It was Valencia's voice. We were going to make a run for it.

I turned around to see everybody hiding in places I hadn't realized were possible hiding places before. Valencia himself was down at the stern running the rudder.

"Thank God!" I whispered as the vessel's motor's growled in the stern. I could feel our speed picking up. Then it started. A burst of machine gun fire flew right into the coconuts on the bow and I ducked further on the deck. If I could have opened up the boards and slipped through, I would have. Then everybody was shooting and I felt like I were in a scene from a re-run of a World War II picture off the Philippines. Pchung, pchung, rat-tat-tat . . . rat-tat-tat-tat . . . kung, bzzzz, bzzz thump!

Valencia was still at the rudder, ducking down, but his arm was visible above his protecting coconuts.

"I'm going over the reefs!" he called. "Pray to the Virgin." I held my breath listening for the sound of our bottom crashing into the coral. It did, but the boat kept moving, and moving, and we went off the reef and over it. A moment later, we were heading straight for Colombia.

"Haa!" ejected Valencia. "I think we're going to make it."

"Good," I whispered.

"I order you to stop," came the strong, self-confident voice over the microphone.

"Non Hombre!" called Valencia still keeping below the coconuts even though the vessels were now some 30 yards apart. The guard boat would still have to go around the reef—her bottom was too low in the water to make the trip over it. We were very light having given up most of our cargo before having been sighted. We could never have made it if we were heavy. The *Nita* was still rounding the reef. If the guard boat made it over the reef, she would be caught. We all waited tensely for the decision of the Guardia captain. He didn't want to risk his precious vessel in shark waters—he turned and went in the direction of the channel through the reefs some half mile away. The *Nita* would make it. The crew and Valencia cheered.

"O.K.," replied the megaphone wielding young Panamanian whom I caught sight of briefly when I lifted my head, "we're coming after you when we get through the reefs and you'd better pray the wind holds. I'll go right into Cartagena port after all of you."

With this World War II was in session again as the guard boat let us know that we weren't too far away to be fired on. They held where they were, and for the next ten minutes, the amount of gunfire seemed incredible to me. I was again cringing in the midst of my coconuts, literally covered with coconut milk from the shot open shells. Everyone else was ducked under or into some newly discovered mousehole. I just couldn't believe anything that was happening and the whole situation seemed very unreal to me although I had been warned that it was possible that we were going to be caught. I expected pirates in full cutlass slashing form to come streaming aboard at any second, with the captain of the cross bone vessel to have a parrot on his shoulder squawking: "Pieces of Eight, Pieces of Eight." We were well into Colombian waters now, but the sky was beginning to darken. If we had a full-scale "choco sano" storm now, we would have had it, and the *Nita* too.

Mercifully, the firing stopped, but the storm came and with it, a howling wind that forced us to take down our sails and depend upon the motor to escape. Fog or some kind of haze dropped soon after the choco sano passed and it was difficult for us to see into the whiteness in front of us. The sea was calm though, calmer than I had seen it in days. Valencia kept at the rudder, never having left it, and "smelled" his way through as he said, compass and memory in hand. Then nightfall came, and still no Guardia boat. Valencia nosed us into a small cove that he said was often used by the canoas in returning to Cartagena. It was a resting place. We had one bit of a big scare when another vessel became visible in the cove. It was the *Nita,* and she thought us to be the guard vessel too. We all laughed and the crews had a happy reunion there with much singing and dancing and drinking of any remaining beers aboard.

We counted our mutual "wounds" and I discovered a casualty of my own. My perfume bottle of Narcissa Negro, still tied up in my belongings at the stern, had suffered a direct hit. We were the nicest smelling smuggling boat in Colombian waters at that point and some housewife was going to wonder why her coconuts smelled of Narcissa Negro when she brought them home from the marketplace next week.

The night was spent in making repairs to both of our vessels. Our sail had been hit a number of times, and the men had to stretch it out and sew it right then and there. All the coconuts that had been hit were thrown overboard. Not too many had been left on the upper decks because of our morning passing operations, but there had been enough there behind which to take cover. Our rudder had also been hit and we had to make some repairs on that. All in all though, Valencia and Rodriguez agreed they had come out of the melee in relatively good condition. I was relieved but rather nauseous from the fright I got that day, and very tired. I was also very sticky from the coconut milk, but couldn't wash up then and there. I'd have to wait for the morning—our water barrel had also been hit. I put out my mat and quickly went off to sleep, leaving those awake to repair the *Matilda* alone while I recovered.

The *Matilda* was somewhat in order by the next morning and I was feeling much better. I must say I thought Valencia somewhat the hero of the day with his actions at the rudder of his *Matilda*. Everyone else thought so too and Valencia was drowned amid much compliments on his being "Mucho Macho" or much man et al. All during the morning's sail to a point just off Sapsuro, he smiled and smiled and sweated and smiled and drank warm beer and sweated. I was very quiet, having found the day before quite different from anything that ever happened in New York City. Here in the relative safety of a small cove the *Nita* and the *Matilda* proceeded to complete their business transactions of the previous day. I felt very good in a strange way—it's that feeling that comes from having risked something—namely a chunk of oneself, for some kind of cause known only to the individual and having come out of it well. I must sadistically report that the day after I was rather in a jovial mood, glad that the whole thing had taken place and that nobody had been hurt.

My gladness was short lived. Carlos came back to where I was sitting.

"The next time you swim in a jungle river and then go up on the bank to rest—get yourself dressed first. You never know who's going to come along or what. AND," he bellowed, "never sleep in high grass. Only on a sand beach. Snakes like high grass very much and the snakes are *bad* back here."

And with that gentle word he strode off towards the bow to watch the water for a good half an hour. I considered myself duly bawled out and rightfully so. We just made it back to the boat and if I had been dressed we would have made it sooner. I sat where I was, feeling relatively penitent.

As soon as the coconuts were on the *Nita,* Valencia passed clear out on the deck and had to be carried back to his mat under the tarpaulin by two crew members. We spent the night, once again, in Colombian waters—home to these men, but far away from the villages of the Cuna that I called home.

Two messengers were dispatched to the Panamanian border to meet with contacts there to discover where the guard boat had gone. When they returned the crew was happy to hear that the boat had gone back to Porvenir and was nowhere in the area. Valencia would be happy to hear this news in the morning since it meant that he would be able to return to San Blas to pick up another load of coconuts that were waiting for him on three islands. During this trip he had made arrangements with certain chiefs to save their coconuts for him. He told them he would be back in four days or so to pick them up.

Carlos came back again to speak to me. This time he was wearing an easy grin. He apologized for his rough words of the early afternoon, but repeated:

"You'd better remember what I said anyhow."

I told him I would and thanked him for being so concerned with my safety. At times I really had to stop and remember that the jungle was dangerous and not my own private playground. It seemed very easy for me to "go native" in the vast beauty of the world of big trees. I loved the forest and the rivers. Being among them many times gave me the feeling that I was in some kind of huge, natural cathedral and that, if not disturbed, the animals would respect what reigned there. Then, of course, there are always those few rogues in church. I also knew by now that I had nothing to fear from the Indians in the jungle. They would never harm me there in any way as long as I respected their law and the jungle they loved. Then, there were the outsiders—the non-Indians, these I did fear if I were alone in the jungle. Any non-Indian roaming the forest was looked on with suspicion by the Indians, if he was unknown to them. It was generally found that such men were up to no good, either panning for gold, or watching the Indian villages for an opportunity to raid the graveyards and take the gold from the dead who lay in peace there.

I knew that it was of these that Carlos had spoken.

The happenings of two days were still very much with me. It didn't seem possible for all that occurred to have happened in that short a length of time. I knew the *Matilda* now. I knew her crew and her captain. I felt close to them and closer than I could have felt if nothing had happened. Trouble has a way of letting individuals know each other quickly.

With the night wind and water lapping softly against the sides of our boat, we slept peacefully that evening.

In the morning, Valencia, chipper and again humming over his cooking fire, woke me up with another cup of that very good coffee of his. I smiled a thank you and he asked me what I thought of the last two days.

"Does this happen all the time?" I asked.

He replied that it didn't, but often enough to keep everybody on their feet. He laughed and went back to his kitchen.

Later that morning, when we were again back in Panamanian waters, he repeated his offer of passage and hospitality at Carthegena. We could stop at Isla Pino long enough for me to pick up my passport and papers.

"My wife will treat you as one of our own children," he had said.

I again thanked him for his offer, but thought it best that I continued with my business along the San Blas coast and then back in the jungle before I left the area again.

Valencia brought the *Matilda* up into the wind and we quickly made our way to Isla Pino. We parted at the dock and the *Matilda* went northwest to pick up her coconuts. Carlos waved goodby from the stern. I was sad to see the *Matilda* go, but the memory of my 72 hours aboard her and of the things I learned about smuggling on the San Blas coast would long be with me.

I went to the Davis hut, greeted the family, then climbed up to my waiting hammock and slept for the next 12 hours. I hadn't realized how tired all the excitement had left me.

When I got up the next day I settled back into the peace and serenity of Isla Pino for a week's worth of time.

When I rose in the morning with the sounds of the birds singing in dawn, I went to the stream to bathe, then back to the Davis hut for breakfast. After this I generally roamed around the forest on the island, or went fishing in the beautiful aqua channel and reefs nearby, or just sat down at the top of the mountain for an afternoon listening to the birds and watching the animals there.

One of my special haunts was the old graveyard at the rise in the mountain. It looked down on the channel and I could see clear to the bottom. Many afternoons I saw big fish in the channel: sharks, porpoises (in which case the sharks got out of there fast) or big red snappers, and what have you. Here I could also look across to the river and the jungle mainland. Most of the time I just spread myself on the ground, careful not to upset any ants and looked at the sky or drifted off to sleep. The Indians, knowing that I was enjoying the beauty of their island and wanting to be alone with it, left me in peace except at meal time—Nana Lonnie would come looking for me and she generally knew where to look. She told me once that she was afraid I'd starve to death on one of my walks in the forest, if she didn't come to bring me home to eat. I wouldn't have—there were many fruits and delicacies growing about that I could snack on—Maria at Ailigandi had taught me well during our walks in the jungle. If I were ever in doubt as to what was good to eat and what was not good to eat, all I'd have to do is watch the monkeys or birds and eat what they ate. I knew then that it would be safe for me to eat whatever it was. Life was easy, gentle, warm with these people and the forest, and very rewarding to me. The very quality of the peace here and the beauty which is everywhere, even in the people, is something that many people never find or experience in a lifetime.

The quality of being content with the earth was also taught by the land itself here. The Indians knew that as long as one of the villagers could still raise a machete, there would be food and housing from the mainland and the sea.

A certain state of mind seemed to come over me after I'd been in San Blas for two months. There was something I couldn't quite put my finger on here and it was of ultimate value to me when I found out what it was. I knew that it was near the river, in the jungle, and on the islands in the huts of the Cuna. I also knew that it would be useless for me to look for it, because it had to find me.

Then one day during a hunting trip into the Ailigandi jungles it suddenly hit me. Here on all four sides of me, under my feet and over my head was life and death in continual action. The leaves would die, more would replace them; crabs would die, others would be born; the same of monkeys, trees, jaguars, and everything which dwelled here. Then I realized something very important—if left to itself, the balance would always be on life's side. There was more life being born and living, than death occurring. The death couldn't possibly catch up with the life, because life ruled and would rule until the earth itself was no more. After so much was said about the lifelessness in the world, or the horror of death, this wonderful basic truth was like a bath in a cool stream to my soul. The earth was an earth of life, not of death, although the latter was ultimate in that every living thing would eventually experience it. That one thought spoken often enough inside of one's soul can influence an entire day, year, or lifetime. The very existence of life, of another human being, is then something sacred and enormous in meaning.

I also found out what the reasons in my society for living and life were all about. They are the same as the reasons are to the Cuna: to live, to be happy, to have a home to live in, to eat, to sleep, to love, to have children, to die content with the life one has lived. The reasons for life here in the jungle were identical to life back in New York or anywhere for that matter. Only the tools which fulfilled these needs were different.

The Jungle was also a teacher then, as well as just being a beautiful place.

One last truth which caught up with me came from a tree being so high and a leaf so wide. Truth, being, life are constants—a tree is so high, depending upon the shorter tree that stood beside it. This may not be immediately understood by all readers of these words, but at some point, somewhere, it will be perfectly clear and perfectly logical. In a place where a tree grows only *sooo* high, everything else seems to fall into proportion. Love, life, work, play, joy, sorrow—all come into their correct proportion and are not enveloped with much silk, or nails as the case may be. When all the dressing is stripped off an emotion or a reaction to another's action, then there remains the basic thing which *is*. Anyone with the capacity to do this can then deal with whatever comes along and treat it with more wisdom, whether it be a great joy, sorrow, or simply dinner. The Cuna possess this infinitely valuable gift.

11
MINET-MARCELLA

I no sooner got back to Isla Pino, spending only about a week's time there, when a long sleek Panamanian boat and coconut trader, *Woolworth's,* came gliding into view.

Marina, who was still on the island, and I went to visit her late one September evening to talk with her owner—Israel. Besides being a most cordial and talkative gentleman, he spoke Spanish, Russian, Greek, French, Arabic and Carib Cuna for a starter. Both he and his son Fernando were accompanying the boat owned by the father, down the coast to Puerto O'Baldia buying coconuts, or trading such goods as the *Melda* had—pots, pans, knives, cloth etc. . . . for coconuts.

We had a most pleasant time talking and I told Israel of my adventures or mis-adventures aboard the *Matilda.* He was completely convulsed into laughter by the entire history of the *Matilda*'s trip and knew her captain well. The crew joined into our conversation and I liked this boat immediately. The decks shook with laughter the entire four hours we talked, each crewman possessing an intricate and hearty sense of humor of his own. Our evening culminated with an invitation from Israel to accompany the *Minet-Marcella* on her rounds along the coast. I thanked him and accepted, not having had a chance to date to see the numerous villages along the way from Quaitupu to Pureto O'Baldia and wanting to at least spend a bit of time looking at each. I said goodnight to these warm and friendly Panamanians and made my way back to the Davis hut with Marina to tell the family of my plans and pack once again. I went immediately upstairs to my loft and to sleep, knowing I'd have to be up before dawn to get my belongings aboard the large, sleek trader.

Mrs. Davis was upset at my leaving once again, but helped me to get most of my things in order for the trip. I left some things at Isla Pino, knowing I'd be back shortly to spend more time here before I moved on down the coast once again.

I was helped with my bags of equipment to the *Minet* the next morning by Mr. Davis and Peti, his son. A "choco sano" of unusual violence and high winds hit us before we were out in the channel and we had to return to the dock and ride the storm out. It was about eight o'clock when we finally got under way again.

During the stay at the dock, I met a most unusual Venezuelan gentleman by the name of Carlos. He reminded me greatly of the Carlos aboard the *Matilda,* having the same coloration, but of a lighter shade. He had married a girl at a place called Buenos Aires, Panama, and had seven children there and another on the way. He was leaving to go to Venezuela to get a boat there. He was seeking the job of a seaman aboard one of these freighters. After he reached Puerto O'Baldia, he hoped to catch a canoa to Carthegena. From there, he would cross the mountains to Venezuela on foot and go on into the port towns. He had twice before been a seaman and was highly experienced in this line. I was, however, concerned about the fate of his wife and seven children and asked him what would become of them now that he was off to sea for two years at least.

He cocked his lean Spanish head and smiled. His eyes were twinkling with amusement.

"She is not alone," he replied, "Her mother and all her sisters and brothers are with her in the village and my wife is a very good farmer. Our women in the back country, Juanita, are very different from the women of New York. From the time they are children, they learn to take care of themselves. They raise their food under the supervision of their mothers and fathers. My wife is one of the best farmers in all of Buenos Aires. I have left enough money with her relatives to take care of her and our children should an emergency arise. In our district each person looks out for every other person. Felecia is an excellent business woman. She probably will have increased the money I left for her by two-fold when I return home." He smiled and looked out at the raging storm. Then he turned back to me and spoke once again:

"This trip I take is to get enough money to buy a generator and refrigeration plant for my village. It will be the first electrical company in the district. My wife and I will have a better life for ourselves and our children with the sacrifice of these two years of our life together. This is why I go, for her and our children. If I thought she would be afraid to be alone, or if I thought she were unable to take care of herself, I would never leave her." A tree fell on Isla Pino and split a dug-out canoe. No one, however, was hurt.

"You know, Juanita," started Carlos again, not even mentioning the tree, "when I say to my wife, 'I must go for the money for our electric plant,' she say to me: 'O.K., but first, I want you to put down on a piece of paper a boy's name and a girl's name, because we're going to have a baby while you're gone and I want to know that you like its name.' "

I thought to myself that there were many strong people in this little country of Panama.

Israel arrived with a cup of coffee and I sipped it, then we pulled out of Isla Pino, the choco sano going past and dying, and soon we were in the open water, passing the islands of Gold Key and Quaitupu on our left.

We were no sooner out in the sea than a school of porpoise joined us. These lovely and graceful fish ran circles around the boat, then swam up near the bow for a good hour. I went up and sat at the bow of the boat. If I looked straight down, I could see the fish arching so effortlessly in and out of the water that it seemed almost impossible that a fish had that much strength. They were loads of fun. There was one porpoise in particular that caught my attention. It lifted its entire body from the water, then ran backwards on its rear fin standing straight out of the water and flopped back into the sea. During its amazing display of agility it was making sounds like a puppy barking, or like a duck. At one point I barked back at it and the fish got all excited. In one fluid motion he was beside the bow and talking with me in some kind of strange but friendly fashion and I had a feeling that he knew I liked him. We both got as excited as the other barking back and forth to each other, I hanging down from a rope on the bow and he standing out of the water and muttering his excited barkings. I was having so much fun with that fish, I wished I could have caught him and brought him home with me, for he seemed to display more than average intelligence. I laughed at him and he particularly liked this sound and in his quivering friendly fashion, answered me.

The porpoises were out in front of the *Minet-Marcella* at one point and I couldn't shake the image that in some way they were harnessed and pulling us along in the aqua water. They finally left our company and my porpoise and I emitted one last series of barks at each other, and then they were gone. We were entering shallow water.

I turned to find Israel smiling down at me.

"That's the first time in all my life I've ever seen anyone talk to a fish and the fish answer back, all in running motion." I felt embarrassed.

I went over and sat on an oil drum under the captain's bridge. The rhythmic rise and fall of the *Minet* was hypnotic. My thoughts turned to the people I'd met and the villages I'd visited in San Blas. It seemed as though I'd been here for a long long time—years. In reality it had only been a short period of a few months. New York and Boston seemed very far away in miles, years, and time itself.

The dark Colombian cook brought me a cup of hot coffee and a plate of tortoise and yucca mixed with plantain. I ate hungrily as I always did when at sea. It was very good.

I was eating peacefully when some kind of animal moved and let out a never-ending stream of breath at my feet. I naturally was startled, but looked over to the right of me to find a tortoise tied up there. It was evidently being saved until we ran out of meat—then it would be slaughtered and we'd have a feast for another week at least. I had been warned not to pass too close to the large sea turtle when I boarded the *Minet-Marcella.* It had, the previous day, inflicted a nasty bite on the captain's heel. I went along the other port side of the boat and brought my dishes back to the galley, then returned to my oil drum seat to examine the tortoise at length. He was a good two and a half feet long and weighed about 200 pounds. He was on his back and both his front and back flippers were tied together with strong rope. He couldn't move very much. Actually, as much as I liked his meat I thought this was a heck of a way to treat the animal. I poured a cup of water out into a cannister cup from the fresh water tin and poured the water over the giant's head and into its swiftly opening mouth. It still held its mouth open after the water was gone, so I went back and got another cup and gave it to him gradually. When this was gone, the tortoise sighed and closed its eyes and presumably went to sleep for it continued to breathe every few minutes or so.

Israel had told me that the *Marcella* was heading first for Puerto O'Baldia, then would hit the mainland villages on her way back—that's why we were outside of the great reef. We could run blind out here without fear of reefs once it got dark.

I got bored with sitting on the oil can and went back to the rear hatch cover to talk with the crew there. The radio was on and Enrique the tall white-skinned Panamanian from Colon was dancing to a pachanga blaring forth from a radio station in Cartagena, Colombia. He was to keep me laughing during the entire trip aboard the *Minet-Marcella* with his wild antics and flair for the funny in any situation, no matter how gloomy.

Carlos D'amil, our Venezuelan seaman, came back to tell me a few more tales of life in the Panamanian bush. It seemed that if one man insulted another, the two of them went to the river, climbed onto a log that was pushed center-stream, and fought it out with machetes until one was wounded, thrown from the log, or dead. There was still some pretty wild country left in Panama—namely four-fifths of its entire area. More than half of Panama is uninhabited jungle.

A thought I wish to mention on the day's activity is the attitude of the crew of the *Minet-Marcella.* No matter how bad the work got, lugging coconuts here and there, during our stop over at a small island off of Quaitupu, their patience and continual good humor was a joy to be around. These men would be down in a stifling-hot hold receiving the baskets of coconuts from their fellow-crew members on top deck and yet there would be no cursing or shouting for a rest or stop, only joking and laughing. Sweat would be literally pouring off their bodies. When work got heavy, they joked about it instead of hollering. The crew of the *Minet-Marcella* had this wonderful attitude in everything that they did, be it work or play. Of course, I already knew from previous trips aboard trading boats on the San Blas coast, that a small coconut trader out here is no place for a pessimist or anyone with little patience. You either got along with everybody and handled smoothly every situation presented to you or you made everybody aboard feel that much more uncomfortable. Actually, the same thing went for island living. The space is so small and limited on most of them, that if you happen to have an argument with anyone, you had best get off the island or make up immediately because you invariably run into the person with whom you have argued, ten to 20 times during an average day.

The only person who was contrary at all aboard the *Minet-Marcella* was the cook, and he was not in the least bit disagreeable. It's just that he never muttered a word to me in all the time I was to spend aboard the *M.M.* For that matter, he never spoke to anybody else. He just went about his business of being a cook and let the rest of the world go by. The cooks aboard the trading boats on the San Blas coast are some of the most motley crew of unusual individuals I have ever met. He did very little socializing. He did, however, take the shells of two coconuts that day and bring them to my oil drum seat under the wheel house for me to snack upon. They were greatly appreciated.

The day passed peacefully and I went up front in the darkening light. Nameless villages along the coast were visible from outside the reef because of their numerous campfires. I got up and looked over the side and was startled and surprised to see tiny stars in our wake caused by a kind of plankton in the water. The stars in the sky were glowing blue, yellow, and red. It was a crystal clear and perfect temperature of a night. The strong hum of the *Minet-Marcella*'s engine heart was making me fairly sleepy up on my oil drum, but then Fernando came along.

He sat himself beside me on the oil drum and we sat in silence watching the lovely night go by for a full 20 minutes before he opened his mouth to speak. He told me of his father and himself and their life along the coast. He told me of the troubles, of losing boats to the sea, of his wife and brand new baby daughter back in Colon and how hard it was to be away from them for so long, but worth it for their future financially. His father had been doing this for 20 years and was a rich man. Someday he'd have the *Minet-Marcella* and finish his father's work then pass it on to his son that he would hopefully have in the future.

As he was speaking we suddenly began to hit heavy seas, and I noticed with some alarm that the sky was beginning to cloud up on us—another choco sano out here would be a bit rough on us.

"I hope you're not going to get seasick," he stated more than asked.

I replied that I certainly hoped not.

I remembered a day off Falmouth Heights in Cape Cod, Massachusetts when I had indeed been seasick. It had only occurred twice in my life—then and when I had been aboard the *Muara* some months earlier. My mother and father and I had been visiting friends who lived in this very lovely place on the Cape. I was about ten at the time. Dad and I had gone out in a small rowboat to do some fishing. I had become excruciatingly seasick, and my father, a chief in the Navy, was embarrassed to tears when he brought his only child back to shore literally green with nausea. The sickness left me the minute I was back on land, but I was so upset by the happening and my father's disapproval that I went walking around in solitary unhappiness for the rest of the day. I laughed remembering how upset a ten-year-old could get from failing a father, and wondered how many Little Leaguers were this night solitarily gloomy in their beds nursing the hurt of a "Three strikes you're out!" with Daddy looking on.

Our society demands strange behavior of children. After seeing children here in San Blas as children are supposed to be, I often wonder why our whole treasure of a young American population isn't under psychiatric care. It seems that we never give our children a chance to *be* children, but force the responsibilities of adults on them from seven on, demanding more and more of them, until it's a wonder we don't have a full-scale child revolt on our hands. The youngsters are told on one hand to achieve and always achieve and on the other—not to interfere with the adult world about them. Advertising tells them to be sexually aware from the age of reason on—the Church says "Horrors!" to such an attitude—parents are either too lenient or too strict on sex or any subject in general—everybody cares about "Gerald's sensitivity and need for expression," and Lord forbid, if the child doesn't draw a picture of a cow at the age of three his parents think him mentally defective. Yet, when the child shows any initiative on his own and goes out looking at the world around him his parents drag him back to the books, or to the Little League Baseball Field, or put him in this advanced class and expect, and expect, and expect! The intelligent child is disciplined in his intelligence and told what to learn. The dumb child feels rejected—the smart child is an outcast in his age group—the dumb child, a comrade against the world of adults. This goes on and on until the child finally doesn't know who to believe—his parents, Madison Avenue, the preacher in his local church, or Henry Miller!

The children grow up with the H-Bomb hanging over their head and this Paper Tiger threatening the other Paper Tiger. They grow up under schedules which are often more full than their parents' schedules. If they have free-time it is promptly filled with a course in art appreciation or "How to Enjoy and Read Shakespeare." I am not against art appreciation or the enjoyment of Shakespeare, but I am for time to look at clouds and hunt lions in the tall grass in the yard—or run down the street and look at the rest of the people in the world—or maybe go roaming off playing hooky from school for a day in a year.

Our children are constantly beset by opposite demands upon them. They are given little time to develop *themselves* into individuals, although they do turn out to be carbon copies of this and that college's graduates, knowing this and that fact, but not having much experience in the realm of simply living. They've never or rarely had time to live. Most of our children are afraid to be alone or to have time on their hands, finding themselves bored or frightened at the prospect of a few free hours and needing to fill this time with T.V., a movie, or maybe they'll hang around with the rest of the boys or girls exchanging this and that piece of gossip and wondering what they're going to do tonight?

No group, society, or race upon the face of the earth has as much trouble raising children as we do, and it is for one very simple and basic reason—premature demands upon our children. I believe every source of trouble we have with them can be traced back to this basic fact. If someone would only settle back, someone with the authority to say such a thing, a Dr. so and so, and tell us bluntly to stop draining the mentality and lives of our children away with unreasonable demands upon their resources, then we'd probably be 500 per cent saner for it and lead a much more enjoyable life.

I was brought back to the *Minet-Marcella*'s deck by Fernando's asking a question. "Humph?" I asked.

"In case you're sick—go and ask the cook for a piece of lemon and chew on it. Stops sea sickness like nothing else does."

I thanked him for that helpful bit of information and settled back to relax on my oil drum.

Enrique pachangad to the bow and informed us that we'd soon be in port. The two cat's eyes, the lights of Puerto O'Baldia, were in sight. They gleamed like the eyes of a jaguar in the night, the dark form of the mountain behind them increasing the illusion of a giant jungle cat waiting at the end of the trip to swallow us whole, radio Cartagena and all, into its crouching form.

I had had the same impression of my first sighting of Puerto O'Baldia on top of my coconut perch aboard the *Matilda,* a little more than a week previous to this.

Twenty minutes later the *Minet-Marcella* dropped anchor at Puerto O'Baldia. The sounds of a party were coming across the water from the border town. The musical sounds joined with our own not-to-be-ignored offerings from Cartagena and everything seemed much livelier up here now than it had been when I passed this way aboard the canoa.

Several dug-out canoe loads of happy and smiling Panamanians paddled out to meet their friends aboard the *Minet-Marcella.* Evidently Israel was possessed of a very popular crew. There was much back-slapping and "Come ashore for a drink and aiiiieee, you should see what's ashore," with raised eyebrows from the newcomers. The welcoming committee left us an hour later and at least six beers apiece, then we prepared to bed down for the night. I would get a chance to visit the town in the morning and was anxious to do so.

My hammock was slung for me by Enrique over the central hatch cover. I slept in my dungarees and mola knowing that it would be cool in the morning and that I didn't have a blanket.

I no sooner got into my hammock when I made a miserable discovery. The boat had turned around in the harbor to face the wind and we were rocking quite noticeably. Trouble was that the boat would rock one way and my hammock would go the other. Soon I was weaving feverishly through the hot air and more often than not, hitting both walls on either side of me—Israel's and his son's cabin to the bow, and the store cabin to the stern. Not only that (don't look now Daddy), my stomach was beginning to get that disgraceful feeling. The breathing of our captured "tortuga," now put to sleep some five feet from my hammock, sounded like a proverbial foghorn. Cartagena was singing me no lullaby from the stern and I felt miserable. The crew were in the stern, no doubt seated around the stern hatch-cover playing cards.

Ten minutes of misery later, my stomach decided to play Mount Vesuvius and I quietly crawled to the port side of the boat, that being the side of the boat having no wind directed at it, and hung my head over while my insides revolted. When I calmed down somewhat, I decided that the swinging in my hammock was going to get me nothing but black and blue marks and more of this, so I sat up on some bags of copra and smoked a cigarette.

Puerto O'Baldia was quiet now. Several other vessels, both Panamanian and Columbian, were anchored out in Puerto O'Baldia bay and all was quiet there. I threw the cigarette away, it tasting horrible at that moment, then drew my knees up to my stomach. The smell of copra clearly wasn't helping me. I didn't want to wake the cook up and ask for lemon (he was already in bed in the galley). As a matter of fact, I didn't want to speak to *anybody* at that point. I wanted to stay quiet and exactly where I was feeling somewhat better in that pre-natal position. I fell slowly to sleep.

I woke up several hours later to find I'd been using a bag of copra for a pillow all night long. I felt fine though. I crawled back to my hammock before anybody could discover me sleeping on the copra and was there only five minutes before Enrique danced by.

He poured himself a tumbler of water from the water tank near the central hatch-cover, then danced back to the stern. The sound of activity aboard was beginning to fill the air, then suddenly our not-to-be-without companion, Cartagena, Colombia, joined us. We were all on our feet ten minutes later.

After I dressed and washed up in the stern head, I went to my oil drum in front of the bridge to watch the sun come up with breakfast the cook had so opportunely handed me as I walked past his window. The sun was turning the sea and mountain a bright color of gold.

About an hour after breakfast, after the *Minet-Marcella* had been washed down and gotten into some kind of order, Carlos, Fernando and I went shore, via the *Marcella*'s whale-boat. We put in right behind the general store then walked to the town's main street and looked at things. Puerto O'Baldia looked like a typical small Spanish-Panamanian town. It had cement sidewalks and two-story buildings—small shops lined the streets—there was a gold shop, a bakery, a grocery store, a government office in charge of, of all things, any cattle in this jungle area, and last but not least by any means, an authentic bar and poolroom. I left Fernando and Carlos there, to return later, and went about tasting the flavor of the first somewhat civilized town I had been in in a long long time—months. I also wanted to buy a pair of earrings. I had strings in my ears for a week, some Indian having pierced my ears for me on Mulatupu Island when I was there. They were pretty well healed by now and I wanted to get the earrings in as soon as possible. I went into the gold worker's shop and bought a small pair of 18-karat hoops and went on down the street. After my walk, I returned to the tavern to find a young American boy sitting with Carlos at a table and looking none too happy about life and the living of it.

Carlos introduced us. The boy's name was Dick. He was on his way to the Rio via the Amazon. I accepted this in due course. I had met three Americans passing through San Blas on boats—all of them were heading for the Amazon. I was beginning to wonder what the huge attraction was and asked Dick. Four beers later he told me. He was from Los Angeles. There had been a Brazilian girl in Los Angeles and a two-year romance. She returned home, her letters stopped coming, now he was on his way to either win his love or lose himself in the whole bloody Amazon. Incidentally, he was all of twenty-one years of age. We also found out that he had 15 dollars to his name and intended to get to Rio on it. Carlos and I talked to the boy for a good two hours convincing him that it was sheer folly on his part to expect that he was going to get to Rio on 15 dollars.

He couldn't even find a way to get from Puerto O'Baldia to Colombia! He'd never travelled in a jungle before and intended to traverse the entire Amazon on his way to Rio and Love. He told us that if he could get to Bogotá, Colombia, that he had friends there and they had written him pledging their support of his project—as he told them—to get to Rio and study piano. Dick was a musician.

Carlos, shooting me an amused look, thought that he could get Dick to Bogotá safely enough. Actually, it was much better than here anyway, at least if the boy couldn't get any further there was the American Embassy. Carlos would be passing through Bogotá. He agreed to guide the boy there and deliver him safely to his friends. Dick's face promptly brightened and he ordered another round of beers, this time on him, for all of us. Carlos laughed and said that he'd get them for us. I was delegated to talk with Israel and ask him to arrange passage for Dick on a Colombian canoa that Carlos intended to travel aboard.

Two young girls, both Cuna, entered the door of the tavern and greeted me and I greeted them.

"I didn't know that you knew everybody in the whole tribe?" laughed Carlos.

"Don't I wish I did, and also don't I wish I knew what they were thinking!" I answered.

"What is that supposed to mean young lady?" he asked still smiling.

I proceeded to explain the age old Indian trick of saying the opposite of what they mean in any situation with strangers. If they don't like you, they'll say that they do. If you ask directions, they'll point in the other direction. There were times when a lot of patience was necessary in dealing with the tribe. Especially when they didn't know me from a hole in the wall right after I'd arrive in a new village. The people who knew me were friendly and open with me, but not strangers.

On each new island I'd visit, I'd have to go through a series of trying incidents before the Indians got to know me and got to know I meant them no harm on God's green earth—only good.

Their first and immediate reaction was that I was a "Uaga Ome" or an outsider's woman. There is no more malicious term an Indian can use for a strange woman than this. Children would taunt me with it, women would hurl it at me from the doorways of huts. The rule is, after so many centuries of bad dealings with outsiders, that you are bad and evil until proven good. I had the Spanish conquerors to thank for that. Quite a bit of unfriendliness was generally displayed for a few days after my arrival on a new island—the trick was to never lose one's patience. Once you lose your patience, just one time—just once—months and months of working toward friendship with the Cuna would have been lost. Even in bad incidents the trick was to laugh—laugh and laugh some more. Generally, everybody laughed with you and gradually accepted you.

"Uaga Ome!" I thought, "How many times in how many different places had I heard that name hurled out at me—probably hundreds of times. Then after I'd been in a village for a week or two I didn't hear it again. It would be 'Sipu! Takwele,' White One—come here, or just plain Juanita."

We took Dick back to the *Minet-Marcella* after explaining the situation to Fernando and asking him what he thought his father would say. He thought all would be well. We did have one trying moment. Dick had been trailing his lily white hands in the water and I let out a shriek for him to get it out quick. A shark's fin passed by us and Dick broke out into a sweat. Fine piano player with no hand. Carlos bawled him out thoroughly for his stupidity and told him never to do that again. This was shark water. When we got aboard, Dick went promptly off to the world of sleep on the back engine cover. The smell of tortuga was in the air, and dinner would come soon. Fernando went back to shore to help his father with business and I settled down to a good lunch.

After lunch and arranging to get Dick to Cartagena, Colombia, we pulled anchor and went off to Puenta Tiburon. It was so quiet there, and I remembered the way it had been just a little over a week before. We were in no danger now, we being in the bay legally.

Dick, Carlos, and I went to the river to bathe and do laundry, they taking the downstream and I the upper part, sheltered by some bushes. An hour later, our clothes were almost dry, having been hung up on bushes to dry; only my dungarees were still wet. Then we took Dick on over the mountain to check on the canoa they were to take. The trip was, if that was possible, even more exhausting than the last time. Carlos remembered passing this way before, almost seven years ago to take a brief trip to Colombia on business and had spent the night with a Colombian family at Sapsuro. Not only did Carlos find the family, but they remembered him vividly and greeted him with great pleasure. One of the boys in the family still had a picture taken seven years ago of himself and Carlos standing out in front of the same house where we now stood.

The boys quickly located their canoa while I stayed safely within the house fearing to come into contact with the local Guardia again, and when they returned I was informed that all was well and arranged. They would come back later that night with all of their belongings. As it was getting dark, we wanted to get over the mountain as soon as possible and back to D'Armila, the hidden border town on the Panamanian side of the border mountain. The trip back was tricky, as each of us slipped at least a half dozen times in the darkness. Fortunately, there were no snakes about to make life more difficult. After stopping for some cold sugar cane drink at D'Armila, we went back out to the boat.

We had missed the evening meal by going over the mountain, but "silent Sam," as I nicknamed our cook, was an angel and had saved a goodly portion for the three of us to split.

After supper, Carlos and Dick went with Fernando to shore and we said our good-byes. I sincerely wished them the best in their voyages and hoped to meet both of them again sometime. Carlos whispered that he'd look out for Dick and then they were off. We waved them out of sight.

Israel decided to return to Puerto O'Baldia for the night and we pulled anchor and were off once again. I missed Carlos, for he had been delightful company during the trip up here and full of all kinds of interesting stories of the Panamanian bush. We dropped anchor where we had spent the previous night and I'm pleased to report that the water was much calmer and I slept peacefully in my hammock all night long.

The next morning we were again up before dawn—coffee and freshly made delicious bread was our morning meal and we were off down the coast of San Blas once again, Cartagena following us all the way from the stern. This time Pablo and Enrique were dancing back there—Fernando playing some kind of drum section, Arab style with spoons. It seemed that there was a village named Amiela on the coast that was relatively inaccessable because of reefs lining the entire area. The Indians would have to row out and meet us in their own dug-outs.

The next few hours were spent being tossed all over the entire Caribbean Sea. I sat on the stern engine cover frantically clutching my knees to my stomach and madly chewing through four lemons.

Israel seemed unperturbed by all the rocking about and sold his wares to the Indians who arrived a half hour after we dropped anchor off the reefs. Israel's store was going to hell in a handbasket. Pots were falling off the walls, whole boxes were sliding back and forth. All kinds of things were sliding off shelves, but the selling, buying, and trading went on and on and on. Even the crew was beginning to get worried. One wave came along that settled everything—it nearly capsized the entire *Minet-Marcella* and Israel wisely decided to pull out and go back to Puerto O'Baldia to wait a bit and see if the sea would decide to calm itself.

Well it was that afternoon that "he" arrived in a dug-out canoe blessing all of Puerto O'Baldia in general and wearing a necklace of rosary beads about his neck, singing a forgotten Spanish love song at the top of his lungs in some kind of off-key way.

I was resting on the central hatch-cover. Enrique and Pablo

were asleep since it was siesta time, on the rear engine hatch, and everybody else was ashore.

A small dug-out was making its way across the bay out in our direction toward any one of the five boats anchored there and I watched it disinterestedly. It was a lazy quiet kind of an afternoon and there was only the sound of the waves and the rope on the anchor rubbing against the bow in the air. Then I heard the song and looked up to find out where it was coming from. Maybe Enrique had just gotten up and put on the radio. There he sat in the bow of the dug-out canoe, with a plaid paper suitcase in his lap. His black moustache, his wild eyes, and the wave of black hair coming down over one eye reminded me of Adolf Hitler. He was singing to nobody in particular and heading straight for our boat.

I sat up and fearfully awaited further developments. The man was obviously a bit strange. That turned out to be the understatement of the entire San Blas voyage of the *Minet-Marcella*. The man rowing the boat in the stern looked at me, stopped rowing briefly to make the circular sign at his head for "crazy" in any language and continued to row out toward us. Now I was really beginning to be alarmed.

"If he's nuts, then why are you bringing him here?" I thought.

The dug-out came abreast of us and "Adolf" climbed aboard. He proceeded to sweep me a waist-low bow and uttered something in some kind of language ending with Madame, but I knew it wasn't French—no French that I'd ever learned anyhow. He proceeded to bless with his right hand, and in this order, me, the bridge, the tortoise, the deck, and finally his companion, who was by this time rowing frantically back across Puerto O'Baldia Harbor. I got to my feet and backed off as he advanced. He pulled out his "spare" rosary (I found out later he had a full baker's dozen of these in his luggage).

I stood my ground ready to fight for my earth-life and scream if he came a step closer. He did. I decided to make this a cut and dry thing.

"You are out of your mind. Get away from here and don't come near me or so help me I'll brain you." He leapt into the air and came down directly in front of me and I uttered a shriek of surprise. He then proceeded with plaid suitcase to the bow and began to talk with himself, found himself very funny and laughed and started to pray and sing at the same time. I ran to the stern.

I shook Enrique awake.

"Mmmmmmmmmmmmmmm," he mumbled.

"Enrique," I began not quite knowing how to word this statement, but choosing the most direct route in case our new passenger planned to start a fire to warm himself off the *Minet-Marcella's* bow, "there's a crazy man singing with a pair of rosary beads on the bow."

His eyes flickered open.

"Que?" he asked startled.

"There's a . . ." I started to repeat.

"I heard you the first time—are you alright?"

"I'm fine—but I think you'd better go take a look at him."

He quickly shook Pablo awake and explained what I had said. Both men were immediately advancing on the bow with me carrying up the rear.

They both came back looking somewhat shell-shocked.

"Well?" I questioned.

"Madre Mio!" stated Pablo.

"LOCO!" stated Enrique, and he continued, "but, he's coming with us to Colon. Israel sent him."

"Jesus God!" I muttered and sank to the central hatch-cover.

Fifteen minutes later Adolf interrupted his song briefly to come back and hold a conversation with himself in front of me. I had prepared for such an eventuality and sat calmly, my machete across my lap and let him rant and rave, not paying a bit of attention to him. I acted as though I could neither see nor hear him, which was the best policy. He started to come close to me again and I took the machete in my hand, intending to use it if he came any closer. I still did not look at him, but it was obvious that I intended to do battle if he bothered me physically at all. He retreated and went back to the bow.

From then on he addressed me as "La Reina" or the Queen. I felt sorry for him, but I wasn't about to have half my day occupied with his mad ravings or being bothered by him. He never came near me again during the duration of the trip, although he did try to start several conversations with me, all of which I paid no heed to whatsoever.

Israel arrived back with Fernando soon thereafter.

Fernando climbed on to the deck and shot me a "Is he here yet?" look and I motioned with my head toward the bow.

"Loco," he whispered.

"You're telling me?" I replied.

Adolf was *still* singing on the bow.

We pulled anchor and soon after left Puerto O'Baldia for the last time this trip around and headed down the coast toward the mainland village of Anachacuna. We spent a few hours at anchor in Anachacuna Bay, then headed on to Careto for the night.

It was in this area of Careto that a Scotchman, William Patterson, had made a futile attempt to establish a colony more than a century ago. The Indians had accepted the Scots readily enough, but diseases such as malaria and yellow fever had virtually wiped out the colony before it could really get started. The Scots returned home—not with the expedition's doctor though. He remained with the Cuna helping them for a great many years. I have been seriously thinking lately that Ibeorgan and this Scottish doctor may be one and the same individual. Everything certainly seems to add up to that—kilt and all.

When we arrived at Careto Bay, we found another vessel at anchor there—a Colombian canoa. I found out later that this boat was bringing in a load of supplies for several Colombians, an entire band of them, who had set up camp and were evidently homesteading nearby. I was leary of the whole thing. No Colombians, not even Panamanians who were not Cuna, were allowed to live on Cuna land in the San Blas area, for the area according to the 1925 Treaty with Panama had official reservation status. I knew the Cuna of Careto were not taking kindly to the entire affair and I found out later that the two elements hadn't been getting on well together at all. A few fights and one actual exchange of gunfire between the Colombians and the Indians did take place at a later date.

Supper was a quiet affair, after which we all rested and relaxed sprawled about the *Minet-Marcella*'s sea-going anatomy. Suddenly Adolf sprang to life and started to sing. Then he proceeded to tell each and every member of the *Minet-Marcella*'s crew his life story. When the crew finally got together these were the different stories they got from Adolf: He was a schoolteacher on his way to Panama to take a job (we later found out that he made the trip from Colombia on the mere rumor that there was a position in a school in Colon open); he had a plantation in Colombia and it had burned down and he was now on his way home to San Salvador after 15 malaria-filled years in the interior jungles; he was the illegitimate son of a priest, and his mother was a nun; he was the Peruvian Ambassador to San Salvador; vice versa; he was really a very rich person traveling incognito.

His singing went on well into the night, along with the tortuga's monumental breathing. It does the crew credit to say that they stood Adolf and thought him very funny. They let him rant, rave, and sing and bless as he would during the entire trip without once telling him to stop the infernal racket.

I had, at some point during my trip down the coast after hours and hours of looking at the jungle mainland, decided that I wanted to accompany the *Minet-Marcella* down the coast to Porvenir Island and back over to Wichub-Huala. There were several jungle villages back in the Mandinga Bay region that I wanted to spend a bit of time in. I would stop off at Porvenir and Wichub-Huala to re-organize myself and with a little bit of luck, get on back into the jungle in two or three weeks time. I mentioned that I'd like to accompany the *Marcella* as a passenger from Isla Pino to Fernando. He asked his father if this might be possible and the latter came back to not only inform me that I was his guest all the way to Porvenir, but asked if I wouldn't like to spend a few days with his family in Colon, riding all the way back there aboard the *Minet-Marcella*.

I was very grateful for the invitation, but told Israel that I thought it best that I went on with my nosing about uninterrupted for the present. I'd no sooner get used to civilization, than I'd be off in the bush again, and my system would once again have to adjust itself to jungle living. He understood.

Enrique did me the honor of helping me string my hammock over the central hatch-cover and I climbed in and went to sleep for the night. Cartagena, still in my ears, joined with the ever ceaseless melodies from "Radio Adolf."

When I woke up the next morning, the first things I heard, and in this order, were Adolf singing (did he ever stop?) the wind howling and rain beating on the *Minet-Marcella*'s cabins. Cartagena, by now an old reliable friend, was blaring off in the stern.

I got up to find breakfast ready and waiting, pulled my hammock out of the way into the beams above the hatch-cover and went to the galley window on the port side of the *M.M.* for the first day's course—bread and warm delicious coffee.

The rain stopped soon after breakfast, but the air was still quite chilly. The Indians, the rain having stopped, made their way out to the boat in dug-outs to do business with Israel and Fernando. Out in the bay a caravan of some 12 dug-out canoes tied bow to stern were being towed into Careto Bay by a motor boat manned by a dark Colombian. These were tied to the stern of the canoa and she put out from Careto Bay with these behind her—probably on her way down the San Blas coast to do a bit of business with the Cuna there.

Fernando called me. I half turned in my seat on the hatch-cover to find him standing there, shirtless and beaming.

"We're going to kill the tortuga," he informed me. I was still thinking about the selling price of each of the different sized dug-outs I saw go by and didn't pay too much attention to what he was talking about.

"We're out of meat?" I asked just to say something.

"Uh huh," he nodded his head.

"When are you going to kill it?"

"Now," he said and I turned as he spoke to see the tortuga who had so plagued my last few night's sleep with his head on a block and Pablo half naked poised above him with a machete in his arms. The blade swung through the air and the great turtle was suddenly headless. A great wosh of air rushed from him. It could be heard clear across the bay. The head of the sea turtle was still snapping animatedly on the starboard deck and the crewmen were swift in side-stepping it. It could still inflict a nasty bite.

Pablo and the other crewmen started to clean out the turtle

shell to get the edible meat. Within 20 minutes they had completed the job, but the water all around the starboard side of the *M.M.* was quite red. I was truly surprised to see nary a single shark there. As a general rule, they'd be flocking to the smell of such a delicious kill and literally leaping out of the water to get at it. Perhaps there were none here because of the series of reefs surrounding Careto Bay. I caught sight of a movement up near the bow and found myself observing Adolf blessing the turtle's remains and fingering his rosary beads. I wondered what had happened to him to make him so crazy? Watching the whole scene, turtle, Adolf, Indians, Israel and all, I felt as though I were watching a Jean Génet play.

After an hour's worth of trading took place and subsequent reception of coconuts from Careto's Indians, we pulled anchor and headed into the sweet, cool, north wind. We had many miles to go before each of us reached our ultimate destination.

We stopped briefly at the ruins of an old United Fruit Plantation before Gold Key Island. This island, I was informed by Fernando, had been used by pirates for the burying of gold. The plantation ruins were memorable. They were now run over with creepers and the buildings that had been only 50 years ago teeming with life were deserted and dead. I wondered about the people who had lived here. I wondered how they lived and what their relations with the Cuna were like. But nobody could tell me, for the memories of the place remained only in the minds of those who had been here and from the beauty of the place, I knew that somewhere still living in the world were people whose thoughts dwelled here and there among the ruins remembering this and that—sadness, joy, work, laughter. . . . Now they were no more. We pushed on leaving the Ghost Plantation to remain in peace.

We went on running with the wind and again porpoise, to Quaitupu Island, or as the Spanish call it, Caldenonia.

This particular island was completely closed to outsiders and was more primitive than Mamitupu itself. As soon as we docked I found myself in a somewhat hostile atmosphere, hearing the name "Uaga Ome" and other insults hurled at me at every turn in the village streets. I was bluntly told by one man that the chief wanted no whites to walk on the island. I couldn't even bathe or stretch my feet. I had never encountered a similar attitude displayed toward me in any other island in San Blas. I went back to the *Minet-Marcella* and took up court on the rear engine hatch-cover and brooded on my hostile reception. Strangely enough, as it developed, when the Indians did come aboard for trade I was the main attraction of the afternoon. The young Cuna boys came back to speak to me and two proposed out and out marriage. They were lovely, warm and friendly, certainly much more to their credit than their mothers and fathers had been. I asked one boy to accompany me to the village so that I might buy a few hands of small bananas to snack on. He agreed. During this walk I came upon the preparations for a Chicha feast that would take place the next day and stopped to talk with the women. They were peeling plantains en groupe outside the cooking hut door that would be served the next day.

One old woman immediately whispered "Uaga Ome" to another and they looked up sternly. I smiled at them anyway and got no results. I was just ready to turn and go when an old grandmother decided to get belligerent. I was wearing a blue shift dress I had made, at the time, with a red eagle embroidered right in the center of it. The old woman took her worn but still sharp blade of a machete and thrust it against the fabric of the dress against my stomach, almost cutting the material with the force of her thrust and certainly hurting me.

My first impulse was one of rage. I raised my arm to hit her and my hand was already coming down—by impulse. I grabbed her wrist and shook the knife loose from it. Then the enormity of what had just happened hit me and I knew that I had better be damned diplomatic fast or the whole island would skin me alive. I picked up the knife, laughed, and performed a similar motion with equal strength upon the old woman—she uttered a startled cry and turned her sour look on me. In the interim, I laughed for all I was worth. The women in the group roared along with me and I left the group and walked back to the *Minet-Marcella* laughing all the way.

I got to the *M.M.* and was upset for the rest of the afternoon. My own reaction to the situation had so completely taken me by surprise that I was beside myself. If I had struck the woman—which had been my first intention—it would have been suicidal on such an unfriendly spot. I would have been in a tremendous amount of trouble with the Indians, and word of my actions would have traveled down the coast with the speed of lightning. Even the Indians I had befriended would not take kindly to the news. This was no place to lose one's temper. I was further startled at myself for even the thought of striking somebody. I hadn't thought of actually *physically* doing battle with another human being for years, and here I had not only decided to do battle with a rather dangerous and murderous weapon, but almost had. Was I going Indian out here? I stayed on the boat for the rest of the afternoon, trying to figure out both this mystery of a change in me, and the fact that the afternoon before I had taken a machete in my lap with every intention of using the thing had Adolf tried to interfere with me at all. The very thought of hurting someone—even in justifiable rage or self-defense—had thrown my thoughts into a tizzy. Perhaps it was time to go back to civilization! What a miserable place this Quaitupu Island was. I suddenly thought of New York and my friends there. I wanted to spend the night with them talking of San Blas and perhaps even going to see an honest-to-goodness movie and eating steak and having ice cream for dessert.

Oh well, evening came around and fresh tortuga meat promptly lifted my spirits to the point where Enrique, Fernando and I used bits of tortuga meat to fish over the side of the *Marcella.* We caught eight good sized red snappers. We'd have them for breakfast in the morning. I tied up my hammock and continued to fish from "bed" until I added another two fish to our collection. I dreamed that night that the old woman came to the *Minet-Marcella* to ask me to help her peel plantains and I threw her off the dock and into the water.

When we got up in the morning we had our fried red snapper and it was a superb and most welcome treat to all of us. Shortly after breakfast, one of my suitors from the afternoon before arrived on board and gave me an entire arm of ripe lady finger bananas and whispered that the old woman was in very bad spirits and was talking with the villagers that they should do something about that bad woman on the boat who went around sticking knives in people. He told me that the rest of the women had laughed her all the way back to her hut telling everybody in her path what had really happened. The villagers thought it was a very good joke indeed. I was both grateful for this news and I felt a bit triumphant in having come out of the minor melee on top. It seemed that the old woman had a bad reputation anyway—she never gave her husband any children and he claimed that he tried time after time always hoping for success, but she always told him to go sleep in another hammock. I hated to make suggestions, but thought that perhaps the lady preferred other ladies. I said as much to the youth who promptly turned red with laughter and told me that that's what everybody else was saying—first time I ever ran into a Cuna Indian Dyke!

It is interesting to note here that there is very litle homosexuality among the Cuna. I did notice two men on Ailigandi Island who were obviously very much attached to each other, but I don't think they even knew or understood that there was anything strange or abnormal about the whole thing. One was extremely feminine, the local hammock-maker, and the other was an unmarried storekeeper on the island. They never bothered anyone else and since they didn't, their activities went unheralded in the village. They simply were and were left to themselves and not bothered by anyone else. These were the only obvious cases I ever ran into out here.

We left Quaitupu Island before the Chicha feast began at 11 a.m., not wanting to be in such unfriendly surroundings once someone was drunk, and proceeded on towards Mulatupu Island. Israel informed me that we would be spending an hour or so there. There was just enough time for me to check up on my mail and perhaps take a shower at the Iglesias house before continuing our voyage.

We docked and I went immediately to the Iglesias residence. Marguerita graciously made me a snack and told me that there were ten Putomayo Indians from Colombia about town. I found out that Playon Chico was leading in the basketball tournament and said hello to Peter Miller, Jr. who was staying with Ignacio and his wife, then returned to the boat.

There were ten Putomayos in town alright. They were all over the *Minet-Marcella*'s decks in long black dresses (the men) and their multicolored skirts and blouses (the women). In all I counted four babies with the Indian women. There were six men and two boys—considerably more than ten when you got down to it. There were 16 of them with babies counted. The women had a strange charm and wore their waist long hair in long braids down their backs. Each of the men had a large straw hat on his head. Their tunics came down to their calves. Each Indian was carrying brightly beaded pouches from their arms and waists. I suddenly found myself wondering just what they were doing here and turned to find Israel grinning at me.

"You'll have a chance to find out something about them," he informed me. "They're coming to Colon with us." I also noticed, namely because he had just let go of his enormous lung capacity, that we had another tortuga aboard. There was aslo a live chicken tied to the back engine cover.

I laughed and mentally calculated the present population of the *Minet-Marcella*—there was Israel, his son, four crew members, one captain, Silent Sam, our cook, Adolf, 16 Putomayo Indians, one live tortuga, one live chicken, and myself. That was, not counting our livestock, 26 people. I wondered where we were ever going to bed down when the night came. There was sleeping space for only eight of us—nine with my hammock over the central hatch. With all of us, when night did come, it was going to be interesting watching this geometric problem from the security of my hammock. If it rained we were through, that I did know.

The Putomayos got their belongings aboard, then disappeared on Mulatupu Island again to buy some bananas, so Enrique informed me. We were 15 minutes late in pulling out because a general round-up of the Putomayos was necessary. We lost each one two or three times before we finally got them all aboard again.

The *Minet-Marcella*'s motors chug-chugged to life, then we pulled out. The new Indians made themselves comfortable along the decks on the port side of the *M.M.* We pushed on, the salty sweet sea breeze blowing free in our faces and the *Minet-Marcella* dipping up and down in the green sea. Adolf was again serenading us from the bow—it was about this time the Putomayos got *their* first blessing.

The Putomayos were curling up on the deck for a short siesta and I felt rather tired about this time and curled up on top of a coil of rope on the central hatch. I was soon asleep.

Awareness once again came as we neared Isla Pino. We stopped briefly here while I collected my belongings and thanked the Davis family for their hospitality. Once again we lost our Putos, as I called them, and finding them at Isla Pino took us another half an hour—most of them were at my shower stream on the east end of the island. They appeared back on board with more bananas and a few pineapples. I couldn't see how they could possibly starve to death or get hungry within a week's time, judging from our growing number of bananas and what have you hanging from the cabin roof. We were beginning to look more like a banana-boat than a coconut-trader. Israel informed everyone of this fact soon thereafter tongue in cheek.

We were again on our sea-going way. The Putos, now assured beyond any shadow of a doubt that they would not starve on the way to the next island, curled up against the cabin walls and went to sleep. It was catchy. I found myself asleep at our next stop—this time beside an Indian dug-out canoe under sail. I noticed some high handed bargaining going on with much talk and high pitched voice activity from both sides—then I saw why. We now had two tortoises. This was going to be an interesting night, that was for sure. I hoped that they would breathe simultaneously at any rate.

Adolf, wonderously unscathed by either sunstroke or the urge to bless the sharks in the area, started once again to chant us a bit of a diddy from the bow. Incidentally, I had yet to see Adolf leave that part of the boat and wondered what he did when nature called. I hadn't been watching him with any great interest, so didn't know. He was beginning to seem to me like a kind of hallowed figure-head at the bow of a windjammer. If he did move from that spot, I would definitely know that something earth-shattering was about to befall us—as I would have the same feeling and observation on seeing rats leaving a ship before sailing. As long as he stayed put, blessing all and calling forth every saint known to earth to the *Minet-Marcella*'s bow, I knew all was well.

Alfredo and his father were both catnapping in their cabin out of the heat of the day as were most of the crew in their own bed-bunks to the stern. Enrique and Pablo, however, were playing blackjack in their own way on the stern hatch-cover. The engine roar blotted out Cartagena.

Ahead lay the islands of Ustupu and many miles away in Mandinga Bay—Porvenir, Wichub-Huala and Nalu Nega. I would be happy to see Machi, Alfredo, and the family again and hoped all had gone well with them since I last was there.

We by-passed the island of Ustupu-Conception and continued on toward the Ailigandi group of islands to the west.

Some activity began to be evident among the Putos and they got up and came over to talk with me. By joining my bush Spanish with pantomime we were able to communicate. One of the women, a girl of seventeen named of all things, Josette, had an eight day old baby with her. I had thought the child to be much older and was further horrified to hear that she gave birth to the child in a storm aboard a canoa from Cartagena. The child was with fever and Josette was worried. The crew had told her to let me see the child, although I was at a loss to know why. I had no idea on God's green earth of what could be the matter with her. I did, however, find Josette herself running a 104° fever and told the mother to go and lie down and perhaps give her baby to another woman for a period of time. She could have been infecting the child. I gave Josette a strong antibiotic, then gave the baby an infinitesimal piece of aspirin and hoped for the best.

This bit of trying to help was my first mistake with the entire Putomayo Nation. Each and every one of the 16 Putos immediately and simultaneously developed a series of absurd and strange sicknesses. They came to me in mass demanding some of the medicine I had given Josette and her child. I really couldn't blame them. One or more of them would probably be sick at one time or another during the long and tiring voyage ahead and suffer unless they had medicine in reserve against such time. I talked with each Indian, however, to find out who had a legitimate illness or who was a good actor. I had only a limited quantity of medicines with me—a reserve awaited me from the Pfizer Company at Porvenir, sent down via plane by request. When I did finally break down and give everyone an aspirin, each immediately cached his or her pill.

As we neared Achutupu, each was again deathly ill and demanding another pill. I handed them out and thought that the entire thing was over. How wrong I was!

We pulled into the dock at Achutupu. The memory of the dock, a little boy, and red water were still vivid in my mind. I turned away from that side and went over the dock to the island. Funny how water never bares the scars of battle as land does.

The night at Achutupu was historic in the annals of that island with Adolf and Putos and all. The Colombian Indians went all over town trying to sell a concoction of their own—a medicine to keep the skin from getting sun burned, and selling beads, silver rings, and all kinds of knick-knacks. The entire population of Achutupu followed them around from street to street trying to figure out just what this was all about and not succeeding too well.

I spotted one of the younger boys in the Puto group trying to sell eight aspirin. When he saw that I saw, he called out "Muchas Gratias . . . Non?" I decided right then and there not to give out another single pill—not even so much as a vitamin until whoever it was that was sick was dying. Even then, I'd push the pill down their throats personally.

It is to the credit of the Achutupu population to inform the reader that when the Achutupu people found out that these strange looking individuals running about and selling all of this stuff were *Indian,* they promptly took each family by the arm and home for the night. I should imagine that business considerably picked up too. I went over to say hello to the nurse, who by this time had herself a new hut, and was invited to stay there for the night, which I did. It had been the first time in weeks I'd slept in a bed.

The next morning I was up before the sun was and made my way to the *M.M.* I couldn't believe that it was the same boat I'd left the previous night. The decks were living testimony that the Putos had done a record-breaking business over-night on Achutupu. I've never seen so many plantains gathered in one place in my life. They were even hanging from my hammock strings. I also discovered that Israel had wisely vetoed Adolf's efforts to go ashore and sleep that night. Once the Indians discovered that he was crazy—I hate to even guess what would have happened. He was quietly fingering his rosary beads at the bow at this early hour.

It took us another hour to gather everybody aboard and then we were off to Ailigandi. Some of the younger children caught sight of me before we docked and went off into the streets telling the whole of Ailigandi's population that "Juanita" was back. Maria, Ricardo, and a dozen dignitaries were waiting at the dock when we got there. Israel watched my reception by the children and adults with amusement.

"You're certainly popular here, Juanita," he commented. I felt somewhat embarrassed by the reception committee, but secretly happy that my "home" village and I were having an open love affair. I scooped up Ricardido who held onto my neck and fairly screamed with delight. We went off with Maria and her husband to their hut across the island. I heard a commotion behind me. It was Adolf at the bow crying "Viva La Reina, Viva La Reina!" I quickly got out of there.

Soon, I was again in Maria's hut resting in my favorite hammock and drinking coffee. It felt good to be "home" again—even for such a short period of time. Several of the village women entered Maria's hut and soon I was telling them all about my adventures down at the border and beyond. They laughed and thought them to be very funny. Two women were talking and I over-heard their conversation. They were laughing about a strange Indian woman with a tiny baby who was trying to get bread. From the description they gave of the woman, it was Josette and her baby. She was just getting back on her feet from her fever of yesterday. The baby was also in better shape. I explained the whole story about the woman and giving birth aboard the canoa and all to Maria. She immediately bellowed:

"HEEEEEBuuuoooiirrrrR!" or "What!" in a very loud voice and before I could so much as take the next breath, she sent Leopoldo off with a bunch of coconuts through the door, grabbed her scarf and was gone. Sure enough, five minutes later she entered the hut with Josette, and carrying Josette's baby. Leopoldo came in after her with five loaves of bread.

Maria motioned for Josette and her husband who then entered

to sit down. She then served them both coffee and bread until they indicated that they could eat no more.

"Muchas gratias, non?" spoke the boy-man after each and every bite. I felt so close to Maria. Her heart was as big as the whole Ailigandi River and flowing with good will and love of other people. "They call these people primitive!" I thought to myself. To call Maria a friend that morning made me feel very very proud.

I left Maria with the Putos and went to visit my old friends on the island. I found out Mr. Miller, Senior was back from the States and spent some time talking with him about his people. I was startled to find him an albino Indian. He wore dark glasses to shield his sensitive eyes from the bright midday sun. Mrs. Miller, thinking that I'd been starving slowly away since I left Ailigandi, made me a whopping breakfast and stood over my shoulder to insure that I'd eat every bite on the plate. Peter Jr. was still at Mulatupu playing basketball and I left a hello there for him and went back to Maria's hut. I accompanied Josette and her baby and husband back to the *Minet-Marcella.* The family went to wait for the call to leave and perched themselves on the cement foundation of the clinic to await Israel's voice telling us as much. Josette's husband definitely thought the world of his wife and they talked to each other with a light in their eyes that was for no other people.

Israel finally put his foot down, I was glad to see, and told the Putos that if "uno" more banana was put on the *Minet-Marcella,* he'd leave the Putos on the next island. It was a wonder any of us could move with them as it was. I'd have difficulty sleeping with the plantains swinging on top of me and decided to move them during the afternoon's trip. No more were added, but I did laugh when they arrived with pineapples. Israel had said *"Plantains,* Muchas gratias, non?"

We left Ailigandi a half an hour later and that was the last I was to see of this beautiful place of beautiful people for the duration of the trip. The husky rise and fall of the *M.M.* let us know that we were out in the dark green waters of the Caribbean outside of the reefs. All was normal aboard—as normal as things could be wih us anyway. Off the starboard a rather large white shark was sighted and the Indians, crew, and myself went to look at it. It was clearly a monster some 18 feet long without exaggeration—when it turned in the water it displayed a mouth that could have accomodated two people without any difficulty whatsoever. I hoped that it would not enter the shallows about the islands and further torture the populations there with yet another attack.

Due to this bit of excitement, everyone felt very adverse to going back to their places and calmly letting the miles of jungle mainland pass in peace. After blessing the shark, Adolf broke into song, a rather lively one, and the Putos were pleased with the melody. They went up to sit in front of him in a half circle at the bow in the hot sun to listen to him. Soon, each one burst into song and decided to do a bit of dancing and singing of their own. Their dances were spirited and their songs delightful to listen to—the dance a pleasure to watch, was a healthy combination of bush Spanish dancing and flamenco from the tapping of their feet against the bare decks. Soon the Putos had everyone on the *Minet-Marcella* watching their fun from Enrique who deserted Cartagena for the "live" show, to Israel and Fernando, who went up to the captain's bridge to watch the goings-on from there.

Josette gave her baby to one of the other women and joined in with one of the elder grandfathers in the group and both were having so much fun with each other dancing and clapping their hands that all the spectators received enjoyment that much more. Soon Adolf, Pablo, Fernando, the four Puto women, Enrique, and the rest of the Puto men were dancing on the forward bow deck of the *Minet-Marcella*—someone swooped by and I found myself suddenly in the group clapping and stamping my feet with the rest of our rather international bush-potpourri.

A strange sight the *Minet-Marcella* must have been that hot afternoon in September, her bow all alight with at least 20 dancing people, bananas, coconuts, and pineapples strewn about her decks or hanging from ropes tied to the cabin roof. She chugged on toward the west and Porvenir with song and dance pouring from her in such gaiety and profusion that even during carnival time in Rio people would have stopped to examine the grouping, unlikely though it was. Adolf laughed at the top of his hysterical lungs. Enrique had a mop on his head imitating with much success the efforts of a young Spanish girl to get away from a Muy Macho Spanish Man (Pablo). It was Josette, however, who stole the show with her proud and graceful, physically exhausting dance. Most of us stood around clapping while she picked up her long red skirt and displayed her knees to the throng. Her feet, hardened by many years of bare-footedness, sounded the beat, and at one point it was difficult for us to even see them moving, so fast did they tap out their rhythm. We cheered en masse after her performance. It was hard for me to believe that she had had a baby just two weeks ago, and a fever the day before that. She was as strong as three oxen. On we went toward Porvenir that hot afternoon and I later wondered what the fish must have thought was happening over their silvery heads many feet above on the wavy green water.

The next day and night passed peacefully enough docked at the island of Playon Chico. I spent the night with the Baptist missionaries there. The Putos spent the night sleeping all about the *Minet-Marcella* and when we all gathered on her at seven the next morning and got under way, the morning sun was rising in full glorious profusion in the east. We pushed on toward the island of Mapequandi. I hadn't heard of Mapequandi before, but was calmly informed by Enrique that it was a jungle mainland village located at the mouth of a large river some 15 miles from Playon Chico. All of us thought of the same thing at the same time—river—wash up—laundry—swim—cool. I loved the jungle rivers and this one would be no exception I was sure. I'd be able to spend some time here and go about my laundry cleaning in peace and quiet in the shade of the high trees.

Mapequandi turned out to be an exquisite and lovely village. Some of the trees in the area had taken 500 years to grow and the high jungle pushed itself right down to the edge of the water. Fernando, Enrique, and the Putomayos took the first boat over, and I followed with Israel, Adolf, and Pablo.

The Putos promptly made themselves at home at the many fingered mouth of the Mapequandi River. They stripped down, then dove into the water, then returned to the bank for their clothes. These they beat against rocks there and washed the garments out in the water many times repeating this rock beating and soaking before the garments were hung on bushes to dry and the entire troupe collapsed onto the bank to sunbathe and sleep for the duration of our stay. Adolf, accompanied by Fernando and Enrique, went around the bend of the "S" shaped river mouth and I went further upstream via a tiny jungle path until I found a quiet secluded pool of water downstream from a miniature run of rapids. I undressed, took my bar of soap and stepped into the crystal clear, cool, delicious water, spending all of a good hour soaking and splashing about. I got dressed without any visitations from any animals, except the lovely song birds in the trees over my head, and went back down the path. The men ducked their bodies underwater as I passed pretending that I had taken their innocence unawares. I laughed, and ran back to the riverbank to join the Putos in a bit of lazy sunning. The whole area looked as though it were a scene from a film called "Paradise Regained" or "Eden—1964." I slept for a good hour, then walked into the village where I was promptly taken into a hut by an old Indian grandmother and fed to the gills with pineapple and banana drink. I was back in Indian garb, skirt, mola, beads and all, and it was with somewhat of a shock that I found the grandmother addressing me as "Sepugwa," the name for an albino in the tribe. I asked her how she could do this when I had the wrong color hair and she stuck a mirror under my nose, the first I had seen in a good long while. I was shocked at what I saw. My hair was almost white from the sun on the top of my head, although my pigtails still retained much of their red color. I looked exactly like one of the albino women now. I seriously thought that if I had met up with even my closest friends, who were used to seeing me in a piled-hairdo and sheath dress, they would never recognize me.

An hour later we were all back on board the *Minet-Marcella,* considerably the better from our stop-over at Mapequandi. We pulled our heavy anchor and went off again west down the San Blas coast toward the island of Tikantiki. When we docked Israel again made his statement of "Not one more banana or anything else," and the Putomayos went ashore.

When we were again out in the sea heading for Tigre Island I thought again of what I had learned of the recent troubles on the island. Tigre—the ring of the name was suggestive of a wild, mysterious place—her name fit her. The island had been the scene, not too many months back, of a violent, unfortunate clash between Panamanian, Colombian, and Indian elements, resulting in a few deaths and almost an Indian war.

The clash was caused by that great causer of oh so many hatreds between otherwise good and well-meaning peoples—ignorance of each other's ways and customs.

There is an unwritten law in San Blas which everybody dealing with the Cuna know in some way or another. If a canoa, or smuggling vessel, is discovered by a Panamanian guard boat at the dock of any island in San Blas—it is *not,* repeat, *not* to be attacked or in any other way bothered while *tied up at the dock.* This is for one simple reason—invariably a gun battle ensues between the Colombians and Panamanians and a child or Indian woman or young boy may be hit, hurt, or killed inadvertently on the island itself.

Well, one day a little over a half a year ago a canoa was tied up at Tigre's dock and a Panamanian National Guard boat came along out of the blue and took the boat at the dock. They told the Indians to throw off the canoa's ropes from the dock thinking that now that the canoa was no longer tied up, the law had been appeased and it was alright to go ahead with the gun battle or what have you to take the canoa. Well, as it was, a Guardia soldier was left standing on the dock of Tigre Island with a gun. The Indians, curious about what was taking place just off their island and in plain sight, flocked up to the dock area. The soldier becoming alarmed with the increase in the number of Indians shouted for them to get out of there and disperse. Most of the spectators were women and children, and very few of these could understand even one word of Spanish. The guardsman naturally could not understand or speak Indian. When the throng surged forward to get a better look out of curiosity, the guardsman fired shots into the air. The Indians thought he was shooting at them and consequently fled home. Some of the men decided to defend their island against people shooting at them and returned to the dock area where a battle was now going on with the canoa, with shotguns, a weapon which by law they are not permitted to own. Any trading boat captain caught selling weapons to the Indians, with the exception of machetes, is prosecuted. The Indians returned to the dock and fired at the Panamanian who promptly shot back, killing one Indian and wounding several others. The guardsman was killed and then his comrades came to his aid. What followed was unfortunate. Another Indian died, guardsmen were wounded, several Indians were hurt, including some children; in the end, several guardsmen were taken as hostages until such time as the Indians of Tigre could be insured by the Republic of Panama that no one was going to come swooping down on their heads in retaliation for the killing of the guardsman. The result was that units of Guardia were sent to surround Tigre with P.T. boats and plane support and the Indians were told to release the guardsmen or else the wiping of Tigre Island off the face of the map would quickly ensue. The chief of the island fearing for the lives of the entire population of women and children obeyed the order and released the guards and there has been an uneasy peace at Tigre ever since.

A final note to all of this unfortunate occurrence was that both families of the men killed, the Guardia man and the Indian, have been pensioned for the support of their families.

It is my belief that the entire incident could have been again avoided by the use of simple understanding between the two peopeoples and the use of a bit less hasty action on the part of the well-meaning Guardia, who were only protecting their country's borders against smugglers and therefore doing their job.

It is my sincere hope that such an incident will never again take place once the "unwritten-law" here presented is understood and the reasons for its being, namely to protect the islanders, is understood and accepted.

As the *Minet-Marcella* neared Tigre, the sounds of Indian music, the flute and rattles drifted out to meet us.

I have never ceased to be fascinated by the music of the Cuna peoples and wondered if there was a Chicha feast underway at the village. There would be much dancing and song and if so, I looked forward to this diversion. As we tied up at the dock I caught sight of a group of twelve Pan-like dancers in the front square of Tigre Island. There were three golden-skinned boys and nine long-haired, reed-playing, rattle weaving Cuna girls. All of us, Putos included, stood on the port side of the *Marcella* looking at the scene and listening to the beautiful music. Two lines of six dancers each faced each other, then two would break from the right end and dance about all of the others in the group, coming to rest in the center to do their own solo. With that the similarity beween the Cuna dances and our own American Square Dances ended. The dance was in four-four time, every two beats the dancers would change to the other foot. One two, skip, three four, then repeat.

Soon all of us aboard the *M.M.* were out sitting around the square in the shade of the trading store veranda looking at the dancers and appreciating their wonderful music. There is a naturalness of this Indian music played in its own environment. It doesn't clash with anything. It is a part of the Indian nation, it comprises the quality of wildness of the Indian soul with the feeling of earth under one's feet, and the song of birds in the air. I loved to listen to it and if anyone, Indian or non-Indian, listened to it for very long it would put you in a trance. I have seen its effects upon a drunken Indian population. Most of these were in a prophetic trance within one hour after the music commenced.

There was a quality of dignity about the Indian dances. The participants were graceful and relaxed—there was no wildness or strain to the dance and it was as though the participants thought the action of dancing as natural to them as paddling a dug-out canoe or walking.

When the dance was over, spontaneous applause broke out from all sides—I noticed that there were a crew of Colombians in town—probably from another canoa. They clapped too. The Putomayos were enamored of the entire presentation and let their entire selves let the Cuna know how much they appreciated the unique performance.

No less than eight full dances followed, and we loved every minute of it. I then retreated to the bow of the *Minet-Marcella* which was blessedly deserted by Adolf to watch a most amazing and beautiful sunset. Not just the west, but the whole sky from horizon to mountains to horizon to sea was draped in varying shades of gold, pink, red, gold, yellow, orange, blue, purple, maroon, and finally deep royal blue. It was a sight that no camera could have caught. I was amazed and over-awed that such a display could concoct itself out of the air I breathed. I wondered how the sky could ever allow another sunset in the morrow, it seeming to me that nature wore itself out producing this night's show.

Supper passed peacefully and night came and all of us fitted ourselves into our separate mouseholes on the *Minet-Marcella* and went to sleep. Most of the passengers were sleeping out on the bow deck, it being cool and completely open to any sea breezes coming in to cool the land.

I don't know what time it started to rain, but rain it did and the result was catastrophic for all of us. Our collection of animals and passengers got soaked and everybody was miserable. The result of the downpour was a mass exodus to both the rear and central hatch-covers, those areas being covered by cabin roofs. The most uncomfortable assortment of eight pairs of legs and elbows suddenly poked their way through my hammock in an effort to find a dry space below. I tried to live with it at first, but someone below me would always move and I'd end up with an elbow in the ear or what have you. I finally got up and pulled the ropes of my hammock strings shorter, the hammock itself going up and finally coming to rest a foot below the cabin roof. I then performed what can only be described as a magnificent feat of balancing by climbing up and into it without tumbling onto the grand gathering below. Result? No more elbows or kneecaps. I no sooner got into the hammock than I remembered Josette and her new baby. I got out again, found her and explained that I'd take the baby to my hammock and it would be warm and dry for the night. I got back in and she handed me the child. At least it would not catch cold from the rain. The child gurgled cutely and snuggled against me. I got into a position where I couldn't possibly turn over and accidently smother the child and fell quickly to sleep.

Josette's tiny baby girl woke up at about 4:30 the next morning hungrily demanding her breakfast and I clearly was in no position to provide that for her. I called to Josette to come over. She did, withdrew her breast from her dress and fed the child. After the baby had eaten, she was handed back to me and we both fell asleep for another hour or so.

We got underway again right after the sun came up and went on our way toward Narkana Island. Josette found me once again.

The baby had not fared as well as we had hoped during the night and she was again running a fever. I again gave her a tiny bit of an antibiotic and hoped for the best. Again, the entire rest of the *Minet-Marcella*'s Putomayo population descended upon me demanding similar pills. I said no and left it at that. They kept up the demands following me clean up to the roof of the captain's cabin where I had retreated to have a bit of peace and quiet. The result of their continual nagging was that I was beginning to lose my temper. I decided to let go with a "controlled" blast before I genuinely did lose it and hit somebody. I cut loose with a torrent of angry Cuna dialect gesturing with my hands and injecting a few good hearty English words in the course of my torrent for good measure. I finally ended up by raising my hands and evoking all the spirits and devils of evil in the vicinity to come and protect me from this invasion by making everyone who was bothering me fall into the water and be eaten by sharks.

The immediate result of the outburst was that the Putos retreated to the stern as though eight devils in pink dresses were chasing them. There they remained talking excitedly to each other. The crew was at a loss to find out why I was angry and wanted to know what had evoked such a violent outburst from me. I told them what happened laughing at the very good results as I did and they found this quite entertaining too. I remained on the roof of the cabin for two hours studying the shore line of San Blas before I finally came down. When I did and returned to my new seat on the water drum to the starboard side of the *M.M.* and away from the sun, a small Puto lad came up to me and dropped an offering of a ripe hand of bananas and ran all the way back to the stern. I noted that Israel was grinning and his son Fernando was nearly hysterical holding onto his stomach, wiping his eyes, and rocking back and forth. They both caught the significance of the bananas. They were given to placate me, in much the same manner as they would placate a God or angry diety. They thought my medicine for good so worth-while, that my medicine for evil and devils must have been devastating and I must be calmed with all haste before the boat sank. I also noticed for the first time that we had picked up three Cuna men at our last stop. They were heading for Colon. That made 29 people aboard the *Minet-Marcella*. I accepted the bananas and went back to distribute them to the Putos, letting them know that I was no longer angry at them. After this act, I again retreated to the cabin central hatch and sat down to watch the jungle go by, wondering what life was like back in there.

I caught myself mid-thought because somebody was staring at me. I turned to find Fernando beaming broadly from his tanned and handsome face.

"You're going into the jungle, aren't you?" he asked.

I smiled, literally being caught in the act.

His grin grew broader, and he nodded his head, then returned to the stern of his father's boat.

We pulled into the dock at Narkana. The Putos went ashore and Enrique and I had a three hour rummy game on the rear engine hatch. Both of us had an Indian audience who rooted for each of us. I won the first game, but my win was short-lived. Enrique caught on to my system in the second hand and beat me soundly. I laughingly acknowledged his superiority and he offered me a drink ashore as a consolation prize. I accepted. The beer was, as usual, somewhat warm but it was good and I enjoyed it tremendously. Back on board Israel calmly informed me that we would run this evening and not remain the night at Narkana. I would be back on Porvenir Island this very night if all went well. I knew that there were many reefs in Mandinga Bay and asked if this running at night wouldn't be dangerous. He replied that the captain knew the reefs in the bay like the wrinkles on his wife's face. I accepted the news with a great deal of joy.

I thought of the Cuna Inn and Jungle Jim's porch and cold, cold beer or Pepsi. I yearned for one of my own kind—somebody to speak English with. I wanted to find out what news there was of the world, even find out what the weather was like in New York City. This was one of the very few times since I had left Porvenir many weeks before, months actually, that I felt homesick for civilization. I was anticipating what meat that wasn't boiled would taste like, and my God, butter and even pancakes would be available!

"Civilization," I thought, "here I come."

The great reef disappeared from view about an hour out of Narkana. With the departure of the reef came the high sea and waves which tossed us about soundly. The *Minet-Marcella* was up to it, and I felt a confidence and yes, even a love for the trader I had never experienced for any vessel before or since. My exhilaration at almost being "home" again was not shared by the Putos. Most of these were horribly seasick—Josette leading the entire group in moans. Adolf was singing as usual from the bow.

At last the mountain tip of the end of Mandinga Bay and Colorado Beach were visible in the sunset. Still, we had about an hour's worth of traveling to do before we got there. Then I made out the form of the radar station atop this point of land.

A while later I could see the lights of Jungle Jim's hotel and the Panamanian government buildings on Porvenir. We dropped anchor off the island and went ashore in our dug-out. After signing in with the secretary to the goveror of San Blas, I walked with Enrique and Pablo carrying my belongings to the other side of the island.

As I neared the hotel, I could see that Jim had some guests on the porch. He couldn't see me as I was still in the darkness about 20 yards from the porch lights. I stopped, thinking it best not to disturb Jim when he had guests around and was all set to turn back and perhaps see if I couldn't get a ride to Wichub-Huala and spend the night at Alfredo's hut, when Jim caught sight of us somehow and bellowed:

"Who in the devil is out there?"

I moved a few steps into the light so that Jim could recognize me and not be wondering about who was pussy footing around.

"Well, I'll be a hush-puppy's mother!" exploded Jim. "Sipu! Welcome back!"

"Come on up here Sipu and introduce yourself to these gentle-said.

"Is she some kind of Indian from a different island?" asked one of the two men sitting on the porch.

"No," spoke Jim, "believe it or not she's as American as apple pie."

I was somewhat taken aback by the man's observation of my dress, which consisted of dungarees, mola, beads, and sun burnt skin.

"Come on up here Sipu and introduce yourelf to these gentlemen while I get Machi to fix you a drink. You do want one," he asked looking at me as though if I said no, he would have had me tied and delivered to Bellevue Hospital.

I bellowed that I most certainly did. Anything that was cold and available would be most welcome. With this Pablo and Enrique and I climbed up onto the porch. They put my belongings in a pile off to one side of Jim's bar and I thanked them and said a grateful good-bye to each of my friends. After this was done I turned to look at Jim's guests who were both eyeing me tensely as though they'd leap from their hammocks and run if I made one wrong move. One man's mouth was actually hanging open from astonishment, an observation I made and found very funny. I started to laugh.

"You must forgive my appearance," I started, "I've been traveling by trader for two weeks and I know they'd never let me into Sardi's in this condition."

Both of them laughed and the ice was broken. Machi appeared with a (oh blessing of blessings) a scotch and soda with ICE CUBES. I hugged Machi and he me in a big fat welcome. Most of my enthusiasm though was for the ice cubes. I was so happy to see them floating around in that glass. I wouldn't have cared if Machi had served water, as long as the ice cubes were intact.

"Civilization!" I burst forth enthusiastically and raised the scotch and soda and ice cubes in a salute to the entire length of Jim's hotel.

My exclamation was greeted by simultaneous laughter from both of Jim's guests and I turned to find out why. One gentleman volunteered the following:

"Excuse us. You see, to us, this hotel is the furthest possible point *away* from civilization that we could possibly get and your comment seemed overwhelming. Just where have you been, young lady?"

We all had a good laugh and Jim then offered me the use of his shower and rooms to get myself somewhat in order. I welcomed his offer very gratefully and went in, got washed up, put on a dress, and make-up as well as fixed my hair into an upsweep design that had been in style when I *left* anyway. I looked at the results in a mirror and felt young, happy, and feminine.

When I came out I was greeted by silence and the sight of a rather large group of people sitting on the porch. I went and sat down and one of the Panamanian government officials whistled lowly. I adored the sound and turned to smile at him. I had been afraid I'd still look like an Indian; evidently I didn't.

There ensued four hours worth of straight conversation during which time, I must admit, I did most of the talking, so happy was I to find an entire group of people who would understand the English language. I gave a running travelogue of what had ensued since I left.

Jim gave me a room for the night and I went to sleep with that wonderful feeling of good exhaustion. My last thought that night was of the *Minet-Marcella* and her voyage through San Blas. She would be returning to Colon with her crew and most unlikely group of passengers. I knew that she would be back though, and with her would come that wonderful feeling of adventure and riding the sea on the San Blas coast. I would not soon forget the fun we all had enjoyed aboard her.

12

A WEEK OF DAYS IN MANDINGA BAY

Four weeks have passed in all since my return to Porvenir Island and the Mandinga Bay region and much has happened in that short length of time.

So much, in fact, has happened that I will list some of the more interesting events—seven of them—by the days of the week on which they occurred.

It was a sunny Monday afternoon in the beginning of October, and I was full of thoughts of a good catch in the reefs around Porvenir. Donning a bathing suit, face mask, and carrying a spear with me, I went out in back of Jungle Jim's hotel to a tiny L shaped reef there. Jim had previously warned me of the rather numerous moray eels in this area, so I was careful to avoid any "too rocky" part of the tiny reef that morays particularly love to call home. The sea fans and color of the coral and the whole slow moving underwater world was in full view one-third larger than it was because of the normal distortion through the face mask glass. As usual I became half-hearted about my desire to spear fish and took to casually sight-seeing down there. I loved the very swirl of the water against my body and the feeling of almost "flying" that I experienced here. Some days, after I'd spent a particularly long time underwater, I'd be possessed of the belief that if I didn't have a breathing apparatus with me, I'd be able to breathe the water's oxygen. I never became enamored of this desire to the extent that I tried it.

A school of parrot fish came drifting into view, and the scenery was forgotten and I took off after food for the night and perhaps to add a bit to my family's supply of fish for the next day. I left the reefs and started off towards the "plains" beyond the coral "mountains" in pursuit of the fish. They disappeared behind another cropping of coral and it seemed strange for me to find the coral there, in the middle of the "plains." I lifted my head from the water and realized that I had made my underwater way to the outer reef curving about the perimeter of Porvenir Island. I had come clear across the grassy barracuda kindergarten as we "permanent" inhabitants of Porvenir call it. I felt somewhat exhausted. If I had set out merely to explore this grassy shallow for barracuda I would have been frightened before even entering the water. As it was, I still felt the familiar crawling between my stomach and throat every time I swam the reefs in San Blas. I was afraid of the water, not because of the water, but because of the dangers there and a small boy who was once living on Achutupu Island. I hold no claims to bravery—but I am obstinate—therefore I kept coming back into the water.

"Why do you keep going back in then, if you know that there's danger here?" I asked myself standing on top of the reef.

"Because you're living on an island—that's why," I answered.

"Um hum. I know, but why are you living on these islands in the first place?"

"Because of the Indians!"

"You'll have to do better than that. Now just answer one simple question and you'll have the final answer. Why are you *really* here?"

"I don't know—I seriously don't—all I know is that it existed and was and that I'm alive. Maybe I wanted a vacation. Maybe I needed a rest and a period of time in which to examine my whole culture and civilization."

"Why didn't you go to Fire Island for the week-end?"

"Because it's SNOWING on Fire Island, that's why!"

"In October?"

"Well if it isn't now, it would have been when I finally got back!"

"So because it's snowing, or will be snowing on Fire Island, you're swimming the Porvenir reefs?"

"Yep! There are frozen drops of rain falling all over New York and there's sun and green Caribbean water here. Now let me further explain why I happen to be in the water—it's all because of snow, ultimately. If I sat on the porch of the Cuna Inn, or stayed home on Wichub-Huala Island helping Eme or Fulvia peel plantains for the evening meal, I'd feel guilty. My friends, once I got back, would say:

"Gee, you're lucky. All that sun and wonderful water and we up here with all this cold weather. You must have had fun. You did do *quite* a bit of swimming or spear fishing didn't you?" All of them would look at me expectantly.

How can you explain what a shark looks like when it turns over on its side and makes a lunge at your legs, and how you go over a coral reef to be able to walk in the future and your rear end and shoulders are covered with sea urchins that sting like the devil until someone manages to hit them with a calabash or you can gather urine to pour over the hurting black marks on your body. How can you explain that there is no marker above the surface of Porvenir's or San Blas' water saying "Under Water Tour Begins Here" and an arrow pointing below water. "There's no danger," says the sign, "keep close to your guide." How can you explain what your heart feels like, thumping right at the entrance to your snorkel tube when you've just hit a barracuda and he's *there,* right at the end of your spear; and you're holding on for dear life and your lungs feel as though they're about to burst. You've got to hold on or the vicious teeth filled head will turn on you and tear off an arm or a leg. How do they know what it feels like to fight for a limb and there's nobody about, no knight in shining black scuba suit to come and lance the dragon barracuda and carry you home to his castle.

"My hero!" you sigh and fall into his arms. Nuts!

You can't surface to call for help because if you do, then he can turn on you and now you've got him on the bottom and he's getting tired, all three, steel, sinewy, strong three feet of him.

"Do much spear fishing?"

"Ah, Well, ah, No. You see there was this open space in the reefs and this 20 foot shark frightened me pretty badly one day because he was trying to kill me, and the water thereabouts you see, is, ah, pretty bad for cuda so I stayed on the islands and lived with the Indians and went back into the jungle for a bit of hunting and look-see or what have you and stayed out of the water and ah. . . ."

"WHAT! You mean you stayed *out* of the water when it was *WINTER* up here and we were *freezing just* because of a few measly old sharks and a few little barracuda! How can I tell my *friends* that you did that. How can I *tell* them that I know an explorer that doesn't go swimming because of, oh this is absurd, *fish!*"

There was another reason—I was the only American woman about and American women are very sporty and are continually swimming in their pools and at the seashore and where have you. If I sat on my rear-end all day, the local government officials would start saying:

"She SAYS she's an American woman—but you know, I've never seen her in the water, or for that matter in so much as a bikini bathing suit or dancing the TWIST. I've never seen her with make-up or wearing a full length lounging dress out here. I don't know about her—maybe I think, she's not what she says—not twisting at all, and all that. Maybe she's not even an American. Did anyone check her passport when she got here? You know what I think? I think that the *real* American woman drowned when her dug-out canoe tipped over while she was hunting for sharks a mile out beyond the reefs. This girl, she's from God only knows where, *found* all of that documentation and took her identity."

What I'd like to know is, who started all of this ridiculous nonsense! There I would be, calmly, peacefully relaxing and swinging in my faithful trusty hammock, in complete union with the coconut trees, the cool breeze, and birds, when suddenly a government official would show up and say:

"You no go into the water today, Sipu?" He would stand there expecting me to say "Gadds," snap my fingers and exclaim joyfully, "Forgot all about the time," climb into a bathing suit and run quickly for the water, leap into it and come back with a 30-pound red snapper to uphold my claim to American citizenship. Some afternoons I'd run and hide down at Meditation Point for fear that the whole Panamanian population, and Indian too, would come to watch me swimming as all good American women do, in the afternoon. There I would be, waist deep in the high grass down on the point, when a dozen heads would find me pretending sleep, shake me into awareness and ask me why I wasn't in the water. I'd thank them for being so thoughtful as to remind me of my duty and go skipping off to don my bathing suit.

Another day, I hid in a coconut tree I'd climbed specifically and with all intentions of avoiding my set duty. The government officials would find me up there and exclaim:

"Look at the American woman!" admiringly. All American women know how to climb coconut trees and cook a Smorgasbord. They reminded me when I came down that I hadn't had my afternoon swim, and I trotted faithfully and fearfully into the Cuna Inn to put on my torn, battle-scared, blue bathing suit to lose myself beneath the water under their watchful eyes.

There were other specific and set ways of life that all American women were supposed to follow. They were great love makers these American women—a theory I immediately set about to tear from each and every textbook on American women on Porvenir Island.

"What? You don't want to?" Disbelief incarnate would exclaim.

"Well, ah as a matter of fact no," I'd say apologetically.

"But you're from New York?" Eyes Getting Wider would factually state.

"I'm well aware of that fact."

"What's the matter with you?"

"I really don't know, all I know is that I don't want to!"

"How can you say that—you *are* an American woman, aren't you?"

"Well I was born in Boston, brought up in Charlestown, Massachusetts, then I went to school in Brookline and went to Washington, then Mexico, then to New York and. . . ."

"You *say* you're American, but you say 'No' to *everybody?*"

"Well you see, I'm rather close to a man back in New York and . . . ."

"But you're here."

"I *know* that, for Gosh sakes!"

The only logical reasoning left was then the "Madrid Charge" which was to lower one's "horns" and attack. When my red cape had been brought out and successfully used to do any Matador's honor, my bull would then retreat in shock at all American women in general, trying to figure out where he had failed all of Spanish manhood in general. It was very difficult to understand that an American woman was running about in a bush-jungle area for the simple reason that she wanted to study Indans. Any woman traveling alone was suspect to amazing action and willingness, but a woman, an American woman in the jungle? Naturally! Forgive me sisters for destroying our reputation in this little known area of the world!

I did, however, hold up our reputation under duress for dancing the Twist. I was beset one October evening by a group of Panamanians and Indians who wanted to witness this much spoken of phenomenon of American Tribal Dancing, the leader of which was the famous "Twiiiest," as they put it. A guitar was brought out from God only knows where and . . . Ever try to twist to a Bolero? It's an experience which I recommend highly for all those with amazing physical stamina. After a two hour demonstration of this form of dancing, I was exhausted and joyful that once again I had upheld the honor of the race. I threw myself in my hammock back in Alfredo's hut on Wichub-Huala Island and slept until ten the next morning.

Oh blond-haired, blue-eyed sisters to the north! Do you know how hard it was day after day to protect our name from being buried under sand and forgotten. Do you know the nights I spent wide-awake looking at the walls of my hut trying to think of what other, new, preposterous method for proving our reputation that these jurors would invent? If failure has occurred, in the past, it is not because of lack of loyalty—but only from lack of endurance and strength!

Well anyway, I was on the reef and the beach was empty, now

that everyone was assured that they had reminded me of my duty and I was in the water. They were all in bed for a short siesta. The feeling of fear was still within me. How familiar it was. Fear lets you move slowly, swiftly, lets you fight to your fullest when necessary, or to flee the fastest it is possible for one to flee. Yet the very fear was a saving thing. I could imagine how much life would be uselessly lost without it. It was the geiger counter of life, this fear. How often did I fear back in New York—twice, maybe three times a month. Here the feeling possessed me at least once a day—sometimes more. Underwater, it came five times an hour. Sometimes it was constant. Then there was the feeling after the fear—the huge joyful relief that made life seem all the more valuable. Fear, then, was also responsible for a deeper appreciation of life around you. Risk, fear, safety, and each and every bird's song was a rich experience. The very waving of coconut palms in the warm breeze was a delight, because you had ben given a reprieve by life and allowed to watch, allowed to listen, allowed to breathe. The colors of sunset were as though a sacred occurrence and watched with reverence and awe at a divine act.

It was in the midst of all of these delvings into the word "fear" that the real thing once again reared its ugly head. A large triangular jet black shape drifted right below my body blocking the shadow of my own form from the sandy sea bottom.

"Jesus God!" I exclaimed leaping for the highest outcropping of coral in the immediate area, "What's a manta ray doing out here!" But there it was.

"Where do you spear a manta?" I kept asking—"head, near the tail so that barbed tail won't come back and stab me to kingdom come? Where does one hit a manta?" I was frantic. I was still, even at the highest point of coral, in two feet of water.

"Oh Lord, why did I come out here?"

I quickly analyzed the situation. I was on the outer reef. I could go over the other side if the ray came up to jab at me. Were mantas unfriendly? Who cares—maybe if they are, this one's the exception, then again, maybe if they aren't this one's also the exception. Just watch him and stay still. You can always go over the reef and swim along the other side until you get to a different stretch of water, then go to shore.

With this in mind I examined the route of my retreat. What I saw almost caused me to faint. A grey fin cut the water some 15 feet away and the form of a shark, a good eight foot one, was visible beneath the surface and circling. That meant he was examining the possibility of coming in for a midday snack. Both of the sea-dwellers could get up on the reef.

I screamed as loudly as I could against all American womanhood in general.

Of course, everybody and his uncle and brother was sleeping and no one heard me for the wind was going in the other direction.

"So what do you do now?" I asked looking from side to side. I then thought it would be best to get myself underwater and at least make myself as ball-like as possible. Besides, I wanted to see whoever was coming first. The ray was eyeing me somewhat curiously, confident of his ability to handle whatever kind of a fish I was and he had reason to be. My spear gun was half the size of his tail.

The shark settled the whole problem by coming in and making a close pass at the reef, turning over on his side as he did. I decided that a barb in my body was better than having my body in a barb, shark's mouth rather. I slowly drifted off the reef to the manta's side, moving oh so cautiously. I saw the ray's tail flick up and down a couple of times. The fin lunged for the reef. That did it officially and unforgettably! I started to swim like a maddened maniac toward Porvenir Island, not caring what the creature below the surface of the water thought was speeding over-head. When I reached the beach, I threw myself on the sand thinking my lungs and body were just going to fall apart. I didn't care if anybody saw me, I started to sob, and sob I did for a good five minutes.

After getting the whole ridiculous situation out of my system I walked up onto the porch of the Cuna Inn. Jungle Jim was asleep there, so I just took my cigarettes and went off out to the dock behind the hotel. After a half an hour's worth of straight smoking, I felt much better, but couldn't even bring myself to put my toe in the water.

My thought session of life and little fish was interrupted by the sound of rapid shooting nearby. I dropped flat on the dock trying to figure out what new torture was about to present itself into my life, and madly trying to look everywhere at once. I caught sight of Pacheco, the secretary to the governor of San Blas, walking down the beach with a 30-30 rifle in his arms. He called out to greet me and asked if he didn't interrupt my sleeping on the dock, which he assumed I had been doing because I was flat out on it. I said that I had been and asked what he had been shooting at.

"Smugglers?" asked I.

"Sharks!" stated he.

He pointed out beyond me into the bay from whence I came not less than a half an hour previous to all of this. A grey body thrashed in the water and we watched in silence while two other fins shot in and out from it. "Damned Cannibals!" I thought. "The sharks are nothing but damned cannibals. They eat their own." I hoped that it was the same monster who panicked me. I felt an animal desire to go right into the water and help his other "pals" finish him off.

"Too much for one afternoon," I thought. A wave a little bigger than the other came up and touched my feet and I drew back from the water. "Oh, Oh," I thought, "this is bad." I didn't even want to talk about what had happened.

"You cold?" asked Pacheco.

"Just got out of the water a little while ago and I'm drying off," I said. My voice sounded strangely not a part of me at all. I realized too, that I was shaking somewhat.

"Why don't you come back into the water for awhile? I was just going out to do a bit of spear fishing," stated Pacheco.

I knew what had to be done. It was like falling off a horse—you get right back on again or it will take maybe years to climb into the saddle again.

"Sure," I said feeling like dropping dead on the spot.

"Let's go to Jim's and get the guns," he stated. We did.

"Oh well, tra, la, tra, la, At least this way you've got another person with you—it's much safer than going all alone."

Soon Pacheco and I went out into the "kindergarten" on the other side of the island away from our grey "pals." We no sooner got out into deep water when Pacheco grabbed my elbow and pulled strongly backwards, pointing frantically out into the deep water. I looked feverishly around. He was pointing over a sunken log on the bottom of the grassy sand. I could see nothing, but started to back off with Pacheco. Then the "log" opened and closed its mouth. I knew that no log ever had teeth like that. It was a barracuda and the biggest one that I had ever seen in my entire life. He was even bigger than "King Cuda" of Ailigandi's reefs. I was grateful for Pacheco's presence, and the knowledge that two whole human beings were making a smooth retreat was like a soothing balm to my battered spirit. There was no panic in our retreat, only the knowledge of the Cuda's presence and an effort in our retreat not to disturb him. Jim was standing on his back porch when we climbed up onto the L shaped reef.

"What was it?" he asked.

"One of the biggest barracuda you're ever going to see, Grampa," Pacheco said, using his affectionate term for his friend Jim. Jim called Pacheco Grandson and me Grandma.

"Should have shot him in the back of the neck!" commented James Kyle Price.

"Not this one, Grampa," replied Pacheco, "he was just too big."

"Really?"

"Yes, about seven feet."

Jim turned to me smiling and stated: "Well young lady, you've certainly had your excitement for the day. Glad nothing earth-shattering happened."

I turned my head to him and looked at him, not saying a word. Then Pacheco and I looked at each other knowing that Jim probably didn't believe the length of the creature.

Jim left, leaving Pacheco and me in silence looking out over the still, deceptively quiet water. He got up to leave and started walking, then stopped. He turned back and threw me a brotherly look:

"The next time you decide to go out on the reef, don't go alone Grandma.

"The next time the shark's going to get you! I was watching with this," he said slapping his gun.

I looked up quickly and unbelievingly.

"You saw what happened?" I asked.

"Yes, I heard you scream."

"Thank you," I said. Pacheco acknowledged my gratitude with a nod of his head and a smile. He went on down the beach with his gun to look for any stray meat birds that might have wandered out here from the jungle mainland.

I went back to my hammock vowing never to go beyond the L shaped reef again for the duration of the time I would spend in San Blas.

It was on Thursday of the same week that the *Corsario,* a coconut trading boat, went up on a sand bar right off Wichub-Huala. As a matter of fact, it was right out in back of Alfredo's house some 25 yards from the back door.

She had come in earlier that morning to trade for coconuts from the island inhabitants and Fulvia and I were peeling plantains for the mid-day meal when we heard her pulling away from the dock. Suddenly there was silence. Fulvia and I looker at each other in alarm. The sound of much angry cries ripped through the air. Both of us dropped our machetes and ran out to the backyard through the hut and out into the strong sunlight. Sure enough, there was the *Corsario,* one of the biggest traders that did business with the San Blas coast, with her bow up on the sand bar and her crew running frantically about like chickens with their heads cut off trying to frighten the poor boat off the obstacle. Within ten minutes a minor flotilla of dug-outs was out at the boat and the Indians of both Wichub-Huala and Nalu Nega Islands were talking with the captain to see what could be done to help out. Soon the crew began to pass cases of beer, bags of copra, all kinds of trade goods to men in the dug-outs from the area of the bow. Evidently they were trying to lighten her bow to see if that would help any. Soon my friend Marine's blue painted dug-out driven by 28 h.p. came roaring across the bay from Porvenir Island. Pacheco was aboard and standing on the bow holding onto a rope surveying the situation. He went aboard. Even some of the island women were out helping, so I decided to paddle out myself to see if I could lend a hand. I pulled up alongside and her exasperated captain, a Greek named Kakelanos, helped me aboard.

I found out the situation was somewhat dangerous in that it was high tide. Once low tide came around, the *Corsario** was in danger of losing her sea-going life by turning over from sheer weight once the water level dropped. It would be a great loss if she were to be overturned. I couldn't quite fathom how this was to occur but accepted the reasoning of the sea-people as the last word in the situation.

The *Corsario* was a pioneer in her particular field and one of the most unusual boats I have ever heard of. She had a traveling movie house aboard. In exchange for showing Spanish movies to the Indians, she collected five coconuts from every person who watched the films—a most unusual way of trading in any business. She had her own generator and lines and lines of wires aboard. She pulled into a village and Kakelanos promptly went off to talk with her chief and arrange to use the council hall on the island, or the chicha hut, whichever was nearer to the dock, for a movie house. Cables would then be strung from the *Corsario* to the hut where the films would be shown and the show would take place. They had a large motion picture screen aboard, excellent sound equipment and a good projector. It was a unique and imaginative idea and I admired Kakelanos for his spirit and adventurous ideas. He was a fun loving creature of life, as most of the captains along this coast are, and lived his way of life well.

I climbed on top of the cabin roof and made myself comfortable to watch and see what would happen next. The *Wakuna,* another trading boat owned and operated by San Blas Indians, came by and offered to help. Lines were tied to her stern from the *Corsario's* stern, and many other lines handed out to the men in dug-out canoes. A cry went up from Kakelanos to pull and the motors of the *Corsario* were set full astern. The Indians cried out and commenced to paddle furiously, then the *Wakuna's* engine's throbbed. Slowly, inch by inch, the *Corsario* fell backwards off the bar. A cheer went up when she pulled free from 300 voices. Kakelanos handed out free beer to all who had helped for the remainder of the afternoon, getting somewhat potted himself with relief from the near-loss of his much-loved *Corsario.*

* The Corsario, RIP, went down in a storm off the port of Colon in November 1963,

Later on that afternoon I paddled over to Porvenir. I had already minimized the events of Tuesday last and was eager to get back ontop of my L shaped water home. I had a pleasant afternoon and a successful one, getting a good half dozen parrots and red snappers for the family. I felt very good about the afternoon's activities and it was with a song in my heart that I came on shore for the last time, not having found anything on my last trip out. I flipped the safety of my spear gun to "shoot" and aimed the point, a three-pronged lobster spear that I was using that day, into the soft sand on the beach.

I found myself standing there suddenly wondering what in the devil the damned spear was doing in my left calf—two whole prongs of it were buried in the flesh there, the third cut a gash in the side of my leg, but didn't stick in. It didn't hurt and I knew that because it didn't, it was a bad wound—bad wounds never hurt after the initial shock. The nerves had been anesthetized by separation. "Oh Good Grief," I said, still wondering how it happened, but knowing that now was not the time to find out. Those prongs had to come out and they were in up to the barb and beyond—that was a good three inches. I sat slowly down on the beach and tried to pull. No luck. The barbs would have to be cut out and soon, before the wound started to hurt. We had no anesthetic on Porvenir Island and there was no doctor anywhere near us. I knew that Alfredo was working on the addition to Jim's hotel and called out to him. He called back that he couldn't leave his cement and couldn't whatever it was wait until later?

"Alfredo!" I bellowed once again. "Get me a sharp knife quickly. I've got a spear in my leg."

He came out to the side of the hotel and looked at me on the beach. He dropped his rake and shovel and screamed:

"Señor Jim, Venga, Pronto," then broke into excited Cuna telling the whole island I had a spear harpoon in my leg.

He took off in the direction of the hotel as though he'd been fired from a cannon. Jim and Machi soon appeared on a run. Jim examined the wound then straightened himself up.

"Sorry Honey, but we're going to have to get that out of you and it's not going to be too easy on you."

I told him that he'd better do whatever he had to do fast, because at the moment, my leg was numb and I wouldn't feel too much of it. He sent Machi and Alfredo into the Inn for a knife and the first aid kit.

In the interim, Jim turned me carefully over onto my stomach so that he would have an easier time getting to the spear. In the process, he turned a bit too quickly and one of the barbs tore loose, and my leg wasn't numb to THAT. I bellowed that he was murdering me right on the spot. The third barb, however, was fairly well in and once the first-aid material came, Machi started to operate.

Jim bellowed that he was not supposed to cut a piece out of me, but the spear out of me—"Not the flesh!" I moaned and wondered what it would be like going through life without a left leg.

"Jumpin Lucifer!" bellowed Jungle Jim and told Machi to give *him* the knife.

My leg by this time was throbbing and no longer numb.

"Can't see a damned thing without my glasses," offered Jim to set me at ease.

"Jesus God! Give *me* the knife, will you?" I shouted.

Alfredo by this time had taken to chanting on the sidelines. Soon he was joined by two other San Blas men.

"Be quiet and lie still. I'll get this out of you in a few minutes, but how can I do a good job if you're going to twist yourself all out of kilter and stare at your leg. Now lie down and stay still."

I collapsed onto the sand on my stomach and resigned myself to my fate.

Machi reappeared with a beer from the hotel and put it in my hand. I knew it would never take in time so refused it and told Jim to go ahead. He did. The next five minutes were not the most pleasant in my life, but Jim did a magnificent job under the circumstances and all I have to show for it today is a one inch half-moon scar on that leg and it's in excellent shape.

Jim dressed the wound and asked if I could walk on it. I got up and hobbled back to the Cuna Inn and had my beer there.

"How did you do a fool thing like that?" queried Jim.

"I don't know," I answered and told him of how I had aimed the spear as one is supposed to, into the sand and fired.

He went running off the porch saying something about wait a

minute, then he returned. He found out that the spear had hit a piece of coral buried beneath the sand. The spear had hit it and ricocheted back into my leg. When the force of the spear reached its full length and felt the rope pull it back, it had reversed direction and hit the leg.

"Damned lucky Sipu that it didn't hit three inches lower. You'd have a severed tendon to deal with."

A week later, I was running around and back in the water. The leg felt fine.

It was on a fine sunny Tuesday morning that I went to Aritupu Island down at the other end of Mandinga Bay. The Indians of Aritupu were the closest to the river area and I knew that word that I wanted to come into the river would get to the jungle Indians from Aritupu. I wanted to spend a month or two in the jungle region.

The most vivid memories I have of Aritupu Island are:

There's a beautiful Macaw parrot who sits up on top of the Council Hall Roof and sings its heart out every morning at dawn.

It's relaxing sitting here in a skirt with the rest of the women on this hot afternoon teaching English to a dozen local children. It's especially gratifying knowing that I can enjoy all the freedom of a topless bathing suit and not worry about being fined 500 dollars for my topless condition. Nobody even looks twice it's so common, and it would be considered quite silly to put a mola on in this heat.

Why, when I can go around in a mola-less condition does the fact that I am also human and therefore make periodic trips into the ocean due to nature's calling, draw such a gathering? They must wonder if outsiders have the same bathroom habits as Indians do. Well, at least now they know, but I've taken to scheduling myself for before the sun comes up and after it goes down.

I've never been so stuffed with food in all my life. We eat four times a day here. I felt obliged on a couple of occasions to go out with face mask and gun to help with the food. When I do the woman have told me I'm silly. The men will bring in enough to feed me. All that is necessary is for me to sit home and take care of the house and children. It's fun being female around here and I feel more like one than in New York where I am often times forced to compete and appear capable in a man's world. It really does belong to them and I'm all for letting them keep it.

Will people ever stop getting sick around here? I'm rather feverish myself at this point—been treating people all day long—they're even coming down from the mountains with malaria and t.b. I have no streptomycin for the t.b. and can't help. The malaria I've been able to keep up with but not for long. My medicine supply is dwindling once again.

I've been re-named, thanks to what I have no idea. My name is now officially Puna Sepo, Ome Nele, or White Sister, the medicine woman. I don't know who I have to thank for that one, but as of this morning, nobody says Sipu anymore; they say my whole long dragged out title in addressing me at any time.

Today is one of those rare days when a "moment in time" occurs that is unforgettable. I woke up in my hammock this morning and looked out of the door which I am situated directly in front of. A thin red line was blazing like blood in the east. Somewhere in the village a radio was tuned to Quito, Ecuador for we can get it out here. The sad lonely plaintive sound of two guitars came drifting across the whole village, as though singing the sun into being. Then a woman started to chant to her baby and the two songs interwove and joined, not fighting each other. The sun turned redder and the sea and everything for miles around was the same color. In the south the mountains rose, letting me know for the hundredth time that they are there and offering their peaks in challenge. I want to go soon into the river.

My nana or mother in Aritupu Island is a fantastic woman and much respected in this village. She is a "nele" or medicine woman and it is appropriate that the two of us, both being medicine women officially within tribal structure, should be placed together under the same roof. She has been taking me into the mouth of the river every morning teaching me the medicinal value of the plants which grow there. In return, and many people may be shocked to hear this, I taught her the use of three antibiotics. She is quite intelligent and learns quickly. My warnings of "how much" for a baby, young child, young adult and old man have not fallen on deaf ears. I have gone with her every time she goes to give any of the pills. I stand by and watch her treat her patient. She never makes a mistake about dosage. I am proud of her. I have taught her also two powerful American chants to sing, for singing and chanting is absolutely necessary for a complete cure in her culture. One is "Mary Had a Little Lamb," and the other one is "Sixteen Men on a Dead-Man's Chest, Yo Ho Ho and a Bottle of Rum." I can with all seriousness say that "Mary Had a Little Lamb" and "Sixteen Men" have effected and helped in the psychological curing of more Indians in the Mandinga Bay region than they have in any other part of the world. "Pop Goes the Weasel" is also another fine medicine chant. Nana singing inside that hut and me standing outside listening makes me hope that nobody will ever come here to tell them that these songs aren't what they are supposed to be. I am not playing games with helpless Indians. I have given them something worthwhile in the pills and songs. First of all a good cure, and secondly, in keeping with their fine tribal traditions, the songs to go with them so that a patient thinks he's getting the full treatment and therefore thinks his chance of survival are better. They consequently are if *he* thinks so.

When Nana speaks, she sways from side to side moving her whole body and it is a show in itself just to watch her express herself. She has one breast sagging lower than the other, as many of the women do, they favoring the left breast for feeding purposes and I found out why. It is often necessary to hold a baby in one's arms to feed it while stirring the plantains in the cooking pot. Since most of these women are right handed and stir the pots in the cooking fire with that hand, they hold their children in the left arm and offer them that breast to feed from. I wondered about this phenomenon of sagging left breasts for a long time before I discovered the reason for their being so. When Nana talks, however, even if it's to ask you a simple question like "Have you had enough to fill your stomach?" she will weave from side to side and gesture with her arms and legs and body. She needs the entire length of a whole sleeping hut if she is to deliver any kind of authoritative statement. Watching her is like watching a color movie and I am delighted with her naturalness.

Today Nana and I saw a snake at the river. I was alarmed and killed it with my machete. Nana admonished me by saying that I let an evil spirit loose in the air and it would surely go into a coconut tree and kill that tree. I should not have killed the snake unless he attacked. So ended my umpti-umph lesson in jungle law—never kill anything unless it attacks or you need it for food, and never kill a snake near food or coconut trees.

It was on a Wednesday that Jens and Elmondo, world travelers, arrived at Porvenir Island. Jens was a Norweigan boy and Elmondo a Swiss who would be returning shortly to his country to build a mountain ski lodge up there. The boys had been traveling through Central and South America for almost two years. Alfredo invited both boys to stay at his hut on Wichub-Huala for a few days and they readily agreed. Jens, however, lasted only three days in all he being frightened to death of the rat and bat population on the island. Elmondo brought a clarinet with him and my fondest memory of their stay was one night when he was playing the clarinet while Jens played a comb with a piece of paper wrapped around it to make it sound like an instrument, and I played on a rattle, while a choco sano raged outside the hut.

Once again, as it had often in the past happened, the sea came right in the back door and the entire floor of the hut was covered with a foot of water.

"Does this often happen?" asked the dark-eyed Elmondo.

"Only when it rains during the full moon," I replied.

"How can you stand it?" He further queried.

"I live with it," I replied.

They left the next day, both for their respective homes abroad.

It was on a Friday afternoon that a choco sano hit the bay area while I was crossing to get to Porvenir in a small dug-out canoe. The strength of the waves and force of the wind required that I turn into the waves and bail frantically to stay afloat. An hour later the storm abated somewhat and I paddled back to Porvenir with one arm, the other one being sprained in an effort to keep the dug-out afloat. It had often happened that an Indian was lost while out in a dug-out during one of these storms. The bodies were not too frequently found.

When I got to the island I went up on Jungle Jim's porch and sat down.

Jim came out and looked at me.

"What kept you?" he asked. Then taking another look he added: "Have a nice swim over?"

I had a nice supper and talk with two guests, which is why I came, and I went back to the island three hours later.

It was on a Saturday morning that the "Tours Thru the Lens" group of photographers arrived at Wichub-Huala Island. Eme spotted the 15 people and of course there were 15 potential buyers for her carefully sewn molas and moaned. Fulvia and the rest of the girls in the family were at Porvenir. There was nobody but herself to sell to the tourists. Then she spotted me. I backed off apprehensively, but she soon had me pinned down and was swiftly putting a black line down my nose and forcing the blunt end of a nose ring into my nostrils while I hollared that I wasn't going through with this no how. This was accomplished by inserting the open end of the nose ring past the fat part of my nostrils with a bit of grease. Once the nose ring got past this thick part (feel your nostrils—the skin thins out a quarter of an inch beyond that first thick part of skin) it could rest easily in the nostrils and look for all the world like one's nostrils had been pierced and the nose ring added. I didn't really want to do this, because Jungle Jim told me that one of his greatest and most memorable memories of my stay near Porvenir was the morning when he brought over a middle-aged married couple. I had been, as usual, minding my own business and helping with the housework when the couple came charging into the hut with their cameras and with Machi carrying up the rear. Machi had introduced his entire family and then pointed over to where Fulvia and I were peeling plantains saying:

"And that's my wife."

I later spoke with the woman and she was turning all kinds of shades of white when she discovred that I was American and fairly well-educated. She left in somewhat of a shaky condition that made me think that perhaps the plane trip to Porvenir had been a bit much for her. Later on that day Jim came to Wichub-

Huala to tell me that they had to take the lady back to the El Panama Hilton in the city and call for a doctor because she was ready to have a nervous breakdown because of what she's seen.

"That educated and pretty girl married to that Indian man and living like that in a hut and eating fish and. . . oh my God. Get me out of here. I want to go back to the city. Please get me out of here!" she had said. Jim was hysterical and laughing at the occurrence.

"She thought you were Machi's wife!" he exclaimed. I laughed myself silly with Jim, and soon when I told Fulvia of what happened, she cracked up holding her stomach and declaring that Machi would roll all over the cooking hut floor when he heard of it.

But now, this lovely Saturday morning, I wanted no more nervous breakdowns. I wanted peace and quiet but Eme was having none of it. She wanted me to get out in that street and sell molas until I was blue in the face. I was a part of the family and as such it was my honorable and sacred duty to assist her in this time of crisis in the absence of the rest of the girls. Protesting loudly and in my highest and best form of Cuna, I was pushed into the street and told to head for the advancing line of tourists. Of course, when the rest of the village women saw me, they started to giggle and carry on. I was wearing a red scarf, black nose line, nose ring, beads, mola, skirt, beads on arms and legs and I felt suddenly panicky at the prospect of greeting my fellow-Americans with a nose ring through my nostrils. I tried to get back into the yard. Eme was guarding the gate and tirades of angry Cuna emitted from her. Either I sold two molas this bright morning or I wouldn't eat in her hut that afternoon. Fine daughter I was. No wonder I didn't have a husband, I was too lazy to sell molas. On and on she went until I was fairly chased from the area to get away from her cries of outrage at my obvious refusal to pitch in and help the family.

I lost myself, or made a valiant attempt to, in the crowd of Cuna women, but I was a head taller than any one of them. Suddenly one of the tourist women spotted me, threw up her arms and emitted a savage cry of discovery-delight. I froze in my tracks and watched helplessly as she tore through the crowd, grabbed me by the arm and started to pull me out into the open. I tried beating her off with my mola, but to no avail.

"Look what I found. A white Indian—one of those albinos that you hear so much about. Quick, Mildred, take my picture with her."

In the meantime I was bellowing my nose ring into flying straight out away from my face with the torrent of angry Cuna I used to tell Eme where to go and what was I doing here in this horrible situation and she was a bad mother to make me do this. Look what these women were doing to her only white daughter.

"Here darling, now hold up your mola and smile. No, no, don't cry, I'm not going to hurt you dear. Just stand still and hold up your mola and smile. No smile. Smileeeeeeeeeeey dear-heart now won't you. Here's a nice shiny quarter to put on another necklace around your neck. Now we're going to point our cameras at you to take pictures and you stand nice and still now. O.K.?"

The female tiger forced a quarter into my outraged hand and I stood there glaring at the entire gathering, laughing women, clicking cameras, tourists, men, women, and female tigers with twittering nose ring hanging from my angered nostrils. All during this insane situation, Eme stood on the side-lines urging me on telling me to sell molas or she'd brain me. She came up during a film-break, during which time the tourists re-filled their cameras, and got the quarter from my hand. The female tiger with "Mildred," said "Look, that must be her mother. We must get a picture of them both."

Of course Eme accepted the money readily and grabbed my arm as though restraining me from breaking through the crowd and getting into a dug-out and paddling to Meditation Point to get the blasted bloody nose ring off my face. She smiled hugely for them and I continued to glare.

When the picture taking was over, one of the women, Mildred to be exact, bought that mola and Eme handed me another. One more to sell and I'd be back in her good graces.

"Mola bakay," I bellowed wondering what I was going to eat if Eme threw me out. "Buy my mola!" I cried in Cuna and went after the tourists. A tall gentleman examined it. He said "No," bluntly and went on his way. I went after him again. This time my disgust unfortunately came out "Oh Good Grief!" He turned to look at me and said "What did you say?" I cowered fearfully lest I should be discovered wearing a nose ring. It was at this fateful moment that my scarf slipped from my head and came down on my shoulders revealing my two red pigtails. "Oh No," I exclaimed.

"How do you know English?" he asked curiously.

"I learned it from the missionaries," I said quickly.

"Which island!" he demanded.

"Mulatupu," I stated smiling.

"Schools getting better out here."

"Well we're reaching a little higher educational level than we ever had." I forced a sick smile hoping he wouldn't call out to the people.

"You have red hair?"

"Yes, I'm a specific type of jungle albino that's found only in the end of Mandinga Bay and the river there."

"Listen, whoever you are, I know for a fact that no Cuna Indian ever had red hair. I don't know what you're doing here or why you're here, but you obviously don't want the rest of these tourists to know who you are. You'd better tell me what this is all about!"

I did and Mr. Eric Ergenbright, the director of "Thru the Lens Tours," thought the whole situation very funny, but I didn't.

He promised me not to tell anyone until the tourists were ready to leave the island, but asked if he might devulge my identity at that time, just for fun. I was trapped; woefully I told him that he could on one condition. He asked what that was.

"That you buy this thing so that my mother lets me back in the hut to eat!"

He did. Well I won't go into it in too much detail, but when the tourists found out I wasn't the albino they thought me to be, they were amazed and thought the whole thing a very funny trick played on them for their ultimate amusement. I still, however, was not amused and told Eme later that afternoon that if she ever did that again, she'd lose my friendship and I'd go sleep in another hut.

Of all of the days of the week, any week in San Blas, I liked

Sundays best, on Wichub-Huala Island. It was a quiet day, and even though the Indians did not observe Sunday as the day of rest, the pace was easier and life a bit slower and relaxed.

Many different images present themselves to me when I think of Sundays and Wichub-Huala. I think of Juan's Trading Store and the quiet porch off to one side of the building where I and my friends used to come to sit, talk, and drink the luke-warm beer Juan offered us. The National Lottery would be heard over the radio and each of us would look to see if we won or not. Traders came by with tickets, most of the time for sale. I can see Alfredo again scurrying home from Porvenir Island to Wichub-Huala to wait for this broadcast. It was the high point of his week, and don't let anybody try to tell you that the Cuna are not gamblers. Percentage wise, out of an entire race of people a good 50 per cent of the Cuna gamble legally and the other 50 per cent gamble illegally on the Lotteria Nacional.

Alfredo would listen hopefully while the three numbers were announced, his tickets spread out before him, representing most of his week's salary at Jim's. The number would be announced and he'd either be in a completely joyous mood if he won anything, or in a black mood if he'd lost. I remember one Sunday when he chased Eme clear across the island threatening to deliver her fully bound to the sharks if she so much as mentioned *Lotteria* again.

It was on a Sunday that a Nazi war criminal was discovered at the mouth of the Mandinga River at the end of the bay. It seems that Porvenir got a message via radio that an Argentine man had robbed a bank there and was last seen heading through the jungle toward us. They found the man and brought him to Porvenir and put him in the jail cell there below the Guardia barracks. He wouldn't remove his shoes that night to go to bed and the governor told the guards to watch out for the shoes. He might have a concealed weapon in them. As it turned out when they did take the shoes from his cell, the left heel yielded a picture of their prisoner in full uniform with Himmler and Hitler. I never found out who he was since he was immediately whisked off by Panamanian Security Police, but I hope he met a deserving fate. All concerned with his capture received hearty congratulations from the appropriate government offices.

I wondered what his thoughts were. Twenty years worth of running, and then to find his way here and to meet his capture via a tribe of primitive Indians at the mouth of the Mandinga. He had made a last desperate attempt to regain his freedom, but he would never be free from his thoughts of what he had done twenty years ago. I pitied the man.

Sundays, apart from that one though, were uneventful and lived in the slow certain friendly peace of the bay. I grew to love these gentle and beautiful people more each day and hoped, that whatever became of me, that they would be able to preserve at least some of their beautiful ways in the midst of the onslaught of the civilization which must someday come.

13

PANAMANIAN LAW AND THE SAN BLAS INDIANS

Legally, the San Blas Indian Reservation was set up by the Second Law of the National Assembly of the Republic of Panama of 1938, and reiterated in the Sixteenth Law of 19 February, 1953.

The Reservation comprises the following district of Panama:

The northern boundary is the Caribbean Sea from Shark Point at the Colombian border (77:35)to Colorado Beach in the west (78:55). A straight line drawn from Shark Point to the town of Cerro Gandi on the La Miel River would complete the eastern border. A straight line drawn from Colorado Beach to the and including the source of the Mandinga River completed the western border. The Cordilla San Blas formed the southern border of the reservation. This large rectangle included all of the off shore islands from Shark Point to Colorado Beach.

The town of Puerto O'Baldia on the eastern border was excluded from this territory and falls within its own right as a Panamanian town and not part of the reservation.

This law reconfirmed the ancestoral holdings of the Cuna Indians to be rightfully theirs and declared such possession legal. There would be government offices set up on the island of Porvenir in Mandinga Bay and an "entendiente," or keeper of the reservation, would be in residence here. This keeper of the reservation has official legal title of governor of a province and assumed the same rights as governor.

Article No. 6 of Law 16 adopted the measure of paying the various chiefs of different Indian villages in San Blas a definite salary for cooperating with Panamanian authorities, and a title within the governmental structure of the Republic of Panama for such cooperation: I will quote from that document:

"The General Chiefs or Caciques (there are three of them) will hold the Office of Inspector of Police, and each of these will receive a salary of B/90.00 (90 American dollars) a month. The chiefs of villages which contain more than 500 inhabitants will hold the office of First Class Policemen (Commissioners of the First Class) and receive a salary of B/60 (60 dollars) a month. The chiefs of islands and villages with more than 100 inhabitants and less than 500 inhabitants will hold the office of Second Class Policemen (Commissioner of the Second Class) and receive a salary of B/25 (25 dollars) a month."

Such payment has been carried out from my observations in San Blas. The duties of such a "policeman" are fairly simple: he must let the Indians in his village or district know what laws have been passed by the National Assembly of the Republic of Panama concerning the tribe or affecting them in some way. He must help the entendiente (governor) of San Blas keep law and order within the reservation and assist the governor in catching criminals who may seek to hide in the jungle or island villages in the area.

In each village of over 100 population, there is supposed to be set aside a jail in which prisoners are to be kept. (It has been the author's observation that most offenders are generally kept in either the chicha hut or congress hall and there guarded by two or three strong Indian men.) There are no jails per se.

The governor's duties are the following:

He is to keep his employees on Porvenir Island informed of changes in the law and instruct them in the existing laws. He is to maintain law and order in the villages of San Blas. He must meet with the chiefs of villages claiming any misinterpretation of Panamanian law concerning them, find out what the trouble is, then bring the problem before the Panamanian National Assembly for their rephrasing or further consideration. He must visit the islands and villages regularly and keep the National Assembly informed of what is happening there.

Traditionally, the Cuna, San Blas tribe has been ruled by three chiefs knows as "caciques." The law acknowledges their right to rule the tribe in line with the Organizational Charter of the Cuna tribe.

Also defined here in this charter is the right of a particular Indian chief to punish offenders in his village who disobey the Cuna Indian Law. If the offense is serious enough (murder, rape, theft) it must be reported to the governing authorities on Porvenir Island.

(It has been my observation that most offenses, big or small, are generally handled and dealt with right in the village where the crime has been committed. The Cuna have an expression known as the "Right way" and "The other way" expressing their desire to keep their own "dirty laundry" in the village itself. The "Right way" means handling it themselves and judging and punishing the crime there; the "other way" means bringing it to the attention of the Porvenir authorities. A particular chief of any given village always reserves the right, if he is not satisfied by the way a decision has gone in a certain case, to bring the offense and offender up before Porvenir's authorities.)

Rules have also been set up for educational help by the law. Education in San Blas reaches its highest point on the island of Narkana where there is a junior high school. Any particularly gifted student may enter competition for a scholarship to schools in Panama City or Colon in order to continue his education. There are too few, though, who do go on to higher education.

The law continues to describe the dues a trading boat pays when entering reservation waters to buy coconuts or trade with the Indians.

(It is interesting to note that some 20,000,000 coconuts are grown here during the course of a year. If these are sold for the average price of 5 cents apiece, the annual income for the entire tribe is one million dollars per annum. Dividing this amount by the present estimated population in the tribe, 25,000 San Blas

Cuna, the annual income per Indian is 40 dollars American. In an average household of ten people, therefore, the family would get an income of 400 dollars per annum.)

Additional laws state that the governor of San Blas is to help in any way he can, increase the Indian income by trade, commerce, and general business. Unfortunately, this governor's budget for that purpose is very limited which in turn limits his ability to be able to act constructively in bettering the living standard and income of the tribe.

Laws have also been set up stating that two mobile (boat) medical units are to circulate through San Blas tending to the needs of the people. I have yet to run into one, unfortunately. The most urgent need in the tribe is adequate medical facilities to deal with the increasing disease in the area, particularly tuberculosis.

Going from the Law of 1938, and 1953, let me pass a moment over the actual charter governing San Blas drawn up by the leaders of the Cuna in San Blas, called the Organizational Charter of the Indians of San Blas.

The leaders of the tribe and official spokesmen and governing authorities of the tribe are in the order of their importance:

a) The general congress of the Cuna tribe.
b) The local island and village congresses.
c) The three caciques (Saila Tumat).
d) The chiefs of the villages with more than 500 people.
e) Chiefs of villages with more than 100 people and less than 500 people.
f) Local island appointed police.

The general congress of the Cuna tribe, consisting of delegates from each and every village, and the chiefs of the villages themselves must meet at least two times a year on the principal islands in San Blas. A congress can, however, be called if anything of importance comes up concerning the whole tribe or a great part of it. These "congresses" generally last for about eight days. The caciques and the governor are generally in attendance. Thirty days notice is given to the governor at Porvenir when a general congress is to be held.

During these eight days, the three principal chiefs speak to delegations from different islands and find out what the particular problems are from each and every district. These are then brought out and discussed in full meeting with the representatives of the Panamanian government. During this time also, the customs and traditions of the tribe are spoken of and any changes that are to be made are made then. Anyone attending this congress has the right to speak and the congress can run over for weeks until anyone has had his say in a particular subject that interests him or concerns his district.

Some of the subjects discussed in recent congresses are as follows:

The needs of the people with regard to their eventual education and progress within San Blas; conservation of traditions, dress, the Indian religion, music and language; the need to keep the family and villages intact; conservation of the Indian community and other subjects.

It is from these meetings that the governor of San Blas gets his information on what is happening within the tribe. Here he receives requests which he is asked to discuss with the National Assembly of the Republic of Panama. It is also interesting to note that the governor has the right to speak or give his opinion on any given subject, but the right to vote is reserved only for Indian council members from the different islands.

All in all, the laws that have been set up by the Republic of Panama are good and the Indians and Panamanians seem to get along with the present bevy of laws rather well. But I must state that it is still necessary for the two elements to get together at one time or another and discuss *mutual understanding* of one people toward the other; this understanding is still somewhat lacking. It is also my belief that an additional few schools and, of course, adequate medical facilities should be introduced into the reservation, but adequate funds must be set aside by the National Assembly of the Republic of Panama for this purpose at a future date.

14
CANGANDI

Every morning I watched the mountains in the south grow out of the land to dominate the bay with their green figures. I knew that the time had come for the two of us to meet. I was becoming too lazy and secure in my Wichub-Huala home with Alfredo's family. The days and nights blended into each other in an unending chain of complete union with the sea and the jungle and the island on which we dwelt.

The reasons why Indians stayed Indians and lived the way that they did were perfectly apparent to me—it required a minimum of effort to be an Indian—the life was a secure one in one's own strength, a close one with the rest of one's fellow islanders, and a life lived in relative happiness. I was completely accepted into the village by now, being both a medicine woman in the tribal structure and having my own family, Alfredo's. No one even looked up from work of making a basket or cleaning fish when I walked past. My comings and goings were as free as those of all the rest of the Indians, and everybody always knew what the other person was doing and where he had been at such and such a time. It seemed to me by now that I had lived on Wichub-Huala for a good fourth of my life. These people were close to me, closer it seemed than I had ever been to any group of friends or nextdoor neighbors. Funny, the whole population of Wichub-Huala Island could be put into one New York apartment building of ten floors height and yet, the relationships of people to people here were so completely different. I wondered what it would be like having the same friendly relationships with an entire building full of New Yorkers—but that was clearly impossible. Even I desire privacy in the city. That is a New Yorker's most prized possession, privacy. Still, it would be an ideal situation if an entire apartment building full of people got together and lived as a village did, and in the same closeness. I knew that when the time came to leave I would miss these people very much, and I knew they would equally miss me. Yet, there were the mountains, there was the river, and there were the jungle Indians. One morning, Eme, my Wichub-Huala mother and wife of Alfredo, caught me in the back yard looking at the mountains as I had done for the last week.

"Be ni sapuro?" she asked, "You're going to the Jungle?"

"An Penje buketara, Nana," I said, "I think about it a lot."

She stood in the middle of the back yard thinking about what I had just said and examining the dirt near her feet. She sighed and spoke in a low voice:

"Ni," she said, "Go."

I nodded my head, but didn't smile. I knew that she didn't want me to go back in there and for two weeks had been telling me of the fierceness of the animals, and of the fact that many bad, bad snakes dwelled near the rivers and up in the mountains. I had one natural history book with me that had pictures inserted within its pages. She pointed to, and in quick succession, a tiger, an elephant, a giraffe, a rhinoceros, a gaboon viper and a vulture telling me that the jungle was literally crawling with enormous quantities of each. The Panamanian jungle, of course, contains no such beasts. It would be bad for me if I did go. Surely I would be caught by any one or more of these monsters and devoured right on the spot. But now she knew that I was going and she was sad. Later on that morning I heard her chanting a high pitched chant in the formal language of the Cuna, within the sleeping hut, asking the good spirits to keep me well during my trip.

I spoke with Jungle Jim later on that afternoon and mentioned that I would be going back into the Big Mandinga Region soon.

"Why do you want to do that? You can stay here on the nearby islands and study the people just as well, and maybe even better than back in that malaria-filled jungle. You know, Grandma, that's jungle back there—thick, real jungle. You've got snakes all over the place, and some pretty bad ones at that. Get yourself bitten and you've had it unless you've got anti-venom. You got some?"

"No, unfortunately, I don't, but the Indians have a pretty good snake bite medicine. I've seen it work on a couple of occasions."

"Tell that to yourself, you damned New York lounge lizard, when you find a fer-de-lance hanging on your big toe."

"I'll try not to let that happen," I stated getting disgusted again. It seemed that everytime I tried to do something worthwhile, Jungle Jim would veto it at the top of his very very powerful lungs.

"Going off by yourself in the jungle, my God girl, they've got jaguar back there that could, I'm not saying will, just could, kill you in 30 seconds flat!"

"I know that they never attack unless you've wounded one or it's a rogue."

"What are you going to do, stop and ask it if somebody's been shooting at it lately or whether it's getting a bit too old to hunt on its own? Good God save me from fanatics and New York red-headed women! What do you want to go and run around back there . . . they'll drag you out flat on your back, dying of malaria in three weeks flat."

"Jim," I interjected.

"And not only that, you're four days away from the *nearest* civilization and there's no doctor here. What in the hell are we supposed to do if you get carried back here hurt or sick or with a blow gun dart in your other leg?"

"Jim, I'm going," I stated staring belligerntly at him.

"Well, there's not much I can say to you, is there? You're as stubborn as a damned mule. Just do this one thing for me will you please? For God's sake don't go over the Colombian mountains cause they got head-hunters down a few hundred miles over on the other side and with that head of hair, we'd never see you again. The shrunken head of a red-head is worth 50 dollars tourist prices."

I laughed and said "Jim, I'm not going to Ecuador, I'm going into the Mandinga. I seriously doubt if I'm going to travel over 125 miles worth of jungle unless there's a pretty good reason for it."

"Knowing you, ya lounge lizard, you'd go and invent one!" he stated in a voice the whole island could hear.

Machi, laughing, came out and gave us both a beer and we sat discussing how the tourist trade was doing lately. I returned to Wichub-Huala for the afternoon a bit later.

As fate would have it, a man from Aritupu, Nana's husband from that island, came the next morning via dug-out on a wind-blown Mandinga Bay to deliver and sell some plantains and bananas that he'd gathered from the river area. He also delivered a message to me from the chiefs of the Indian villages back in the mountains:

"Daniqoait!" "Come!"

"When can you take me?" I asked excitedly.

"I leave in ten minutes."

"What luck," I thought. I had been thinking that it would take all of at least a week to get off the island and begin my trip. Things do not move swiftly in Indian lands. I was overjoyed at the swiftness with which I was to be whisked off into the jungle and readily agreed to gather my belongings and depart with Linares, as the Indian was called. I was also anxious to see Nana, my Aritupu mother again, and talk with her. Eme, my Wichub-Hualan mother, came out of the sleeping hut and looked at me. She went back into the darkness of the hut and emerged with two hands of lady finger bananas, all ripe and ready to eat. These she put into the waiting Linares dug-out. The weather was a bit rough, and it looked as though it might rain and I wondered about the logic of making the long trip at that moment. Yet, I knew that if I didn't go then, it might be days or weeks before I'd get another chance to leave. I decided to go. I had packed all the things I would need for my stay in the jungle, having checked over a list of these the afternoon before when I made up my mind to leave as soon as the chance came.

Nana Eme and I said our "tage malos" or "See you later" which is the only way an Indian will ever say good-bye, and Linares and I put out into the bay. We no sooner got our dug-out past Nalu Nega Island than I realized that traveling on this day was going to be a bit rough. Water from the high waves was already finding its way over the port side of the dug-out and I had to cover all of my belongings with my tarpaulin-tent-convertable rubber hammock that I have the U. S. Army to thank for. Little did I realize how dangerous and back-breaking the trip was going to be.

We paused off of Nalu Nega Island and Linares started to put up the sail to take advantage of the wind. I hoped he would finish quickly. There was a rather ugly looking outcrop of coral to our starboard and the wind was doing its best to push us right into it. I was beginning to regret my decision to go right then and there. The sail went up and we took off with such speed that Linares and I were both startled. We both realized that it wasn't such a good idea at the same time; then the dug-out almost tipped starboard and capsized from the force of the wind; both of us found ourselves hanging over the port side for dear life to keep our craft upright. I caught a piece of rope from the mast and hung further over the side hanging onto it to keep from being lost under the waves. By this time I was already drenched, but that didn't matter as long as we stayed afloat. Linares was looking somewhat hysterical at the stern and clutched the large paddle against his chest in an effort to keep us headed toward a point of land across the bay. Hopefully we would reach it. I noticed, somewhat apprehensively, that there were no other canoes in sight on the entire bay, which I could only see when we went up on a wave. Neither Linares nor I dared change our positions to get the sail itself down. We were so delicately balanced as it was, that a stronger than average gust would have been disastrous. I did not relish swimming two miles through the water to get back to land in those waves. For 20 minutes we balanced the *Ulu,* she headed straight toward the jutting salvation of the peninsula of jungle mainland to the southwest. We did not say a word. Only once did Linares give any indication that we might be in a bad situation—a gust of wind turned us at a 90 degree angle and he went right over the port side of the stern to keep us from tipping. I was hanging as far as I could up front and couldn't go any further over the side at that point. My hands were numb from the ropes and my muscles were already locked in painful overwork. When we did reach the point, our speed crashed us right into bushes growing out from the land. My right arm received a fairly bad gash from a broken branch from my elbow to my wrist. Fortunately, no veins were crossed with the branch, but nevertheless I was bleeding quite heavily. Linares left me to tend my own wound while he got the sail down before we tipped. I tore off a piece of my Indian skirt and bound the wound, then helped Linares get the dug-out bailed out. We were half full of water by this time. Miraculously, none of my belongings were wet since they had been piled atop of coconuts in the boat bottom and therefore had been kept out of the water. I was still a bit worried about the arm though. I would be of no help to Linares now that it had been injured and the only alternative was to either spend the night here on this point of land, or let Linares push on if he felt he could. I dipped the whole arm into the salt water to ward off any primary infection that might have started, a rather painful action. Linares decided to push on and try to get to Aritupu Island before nightfall. There at least I could tend to my arm and perhaps rest for the night. The traveling we had to do, however, because of the fierceness of the weather, would be right along the coast line, hugging it all the way until we reached a point where we could get to Aritupu Island with a minimum of cross-bay travel on the waves. I was already tired and numb from being wet and from the effort to keep us from tipping to get to this point of land.

We started out again hugging the coastline. Linares used a pole to push us along the shallow coral reefs near shore. Extreme caution had to be used if we were to get past these in one piece, and I was delegated to keep a watchful eye at the bow and direct us with my one good arm in which direction to go so that we could keep off the reefs. This we did for four and a half grueling, fighting, dangerous hours. Then finally Linares decided to try the sail again, being exhausted himself and preferring to risk the waves rather than collapse on the jungle coastline. We had two close calls. Waves swamped us once and almost sunk us, but we both bailed frantically and stayed afloat. The second close one came when I misjudged the position of a submerged coral reef, and when the wave passed we found ourselves sitting on top of it and had to maneuver about standing on the reef until we got our dugout off of it.

We headed across the bay, once again hanging over the side, and within 20 minutes hit the first chain of islands known as Tupsuit, or near land islands near the mouth of the Mandinga River. The family living on the first of these islands called out for us to come. We pulled in and immediately we were taken into their homes and let rest. The family gave me a dry mola and skirt to put on while they washed out and hung up my wet clothes. We were given rice and coffee to eat and drink and these I attacked ravenously, being by this time starved from our efforts to get here. After resting for a good two hours I put on my still damp clothes and we were off once again. We reached Aritupu Island and Nana and her daughters were very surprised and joyful to see me and greeted me with loud cries of "Aiiiiiie, Puna Sipu!"

I was too tired and dazed to return the greeting and relegated myself to the nearest hammock into which I promptly and gratefully collapsed. Nana took one look at my still bleeding arm and sun-burnt exhausted condition and gave her husband a monumental tongue-lashing, the movements of which went in and across and back out of the sleeping hut once again. He didn't much care at that point and collapsed into a hammock on the other side of the hut. Nana quickly concocted a soothing salve for my burn, which was for the most part from the wind, and another salve for my arm, which she washed and dressed for me. As an added precaution I swabbed the arm with iodine before she put on her medicine, hoping that with the best of Indian and modern medicine it would heal in good time. I further had to put on half a dozen butterfly bandages to close the wound.

Nana got me out into the backyard and promptly drenched me with water from an island well to get the salt off my skin and body. I went in, ate another huge meal and went back to my hammock. I didn't wake up until noon the next day.

Friday afternoon, I joined the family for a visit to a nearby island called Narascantupu or Orange Island where they were having a Chicha feast. Nana had gone, however, because a young girl was in a very sick condition. My appearance on the island during a Chicha feast caused all kinds of a commotion. Evidently they were not used to any white people around those parts. For the most part, I was greeted with open mouthed astonishment and curiosity, not fear. Linares promptly exaggerated the trip from Wichub-Huala to Aritupu beyond all truth and soon men were coming up to me asking how Linares fought off the three sharks who attacked us on the previous day and almost killed both of us a number of times. Men looked admiringly at me, believing the whole misguided story, and again I was asked to marry a good half dozen of them. Linares was telling some kind of wild story about my wound, telling everyone that I'd gotten it when a moray eel crawled straight from a wave into the dug-out. Nana asked me if it were true and I replied in Cuna that her husband's head was broken more than a little bit. She replied that she thought so and was off to treat her patient leaving me to the mercy of the chicha hut and the people there.

My most vivid memory of this day on Narascantupu was in this somewhat drunken cheer filled hut. An albino Kantule was asking me for my somewhat battered hand and two fights were going on on either side of us, sometimes landing right in the middle of our conversation. He continued to talk and I continued to dodge from side to side away from the fights, but listening to his request with attention, trying to be polite.

I found out that the young girl, the daughter of the third chief of the island, had malaria and asked Nana to give her some aralein. The chief would not permit the non-Indian medicine to be given to the young girl, even after a hectic four hour conversation I had with him trying to convince him that the medicine would do her good. She died that night. We went home in somewhat of a down-hearted condition.

The night passed peacefully and my arm was healing well. Linares and I got up with Nana on Saturday morning, ate a hearty breakfast of bread, corn drink, and plantains and set off for the river. With luck I would be at a village in the jungle called Mandinga by nightfall. Linares warned that the trip there would be a long and hard one, and that we could not stop for a rest until we reached the village area.

There was no wind and the trip to the river was long and hot, our having to paddle our way across the three miles to the river mouth. Linares said that he would leave the dug-out in an old canal left by the United Fruit people some 40 years ago and we would go the rest of the way on foot. The plantation, which had once been a huge affair, had been deserted in 1925 after the Cuna revolted and hadn't been occupied since. The sun was scorching when we got to the entrance of the river and the net-work of canals. I could see the rotting dock at the mouth of the canal. It had been well-constructed and was still standing. Some kind of small sand flies attacked us as soon as we neared the canal, biting both of us with avid attention to any exposed untouched skin. We entered the canal and started to go up it. I could hear the call of the various jungle birds and immediately my spirits began to pick up, flies or no flies. Giant, many-legged roots of trees line the canal on both sides, and occasional alligators stuck their log-like bodies with telescopic eyes above the surface of the still water here. At one bend of the river I thought I was seeing a mirage, having spotted some kind of a two-story house on the bank which was now concealed by trees. As we rounded the next turn, there it was, and there was smoke coming from the chimney. It was in miserable condition, threatening to fall into the canal at any moment, and I was more than averagely curious about the smoke. Who in God's name was living there? Even as I thought, a woman, Negro and lightskinned, came out onto the "porch," if I might call it that. Her skin was wrinkled like the bark on a century old pine tree and she was wearing a torn faded house dress. Her face was smiling as we neared the house. She had a kind and intelligent face, whoever she was.

"Buenos dias, Senora," she said to me. I was too stunned at finding her there to reply.

"Are you American?" she asked in perfect English with a southern accent.

"Yes, I am," I replied staring impolitely up from my dug-out.

"Where are you heading for?" she asked with genuine interest.

"Well, I'm going up for a visit to some Indian villages a bit of a way up river."

"Well that sounds like fun," she smiled. "Why don't you stop up here a bit for some coffee. Don't happen to have any cigarettes do you?"

I replied that I did and that the offer of coffee was most welcome. I was beside myself with curiosity as to what she was doing here and who she was.

Linares, I noted, was grinning to himself. He looked up sheepishly and told me in an informative voice: "That's Ma!" "Big help," I thought.

I went upstairs after we banked our canoe, but the stairs one climbed in peril of one's life. Unless you knew that the fourth one up was not in too good a shape, chances were you'd break your neck before you reached the top. I clung to the railing, which was in as good a shape as the steps, for dear life. Coffee was already on when I got into the kitchen. I had no idea what to say to this woman or how to start a conversation. How do you say "My God, what are you doing here?" without offending someone.

"How's the weather back here?" I began.

"Pretty rainy lately, but the dry season's coming up soon and we won't have too much rain then."

"We?" I asked.

"Um Hum, I and my husband Jim."

I was handed the coffee. It was one of the best cups I'd tasted anywhere.

"Been around here long?" I asked.

"Forty years now, and more!" she replied handing me the sugar. I hadn't put any in the coffee and I always took some. I was still in a somewhat shocked state from meeting this woman.

"Do you work back here?" I asked stupidly.

"We used to help them there United Fruit people when they were out this way back awhile. But then they went away and Jim and I are looking after things for them until they come back."

I sat in my seat stunned. They had been looking after things for 40 years for a company that didn't even know they were here and would never be coming back? No, this was impossible, this really wasn't happening, she really didn't say that.

I nodded my head to do something to alleviate the silence that hung over the room.

"You wouldn't happen to know when those United Fruit people are going to come back would you?" she asked hopefully.

I shook my head slowly from side to side. How can you tell someone that 40 years of their life has been lived hopelessly. I couldn't do it. Better to leave the hope than kill 40 years, 40 years of living in a jungle.

"That's what our friend Jungle Jim says too. He don't know when they're coming back. He says we should just keep on going as we're going. This is our home. We're happy here."

My estimation of Jim went up ten points. He must have had the same reaction as I had listening to this woman and probably knew them both for a long time. Linares gave a whistle meaning to the Indians, "'hurry." I drank my coffee, left the woman with three packages of cigarettes and went back to the dug-out feeling as though I'd just inadvertently stepped into a Tennessee Williams novel. I looked up at the house once before we left, at the woman standing there on the porch, waved and smiled at her and we went on our way. We had to reach the village before nightfall. The whole contact with this woman was so unreal to me. Some kind of lapse in time had taken place and left these people behind it—here in the middle of a jungle with nobody but the Indians, but at least they had the Indians, and if Linares called her "Ma," then that meant that the people accepted and respected them. I looked back once at the woman, tall, proud, old, standing on her porch waving, then dug my paddle into the murky water and looked on ahead into the jungle knowing that I'd never forget for a long, long, time what I'd just seen and heard. I hoped that no one would ever destroy these people by coming back in there to tell them that the United Fruit people weren't coming back, except perhaps the company, itself, to give these people some kind of a reward for their loyalty and a pension to keep them comfortable. "San Blas, what a remarkable and strange place you are!" I thought.

An hour later, Linares and I banked the canoe against a shallow part of the canal that was protected enough if the water level got high from rain, so that the dug-out wouldn't pull loose and be lost. It had rained briefly the day before, out in the bay, but the jungle got a lion's share of that rain and was sopping wet. Mud was all over the small trail beside the canal, and oftentimes the canal came right up to cover the path. I sank several times to my knees in the muck. I noticed at one point after two hours worth of walking that the path was not only covered wih water, but that there was a small cayman ruling over the pool. We detoured around it. Linares told me that I was to be especially careful when in the water in the early morning and twilight hours when these caymans went prowling about in the rivers. Their jaws had the strength of "six men" according to my guide.

Walking was slow tedious work and I grew tired quickly. We reached a relatively flat stretch of land, that I learned had been sometimes used as an alternate airstrip for the big Pan American planes. After passing this field, we got back into the jungle rain forest and continued walking on for the next five hours up and down hills through the mud, mud, and more mud.

After two hours of this I started to develop blisters on both of the heels of my feet from my sneakers. I had put shoes on, thinking that they would be very necessary for jungle travel. Both of my feet hurt, but I knew that if I stopped to treat them the walking would have been much harder. We kept going. The trees and bushes pushed their tangled way down onto the path. Most of the time we found ourselves hacking away at the undergrowth with our machetes. Our belongings were tied to our backs with strong behuco vines to leave our hands free for any emergency and for holding our machetes. I saw very few animals during the trip. An occasional marmoset would screech in alarm as we passed, or maybe a rustling would go through the bushes, always away from us, and of course there were the birds, our constant companions during the long walk. I must report one fallacy which has been time after time again reported in jungle books in every different kind of language. The jungle is *not* teeming with all kinds of ferocious beasts waiting to leap out from every clump of grass or tree. It is rare when you will get to see an animal in its natural surroundings at all. I would love to report my different sightings and impressions of the jungle animals and feel it almost essential to have had at least one battle, that is always given in a jungle book, with a 50 foot long anaconda. I must report that there is no such snake in the Panamanian jungle. Unfortunately, in all the time I spent in the jungle, I met one large snake, a boa constrictor approximately 14 feet in length, and we both frightened each other half to death, it going straight up a tree, and I turning tail and running away at top speed. Reading through some books of exploration as I have done lately, I never fail to laugh myself silly much to the distress of my friends who wonder if I haven't lost my bloody mind. It's just that now I *know* that they are full of hot air, these harried explorers having battles with one or another of the jungle animals at least eight times a day and sighting every single camouflaged inhabitant in this clump of bushes or that tangley tree.

Much to the distress of adventure lovers, I must report to you that most jungle animals will go miles out of their way to avoid contact with man, or to avoid even smelling or seeing one. An attack by any jungle animal is a rare and almost unheard of thing in the South American jungles, unless there's some rare reason why this animal is acting so. It might be a female with young who feels threatened. It might be a sick animal who feels as though you're hunting him and he must defend himself. It might be that the animal has had contact with man before, probably white man and has been wounded in a battle with one. No Indian would *ever* let a wounded animal go off into the jungle. They always hunt and kill such an animal to avoid having a rogue or future bad contact with the animal on their hands. If it happens to be a jaguar that has been wounded, it must be killed, for it might come down from the mountains one fine morning, full of hate for man, and attack a young child playing in the streets of the village. But as I say, such an occurrence is so rare and virtually unknown to happen, that one may as well say that it doesn't happen.

But as the case was on this fine afternoon, we did have one contact with the jungle animal that was rather exciting, but again, not an everyday or every month occurrence.

Linares suddenly halted and began sniffing the air like some kind of blood hound. He then dropped to the ground and put his ear to it. I thought he'd gone mad temporarily. Then I began to smell something—something like the strong odor of pig.

"Quick," said Linares, "get into that tree." He pointed to a Sapa some 20 feet away.

"Why?" I called back already climbing the first branches of the tree.

"Pig—wild pig!" he answered, climbing up right behind me.

At this point I expected to see some huge pack of giant pigs with foot long tusks emerge from the bush. I'd never seen a peccary before, but as we climbed I caught my first sight of them—a pack of six of them breaking from the bush in front of the path and charging down it. A snorting sounded in the air and I climbed up higher and just looked at the gathering stream below. The first few pigs were female, and the leader of the throng was in the middle snorting his brains out. He was surrounded on all sides by young and female pigs. "A pretty cowardly way to travel," I thought, "sending the females out before the rest to protect him if any harm should be in the way."

Suddenly the "cowardly" male charged a pack I'd dropped in the path in order to climb the tree. He stopped inches from it, walked around it flicking his tail, then snorted revealing some kind of vicious looking fang-like teeth within his mouth. It didn't have tusks per se, but those teeth could do a heck of a lot of damage if they happened to fasten themselves on someone's leg. My leg slipped on a branch and broke it. The sound may as well have been trumpets heralding the approaching caravan of eight kings. The pig lifted his snout into the air and avidly sniffed it. The wind was coming from behind us. The peccary leader then uttered what can only be described as a vengeful war cry and charged the tree, the entire tree, squealing and snorting about its base as though, if he could, he would have uprooted the thing and had us both for supper. He is not, however, prone to act that way. He tired of this soon, and went back to the pack butting it several times. I was grateful I hadn't brought any food. With a snort, he gathered his harem and went charging down the path in the direction from whence we had come. Linares and I stayed in the tree for an additional 15 minutes just to make sure they had gone. When we climbed down we quickly gathered our belongings and walked swiftly away as silently as we could, virtually on tip-toe. Lesson 70—climb a tree if you smell or sight wild pig—they can hurt and have bad tempers.

During the ensuing back-breaking walk, I found the jungle start to swim before my eyes and called a rest, night coming or not. I was going to walk myself into a coma if I didn't. We rested for only a short while stopping to cut a liana vine and have a drink of the bitter tasting water it contained, and were once again on our way. Fortunately, we walked only for a short time before coming to a river again. It started to rain and my arm was now aching, along with my feet, head, and eyes. I knew that I couldn't go much further and hoped the village would be nearby. Sunset was already glowing low on the horizon of the river. I hadn't realized that the sun was going down because of the constant-twilight condition of the jungle floor. Very little actual sunlight ever reaches it. My legs had long since lost all feeling and were walking on their own most of the time without conscious instructions from me. We walked along the riverbank—I was soaking and numb once again, exhausted and ready to call it a day always after the next step. Suddenly I looked up to see a hut right across the river from us. A real hut. We'd made it. The river was swollen from rain and we clearly couldn't cross it in its present rapids state without drowning. Linares dropped his pack and machete atop it and cupped his hands to his mouth.

"Ahhhhhhhoooooooohhhaaaaa!" he called. He repeated this cry and soon a small naked boy appeared on the opposite bank and answered the cry with: "Hoo, hooooo!" Soon the rain swept riverbank was alive with life and somewhere from the shore a strange looking narrow dug-out broke away from the bank being paddled by two men and started upstream. I collapsed onto the riverbank and took off my sneakers. Both of them were blood stained and my heels were ugly masses. The men reached the opposite bank by letting the dug-out which had been paddled some 20 yards upstream, drift and turn with the current. Then they let the craft glide toward the bank at which we were standing. Linares crossed first with most of my belongings. He made it safely enough, then the men came back for me. When we had reached the opposite bank we climbed it and went up to the hut above.

Most of the men were wearing just loin cloths, although the women who had now come out of their huts were dressed in full mola dress as the island Cuna had been. They were smiling and excited about our arrival. A stately woman, evidently the head of the household, offered me sugar cane drink and I drank three gourds of it before the thirst inside of me went away. I promptly got out my first-aid kit and treated all of my various wounds and hoped that they wouldn't get infected. With this finished, I closed my eyes and leaned back against the hut. Linares had flung himself out full on the ground and was not moving for anything either.

All at once, excited chatterings broke out on all sides of me and I opened my eyes and listened to them. The women were all talking and staring wide eyed at me.

"Ige whey nega?" asked the mother of the house. "Where do you think her house is?"

I answered in a tired voice: "Ani nega Merkgi Nega—New York nuga an tupu."

"My house is in America—New York is the name of my island."

"Be sogay kaga tule be?" asked the grandmother. "You speak Indian, You?"

"Ayah, pepegwa," I answered. "Yes, a little."

They were delighted with this discovery and I was promptly given plantains and rice to eat while a small boy was sent scurrying off down the jungle path at full speed to I didn't know where.

"Ige be nuga?" "What is your name?" asked the head woman of the house.

"Puna Sipu," I answered.

Immediately on all sides of me "Aaahhhhs" and "Hooooos" broke out and the head woman of the house asked if I were the medicine woman from Aritupu, friend of this man's wife. I replied that I was.

I asked what the name of the house was. They told me it was the house of Inilupepe, and that the village of Cangandi was half a mile from here. "Cangandi?" I thought, "Where in the devil is Cangandi?" I had never heard of the village—why weren't we at Mandinga Village? Oh, it didn't matter, as long as we were in a village, but I didn't think much of Linares' directional abilities as a guide at that point. The women found out that we had walked here and were horrified at the prospect. I found out that the trip to Cangandi Village generally takes the men two days to make. "How far did we walk?" I found myself thinking, wondering if we were anywhere near Mandinga Village at all. It wasn't until later that I found out we were five miles off course and had walked approximately 17 miles that day, a heck of a trek through jungle in any land. Cangandi was the name of a village, and a river of the same name joined wih the Mandinga River six miles further down toward the coast. I looked up and was somewhat surprised to find that Inilupepe's hut was right at the base of the high mountains. I had been too tired to notice before. The young boy who had left some 40 minutes before came running back into the yard. He carried a message from the chief of Cangandi Village. We were to go there immediately. The men picked up both Linares' and my packs and proceeded to lead us down a path on the south side of the riverbank. After about 15 minutes worth of walking I came upon a graveyard by the side of the path, then five minutes later we were in Cangandi Village. I was shown into a hut and offered a hammock. I sat down for a minute to rest and the last thing I saw was a mosquito net being slung over me. I slept soundly not waking once during the entire night.

15

MANDINGA

I woke in the morning with a start remembering where I was, to find a young Indian girl staring me in the face impishly and with great curiosity. Once I opened my eyes and the fact registered itself that I was looking *back,* she cried out, burst into laughter, and ran away, leaving me shrouded in my mosquito netting once again.

Outside, I could hear the song of at least eight different singing birds and knew that the time was soon after dawn. I sat up in my hammock, pushing my mosquito net aside, and put my feet on the floor. The congregation that awaited me surprised me. Then I realized that I must be somewhat of a curiosity back here, and burst out laughing understanding why they were there. About ten Cuna Indian women and 20 or so children, along with seven men and boys sat looking at me, smiling softly and seeming to be waiting for something. They were there because they wanted to find out what the strange woman would do once she got up.

I stood up and immediately ten or more of the Indian children burst into fearful tears as though I were about to turn into a red-headed dragon and devour every last one of them. They snuggled closer to their calm Indian mothers. The latter congregation were laughing at their own children's fears. I had to laugh again at all of them—they were so child-like and warm. Their warmth seemed to send creepers out into every corner of the hut letting anything about know that they meant no harm to it. My own laughing had evidenly amused these Indians somewhat. They set about to chattering among themselves in the gentle, familiar language of the Cuna.

The hut I had been sleeping in hadn't undergone examination the night before because I had been so exhausted in reaching the village. It was about 40 feet long and half again as wide. Two rows of hammocks hung side by side—about ten of them in all. There were two doors—one in the rear and one in the front and no decoration except, I noted with amusement, two Kellogg's Corn Flakes boxes—one over each door. The usual closets of the Cuna, the hut's rafters, were drapped with Indian skirts, saburets, and blouses, and molas. A few sets of female and male river reed pipes caught my eye above what was obviously the hammock of one of the boys of the hut, because of the animal skins and necklaces which hung there on the hammock strings. I also noticed that my sneakers had been washed of their thick mud and hung up to dry in the rafters along side my hammock. My belongings were piled where I had left them, untouched—my machete, which I had kept at hand all during the long trip through the jungle, had been placed beside my hammock. It had been both cleaned and sharpened for me.

I stood beside my hammock and smelled the clean fresh sweet air that came from the surrounding forest. The absence of salt from ocean water was evident to my nostrils. Then from the back door there came the sound of men talking excitedly. Three men entered the hut. All of them were wearing a kind of baggy homemade trousers under brightly colored shirts—one shirt was red, another yellow and the third again red, but lighter than the first. The Indian with the bright red shirt advanced—he had a bandage wrapped around the left elbow of his arm.

"Be nuga Puna Sepo?" "Your name is Puna Sepo?"

I replied that I was known as such in the land of the jungle.

He proceeded to tell both me and all the people in the hut that word of the power of my medicine had come even as far in as Cangandi from the islands. He also told me that he knew that I had been to Ailigandi, and to Mulatupu and that I had been aboard a canoa when it was found by the Guardia. He also knew that I had been across the Colombian border and that when I returned I roamed the island of Isla Pino. He knew that my San Blas home was at Wichub-Huala in the hut of the second chief, and that I was a friend of the man called Jungle Jim. He knew that one day I killed a snake at the mouth of the Mandinga River and that I had been seen hunting the water near Porvenir for fish food and that I was a good hunter for a woman. In all, he proceeded to tell me in exact, unexaggerated detail most of the things I had done since I set foot in San Blas, including shooting my own leg with a spear gun, which caused some flurries of laughter in the room.

I was amazed. I had no idea that the jungle grapevine could be so accurate in acquiring news of my past actions. I was beginning to be very glad that I did have a good reputation among the Cuna, and that in all instances I had respected and obeyed their law.

"Ani nuga Themosthenes. Ani saila Cangandi—My name is Themosthenes. I am the chief of Cangandi."

This, needless to say, stopped me. I certainly hadn't expected to meet anyone with a name like Themosthenes in the middle of the Darien jungle, but let it pass by without comment. After meeting the United Fruit woman the day before, I was willing to accept anything that happened back in here and be prepared for it. I had, in my travels, met up with a young Indian boy named John Kennedy and a young Indian baby girl called Caroline.

Themosthenes proceeded to introduce the two men beside him. One was called Querpepe. He was the chief medicine man of Cangandi. The other was called Riekena—he was the chief medicine man of Mandinga Village to the south. I was told by Themosthenes that after I had washed up and changed, then had something to eat and drink, I would be called in the council hall for a meeting with the village elders and dignitaries, as well as the people of Cangandi Village. He flashed me a wide, lovely smile to welcome me once again, then left the hut with his delegation, followed by a flotilla of babies and mothers who decided that I was to be left in peace for the time being.

With their departure, a woman entered the hut looking like

what I can only describe as a frigate under full sail. It wasn't that she was dressed any differently than the women who just left. This woman was huge, very tall—about five feet eight—extremely tall for an Indian woman, and she carried herself with the impact of an African queen—proudly and defying anyone in her path to cross her in any way.

"Obay ni," she stated. "Go for a bath." At first when an Indian used to say this to me, I took it as meaning that I not only looked dirty, but smelled that way too. Then I got used to the fact that an Indian woman, man, or child will rarely say more than is necessary to communicate a thought. By now I supposed she assumed that I had spent several months in the area, that I knew everybody took a bath the first thing in the morning and again at about eleven, three, and at six o'clock when the sun was going down.

I took out a towel and got a bar of soap from my tiny writing case, fetched some clean clothes from my pack and followed her to the river. She expertly untied her small grey skirt from her waist and lowered herself into the river, not exposing a single ounce of fiesh that had been covered with the pecha, as the slip-skirt was called. I took off my still mud-covered clothes, wrapping a small saburet or outer skirt about my waist and dove in. The water was marvelous and I exploded to the surface in center stream blowing water like a sperm whale. She laughed and the laugh echoed into the forest around us. What a wonderful way to begin a day, in a pool a mile long at least. The woman spotted my soap and smiled. I knew they couldn't have much of it, if any, back here but she obviously knew what it was. I tossed the cake to her after lathering myself thoroughly, then dove back into the river water. When I surfaced, free of soap and the mud of the day before I swam to a rock on the other side of the river from the village and installed myself there to dry for a few minutes. Over my head in the sky two macaws called their cry to each other:

"Where are you?"

"Here I am, here I am."

It was so evident to me now that given a bit of time, one can actually learn some of the meanings of the sounds of different animals. The monkey's language was the easiest to learn. They have different kinds of chitterings for "Mother, where are you;

here is food; look out, look out; let's go home; give me that banana or else" and many other sounds, the meaning of which is easily learned by those who live in the forest.

I noted with amazement the comparative lowness of the river this morning to what it had been the evening before, after the rain. There was a ten foot difference in the height of the water within an 11 hour period of time. I knew from past experience that the river can rise quickly when it rains. If one is returning to a village and the village is near a river one half an hour away when the rain starts, more likely than not, one will not be able to cross the river when one reaches the banks. A dug-out canoe, paddled by someone who knows what they are doing, is necessary in order to get to the village. One can swim, but it is dangerous because of the debris in the river water, logs and all, that come down from upstream at a fast pace at this time. The tall Cuna woman was completely covered with soap from head to toes when I looked at her again. She went under water as I had done and succeeded in swimming the entire width of Cangandi river submerged—no little feat, as the river was at that moment 70 feet wide at the village.

She surfaced with a fish in her hands, one of the numerous little "sabalos" as the Indians call them that swim close to Indians when they bathe in the river. They picked at you lightly, getting salt and whatever food they can find from your body, but never would bite—they were incapable of it. They would, however, seriously frighten anyone who went into the river for the first time and whose head was full of thoughts of piranha, the deadly little sword toothed fish of the Amazon regions. There were none of these in the Cangandi—at least I never came across any. One man though, later in my stay at the village, was attacked by some kind of fish at the mouth of the Mandinga—his entire left calf had been ripped open by whatever it was. I was more inclined to believe that a cayman, the small alligator-like inhabitant of the river, did it rather than a fish. As it is, I have no way of proving the story one way or another, except that I did put the man's leg back together and knew that something had attacked him.

"Takwele," spoke the woman. "Come." She started to drift off with the current downstream. I dove off my rock and followed her,

When we reached the bend of the river I thought she was crazy. She was in a shallow stretch of rapids that lead to an even worse stretch 15 yards beyond. White water boiled over the rocks there. She was ten yards in front of me, and I watched her unbelievingly. She let her body loose, put her head in the water and proceeded to float, like a log, downstream straight for the rapids. I decided that what ever game she was playing, I was not going to join in and tried to swim back to the bank. I couldn't. A current had me and was swiftly taking me over the course the woman was now swimming. I saw the rapids coming and couldn't do a thing but what the woman had done, keeping my hands well out in front of me to try to side swipe rocks as I came upon them. Then I was in the white water. The force of the current was strong and I was carried here and there slamming against the rocks. I was through—I hadn't been in them for more than 20 seconds. We swam ashore and the woman smiled at me and asked me how I liked the children's playground.

I forced a small not too strong smile and said that it was nice, secretly thinking that the rigors of jungle life at Cangandi might prove a bit too much for me.

Well, that was that and I wasn't hurt by it. Evidently that's what the children did during the day. "Tra, la, tra, la" I thought and proceeded to examine the green foliage on all sides of us. We both got dressed into our clean clothes on the riverbank and walked back up the incline to the village. The village was about 30 feet above the present level of the river. That meant that the river probably got up 20 feet higher during the rainy season than its present level.

We went into the cooking hut and the woman turned toward me.

"Ani nuga Wardada, ani be Nana san be nika nega Cangandi." "My name is Wardada and I'm your mother while you have a house in Cangandi."

I acknowledged as was customary with a slight incline of my head and "Mmmmmm."

Wardada made the drink for the morning from cocoa, which she ground, and some sugar cane juice she had in a small gourd bowl to one side of the cooking fire. I helped Wardada get the fire going by fanning it with a woven grass fan. We soon had our cocoa drink ready and I had two cups of it. A seventeen- or eighteen-year-old boy entered the hut. He smiled warmly at me and put an iguana down in front of me at the cooking fire, then walked out of the hut again with his spear.

"An machereti—nuga Antonio." "My son—his name is Antonio."

Evidently, this was some kind of offering, since he placed it directly in front of me and not near the fire where game is generally deposited.

Wardada saw the blank on my face and explained that her son had been given the task of hunting for me while I was in the village and he had lost no time in proving what a good hunter he was. The iguana was also a token of friendship. When such a gift is received, generally the receiver reciprocates by giving a gift of his own—then the two are bound in friendship. Down in the islands of San Blas, the original gift would have been three eggs, since those were the best food one could give to anybody and were highly valued. I reciprocated by giving back three eggs to whoever left them with me on the next day. Here I went into the sleeping hut and got out one of the hunting knives I intended to use for trade. I found Antonio and gave the hunting knife to him saying:

"Ei nuadi" or "good friend" to him, thereby solidifying our friendship.

The small girl whom I first saw peeking in under my mosquito net earlier this morning came in and smiled at me. Her name was Sipu Pepe Wardada. That was equivalent of Little White One—she was lighter than most Indians, but considerably darker than my own rather sunburned white skin. The child, Sipu Pepe, Wardada, and I left the cooking hut and walked over to the council hut. When we entered, Linares, whom I had not seen since I woke up, came over to shake my hand and show me to a seat. I was shown to one of the council men's places, but refused, wanting to sit with the women.

Themosthenes was in a jovial mood and was telling jokes all around judging by the laughter of the men who were listening to him. He couldn't have been more than twenty-five or twenty-six. That made him the youngest chief I had ever met in San Blas. I was promptly made at home by Themosthenes who was swinging in a hammock in the center of the hall. He didn't disturb himself, but cracked a few jokes about the white Indian woman's ability to walk like a gold Indian woman through the land of the forest. The men thought this very funny and laughed all around. I could tell that Themosthenes found a liking for me and hoped this would induce him to let me stay in the village for a few months—two at the least. His word was law. If he said no, then I would have to leave—if he said yes, then I would stay. I doubted that he would refuse my request of the village. No village yet had turned me away, but there were some I had been told, in which no outsider had ever been allowed to remain. I had never found it so. Whenever a stranger arrives in a village and requests food and shelter for a period of time, no real Cuna village, particularly the more primitive of these in the jungle areas where the law was carried out in full, would ever turn him away. They believe that the very river at their door would rise and cover the village, or that the cooking fires would go out or refuse to be lighted. The Great Father and Ibeorgan did not look kindly upon disobedience to the laws of hospitality.

A young Indian boy blew on a conch shell that had been evidently brought up from the islands, and villagers began flowing into the council hall. The hut itself was at least 100 feet long by about 50 feet and quite large—large enough to hold comfortably the 150 people who finally did assemble there. I noted with amusement the presence of a radio, a transistor radio, right beside Themosthenes' hammock in the center of the council hut. If a village could get together the coconuts, and generally every village had several hundred coconut trees which belonged to it, the first thing that would be bought with the nuts was a transistor radio—the biggest status symbol among the Cuna.

There were two hammocks beside Themosthenes and I recognized one of the men I'd met earlier that morning, Querpepe, the medicine man of Cangandi Village. The other man was unknown to me.

Soon the people who had been quietly talking among themselves and watching me quieted down and Linares was called forth to tell the people why I was there.

Linares told them that I had come to study the ways of the Cuna of the forest. This was, he explained, so that I might go back to my own people in the United States and tell them all about the Cuna and their life here in the jungle which gave them food and shelter. Then our two peoples could understand each other much better. Anyone who wanted to, could call me aside while I was here and ask me about my own village, New York, and the life there.

I noted Themosthenes' head going up and down as he nodded listening seriously in silence. When Linares had finished saying the above in half an hour's worth of formal, flowery Cuna, Themosthenes went into a huddle with the two men on either side of him. It took less than a minute. Themosthenes sat up in his hammock and talked for 45 minutes. It meant yes—but it took him 45 minutes to tell the people why he said yes.

"Because you have been a good medicine woman and helped our people, because you respect our law and the forest, because you do not come asking for gold or money, but wisdom—we say yes."

How long did I want to stay? A year, two? I quickly stated that two months would be long enough for me. That was fine he said.

After this was agreed upon, I was introduced with much ceremony to the other members of the village council—to Esmilato, Elder; to Ginonole, Elder; to Querpepe once again, medicine man; and to Maqualetti, Kantule or singer of songs.

I was also told that the hut I stayed in last night was that of the Castilla house and that this would be my home for as long as I remained in Cangandi Village.

The young son of the house, Antonio, would be my provider and would hunt for me as long as I remained. Wardada would be my mother and would treat me as her daughter. Why didn't I have a husband? Why didn't I yet have children? He didn't give me time to answer, but went on to the next thing in his mind. Did I bring medicine? Yes, I stated quickly. Good, he thought, and I'd help the medicine man for as long as I stayed? I nodded my head yes. That was very good, now, there was to be a big Chicha feast in the village of Mandinga down the river a little later on. Did I want to come? Of course, I told him. That was very good. I was to go back to my hut immediately and change if I wanted to come. I would be going in Themosthenes' canoe. I wouldn't have to walk again and hurt my feet like I hurt them yesterday coming here.

"Querpepe!" spoke Themosthenes. The man sprung upright in his hammock.

"I want you to look at Puna Sipu's feet and put your medicine on them so that they will get better fast."

Querpepe was out of his hammock and inspecting my feet as soon as Themosthenes finished speaking. He had, just in case, brought some medicine with him.

"Why do you wear shoes, anyway," started Querpepe, "they just hurt your feet—and how can you climb or grip the ground with your toes when they are covered like that. Shoes are very bad. You should not wear shoes. Secondly, you should have rested and not made such a long trip in one day and through the jungle. You should have come up in a dug-out canoe like most of the women do." Why was I hurrying like that. He thought my head must be broken a little bit. He didn't stop talking until the yellow pulpy medicine was all over my feet and he was finished.

All in all I was touched by his concern for me. It wasn't superficial or a courtesy. He was really worried about my feet.

Actually, I was quite touched by all the people here. The openness and complete sincerity of the jungle Indians was unknown to me. The island Indians had this quality, but not to the extent that the jungle people had it. Already I trusted these people completely, even with my life, and I didn't even know them yet. Each person I had come in contact with so far had a distinct and wonderful personality of his own, even the little girl Sipu Pepe. I turned to look at her. She had a pipe between her teeth and was grinning at everyone cutely imitating the old grandmothers in the tribe who actually smoke pipes. I laughed and Wardada looked at her daughter. She quickly took the pipe away from the little girl, put it in her own mouth, and proceeded to stuff it with tobacco.

The council meeting broke up and I returned to my hut to change into my best mola and skirt for the day's festivities.

The Chicha at Mandinga was a spectacular, marvelous success and I can't remember when I enjoyed myself more at an Indian gathering.

Themos, as I called him for short, and Antonio arrived at the nearest point on the river to Mandinga Village via dug-out canoe. We tied up near the left bank of the Cangandi River right below the hut which belonged to the medicine man Riekena, who I met earlier that morning over at Cangandi. This man didn't seem to be too particularly thrilled with my being anywhere in the area and I had to tell myself to be careful this time, remembering the run-in I had in the Ailigandi area with the medicine man from Mamitupu Island. I climbed up the riverbank and found myself outside of a hut that I saw from the river some minutes earlier when we turned the bend. It seemed deserted and falling to pieces, but the hut directly in back of this belonged to Riekena and there was plenty of life in that direction. I immediately took note of the size of the sleeping hut. It was the biggest I ever saw anywhere, capable of sleeping at minimum 50 people comfortably in hammocks.

I was led by Themos over to a cooking hut belonging to this sleeping hut. Here I met a woman who was to become very close to me before I left the jungle area—her name was Nana Pepe Soule or "the mother who is not small." It was a very appropriate name for the roly-poly short but effervescent woman I met there. She was by far the fattest little woman and one of the most motherly I have ever met anywhere. I paused at the cooking hut door to marvel at her fatness. Most of the Indian woman are beautifully proportioned and as strong as bulls. She turned to me, flashing a half mouth's worth of teeth, and her eyes were beaming with that wonderful warmth that everyone had here. She immediately decided that an hour's trip downstream must have been exhausting and that I was most probably starving to death. I got a plate full of plantains and fish mixed with iguana meat put into my hands before I could so much as open my mouth to say hello.

"Be pepegwa pepe soule be—eunay—be nikowait nuadi meme san be nika susu." "You're small more than a little bit you—eat—you'll have good babies when you have a husband," she declared.

"How does she know that I'm not married," I wondered—then it occured to me, but of course, the jungle grapevine—that *New York Times* of the jungle.

During the course of the conversation which followed I discovered the reason for the large sleeping hut. Nana Pepe Soule was almost sacred to the tribe. She had given birth to 15 daughters, each lovelier than the one to come before. Eleven of these had married and most of these had children. This house would be one of the richest in all of Cuna country, with each of the girls marrying a boy with many coconut trees and the ability to buy her much gold. The boy, as is the custom, would move into the girl's mother's house, there working for Nana Pepe Soule. This woman and Riekena had started their own village here on the riverbank just by having all of those girl babies. The cooking hut itself looked like an Indian cafeteria—it must have been a half a day's work just to prepare the drink for the morning for a family that size.

The woman herself, Nana Pepe Soule, even if she never had a child was one of those women who is a mother—just a natural mother. The moment I set foot inside her cooking hut I felt as though I'd been adopted. She just assumed complete control and responsibility for me without my having opened my mouth except to smile at her. She was the kind of person you smiled at without thinking about it.

There were some nine children running around in the yard between the cooking hut and sleeping house. They were content with what they had and could amuse themselves with almost anything. Indian children received and needed almost no supervision. If supervision were necessary, say when the children were walking through the jungle and saw a bad snake, then the eldest child in the group automatically assumed control and the others obeyed her or him instinctively. The eldest child would tell the others to stop, then back track on the trail very quietly to let the snake go by in peace. From what I had seen so far of the Cuna, it was a joy to raise children back here. I have yet to see a bad Indian child. Their system worked perfectly for them. After thousands of years of trial and error, it seemed as though they finally found the answer to anything Dr. Spock would have to say about their own particular form of child-raising.

After thanking Nana Pepe Soule, Antonio and Themos and I got under way again, walking across the strip of land that divided the two rivers, the Cangandi and the Mandinga. Walking this strip of land was not as easy as it sounds. We had to ford one stream and got ourselves muddy, then another. The latter stream had a log bridge in use, but the bridge was also used by an army of red ants who didn't like the idea of anyone trespassing and made crossing not only a balancing act, but an endurance course. Red ants can bite with fair sharpness.

We came out after 40 minutes of walking to the riverbank of the big Mandinga and across the path was the village. I could already hear the sounds of flutes drifting across to us. We swam across the river, getting the mud from our clothes as we did, and reached the opposite bank where a huge tree had recently fallen. Themos said with much sadness that the tree fell during a rain storm killing one man who was coming downstream in a dug-out canoe at the time. The roots of the tree had evidently come loose from the driving force of the current in the rain-filled river.

We climbed the opposite bank of the river and went into the village.

The chicha hut of Mandinga Village was right beside the river and was already full with at least 400 or so people. The feast would take place at "yoruku" or noon by the sun. All three of us were ushered into Mandinga's chicha hut and fed with rice and coffee drink at a table set up right near the door for that purpose. It is the custom of the Cuna to first feed any new guest who arrived in the village during the Chicha, whether they were hungry or not. I personally was stuffed to the eardrums by this time, so just nibbled at a few grains of rice and downed half the cup of coffee. I mumbled "Mmmmmmmm" to say thank you and handed the cup back to the woman who had served me.

After we finished our snack, the chiefs and dignitaries of Mandinga Village came over to say hello. We talked for a couple of hours before the feast began.

There was one heated topic which brought forth many howls of laughter from the villagers—the height of buildings in New York. I drew pictures in the sand outside of the chicha hut to show the chiefs what my village looked like. They took this all very well—until I drew a man beside one. "Be kakansan Pepe Soule be," had been the comment. I was "lying more than a little bit." These people could conceive of nothing higher than the tallest tree in the jungle. A building like that which I had drawn was clearly impossible to build. Even those Indian men who had been to Panama City, and they were rare, thought I was building my speech upon water, as they put it. And as far as the rest of the villagers were concerned, they were the authorities. I dropped the subject being clearly unable to prove it, and went on to the subject of hunting. A lively discussion then followed with each dignitary telling me what he had hunted where and acting out his hunt in full vivid detail. The chief Kantule killed a jaguar. He had shot it, then it turned on him and he fought it with a spear. The medicine man Riekena had killed many pigs. By the time each man had finished telling his story, it was almost noon and we retreated to the chicha house for the opening ceremonies, which were very much different than those down on the islands.

The chicha hut was divided the same as it had been at Ailigandi. There was a man's side, then the Kantules in the middle, then the women at the other end. After several long rolls of tobacco had been smoked all about the room the Kantule invoked the spirits to come and purify this ground from any devils nearby. The rattles were introduced and I noted that they were red, probably soaked in chicken blood as those had been in the island ceremony.

The Kantule then proceeded to sing part of the song of life of the Cuna peoples. I understood and spoke enough Cuna now to understand what he was saying:

"God (Olowaipepelili) once had a nocturnal emission and from this there was born the earth. She and God then gave birth to three groups of living beings—the devils of the underworld, the fish of the sea, and the Golden Ones, the Cuna peoples."

After the complete song had been sung, the Kantules put aside their rattles and took long beautifully carved canes in their hands—most of these represented snakes curling up the stick to the head, the head of Achu Sapuro or the forest dog, which was a jaguar, jaguarondi, ocelot, or margay. Standing on the north side of the chicha hut, they then proceeded to run back and forth from their central hammocks to the jugs of chicha across from them. They did this three times.

At the end of their third run, when they reached the chicha jugs, they were each given a gourd of chicha. After they drank the chicha, they hooted and passed their canes on to other Kantules who repeated this same process. Soon everyone was once again drinking to celebrate the coming of age of another Cuna girl.

The afternoon was full of pleasant, increasingly incoherent conversation with the women of Mandinga Village. We would alternate our drinking with hourly dips in the river. We became relatively close that afternoon, each person both answering and asking questions in complete open sincerity. I have always held that if one really wants to get to know a person well, it is a good idea to have a few drinks with them. Then you can see them as they really are, and they can see you as you are. It makes for more interesting, sincere relationships with anyone you believe might be worthwhile.

The circle of drinking, then going for a swim was repeated six times that day before my villagers and myself went back to Cangandi.

Lunch that day was interesting—papaya (delicious), rice, coffee, bread (Indian, home made and very good), and bananas. It was eaten in the big community cooking hut by several of us. We talked to each other about what kind of cooking was done back in my village, then went on to keeping my hut clean; did I have trees like these in my village; how did I ever get enough to eat if I didn't; did my father have many coconuts and/or much gold; why didn't I have a husband; how many sisters did I have; what did I wear in my village; did I have many beads?

A huge fight suddenly broke out at the door of the chicha hut between two men who seemed intent on murdering each other. Four of the women with whom I was conversing, looked at each other, laughed, then took their beads from their necks and gave them to friends to hold. Each man's wife then leapt into the fight separating the two men and then, with the help of sisters, daughters, and mothers, quickly pinned the man to the ground. When the two of them had been duly downed, the eldest woman present who was a relative of the man would stand "akimbo" over his stomach and gesture profusely with her arms, bending back and forth from the waist. The rest of the family had either an arm or a leg or some part of their male relative's anatomy in hold on terra firma.

This eldest woman who was gesturing—in each case now, both of the men's mothers-in-law—then started not really hollering or hen-pecking the men, but chanting to them in a sing-song, high-pitched voice:

"You don't think of your father or your grandmother, or your babies or your wife. You fight like a silly monkey who fights over a banana. Think how sad your wife must feel seeing you act like this. If you are hurt wasting your strength fighting, then your body will not be strong enough to go to the mountains tomorrow and get food for your family. If you are hurt badly, then your wife will have to find another man who can feed her and your babies. When you married, the man you are fighting married. You played together when you were children. When his wife had a good baby girl, your wife had a good baby girl. How can you fight your friend who has lived and hunted beside you. Maybe your head is broken more than a little bit."

Within five minutes, both of the men were actually crying big huge globs of tears. The women released their men and the two went flying over to each other, hugging each other as though they were long-lost brothers. They had their arms around each other when they went back into the chicha hut to have a drink. The women looked on contently, then came back to the cooking hut.

"When are you going to get married and have good girl babies? Do you have a big river near your hut in the village? What is your mother's name? Your father's? How many blouses do you have? How many skirts do you have?" and so on into the afternoon.

I had watched the breaking up of the fight with much amusement. Later in the day, when and wherever a fight broke out, the women were there pinning their men to the ground and singing to them. They soothed hurt feelings, carried their out-cold men home to their hammocks, and on one occasion carried a cantankerous relative who refused to be placated down to the river and threw him in. Who needed a police force with the women around? I've never seen a more well-ordered National Guard unit as the Cuna women were instinctively.

Thoughts in the afternoon of the Chicha at Mandinga:

"Peace, Oh Great Red Ants cutting off the path between the

chicha hut and the Mandinga River. I'm trying very hard not to step on you."

"What kind of bird sings like two angels, is all green on top, has red-tipped wings, a long graceful neck, and long black legs?"

"I wish somebody had told me that there were small caymans in the Mandinga River."

"The expression 'Oh, go jump in a lake' is very appropriate around here. Most everybody does it at least two times a day."

"(In the chicha hut and overheard while watching a woman chanting to a sun she can't see because of the roof, and crying.) She's crying because she's all alone now. Her grandfather, her grandmother, her mother and husband are all dead. She has two babies to feed. The chief is going to give her another husband tonight. His wife died six moons ago and he has three little girls. She is very lucky to have such a good man with three good daughters for her hammock."

"Funny, the more I look at the chicken houses around here, the more they begin to look like missile nose caps. They are made from banana leaves and twine in the exact shape of a nose cap."

Late in the afternoon Themos called together all of the people from his village because of an impending storm. We could see and hear the lightning and thunder not too many miles off and the storm looked as though it were going to be a bad one. If we didn't leave then the river, which was already climbing the banks, would be uncrossable and we'd all have to remain in Mandinga for the night. Besides, Themos was worried about his dug-out. It was not too securely tied at the bank of the Cangandi, and it might pull loose if the river rose.

We quickly swam back across the Mandinga and were crossing the strip of land between the rivers when the storm hit. We all started to run, and run we did until we got to Riekena's hut. It was understandably empty—everybody had gone to Mandinga Village for the Chicha. We all stood under the shelter of the cooking hut roof until the rain let up some what, then a few of the men decided to run back to Cangandi instead of taking the dug-out. I was handed a banana leaf to use as an umbrella and then we were off, swimming the Cangandi and running slowly (everything was slippery: grass, dirt, plants, rocks, making even walking a navigational feat) through the jungle. The rain was suddenly blinding again and I had a hard time keeping track of the boys, women, and rest of the strong young Indians. There were several women behind me—some carrying a baby on each hip, but nevertheless, running sure-footedly and gracefully through the storm. We recrossed an already swollen Cangandi in dug-outs. I went running into my hut to find Wardada quietly resting in her hammock and feeling her chicha. She informed me that there was corn drink and bananas in the cooking hut, then turned over and gave me a sigh signaling the end of all conversation for the rest of the day. I went and ate, then climbed into my own hammock. I was lost to the forest world until dawn the next morning.

16
JUNGLE INDIANS

The days have been passing quietly and peacefully. Little Sipu, Wardada's adorable daughter, and I went out exploring in the rain forest yesterday minus Antonio Pepe who is recovering from yet another Chicha feast which ended two days ago. Sipu Pepe was quietly playing with one of the family dogs this morning when she saw me relaxing contently and looking at the trees and decided that if she were going to find out anything about where I came from or what my parents were like, it was necessary to teach me a few more words of the Cuna dialect. The first step in this lengthy process, she reasoned, was to teach me the name of every bush, plant, tree, insect, and piece of wood in sight and we were off at a full run to do this. She's about 11 years old or so. The child is one of the most active and playful children in the village, but she's also a miniature mother and woman. She can hold her own in any word battle with anyone in the village and is respected by her playmates and the elder folks. She's not physically beautiful at all, but has a beauty about her which can't be bought in a store or in a plastic surgeon's office. She has amazed me more than once with her statements about life, plants, animals, the river, life after death, and the raising of children. Her knowledge is almost frightening. She's like a warm wind in the early spring, playful as a tiny kitten, and as full of common sense as an eighty-nine-year-old grandmother. I would be proud to call her sister or daughter. This child is highly unusual—even for an Indian child. She is effervescent with delight in life and proud of the fact that she's fast becoming a mature woman. Sipu Pepe wants eight children—all girls. She has decided that she'll marry none but a wealthy San Blas boy who can give her much gold and many beads for necklaces. He must be a good hunter who will bring her and her mother Wardada much meat as her brother Antonio does. She and her brother are very close and the relationship of respect and brotherly-sisterly love is touching to watch.

Her brother Antonio is bright, friendly, and a man in the true Cuna sense of the word. Since he has a plantation of his own way up in the mountains, capable of feeding four adults, he will be given a wife soon and I'm sure he will make her a good husband being both considerate and possessed of a marvelous sense of humor. Antonio and I went up last week to visit his plantation and I was so highly impressed by what I saw that I must describe the place here. The boy has cleared the entire side of a jungle mountain of some 300 feet in height. Once there were trees growing there that were 20 feet in circumference at their base. There had been growths of every kind winding their way down the mountain side. There were rocks and vines, insect nests and snakes, animal lairs and birds' nests. He moved not only the animal nests, and young to another part of the jungle, without hurting any of them since he didn't need them for meat, but he also removed the jungle from a whole side of a mountain—an accomplishment which took him and his father who occasionally helped him five years to do. In the jungle's place grew plantain trees, banana plants, orange trees, rice, pineapples, and all kinds of little fruit trees were fast maturing on the mountain side. It was amazing to see the work that went into getting the land free of jungle, and plants to grow here. Two times a week Antonio Pepe made the trip up into the mountains to the plantation to clean the land and insure that his agricultural green thumb was in good shape. He showed his accomplishment to me with shining eyes and considerable pride, both of which were not enough to express what he had done. We looked down from the mountain into the valley below, log-strewn as it was. I shook my head slowly from side to side and laughed, not knowing what to say to laud this huge project.

Antonio turned to me and asked, "Naudi?" "It is good?"

"Ayah, *Nu-a-di!*" I enunciated. "Yes, it is *g-o-o-d!*"

His smile widened and he did a little dance all of his own at the top of the mountain for a good minute. He was happy that somebody else, not one of his own people, thought so to.

Antonio's relationship with me is warm and open. We have become good friends, and I trust Antonio in a way I haven't been able to trust anyone yet. He is a younger brother to me, and he treats me with the respect due an elder sister and friend. We go off into the jungle almost every day looking here and there. He points out the animals which my untrained eyes cannot pick from the forest. He signals listen, and we stop and listen to the song of some bird cherished in his heart. We have seen snakes together and always watch them from cover, looking to see where this kind and that has its home and how it will eat. He shows me the food which is growing wild in the jungle and which is safe to eat. He tells me what plants to keep away from least I should be pricked and have a painful poison cut from them. He has brought me to places in the jungle that have a special meaning to him, to a tiny waterfall cascading down the side of a mountain, a point in the forest where we can see the ocean and the land to the sea. We could pick out the islands up there on a clear day. He will see a particularly beautiful bird and imitate it, cocking his head from side to side and putting his arms by his side occasionally lifting one "wing" to clean it or spread it with his nose-beak. He will find the tracks of a meat animal or a dangerous animal and draw the beast in the soil with a stick so that I may know what caused the tracks. His pictures are possessed of a primitive, wild quality with a dash of humor. They always amuse me and make me laugh. Antonio loves to draw these pictures to make me laugh, and will oftentimes add a horn here and there or an unusually long tail which he shows tangled in a clump of bushes so that the animal has difficulty moving here and there.

He is brave too, but appreciates the inhabitants of the forest as only he can. One day we were walking up to his mountain plantation and our path was crossed by a huge, jet black jungle cat. I had no idea what it was, but Antonio told me later that it was a black jaguar. He said that it was not seen often in the jungle. The cat paused in the path, lifting its regal, beautiful curved head to look at us. We stopped and were silent looking at him. The cat was proud and there was a quality of strength about it. I have never seen a wild jungle cat look so beautiful and sleek as that one which stood in the semi-sunlight of the mountain path. After it had examined us, it walked on into the jungle, not running, but walking, knowing that we meant it no harm and that he was capable of holding his own even if we did. After the cat had passed Antonio turned to me, that appreciative light in his eye:

"Aiiiie! Nuadi, uhhooo!" The equivalent in English would have been "Wow! that was really lovely wasn't it?"

I replied in dialect that "Aiiie. Nuadi!" It was good.

Two days ago I cornered him in the chicha hut because he was drinking too much and had already been into one fight with the local medicine man. I burst forth with an angry torrent of Cuna, telling him that because Wardada was at home, I was now his closest female relative and therefore, if he got into any trouble, I'd have to carry him home. I told him to stop drinking like monkeys eat bananas. A group of women who had observed the entire word battle burst into merry laughter and commented that I'd better watch out because soon I'd have a Cuna husband if I kept acting like a Cuna woman. Antonio, however, found the whole affair very amusing and stopped drinking to respect his mother's wishes. Actually, I was avoiding the opportunity to nail Antonio to the ground and speak to him as Wardada would have. I could never have held him down long enough to give him a speech, and Wardada had left the chicha house in an inebriated state telling me that it was my sacred honor and duty to keep Antonio out of any more fights.

Antonio Tumat, the father of the house, is a strange one. Most of the day he just sits around looking at the wonderful wonder of the radio. Cangandi plays host to two of them, the village's which is in Themos' hut, and this one in the elder Castillo's hut. He is certainly proud he has one. It was the first thing I was shown in the hut by my host, even before I met the family. I have found out that although Sipu Pepe is Castillo's daughter, Antonio is not his son. Wardada divorced a Cuna man living down on Carti Island in the bay. Antonio is his son. In divorce Cuna style, the mother always keeps both the children and the hut which is her home. The divorced man is always forced to move out of the hut and find quarters elsewhere—either with his mother or father or a friend, until he can remarry and father more children. The child Sipu Pepe, however, is such a swan. I cannot see how Antonio Tumat, the Silent, could have fathered her. Then again there is a possibility that he didn't. Wardada will never tell though.

This radio, or rather these radios, rule the rising hours of Cangandi Village. They are battery run, and when the batteries run out Themos or Antonio Tumat will go down to the coast and buy a whole new radio thinking the other had just broken. They don't understand yet about batteries, even though I've spent hours trying to explain that you really don't have to throw the whole radio away everytime it doesn't run. Oh well, civilized Cangandi!

Every morning that I awoke in the jungle, it was the song of the numerous birds which awakened me. Then would come the sound of both radios being tuned into the same station—a Cuban Campesino program broadcast from Miami, Florida. This was at about five a.m. in the morning. Of course, these were free Cubans singing the folk music of their country, asking "What's happening in Cuba—I see a red banner there."

Most of the Indians of Cangandi Village knew little or no Spanish, but they loved this Campesino music. I should have imagined that the quality of chant and sincerity came through and that's what they appreciated about the songs.

It is a strange phenomenon, this love of the Cuban Campesino programs by the Cuna tribe. I heard these programs all the way from Puerto O'Baldia to Mandinga Bay. The whole tribe listens en masse at five a.m. in the morning and at seven in the evening. The songs begin our day and end it.

At any rate, this is how we began our days in the jungle at Cangandi, but that ended any civilized methods or appliances up there. Themos' hut is situated right behind Antonio Tumat's and he also tuned his radio to the Cuban songs. Consequently, I was treated to a most unusual listening experience in the jungle—stereo Cuban folk music mixed with birds and jungle. I often wondered if any of the animals in the jungle came down from the mountains to listen to the man animal's song at dawn. In the days and weeks that followed I realized that there was one bird that did come over, it seemed, for the purpose of listening to these programs and to "Sing Along with Free Cuba."

It was some kind of a marvelous parrot who sat and chirped his delight of the music in the tree outside the front door of the hut. He would arrive promptly at five a.m. every single morning and sit there in the tree singing with the songs until five-thirty at which time he went on his way. I caught sight of it one morning, leaving the hut expressly for this purpose. The bird was a cassanga parrot, or "wagi" as the Indians called it. It was a meat bird, and hunted hereabouts, but I couldn't see how anybody could eat such a marvelous and happy singing bird as this. He looked like a miniature version of the large macaw, so I nick-named him "Junior." I had a special affection in my heart for this bird and began to listen for him every morning singing from the lemon tree. If he didn't come (which never happened) then I would have felt that my day was incomplete and that there was something missing.

After this program would finish, Wardada, Sipu Pepe, and I would go down to the river for our morning bath. Rain, shine, storm, or raging river we would go to it for our bath. I remember one morning that an almost tragic occurrence happened because of the swollen rain-filled river. Wardada and I and little Sipu went down to the river and Sipu Pepe dove into the water in somewhat the same manner as her intrepid mother Wardada would do. When she came up, she not only discovered that the water was way over her head, but that the current was too strong for her. She went under with a yelp of surprise. I was high up on the riverbank and Wardada was undressing at the base of it. I cried out to her that Sipu Pepe was being carried off by the river, knowing she was closer to her daughter than I and could reach her first.

Wardada stood for one moment, then went into the water with a cry of "An mimi!" "My child!" I started to cry out loudly for the whole village to come and help and soon Themos and Antonio were at my side and looking feverishly at the scene below them. Themos went tearing down the river bank and into the river fully clothed. He was the chief and therefore responsible for the lives of each and every villager in the district of Cangandi. The women were the treasure of the village and if two of them were lost, a child and a mother, sorrow would hang heavy on Cangandi for many weeks. Wardada and Sipu were lost from sight as they, both clinging to each other, went around the bend of the river with logs and debris from the night's rain. Antonio and I, followed by the entire population of Cangandi Village, went tearing along the riverbank path to get to the next bend before the trio did. We got there just in time to see Wardada holding her daughter, go around the next bend downstream toward the big rapids there. If they reached this point, they would all be lost as the water there was white and raging. They had already passed the children's playground, now many feet below water. We ran on through the high grass again. We got there ahead of the trio, who were now separated by only a few feet of water, only by a super-human effort in running. Themos reached the two women, and Antonio, seeing that Themos couldn't pull them alone, went into the water above them and swam madly for his family. The water and now four villagers turned the next bend into the rapids and I knew that if they couldn't get out now, all of them would be lost. The centrifugal force of the water threw the four of them against the river bank and Antonio, whose legs were wrapped around his mother's waist, grabbed a tree branch and hung on for dear life. Themos then grabbed the same tree, only another branch and they stayed there, swaying back and forth dangerously in the current. Themos called out something to Sipu Pepe. Her hands slipped to his waist so that he could have both arms free. Her mother let go of the child and hunt onto Antonio's legs. Little by little, arm over arm, Themos reached the tree trunk and pulled the child from the water. Then he went back into the water, and both men, Antonio and Themos, went arm over arm with Wardada holding onto a leg of each, until the trio reached the safety of the tree and shore. A cheer went up from the crowd. I had just witnessed a feat of heroism beyond anything I had ever seen before. A dugout was sent to fetch the villagers and they were taken back to Cangandi. Sipu Pepe was somewhat shaken by the incident, but by the next morning she was happy and beaming as always playing with the family dogs, "Achu Chichi" and "Achu Sepugwa," meaning Black Dog and White Dog in that order. I was in my hammock at the time resting. I looked over at Wardada who was seated on a small carved foot high seat at the doorway sewing a mola. She stopped sewing for a moment and looked out at her daughter, listening to the dogs play growling and the child laughing. She sighed deeply and went back to her work.

Anyway, after our morning bath in the river, which never again got to be so frightening, we would go back to the hut and the men would come down to the river for their baths while we prepared the morning drink of sugar cane, coffee, cocoa, or corn—all raised right here in the village. After breakfast of the morning drink, the elder Castillo would retire to his hammock and listen to his radio. At about 11, he went off for an hour into the jungle to get the plantains or bananas for the mid-day meal. Antonio also performs this action, as well as gathering any additional wood needed for the cooking fire. No words are ever exchanged in the household about how much is needed of what. The men just look and see and bring it in from the jungle.

Today two more people have been added to our hut. A very old woman with a young Indian girl of about five or six. I went over to greet them and ask their names, but the old woman wouldn't even answer me and the child looked up fearfully at me. I left them to themselves. Today I learned a bit more about them. It seems that the child is the granddaughter of the elder woman. This grandmother once had two children—a boy and a girl. The boy married, then during a walk one day in the jungle a few days after his marriage he was bitten by a bush master and killed. The woman's husband was at this time dead, as well as all of the rest of her family—mother, father, and sisters. She had no brothers. Well, the daughter of this woman, a very beautiful woman from what I can gather from Wardada, married a very rich boy from the islands and soon was with child. When the young daughter gave birth to this little girl now in our hut, she died. The old woman's only living relative became the young child and indirectly, the girl's father. The latter was so distraught by the death of his wife that he left the village and the child in the grandmother's care. The father came up from Playon Chico which was his home island once a year to leave a substantial amount of paper money with the old woman for the care of his child. The woman and her granddaughter had no hut to live in, however, and traveled from village to village living with friends. Wardada was one of those friends and had readily taken the family in. In the interim it was being discussed in the council hall to build her her own home right here in the village.

The woman has been with us for a week, and I'm afraid that things haven't gone too smoothly between us. Her little girl, who is called Small One, was out playing with Sipu Pepe and me two days ago and enjoying herself immensely. The grandmother came out of the hut and spoke sharply to the child telling her not to be a friend to one of the children of those who had killed her grandfather and grandfather's grandfather. I was completely taken aback. The woman evidently thought I knew no dialect. There was much bitterness in her, but I was not to blame, nor was Ireland.

Well this afternoon Small One was again playing with us and for the umpti-umph time, the child was taken away with the reprimand that she was not to play with "Uaga Ome" or the old taunt, Outsider's Woman, a vast insult in San Blas.

"Why don't you go ask the council if I am evil and am being bad to you and your people?" I asked angrily. She spoke to me for the first time.

"Uaga Ome!" she spit.

"Does that give you the right to teach against the laws of the village?" I asked. "You teach hate to the child, not love. You are supposed to teach her the laws of the people and about life around her, not hate. You teach against the laws of your own people."

She calmly spat on the ground in front of me and took the child away. I was left in a complete rage at her and from that day on made no other attempt to speak or communicate with her in any way. I avoided her like the black plague.

Wardada was cooking at the fire this midday. She looked up at me from the cooking fire, sighed deeply and began to speak for no apparent reason.

"There is much pain in the old woman." She poured a gourd of cocoa drink out from the pot and handed it to me.

"You must think of the songs sung in the council hall—you know that it was not long ago that our people were killed for their gold. This woman is old. She remembers even recently things which happened. Her grandfather was killed, shot by an outsider. The child is all she has—as my son and daughter and husband are all I have. You must think of these things and I know that your heart will see the good. You will not think of the morning when you both exchanged angry words and have since refused to face each other."

I nodded my head and did not answer. She was right as she always was. Wardada never spoke until she had something to say. Later on that day I found a land turtle in the forest, a good pet for an Indian house. I called Small One and told her to give the turtle to her grandmother. I found the old woman in the hut later on that afternoon talking to the land turtle who had its head, still suspiciously half in and out of its shell. Then the head came all the way out and she laughed. It was the first time I'd ever heard her laugh. Two days later, I had been hunting in the jungle with Themos' shotgun, rather unfruitfully, and I came home exhausted. The old grandmother entered the sleeping hut where I was resting in my hammock and handed me a gourd of coffee drink. I took it, drank it, and gave it back to her with a grateful "Mmmmmmmmm!" which means thank you here abouts. It was her way of saying that the hatchet had been buried. No words were spoken, as usual, but the next morning Small One accompanied me on a walk to Mandinga Village and life was without complications once again.

When I visited Nana Pepe Soule that day I learned a bit more about the old woman. She had been very beautiful and the wife to four men, each of them dignitaries in the tribe—three chiefs and one Kantule. The story of her life was becoming more fascinating by the day to me. All of her husbands had died violent deaths—one had been shot by another Indian, the second died in the jungle in some mysterious way that I couldn't catch, the third died when he fell out of his dug-out in the river and drowned after passing through the rapids, the fourth, the Chief of Narascantupu Island, had been done away with by an attack of malaria. All of this had happened within an eight year period of time. It was said and rumored that the woman was so beautiful that God did not allow any man to remain in her hammock for more than one year before he went to the house of the Great Father.

Themos is another entertaining character of Cangandi Village. Yesterday afternoon he was in a rage, for what I have no idea. He stood in the center of the village which is between Antonio's hut and his own and ranted and raved protesting loudly against the whole world for a good half an hour, literally jumping up and down. He chopped down a few bushes with his machete and tossed a few stones and rocks about. Everyone had cleared the middle of the village to let him get whatever it was out of his system, but everyone was watching and giggling indoors, particularly Sipu Pepe who was hysterical. She was seated near a crack in the wall in the back holding onto her stomach and giving us all a running commentary on what the "saila" or chief was doing next. Suddenly there was silence from out there and Wardada and I rushed to the crack, being women and curious at heart. I was on top, Wardada was in the middle and Sipu Pepe was on the ground looking out through the crack in the wall. There was Themos standing absolutely still in the center of the village looking at all the cut bushes around him on the ground. He put the machete on the ground and started to laugh as though he'd lost his bloody mind. He laughed so much in fact, that he had to sit down. He continued to laugh amid flurries of responding laughter from all over the village for a good five minutes until tears ran down his face. He was laughing at his own display of rage and found it too funny for words or standing on two feet. His wife Eta came up behind him and stood there looking at her husband with folded arms and head tilted to one side, an amused glint in her eyes. He got up and went home with her still laughing.

Actually, the only time I've ever seen the chief of Cangandi Village in anywhere near a serious state is in the council hall. Even then he continually says funny things sending even the most serious council meeting into laughter. The only sad thing is the small white scab on his left elbow. It looks like a t.b. scar and I can't bring myself to tell him that it might be dangerous to his life. He's happy now—he'll have a few more happy years left to his life before he is in the same state as his wife's mother who is bedridden with the deadly disease. I don't think he knows that he has it. It is better that he does not. I have nothing to treat it with.

His mother-in-law is one of my favorite people anywhere though. We have often talked together, she telling me about the Cuna religion and history and I telling her about my own way of life which she finds amazing and very hard to believe—especially the fact that my island, New York, has more people than all of San Blas living on it. She finds this impossible that such an island holding all the population of San Blas could exist. Even in her bedridden state, she is the head of her household, bossing even Themos around when she thinks he needs it. She is possessed of a marvelous sense of humor, even though I know that she is in pain during most of her waking hours. She is a wonderful and strong person. Her greatest joy lately is watching over Themos' brother's wife, Tilar. She is with child and will deliver soon and Nana Tumat as the old woman is called says that she will live long enough to make sure the child is a girl, then she'll go to the house of the Great Father in peace.

November 1, 1963

All's well in Cangandi. But it's been quite a day for excitement.

Sipu Pepe and I were taking a walk this morning up to see Nana Pepe Soule near Mandinga Village. The young child was all excited knowing that with me along, she'd get fed twice as much as she generally was during one of these trips. I've never seen anyone as crazy about food as she is. Eating, though, I must admit is one of the primary reasons for life back here in the jungle. After I'd been here for a month or so, I began to have dreams about jelly donuts or pieces of bread. At every meal I stuffed myself, fearful of when I would eat again, but nonetheless sure that food would be brought into the village. I needed meat more than anything. I began to miss this addition to my normal diet immensely. The river has been low for a few days now and we aren't getting any fish. My whole diet is formed by plantains and bananas. That's what has driven me off into the jungle on my own, hunting. I'm not hunting for sport or for the joy of the "hunt." Any animal that had more than four bites of meat on its body became my prey and is. I stalk them with a kind of animal urge inside of me which I now understand very well. I was stalking a boiled side of tapir or perhaps a roast piece of wild pig. I have never hunted back here yet for a skin to plomp on my floor or hang on my wall so that one of my visitors or friends can say: "My, that's an interesting trophy you've got there. Want to tell us how you got it?" I have not saved a skin yet, nor do I intend to—damn waste of good salt to preserve it until I could get it to a tannery, and it's not edible at any rate—waste of work to no good end.

At any rate, Sipu Pepe and I were making our way down the riverbank still quite near the village, to cross the Cangandi River and go on our way when suddenly the child shrieked "naipe" or "snake" and there it was, almost underfoot and coiled. There was no time to let it pass, it had been coiled and was frightened and would surely strike. I threw the child behind me with my arm while I brought my right arm with machete down with all of my strength into the center of the pile of snake before me. I cut the animal into three pieces where it was coiled. In my own fright, I struck again two times until I had hacked the snake beyond any recognition. The head still convulsed and snapped shut, then opened and snapped again.

Of course Sipu's screams of snake had brought down half the village to the scene of the great massacre. I turned to find the child convulsed on the ground caught up in hysterical laughter holding her stomach which was her own private custom and way of laughing. I couldn't see what the devil was so funny about a snake almost biting one or both of us though and asked as much. The Indians who had arrived with spears, found the head in the pile of snake fricassee on the ground and I found out why. It was a harmless boa constrictor and totally non-poisonous. Given half a chance, the poor frightened thing would have leapt away into the bush as I would have leapt from the water of Porvenir had a shark nudged me on the shoulder with his dorsal fin and said "Good Morning."

I was beside myself with embarrassment to say the least. All of this heroic nonsense of throwing Sipu back on the ground while I valiantly dismantled the monster which threatened our life and home was ridiculous! The villagers were in an uproar laughing and I shrank quietly away, grabbing Sipu Pepe by the wrist and continuing our trip to Mandinga Village.

I was put out, and fairly so, however. I should have looked before I killed, but nevertheless the snake could have inflicted a nasty bite on either of us, and I felt as though this were sufficient reason to murder him out of our path. Later on that day, my own personal embarrassment for the great massacre put away, I thought the whole situation hilarious.

Back in New York now, I'm never able to watch another Late Show movie on jungle expeditions. I invariably laugh myself silly and nobody can really understand why. Well, I shall tell you: First of all, the camera invariably focuses on all kinds of teeming jungle life, hiding along the path that the expedition is to take. Lions, tigers, jaguars or what have you, monkeys and snakes literally swarm the area to an extent that makes me wonder what they manage to do when eating time comes round. There would be no food left after a week's worth of all those animals living on that particular stretch of jungle. The undergrowth is fantastic, the trees, the tallest grown anywhere, angled and hidden beneath vines and vines of behuco. Piranha the very deadly little fish of South American fresh waters leap out of every small puddle of water. Insects are devouring the participants of the expedition, now in sight. Now the general movie line of expeditions goes so: first there comes the trusty white hunter or native guide, or the hero, who dressed in a pith cap and expensive safari dress walks fearlessly into view, his handsome face looking everywhere for the slightest danger and missing nothing. He carries in his arms an elephant gun elephant country or not, just in case one does inadvertently show its snout in their path. There follows (if the hero has come first) the trusty guide; then dear watcher, there is the comic, funny man right behind the hero. This is the man who keeps saying "My God, what was that?" after every sound, and you can be rest assured that sound effects, the whole department, has outdone itself on this one. This is the man who lets you know how *you* would feel in this deep, dark jungle.

Then dear watcher, there she comes, the star of this whole segment of film, the blond-haired, blue-eyed daughter followed by her father, the aged anthropologist who is going to die anyway from something before the end of this film, or else! There she is, lovely, beautiful, innocent and her hair is in perfect shape, her make-up flawless in this wild jungle land. Daddy is puffy, and puffing from the effort to keep up with the hero's pace. He doesn't know yet that he's going to have to die in order to let the hero protect the lovely blue-eyed blond and marry her. Such is our trusty line, followed by at least 100 native bearers with packs on their heads. Now now the action, the suspense, the horror begins. The camera pans ahead a hundred yards to focus on the biggest boa constrictor ever to hit Hollywood. There he is, hanging over the branch that overhangs the path that the expedition shortly will follow. Get ready, here is the big scene; you know that surely something is going to happen!

There in the ever decreasing distance comes the trusty long, gun-bobbing line. Then they get closer and closer, the boa flicks his tongue out once or twice just to let you know he's alive and kicking—all 20 feet of him. Then you hold your breath, you writhe in your seat. *Who* do you think is going to get it? One by one the hero, guide, and comic pass beneath the deadly branch so loaded down with boa that you think it's going to crack. Then there she comes—the blond. Whammoooooo! Everybody knows that boa constrictors love blonds. He has her in his coils and she screams for help. The hero focuses his gun, shoots from the hip at 200 feet and naturally gets the snake right in the head. It falls away from the girl's fragile body. She hasn't even lost her pith cap in the encounter. She either faints then and wakes up and says "My hero!" or runs to the hero and shouts "My hero!" and then faints. Either way she faints. Then the anthropologist father comes up and says "My Son, it is a great heroic deed you have done today in saving my dearly beloved daughter." The mystery, the waiting is over. (Enter trumpets.) The girl's been saved, the monster is dead and Righteousness rules as it will in the end. You, dear watcher, sit back in your chair exhausted by the suspense. I sit back in mine in such hysterical mirthful laughter that the neighbors are ready to call the cops.

Now for the truth—first of all, no self respecting boa constrictor is going to attack an entire man when he can't even swallow one, not even the biggest can. Secondly, once that poor snake heard all that commotion coming down the path, he'd do one of two things. He'd (1) slither with all his strength into the jungle *away* from the ungodly racket, or (2) go up the tree, if that happens to be home and hide himself in his hole. The last thought in his mind would be to get *mixed up* with whatever is coming toward his tree! Attack? Not on your life! It's a wonder the poor boa they used for this film sequence didn't have heart failure after all of that.

I have heard and read about so much nonsense concerning the snake world. First of all, in every jungle book dealing with the South American jungles there is at least one battle described with an anaconda in the area of 100 feet or so. The biggest anaconda that can reputedly be given acceptance was 37 feet long. And *that is* the biggest. Boa constrictors generally will grow not too large—the largest being some 18 feet in length. Most of those I saw or encountered in my jungle were about eight to 12 feet long, relatively small by the standard. There are no anaconda, happily, in the Darien jungle. While in Cangandi Village Themos, Antonio, and Antonio Tumat did see something which surprised us all; it was a tremendously large, grey colored snake on the banks of the Mandinga River who went directly into the river when he saw or heard us. The length, and I'm being conservative, of that particular snake was in the area of 20 feet. Themos, just to prove to his wife later in the day how big the animal was, stretched himself out on the ground exactly where we had seen the snake, from the base of a large tree to the river itself and it appeared to be four times the height of Themos who is as tall as I am, five feet, four inches. In checking later with reptile houses of two zoos in the New York area, I find that they were very reluctant to even give the snake a name. The largest boa on record, and this was caught on the island of Trinidad in the Caribbean, is 18 feet six inches in length, and there are no anaconda up as far as Panama. Yet it was there, and I will call it a boa constrictor. My only regret is that we were unable to catch this snake to give weight to our story by photograph or actually bringing it back intact and alive.

But even this snake, which was the largest I have ever seen in the jungle, was frightened enough to go into the water. It didn't attack and would not have in any case. So, at the risk of spoiling many a Late Late Show, dear reader, the bitter truth has been said. There's a boa constrictor on my conscience crying out for vengence at the injustice of an early and violent death.

November 2, 1963

Went hunting with Themos' shotgun this afternoon, since my own is not faring well back here and for the umpti-umph time is out of kilter. My shotgun is a 16 guage and Themos' is a 12. His seems to be much more appropriate for the game in this area at any rate. I was walking along the river bank on the way to Inilupepe's hut when I spotted a raccoon. I was totally fascinated with seeing it there, I thinking that raccoons were native to the temperate zone.

I lost a chance at a good shot. Raccoon makes very good eating as I was to discover later. I went on to see two squirrels, a red variety, but missed both of them. My ability as a huntress, to say the least, leaves much to be desired. I sincerely hope I improve somewhat or I'll go out of my bloody head from eating plantains and bananas. When I finally do go home to New York I never want to see another one for a good three months! I'm also missing jelly donuts too!

Well, as it was, the afternoon would have been a complete loss had I not spotted several unsuspecting macaws up in a leafless tree near the river. I knew they made good eating, although they didn't have much meat on their bodies. Their meat was sort of sweet, but nonetheless it *was* meat and that's all I concerned myself with.

I came on them as silently and slowly raised my shotgun, aimed, and fired. The boom of the gun sent all the birds into the air, save one, who fell wounded into the lower branch of the tree. I felt elated and went to collect my bird, feeling good about being able to give Sipu Pepe and myself a few bites of meat this night. When I reached the tree, a totally confusing thing happened. The macaw was beautiful, even in its wounded state. Breathing heavily, it clung with its feet to the branch, one wing outstretched and shattered. But it was looking at me, and looking with a kind of stare that is hard to describe if one has never seen it. Its eyes were terrified and begging and yet accusing. It seemed to be asking me why I killed it when I knew it didn't have much meat to offer me. It seemed to tell me that all it ever did to me was sing in the morning, and in return I had killed it and destroyed its song. I stood cemented to the ground, not being able to take my eyes off the bird in its final moments, nor could I move from the spot. Then it fell, slowly, head dropping little by little; a shiver went through its body and it raised its head and expired. I felt suddenly sick and ashamed. I wanted to take the bird in my arms and comfort it. I wished that it weren't dead and if it hadn't been regardless of how mad the villagers would have thought me, I would have taken it back to the village and tried my best to save it. I felt like some kind of murderer. Yes, I had killed it out of the urge for meat, but that was an excuse of sorts. I had been frustrated by my lack of luck that afternoon and had turned the gun on an animal I ordinarily would not have hunted. Yet, it was dead, and so that it would not go to waste I brought it home and gave it to Sipu Pepe who was delighted with the gift. I refused the offer of a piece knowing that I'd never be able to keep it down. I never raised, nor will I raise any weapon toward the beautiful macaws again for as long as I live. Actually I'd make a miserable hunter because every time that I had killed an animal I felt a twinge of guilt in the act, as though I'd destroyed something irreplacable and beautiful. Yet, if I didn't have the meat from those animals I'd be pacing the floor of the kitchen hut, looking with open disgust at yet another meal of plantains or bananas. We had fruit, yes, but fish was rare in the village, and to sustain life on just bananas and fruit for two months is a frustrating and not too pleasant experience—so it was into the jungle once again to hunt.

That night as I rested in my hammock prior to falling asleep, I became homesick for civilization once again. I wanted a glass of milk, a piece of huge, thick, juicy steak, potatoes, ice cream, butter, chocolate. I wanted to walk a street with cement and no snakes. I wanted a bed of fluffy pillows and a rug under my bare feet. I wanted to sit on a Friday night at Fenjons in the village and listen to Manny playing his uke. There would be a room full of 200 people clapping, singing "Cherie Je T'aime, Cherie Je T'Adore . . ." and there would be 25 pairs of spoons clamping together beating out the song. The room would be so full of song and good cheer that the living of life would become again verified as a wonderful thing. Then of course there were jelly donuts. One jelly donut that night would have set me at peace with the jungle world around me. I fell uneasily to sleep.

As the days go by I am beginning to feel more and more accepted into this strange other world I live in—the world of the jungle Cuna. Lately, and often, Wardada asks me when I plan to return to my mother's village and if I will return at all. I tell her that in two weeks time I'll head on back. She asks why I must go so soon, and I tell her that it is necessary—my mother and father probably miss me as much as she would miss Sipu Pepe if the child were away. She thought about this a moment and agreed reluctantly. I think she feels as though I should stay and settle down and become a good wife and mother.

It's funny how attached one can get to a group of people. I could no more forget Cangandi, with Sipu Pepe, Antonio big and small, Wardada, Themos, and all the rest of the villagers than I could forget my name. The love I feel for these people runs deep.

Life here is physically demanding. Every time we move—even take a walk—it takes stamina, a certain kind of it. The country is quite hilly and a walk into the jungle can leave me dripping with perspiration and ready to drop from exhaustion, but much less so now than when I arrived here. My body is getting used to the demands made on it to keep up with a hunting party or when just climbing up a hill. I don't even need Antonio Pepe to start out for a walk at any distance now. I know the paths, the different routes of travel in the area, and have often gone out alone to be alone with the forest. It's an awesome place and can teach much if one is left alone with it for any length of time.

The river is flowing torrentially today. We had quite a heavy rain last night and this morning. The Indians are looking at each other and acknowledging this fact by saying:

"Wey tewar urway pepe soule!" "That river's fighting more than a little bit."

If it does rain back here it rains at night, then early in the morning. The sun will come out on time and shine until two o'clock in the afternoon, then it will rain again for about an hour or so, then it stops and the sun comes out again. I haven't noticed any deviation from this pattern within the last month and few days.

November 15, 1963

Two nights ago I assisted at the birth of a baby girl born of Themos's brother's wife. The whole village is happy about the addition, but none happier than Themos's mother-in-law who is beaming from her hammock. I was out walking in the forest when a young village boy, naked and sweating, came running up the path to tell me that I was needed back in the village quickly. I ran most of the way back not knowing what unearthly thing had happened, and found out when I got there that Tilar was about to have her baby. She was about 15 years of age and this was to be her first child. The girl was well into labor when I arrived into the hut, the contractions clocking at every five minutes.The village mid-wife was standing by and ready to assist in any way she could, which was no way at all in birth Cuna-style. All of the mothers of the village were running about preparing for the event. An old dug-out canoe was dragged in from the back yard of the medicine man's hut and the birth hammock was already slung in the hut. Both of these would be used in the ceremony of birth among the Cuna peoples. Other women were coming back and forth from the river with gourds of water to fill the canoe full to the brim. I didn't like the significance of the canoe and what the people were going to do with it, but I had no say in how the child was to be born. I had to be there, that's all, so that Themos's brother wouldn't die of a heart attack in the interim. He had long since been sent to Mandinga Village to await news of the birth, and all of the village children had been told to keep out of the area. None of these were ever allowed to witness a birth. Sometimes pregnant women themselves didn't know they were going to have a baby because nobody ever told them that that's how you got one. They just were left to think that they were growing progressively fatter and that was that. Sometimes the ways of the people are very hard for me to understand, but I accept them nevertheless. Two years ago, at Mulatupu Island, a young woman had gone out to nature's call, very very pregnant, not having been told or knowing that she was going to have a baby. The girl was found the next morning by the people; the baby she gave birth to there in the sea was never found. She was, of course, dead. A very unfortunate occurrence indeed.

Themos' brother had weeks ago asked if I wouldn't sit with his wife when she had her child and I agreed. He seemed to be much relieved by my agreement to such action, although I knew nothing about delivering a child. I had never been present at a birth before. I had a layman's knowledge of what the process would be like from medical books and that was that. I told him that I couldn't help out in any way, but that didn't seem to bother him as long as I was *there.*

Tilar was made to rise from her own hammock and get into the birth hammock. This hammock had a hole in the middle of it. She was fully clothed from head to foot in her best clothes, skirt, mola, gold earrings and all. She was very calm about the whole thing, and even when the contractions did come, she did not cry out or become alarmed. The midwife positioned herself beside Tilar and the rest of us sat on small carved seats around her hammock. The canoe, full to the brim with water, had been placed directly below the hole in the hammock, and it would receive the child when it was born. This was of course, a very shocking way to come into any world and I was very much afraid lest the child should be injured in falling through the hammock into the dug-out full of water, but I could do nothing for fear that I'd have a complete revolt in the hut of every woman there. This was *The Way,* and that's all there was to it.

The only man left in the area was Querpepe, the medicine man, and he was outside the hut. He sat on a small carved seat chanting the Song of Life and Birth of the Cuna peoples and chasing devils away lest one should by chance enter and steal Tilar's soul. He sat with a pot of green pepper incense in front of him but with the wind going in the other direction so that it wouldn't come back into his face and smother him as only a green pepper smoke can.

We waited in silence while the contractions came more frequently. Somewhere in the forest, the macaws sang their song. The hut was hot and sweaty and the songs of Querpepe drifted into us from the hut door.

We waited, then the contractions came one right after the other. We had been in the hut three hours then. Suddenly the old grandmother in her hammock across the room started to chant and the elder women in the room did likewise. It was a sort of joining hands with Tilar to help her give birth to her child. When the child came, Tilar gave her first and only stifled cry of the day. The child landed squarely into the canoe full of water and the chanting stopped momentarily. The child was let stand in the water for a full minute before anyone made a move to get it out of the water. I was becoming alarmed when the midwife went to the child and swiftly chewed the umbilical cord at two places. After appropriate knots had been tied, there remained a piece of the umbilical cord. As the baby cried shrilly into the afternoon, this cord was buried beneath Tilar's hammock in the rear of the room. The child had since been cleaned and wrapped in banana leaves. A thrill ran through me as I looked at the child, the dug-out, the mother. I felt privileged and amazed to have been witness to the whole wondrous process of a Cuna birth.

Then a very strange thing happened. Tilar began to chant in the formal council hall language of her people and all the women looked at her in horror, where there had been expressions of joy a moment before. The midwife, whose duty it was to announce what kind of child it was, hadn't even had a chance to announce this fact yet. In a weak voice the chant went on:

"Before the next moon is full," began Tilar, "my own mother will have joined my father in the land of Ibeorgan. A new life has come, the old one must go. Nana! Nana!" she cried, "Mother! Mother!"

All eyes turned toward the old woman's hammock. She had heard, her eyes were wide open as she looked at all of us. It was clear that even she and everyone present believed Tilar's words. Any woman giving birth is prophetic and can see into the world beyond. The old woman would die within two weeks' time which would be when the moon would next be full.

No one moved in the hut. The baby continued to cry shrilly. The old woman got herself into a sitting position.

"What kind of a child is it?" she asked. "You would keep a woman who is dying waiting?"

"It is a healthy and whole girl child," announced the midwife.

"Nuadi," said the old one. "Good." "My daughter as my grandmother and my mother have done, gave birth to a first child that was a girl."

"And Tilar?" asked the old one.

"She is strong and her body will soon be walking like her mother's did before her."

"Then stop standing there and go tell the child's father that he has a strong baby girl and that his wife is well. Then go home and feed your hungry families and tell your children that a child was found this afternoon in the jungle and it has been given to Tilar as a present from the Earth Mother."

All the women, as if awakened from a bad dream, then began to chatter excitedly among themselves. All went well and a good girl child was born to Tilar. They were happy remembering when they had given birth to good strong healthy children in times past.

Before I left the hut to go home and help Wardada start the evening meal, Old One called me to her. She didn't say anything further for a long time, but sat in silence examining as she must have examined so many times, the rafters of her hut. Then she turned her wise old dark eyes on me and spoke:

"You know Sipu, Themos has the same devil as I have."

I didn't answer, but looked at the ground. She knew then that Themos had the same disease as she, t.b.

"Do you have medicine for this devil?" she asked. I shook my head, hesitated, then told her that there were other medicine men, with much more power than I had in my tribe to the north.

"Is it possible then to bring one of these great men here?"

"I don't know, but they have a medicine, a strong one to fight this devil. It may be that I can get some and bring it here for you."

"No, it is not for me. I will join my husband soon, but for Themos . . . if this devil which fills my body fills his, my daughter will chant the death song at his grave before many moons and seasons have passed."

I hesitated again, then spoke to her:

"It may be that Themos will have to leave his people and go away for a time to the medicine huts of my people."

"He must leave the village?" she asked unbelievingly.

"I don't know, Old One," I replied.

"Why don't you know?" she asked.

"Because I know very little. Sometimes it takes a long time to drive such a devil out of a body. Sometimes it is necessary to go to a place where there are medicine huts that do nothing but drive this devil from bodies. I cannot say more than a little bit because I do not know much where Themos' devil dwells."

"But this medicine? Can you get it and bring it here for him?" She was now sitting up in her hammock again.

"I will try, Old One," I stated.

"You do not speak as the river runs, but as the rock sits! Say to me that you speak as the rock sits and that you will keep your word with me!"

"I speak as the rock sits, Old One," I answered.

"It is good," she answered. "Nuadi," and she waved me on my way toward the family cooking hut with her thin hand.

November 20, 1963

Well, we had another puberty feast in the village. It seems that all the young girls are maturing in one huge surge.

All went well, with one exception. Riekena, the medicine man from Mandinga managed to cause a bit of near trouble.

I was sitting and drinking with Wardada. She had been bubbling all afternoon under the influence of chicha, as usual during these festivities, and declaring "An Mimi!" which meant "My Child!" and hugging me. Officially, when a Cuna woman makes this declaration of an orphaned child in a full group of Indians, it is an official declaration of adoption, so as it stands I am Wardada's girl child in the village of Cangandi.

Well in the midst of all of this joy and mass drinking Riekena, who had long since left the land of the sober, came on over to the women's side of the hut and began badgering me without apparent reason or provocation.

"Outsider's woman!" he declared.

I lifted my head from a conversation I was having with Tilar who is now back on her feet for good periods of time and very much overjoyed with her baby. I looked at the man, trying to figure out what I had done to him to merit such a statement.

"Don't you fight like all outsiders fight around here or we'll kill you," he continued.

I was somewhat upset by the statement, but decided to handle it as quietly as I could without bringing all the rest of the village into the argument. He was obviously drunk and in a nasty mood.

I quietly informed him that I had no intentions of starting any kind of an argument and if he really wanted somebody to fight with, why didn't he go over and fight with his wife. I had done him no harm, why say such things to me?

He went away.

Fifteen minutes later he was back and at it again.

"Don't drink so much (I'd had a thimble full of chicha drink at that time). All outsiders when they drink start fights."

I out and out told him to go away and jump in the Cangandi River to cool himself off. He was hot more than a little bit!

He went off in a huff.

I shortly saw him treading his way across the chicha hut again, this time with a small hunting knife in his hand which threw me into no little panic. First of all, no weapons from blow guns to spears were ever allowed in the chicha hut during a feast just in case two men get into a fight. Before he reached me I measured the distance to the door and made sure my path of escape was clear, just in case, then let him get to within five feet of me and start talking. Immediately I started to protest in my loudest voice. All the women of course turned to find out what the hollering was all about.

"You're drunk more than a little bit!" I stated loudly. "I'm not married and have no husband or man and you are saying things to me which no man should ask of a woman who has no husband or children."

Well I have never seen the Cuna women's police force move into such quick action. Immediately a dozen of the village women were on their feet and threatening to bury Riekena on the spot where he stood if he didn't put down that knife and stop speaking to me badly. Wardada, shocked out of her stupor, was on her feet. She lunged at Riekena and took the knife out of his hand and I stood in horror as I watched her make a drunken pass at him with the knife. Fortunately, she missed by a few feet. A good half of the women were over at the other side of the chicha hut speaking with Themos. He came up and over to our side and gave Riekena a tongue lashing that would have shocked a civilized society. He was furious. He ordered Riekena from the hut and village and told him never to come back into it again. If he found out that any harm had come to me in any way, he would have Riekena buried for it. Well, Riekena started to cry right where he stood, telling everybody that he really meant no harm and wouldn't have even thought of hurting me at all. He said that he would never have spoken such words to me and that I didn't listen to him good. He eyed me fitfully and with fright, then rejoined the men on the other side of the hut. The whole incident was soon forgotten, but Riekena and I will never speak with each other again, that I do know.

Later on that afternoon the old grandmother who lives in our hut with Small One went into a trance and prophesied that death would soon visit the village. Everyone has taken this as a further proof that Old One, or Nana Tumat, is going to die. During the past few days she has been weakening visibly. Tilar, in a tearful voice, has told me that she is sure the old woman will die soon.

I got into another word battle with the chiefs—this time about snow. I described how it fell, looked, and stayed on the ground and once again I was told:

"More good stories—this time built on water which is cold, cold." This very clever thought was the contribution of Mandinga Village's chief.

November 21, 1963

This is the second day of the Chicha feast and I was told early this afternoon that there was to be a marriage ceremony later on in the evening. I was excited about seeing this, for I had not been witness to one such event since I arrived in San Blas. I was told secretly, for the young people did not know as yet that they were to be married, that the girl was one of Nana Pepe Soule's daughters, Titi Olo. The boy was from our village, Querpepe the medicine man's son. Wardada told me that she'd boil my skin if I said anything to either of these young people. I said that I wouldn't. This would come as a shock to both of them, that was sure. The boy is a strong lad, Antonio's age, about seventeen, and he is already growing more than enough food to feed five people in the mountains. He will make the girl a good husband.

Wardada and I, with excuses that we were making a trip to the river, left our hut and went to Mandinga at dusk. It was already somewhat dark when we crossed the Cangandi River and made our way along the river path there. This way we could watch the whole ceremony from beginning to end. I was delighted with the prospect.

When we arrived across the river from Nana Pepe Soule's hut, we took off our skirts and crossed the river once again, made our way up the bank by the light of the moon and on up to Nana Pepe Soule's cooking hut. There she sat in all her obese, wide-smiled glory and soon two cups of hot chocolate drink were handed to us and she was chattering away gaily.

She told us that all of this had been planned two weeks ago, when it was known that a Chicha feast was to take place in the village of Cangandi. She had gone to Querpepe telling him that his son would make her daughter a fine husband and it would be nice if the happy event could take place during the up-and-coming Chicha feast. He agreed. It is hard for me to believe that Nana Pepe Soule is Riekena's wife because she is so different from him in spirit and friendliness, but nevertheless it is a fact. Riekena was to go and kidnap the son of Querpepe tonight, with the help of several village friends. Nana Pepe Soule further stated that we had arrived at a very good time, as she was just about to tell Titi Olo that she'd found a husband for her and that he was coming tonight to fill her hammock. I was a bit taken aback by this. The girl, at this late hour, didn't know anything of the ceremony? I said as much to Nana Pepe Soule. She told me that she had warned the girl a week ago to be careful and watchful when the next Chicha feast came, for she might have a husband— but then she'd been doing this for two years.

Nana Pepe Soule called out: "Titi Olo, Takwele." "Come here!"

A young and very pretty girl came into the cooking hut. She looked from her mother to Wardada to me and back to her mother again. Then her eyes opened in comprehension that the White One wasn't just visiting at this hour of the evening. It would have to be something special to make women walk that far at dusk and that something special was probably her own wedding.

"Put your best mola on after you wash well in the river," began Nana Pepe Soule. "A Man comes to lie with you tonight in your hammock. He is your husband."

The girl turned and went away saying "Ayah" or yes, in a small voice.

"That was that!" I thought. I wondered what my own reaction would have been if my mother, when I was fourteen, had told me something similar. I probably would have bolted for the door and stayed away from home for several days.

But here, the girl calmly accepted the news and went back to her hut to prepare for the affair.

An hour later there was a commotion from across the river. Riekena and several village men were pulling behind them and with them the obviously reluctant groom. He kept shouting at the top of his loudly protesting lungs that he wasn't going through with this. He didn't want a wife. He wasn't growing enough food to feed a bird, never mind a whole woman. He liked Cangandi and didn't want to leave. Why were his friends, his life-long friends, his pals doing this awful thing to him? Why did his chief permit him to be carried off bodily to a whole houseful of women? "I want to go home and sleep in my own hut!" he finished.

"Eeeeeeeeeeeaaaaah!" sighed Nana Pepe Soule slapping her bulbous palms down on her equally bulbous knee caps. "It's always like this with the good men." She smiled and got up to get some gourds of chocolate drink for the advancing men.

A wail went up from the sleeping hut. It was Titi Olo. She was also protesting loudly against the whole Cuna race. Since the boy obviously didn't want a wife, she too wasn't going to go through with this. He would do without one. The sound of laughter went up from the other women in the hut who were helping the girl to dress.

Wardada and I went over to look into the sleeping hut. Titi Olo was sitting on the side of her hammock weeping vehemently. Fifteen minutes later Querpepe's son was bodily carried into the hut on the backs of several men and dumped unceremoniously into the girl's hammock. Titi Olo cried out that she didn't like the boy. He cried out that the last thought on his mind was the girl. Everyone kept telling them to stay awhile together in the hammock and find out whether they liked each other or not. Titi Olo emitted such a wail of despair at the thought of the action suggested that Querpepe's son bolted out of the hammock like a man from a haunted house and tried to run out of the hut. He was headed off at both doors by the men who promptly carried him back and dumped him into the girl's hammock. A small fire was built under the hammock then Nana Pepe Soule came into the hut. Titi Olo was sobbing quietly. The boy was looking about feverishly for an escape route. She came over, Nana Pepe Soule, and started to rock the hammock back and forth gently, speaking to them in a motherly low voice:

"Now both of you, my son and my daughter. Stay awhile in the hammock. It is not necessary for you to do anything else but stay awake and perhaps talk to each other a little bit. There is much to learn. Soon all of these people will be gone from the hut and you can be in peace to do anything both of you wish to do."

With this she motioned all of us out of the hut and we left.

Wardada and I made our way back to Cangandi Village in the dark rain forest.

November 22, 1963

What can I say that hasn't been already said millions of times on millions of lips. The shock, the disbelief, the feeling of loss, anger, pain. Yes, even here word has reached us of President Kennedy's assassination. I was out walking this afternoon when I suddenly espied Themos running up the path behind me. He was out of breath and looked upset. He told me that my chief had been killed, murdered by a man with a gun. I was naturally shocked, believing "my chief" to be Alfredo, the chief of Wichub-Huala Village. I said as much, that I was shocked to hear of Alfredo's death and wanted to know how it happened. Themos said "Soule, No—your Chief Kendy!" as he called him. I thought that the man had lost his mind. It was clearly impossible that the President of the United States had been assassinated. I rushed back to the village and to the radio and sat in shocked, stunned, unbelieving silence as report after report in Spanish told the story, hours after it had happened. Then I just sat there, turning the radio off. The reports said that a Cuban had done it. Did this mean war? What was happening to my people. The country must be in a turmoil. Who had done such a heinous thing? Johnson was now president. Were we at war with Cuba? What was happening? I turned the radio back on and found a very faint English broadcast and listened.

One by one, then, the villagers came into the hut until it was full with every living man and woman and child in Cangandi, and even some from Mandiga. Then Themos flew into a rage, got his shotgun, and asked me to tell him where the island of Cuba was. I told him in a low shocked voice that a council of our own elders would try the man who killed our chief and judge him.

Then Old One started to chant, then the women joined her. It was the Death Chant of the Cuna peoples. It went on into the afternoon while the people joined me in my own grief and sorrow at the unbelievable event.

A special council meeting was called this evening and the people sat in silence out of respect for the passing of a chief. Then parts of the Death Chant were sung by the Kantules. Themos told me they did this to make it easier for the soul of my Chief Kendy to go to the land beyond death. After the meeting I stood in council and thanked the people of the village for their beautiful hearts in thinking of the sadness of my people at this time. I thanked them in the name of all of the people of my tribe, and told them that I would go back and tell my people myself of how sad they had been for them, and how they had helped to send the soul of my chief to the land of Ibeorgan.

That night it was a long long time before I slept, wondering about what was happening, how it was being taken in New York—but most of all feeling sorrow in my heart for a wife and mother who had been one of our greatest First Ladies.

It's been a week now since the tragedy and life for me is getting back to normal now that I know that we aren't going to war or that my country has not stopped functioning from pure shock. A few interesting things have happened in that time which I wish to record here:

The day after The Day, Nana, Wardada, came to me and said:

"Sipu Tumat," she said as she sat down in the sleeping hut, "if there is a big fight between your country and Cuba, say that you will come here and stay in Cangandi until it is over. You can bring your mother and father and family. We can take care of them."

I loved the woman. "Wardada," I began standing and smiling at her, "you're great," I continued in English. Of course she looked at me strangely, but knew whatever it was it had been good from the expression on my face.

As a follow-up to the wedded bliss of Titi Olo and Querpepe's son I have obtained the following information.

The children stayed awake all night long under Nana Pepe Soule's watchful eye. They had to. An early sleep on one's wedding night was a sign of an early death. In the morning, the boy had gone out of the hut and back to Cangandi Village. At noon Titi Olo arrived at Cangandi bearing a gourd of chocolate drink. She stood outside of the boy's hut and called him to come forth and drink. He came out and did so. Then Titi Olo told him to get his hammock and possessions and come and live with her in her mother's house. He quietly and soberly packed his gear and trotted after her. That night the youngsters could sleep early or do whatever else they felt like doing, but nothing happened. The next morning, no one spoke to him; he had not as yet delivered the balsa log to the cooking fire of Nana Pepe Soule that told her that he found her daughter a very good wife and accepted. The same thing happened the next night and Nana Pepe Soule was beginning to worry. All the young people were doing was talking to each other. The next morning, Querpepe's son shyly asked Titi

Olo to come and help him carry home plantains, and hope rose in Nana Pepe Soule's heart. The girl did as she was asked and they were gone into the forest for a good six hours. When they returned, the girl was blushing and Querpepe's son was smiling widely. Nana Pepe Soule beamed radiantly at the obvious evidence of the consummation. The boy returned to the mountains alone and when he returned to the hut, he was carrying a balsa log for the cooking fire. This he laid at Nana Pepe Soule's feet. She looked up and laughed and asked him:

"You find my daughter a good woman and wife for you?"

The boy flushed pinkly and bolted back into the forest again. When he returned he and his young bride sat and talked as they would for the rest of the day and every afternoon thereafter until one or the other left for the house of the Great Father.

The marriage customs have changed considerably in the past few generations in San Blas. At one time, there was followed a most unusual and incestuous practice of leaving a bride to be with her father and in her father's hammock for a week prior to the wedding so that any hardships of "breaking in" could be tended to by him. To my knowledge, this practice is no longer followed and a young groom is left to his own devices on the fateful night.

17

HUNTING THE HIGH JUNGLE AND "JUNIOR"

The weapons of the San Blas are blowgun, spear, bow and arrow, shotgun, and machete.

To this day in a few mainland villages, the blowgun is used as a hunting weapon. For the most part, though, it is passé. There are very few individuals left who know how to make one or use it at all.

This blowgun is a six to 12 foot long hollow tube made from river cane and black palm wood. The making of one may take anywhere from three months to a year depending upon how long it takes the palm wood to age. The inner tube is made from river cane hollowed out with a hot coal and a bit of the blade of a machete set into a long stick. This is covered by the black palm wood and joined with tar from the mountains. This outer coating of black palm wood prevents the cane from cracking from either too much moisture in the air or a swift change in the weather. A mouthpiece is joined to the tube at the end that has the widest diameter with tar so that it will be airtight.

The bullets for his gun are darts, tipped with a poisonous solution which paralyzes an animal, made with the root of a certain type of behuco vine. These roots are crushed, and ants and other stinging insects are added and believed to add potency to the solution and the entire gourd is let sit from one to three months. The mixure is then "tested" by applying this solution to a dart. The hunter goes out and hits a monkey or bird with the dart and finds out how long it takes the animal to drop from the tree. If it is satisfactory to him he then has all the material he needs for "bullets" for a good four months.

The blowgun has gone out of use in Cangandi, but there was an elderly Kantule in Mandinga Village who still used one and I went to talk with him so that he might tell me a bit about this weapon. I was allowed to accompany him while hunting, he carrying the lengthy ten foot tube on his shoulder and a container of darts, made with the skin of a tapir, on the other. We sighted a "selee" or black wild turkey and he quickly set the gun on the trail and took a dart from his container and inserted it into the "muzzle" of the gun. The gun was picked up, aimed, and the dart was dispatched true to course with a "pppttttuuu!" sound produced by blowing a gigantic breath of air into the mouthpiece. From what I saw that day, the weapon was deadly accurate on the smallest bird which oftentimes I couldn't even see at a distance of 30 yards.

I was, however, concerned about a few details of the gun. What if a man inadvertently pricked himself with a dart? That would kill him as surely as it would kill his game. I was given a dart to examine and the Kantule pointed out that safety measures had been made to avoid this happening. The actual tip of the dart was not coated with the blackish poison. It started about a quarter of an inch *beyond* the tip. Therefore, if a hunter did inadvertently scratch himself with the dart, more often than not, he wouldn't be hurt. I also wondered how such a long projectile could remain in an animal when it was running and most probably brushing against trees, leaves, and branches. I was shown a tiny notch about two inches beyond the poison. If a animal did brush against a bush with enough strength to break the dart or pull it from his wound, the dart would break at this notch insuring that the poison tip would remain in the animal.

Then there was one final question. How could one eat an animal that had been killed by poison? He said that he could actually drink the poison, as long as he didn't have cuts on his lips or in his mouth. If the poison got into his blood first, without reaching the stomach, then he would die. As for eating the meat, the poison lost its kick when cooked and he told me that an entire batch of this solution could be destroyed by simply boiling it.

Another weapon still used generally by the Cuna is the bow and arrow. Young village boys are given small versions of the larger adult weapon as soon as they can walk. All over San Blas and on every island the younger village boys put their practice with this weapon to practical use, that of acquiring singing birds for the family. The usually pointed end of the arrow was enclosed with a blunt piece of wood and if a bird were hit with this, it would fall stunned to the ground. The bird was then placed in a basket until a cage could be made for it.

From my own observations, however, the birds were generally given the run of the island and had their wings clipped. Each family knew which bird belonged to whom and of course the birds themselves would know where home was by remembering who'd been feeding it.

The adult weapon is used less frequently now than 50 years ago. The arrows used in hunting are straight pieces of black palm, as the wood of the bow is, and these arrows are feathered with chicken feathers to insure a straight course in the air. No poison is used on the arrows and their use is identical to our own in the States. The string of the bow is made from finely woven behuco vine.

A third weapon used all over San Blas by the Cuna is the spear. Nowadays, the spears are tipped with iron points bought from trading boats along the coast. This weapon is generally used on all ground animals such as snake, pig, coati mundi, and what have you. The bow and arrow is used for the tree animals.

The fourth and most valuable device for the protection of an Indian against anything, and used for building huts, and farming is the machete. No Indian home is without at least four or five of these two foot long and razor sharp blades. Any old blades can still be used in the cooking hut by the women for cutting meat, cleaning fish, peeling plantains or cutting open fruit.

The machete is amazingly versatile. You can cut trees down

with it, dig, farm, and protect oneself against snakes or what have you. The machete is truly "the" weapon in the jungle.

For hunting small ground animals from coati mundi and agouti to a ground feeding bird, and catching those alive, a variety of different sized traps are used.

River cane is brought to the village and this is split in half with a machete. Now for catching say a dove, two strips of this split wood are cut down to a foot and a half's height. These are put down on the ground a foot and a half from each other and in a parallel position. Behuco vine is used to connect the two poles so as to produce a dome-shaped "lid." Remaining openings are closed with strips of wood and the trap is ready to be carried off into the jungle and baited. With a dove, it is good to use corn kernels scattered around a wide area and leading to the trap. The trap is placed on the ground and one side raised just a little bit to permit entry of a dove. A two-piece twig of wood is positioned at this lifted edge and will be used as a trigger for the trap. A very thin and fine piece of behuco vine is tied from the bottom pieces of wood on the opposite side from where the trap has been lifted and come around to just touch the "trigger." Any animal crossing this piece of vine would exert enough pressure on the trigger to cause it to collapse and the trap will fall flat to the ground, thereby trapping the animal. The cane itself is heavy and can keep the animal trapped and protected from any other forest animal until the hunter comes to collect his game. Antonio Pepe caught two doves in as many days using this method which is quite effective. Bigger traps made in the exact same way, only using three foot long pieces of cane, can be constructed for catching the bigger animals, up to and including a small jungle cat.

Trapping the larger animals requires a bit more work and patience. I will use a full grown tapir as an example. First of all it is necessary to find out which way the animal goes and which trail he uses to get to and from his watering place. As soon as the sun is an hour in the sky and one is sure the tapir will have watered by then, the hunter will go to the trail where he has found tracks or has spotted the tapir. He will dig a hole to a depth of about five to six feet, fitting as closely as possible the dimensions of the tapir. This is camouflaged by laying thin tree branches, then banana leaves, then a thin covering of dirt and general "path" material over the hole. When the tapir next comes down this trail, he falls through, and the depth and closeness of the hole to his own form prevent him from climbing out of it until the hunter can come. Sometimes it will be a week or so before the beast can be trapped. The danger here is, of course, the fact that a jungle cat may come along and find the tapir and dispatch him, thereby causing the meat to be lost by decay. Checking this trap every day manages, even if this does happen, to save most of the meat.

The traps are clearly marked by three parallel cuts in a tree just before the trap and on all sides of it. This same marking is put on the other side of the trail on a tree and on all sides of it. Regardless of which direction an Indian is approaching, he can see and thereby avoid coming upon the trap and injuring himself in it. When a man builds such a trap, he generally further insures against accidents, by giving its location in the council meetings in the village.

Now if the village is having difficulty at some time with a jaguar who insists on chicken for dinner, yet another method is used. A live chicken is tied to a stake in a wide clearing near the trail believed to be used by the jaguar. The men station themselves in trees with shotguns or spears. Generally this kind of hunting is done in the time of the full-moon to allow the men as much light to shoot by as possible. If the village is lucky enough to be possessed of an albino man, he can see clearly in the dark and is delegated the job of doing away with the animal. It may take as much as a month's worth of time before the animal comes along, and an occasional attack on the wrong kind of animal who attacks the chicken often occurs.

The Cuna are not as apt to hunt as are their Choco Indian brothers over the mountains in the Darien, Chucunaque River region. But occasionally the urge will take hold of a group of village men to hunt and this urge may last for a full month with much meat coming into the village at this time.

One of the best hunters in Cangandi Village is Antonio's half brother Achido (son of Antonio's father on Carti Island and his father's other wife). The boy is a year younger than Antonio, but already has a wife named Punolo Pepe. Actually, to call them villagers is not correct, for they spend about four months out of the year in the village, the rest of the time being spent in the jungle roaming about as they will, using the small rivers off the Mandinga and Cangandi for their roads. Achido is a happy-go-lucky boy and a good husband to his wife per her say-so. Achido came to the village one afternoon with his wife and within two hours had a raccoon, two iguana, and a squirrel in the cooking pot by his shotgun. Punolo Pepe and I talked for hours that day about the back country and her life there. I was at that time drying out my absorb-moist to protect my film when she picked up two balloons, a red and blue one, that I had been using when I ran out of prophylactics to protect my film from moisture. She was fascinated with the colors and I blew the balloon up for her. She laughed heartily. One balloon, the little blue one, was fat and round and full. The red balloon was elongated. She liked them so much that I tied knots at their ends to prevent the air from escaping and she tied them to the rafters over her hammock. When Achido came home, she pointed to the bright balloons and said:

"Look what the White One gave me. One is a female ballooona and the other is a male balloooooona."

Both of the young people laughed until they cried and were still giggling to themselves that night after we went to bed saying over and over again "balloooooona" and laughing. The next morning Punolo Pepe gave me a mola dress to thank me for the gift of Ballooona. It had a lively brightness to it and occupies a prominent place in my collection of Indian wares.

There is another form of hunting by spear that can also be called fishing. One day Antonio and I went to a mountain about five miles upstream where he has his "tree." Antonio Pepe is a carpenter by trade and sells paddles to the island Indians for their dug-out canoes. They are carved by machete out of the red sweet-smelling wood of the "sapa" tree, a kind of pine they have back here. He can make two big paddles and about four smaller ones during one back breaking day's worth of work. These he takes to the islands on periodic trips and sells them for 50 cents for a large paddle, or ten coconuts, and 30 cents for a smaller one or six coconuts. I always accompanied him on these trips to more or less look around in the mountains while he worked on his paddles.

We were coming home one late afternoon from the mountain when suddenly Antonio let forth with a blood-curdling cry, grabbed a spear, and went over the side leaving me to paddle the dug-out alone through the rapids downstream. I thought the boy had lost his mind and willed himself to the river. I had no idea what this was all about as he had never performed such an action before. I looked around in the water worriedly for him. He came up in a small pool of water with a good-sized "sabalo," a good eating fish, on his spear and paddled over to the dug-out which I had banked rather than run the rapids alone. He took the fish off his spear by pulling the tip of it on the side of the dug-out and was off again with a cry of "Uha buketara!" or "Many fish!" He reached a shallow stretch just before the rapids and stood up in the water. Time after time he threw his spear until we had nine fish in the dug-out. I held the dug-out against the riverbank watching him. He stood there, his legs apart, his fine golden body and back arching, the spear above his head and pointed toward the water in his right arm. He swayed from side to side and when a fish was sighted, he threw the spear crying "Haaaaaiiiiieee!" On both sides of him, the beautiful tall green awesome rain forest rose majestically, tangling itself into the very river. It was late in the afternoon and the sun was hitting Antonio and turning his skin even more gold than it normally was. He looked like some kind of a statue come to life, his muscles taut and ready, excited at the hunt. He was absolutely beautiful standing there. Cuna means Golden Ones, and now I could see that the name was the best they could have chosen for themselves. Antonio was golden and one and as much a part of the rain forest as any tree on the bank or any bird flying in the air. He was one with the forest and the forest was one with him. He was Indian and the lord of all that surrounded him.

When Antonio Pepe had caught his last fish of the day he put the fish in the dug-out, and, so happy with his catch, he raised both arms with the spear and shouted "Hooooooooiiii! Hoooy! Hoaaaiiiieee!" at the whole rain forest. He was a sight worth traveling 2,000 miles to see that day. We pushed off our dug-out and went home.

I opened my eyes and the birds were their usual effervescent selves in the backyard of our hut. It was morning and it wasn't raining. I turned over just as Antonio Tumat, the father of the hut, put on his radio and tuned into the Campesino programs. I lay there listening and waiting for "Junior," the cassanga who came down this time every day to start singing out in the lemon tree. He did. The two songs joined and I yawned. Suddenly a series of frightened indignant squawks replaced the song of the bird and I heard Themos' voice out there. I leapt from my hammock and went out to the backyard. Themos was about to dispatch the bird with his machete and I bellowed for him to stop.

"Heboir?" "What?" he asked.

"Don't kill that bird!" I stated.

"Why? This is good meat," he said.

"But he sings to me every morning."

Themos clearly couldn't see what that had to do with meat, but I wasn't going to let "Junior" die.

"I'll trade you for the bird, Themos," I stated.

"You want to buy this bird?"

"Yes, what would you like of mine for him?"

"But he has only a little meat on his body!" he stated perplexed.

"I just like to listen to the bird sing!" I explained not knowing what else to say about it.

Then I had an idea. Themos had been for weeks eyeing my brown attaché case with avid longing.

"I'll give you my case that holds papers if you give me the bird!"

The bird then, to punctuate my statement, bit Themos on the thumb and the latter threw him back into the trap in which the bird had been caught. He stood up.

"If I give you just this one bird you'll give me the case?"

"Yes!"

Themos then picked up the trap and handed it to me, beaming widely. I now had a bird. What I was going to do with it, I had no idea. I went into the hut, emptied out the case and gave it to Themos, sealing our bargain. Wardada thought me mad to make such a miserable bargain for a mere bird and said: "Your head's broken more than a little bit!" showing me that she disapproved, but that was beside the point. I wanted that bird alive, even if it were just to turn it loose again. I took the bird, cage and all, into the hut, emptied a basket of mine and put him under it. The bird eyed me from the wickerwork of the basket, then emitted a series of angry mutterings, and tried to lift the corner of the basket. Captivity clearly didn't agree with him, but if I let him loose immediately Wardada would have given my brain up for lost. I laughed and put a few things on top of the basket so that he couldn't lift it. He was quite a beautiful creature, most of his body being green and his head a vivid blue. Small growths of pink feathers almost encircled his neck. His beak was hooked and a pinkish brown in color. I wondered if it could be tamed. With this thought, Junior backed off to one end of the basket and charged the side of it with the top of his head. I laughed. When he knew this wasn't going to work he emitted a series of indignant cries, protesting loudly against this miserable treatment of baskets and what have you. I placed a banana under the basket and got nipped as a thank you from Junior. I lowered the basket and went about my business for the morning.

When I returned early in the afternoon, I found Junior out of his basket and walking around the hut as though he owned the place. I was afraid that he was going to take off to the rafters, when Wardada informed me that she'd clipped its wings so that it couldn't fly away. I was angry with her for doing such a thing, and now I knew I couldn't give the bird back to the forest. As the day progressed, I realized that he was quite a personable creature. If anyone walked near him he would back off chirping warning sounds from his beak. If the person continued to walk toward the bird he attacked, wings out, and bit their toes. He was then clearly able to take care of himself in a human situation anyway.

Within a week Junior got used to being picked up and handled by me. He slept in the rafters at the end of my hammock, but vampire bats began to bother him too much and I finally had to build him a small cage up there from pieces of river reefs and behuco vine. There he would go at night free from pestering bats. Every morning he'd sing and chirp his gentle beautiful song at dawn, come down out of the rafters via my hammock ropes and walk out to the cooking hut. He'd climb up onto a cooking log and loudly demand his breakfast. I gave him a small thimblefull of whatever drink we had that morning and a piece of banana. I had to watch the house dogs though. One morning Achu Sepugwa, or the white dog, stole Junior's banana right out from under his beak and the result was disasterous. The bird, outraged by such an action on the part of a mere dog, attacked the white dog and bit him squarely on the nose. The dog left emitting such cries of pain and fear that he brought all of us to our feet to find out what had happened. When we got to the hut the evidence was sufficient. The banana had dog teeth marks in it and had been moved. White dog's nose was bleeding. We laughed merrily. The dog never went near the bird again.

Junior and I fast became inseparable. He choose me out of all the people in the hut as his own personal human and that was that. He wouldn't even permit anyone else to pick him up but me. When I left to go swimming in the river or hunting in the jungle, Junior came running down the village streets after me and the people would say "Your bird misses you already." I'd stop and Junior would climb up my skirt mola and to my shoulder. There he would sit chirping happily.

When I'd come home from a walk in the jungle in the afternoon, the bird emitted a cry of delight and came running down the village street to meet me. His wings would be outspread and his beak almost touched the ground in his efforts to gain momentum. His feet ran quickly and when he reached me he'd demand to be picked up with numerous chirpings. Then we'd play, he nibbling on my ear and talking and I tickling him on the back of his very blue head, an action he adored. He was also my barometer. If it were going to rain, Junior began to sing his "Rain's coming" song and I'd know even before the sky clouded that it was going to pour.

One day I went off into the jungle leaving Junior at home as usual. When I returned, the bird came out to meet me and play as usual. He stayed right on my shoulder refusing to be put down and there he remained all during supper. He had a special series of songs to tell me how the day had gone and talk to me. He was by far the most conversational animal I've ever seen or been near and

I grew very fond of him. Later Wardada told me that the bird watched me going off into the jungle and tried to catch up with me. He stayed right at the edge of the jungle trying to spot me for a good hour before he came silently home to wait for me on the doorstep of the hut. Two more times he went to the edge of the jungle crying loudly for me to appear, then returned home. I never left the bird home after that, but took him everywhere with me. On one occasion I took him on a walk into the jungle and he gave out his warning cry, telling me of the presence of a snake in a branch of a tree I wouldn't have noticed had the bird not been with me.

Life with Junior, however, was not one of complete milk and honey. He had one habit which infuriated Wardada, that of climbing into the pepper trees in the back yard and chewing on the unripe peppers. If he just ate one she wouldn't be upset, but he'd take a bite out of one, drop it, then go on to another, then another, then another. I'd hear her cry in rage and go rushing to the backyard before she murdered him on the spot. I could not, however, keep Junior out of the pepper trees, nor could I change his pirate-like ways.

His stealing one morning was almost the end of him. It was early morning and I was in resting in my hammock when Junior climbed down from the rafters and right over my face, playfully nibbling on a piece of red hair as he walked. Then he reached my stomach and jumped onto the floor and went out to the cooking hut.

A moment later, Wardada emitted such a shriek that I thought Junior had pulled down a whole pepper tree. I sat up in my hammock and saw Junior, running for his life toward me. He entered the sleeping hut with something in his mouth, ran right up to me and dropped it. I almost fell out of the hammock when I saw what it was—Wardada's nose ring. She came running out of the cooking hut with a machete in her hands crying out loudly for Junior's early violent death and the early violent death of his mother, father, brothers and sisters and any children he might have had since he lived. The bird quickly climbed to my shoulder and sat there uttering small cries of alarm.

Wardada came up to me and told me she was going to murder

the bird. He had taken her nose ring off a log where she had put it for a moment, and stolen it, a horrible crime in the Cuna tribe. I took Junior off my shoulder by the legs, knowing I was going to have to think fast if I wanted him alive. I then walked to the side of the room with Junior squawking loudly in his upside down position and picked up my own machete.

"Because you have done a very bad thing" I began holding Junior in one hand and the machete in the other, "because you have stolen gold from my own mother, you will die. You have been my friend for many days, and have kept me company and I grew to like you, now I must kill you so that you will not hurt my Indian mother again by stealing gold!" With this I raised the machete further into the air.

"Soule!" "No!" cried Wardada. "The bird is your friend and *this* time he will not die."

I put down the machete and put a highly frightened indignant Junior on the ground. He climbed into the rafters and spent half the day sulking there.

On another occasion, when there had been a Chicha feast in the village, Junior was as usual on my shoulder in that hut. He climbed down one day to taste a bit of the chicha I was drinking, took a little, then climbed back onto my shoulder. Five minutes later he fell off my shoulder into my lap and I thought he was dying. He lay there, his wings outspread, whistling sharply. I uttered a cry of surprise, then quickly took the bird down to the river to revive him. When I dunked him, he bit me, fell to the ground where he shook the water from his feathers, part by part, then squawking vehemently, made his way back to my sleeping hut and the rafters once again. He had simply been a bit drunk as only parrots can get drunk, as I found out later from Jungle Jim.

When a "hunting fever" possessed nearly all of the men in the month of November, I decided to join in and construct a bird trap of my own. I spent three days doing so under the watchful eyes of the Indians in Cangandi Village who thought the trap not capable of catching a fly, much less a whole bird. I sat my trap in a tree near the village and baited it with banana and went about my business. Later on that afternoon a small boy laughingly found me and told me that my trap had caught "something." I went back to the village and to the tree to find half the population of Cangandi laughing and pointed to my trap. I had caught an iguana. Three days later, Junior managed to get himself caught and a week later, I had another iguana. Not one single wild bird met its fate via my Kelly Bird Trap which I don't think I'll patent. However, many of the village men were imitating it in hopes of catching iguana in the area.

18

DEATH IN CANGANDI

Themos' mother-in-law, Nana Tumat, the big grandmother or the "old one" as she is called, sent for me this afternoon as I was preparing to go again out into the forest to *try* and get some meat for the family and myself. Themos had lent me his shotgun and he made six cartridges full of shot for them. I went into her hut and sat down on a small wooden seat beside her. Eta and Tilar were at the other end of the hut tending a cooking fire looking none too happy.

"Sipu," she began, "did you send for the medicine for Themos?"

I told her I hadn't as of yet, but planned to have it by the time I returned to Porvenir.

"It is said," she spoke once again, "that I am to die soon. I know this is so."

"She hasn't eaten anything for two days and she refuses to take of even a glass of the morning drink!" spoke Tilar from over my shoulder.

"What is the house of the Great Father like in your land?" asked Old One disregarding Tilar's words.

She was resigned to die and she accepted this completely. The hope for life was gone, driven out of her by the pain of a sick body.

And now she wanted her own thoughts on life after death reconfirmed so that she might go in peace.

"The house of the Great Father is a long, long way from Cangandi," I began in dialect. "Your purba will travel far before it reaches this place of peace and much sunlight. Near the Great Village is a huge river where many many fish live and are caught by just throwing a spear into the water. The Great Father has planted many coconuts near the village and has set aside many many trees for those who come there. You will have much money to trade. The Great Father's banana trees are so numerous that it would take a month to walk through the place where they grow. He will feed you well and he has a medicine man so powerful that he will heal your new body of all the old wounds. At night by the fire you listen to Ibeorgan teach the ways of the new land, which are very like those of the old. You will swim and laugh in the good river. There your husband lives and there live all those who have gone before you. You will be as happy as in the first months of your marriage."

"The Great Father has bread in his house?"

"Yes, he has so much bread, 50 men work every day to make it for the villagers of his district."

"He has a medicine man to make me walk again?"

The tubercular sores had deformed her right leg to such an extent that she could not walk. I replied that the medicine man would make her walk again.

"I will swim and walk by his river?"

"Yes, all you want!"

"Naudi!" "It is good!" she spoke and sank back into her hammock weakly.

She turned her eyes toward me and saw the shotgun.

"You go into the forest?"

"Yes, I go to see if I can find meat."

"You will come back soon?"

"Yes, and whatever I catch you will help me eat, Old One."

She smiled and said "Ni!" "Go!"

I spent a little over an hour in the forest when I saw a large raccoon in a tree. I shot and hit him and was elated. He was a good 15 pounds heavy and would provide us with more than enough meat for the evening meal. The meat was the third best in the area. Tapir meat was the best, followed by iguana, followed by raccoon. I decided to stop in at Themos' house on the way home to show my catch to the old woman, but hunted for an additional couple of hours to see if I couldn't get something else specifically for her family. I didn't even see another meat animal. I knew that she wouldn't refuse meat if it were offered to her as a gift from a friend. Then her spirits would perk up considerably.

As I neared the village, my heart froze. The Death Chant was being sung. I ran the rest of the way and straight toward Themos' hut. When I entered, I saw a circle of women around Old One's hammock. All of them had their "tu nuadi," or good head scarfs down over their faces and they were chanting in a high pitched sorrowful voice and crying. I put down the raccoon and shotgun and went to the hammock.

She was dead. Her eyes had been closed by one of her friends and already her skin looked tighter on her face than it had been when I left.

"Oh No." I said and joined the women in their sorrow at Old One's passing.

When I was young and needed milk to drink,
Nana gave me her breast.

When I was a young girl Mother taught me
to cook and sew.

When I was a young girl
Mother taught me the ways of
my people.

The children were remembering in their chant, what their mother had done for each of them in turn when they were small.

When I was a woman, Mother
helped cut my hair, then found
a good husband for me.

When I lost my new baby, sang Eta
Nana stayed with me and told me of
the many new good babies who would
come to me.

It was very sad. The high-pitched heart-broken chant went on for 20 minutes, then stopped as though by signal. It was time to prepare the body for burial. No time could be wasted. It would take two days for all the preparations to be complete and the body then would have to be willed to the earth before the heat of the jungle got to it.

Freshly cut banana leaves were placed on the dirt floor beside the dead woman's hammock and we lifted her from her death bed and placed the body on top of these. Her best clothes were chosen out of the woman's belongings by her daughters. A solution of sweet smelling herbs was prepared in a gourd and the body was undressed except for the woman's pecha or slip, which was left in place, and the body was lifted and drenched with this solution. Her hair was then cut and combed, her nose ring placed in her nostrils and she was then dressed in the best of her possession. Her gold earrings were placed in her lobes and gold necklaces in much profusion were placed about her neck.

While we were dressing her body, banana leaves had been brought in and laid into the hammock of the dead woman. Wardada and Eta took care of this. Then we carefully lifted the woman's very light, wasted body into her hammock. All of the woman's necklaces of beads were then added to the gold around her neck.

Then the body and face were carefully covered with the woman's skirts and all her remaining clothes and possessions. It was found that the woman had many beads and necklaces which were unstrung and these would be tended to later.

As soon as these first preparations were complete, another round of spontaneous chanting broke out from the women who once again buried their faces beneath their red scarfs. No men were present. If a man had died they would be in charge of these preparations.

As the afternoon progressed the village women and the dead woman's daughters went through her scant possessions. There was cloth to wash and dry and beads to restring.

The wife of Querpepe entered the hut and began to string and weave some kind of complicated rope of six strands of behuco vine with the help of three young village girls, Sipu Pepe included.

A small tree branch was being carved by another woman into an Indian ladder. I watched the preparations from the side of the hut with sorrow yet interest in what was happening. When the tiny ladder was finished it was hung from the end of the hammock where the woman's feet were placed. It was believed that the soul was small, and resided in many pieces and parts of the body. When all of these pieces joined together the soul was about the size of a hand. When buried, if the soul was still within the grave it could use these steps to walk into the light of day again to begin its journey to the house of the Great Father.

When the vines of behuco had been woven into a rope, or rather two of them—one short one and one long one—these were tied about the woman's hammock, one horizontally about her chest area, and the other from the head of the hammock to the foot.

The children were fast at work restringing beads and making small circles of beads in red, green, and white. These were put directly on the woman's fingers and toes, three ringlets to each appendage, the red first, then the white, then the green.

Benches were carried in from the council hall and placed about the room and in a rectangle about the dead woman's hammock. All during the afternoon and early evening the periodic chanting went on. In all, six chantings had taken place by seven p.m. and the woman died at about two-thirty in the afternoon.

As the evening went into night I began to note with considerable interest the attitudes of the people in the hut. There was no horror at the fact of death, but only a heart-felt parting with a loved one. Her daughters and sons, when not keeping watch with the body, went about their normal household duties, and these had increased somewhat. The death now began to take on a kind of "social event" status. Pots of cocoa drink were being prepared and passed out to every visitor in the hut. A huge pot of plantains and fish was also being prepared so that any visitors from nearby Mandinga and Nana Pepe Soule's hut could eat when they arrived.

A young boy walked into the hut and I overheard his conversation with Wardada:

"What are you doing to Nana Tumat?" he asked.

"She's dead now and we are preparing her body and soul for the trip to the house of the Great Father."

"Mmmmmmmmmmm," replied the child. He looked around and found a group of children stringing beads. He went over, sat down and without being asked to, and began helping them. Men now walked in and out of the hut helping with the work now that the body had been prepared for the grave.

I looked around and found Themos sitting in a darkened corner of the hut across from me watching the actions in the hut. He then stared at the Old One's hammock. He examined the white scar on his elbow and looked from it to the hammock. He sighed deeply and sank back in his seat in silence watching the scene in sorrow. After about five minutes of silence he spotted one of his friends in the crowd, called out to him, smiled, and went over to greet him. I think he knows now that he has the devil that has taken his mother-in-law.

Several of the men in the hut were by now engaged in carving large, two foot high medicine dolls. It is believed that the soul of the Old One is still within the hut and will be here until the body has been buried. That is why each of her children sing and chant in a loud voice at the hammock, so that their mother might know now the thoughts that never were said in life. The dolls are to be placed near the hammock and the Kantule and medicine man will chant later in the night to give them life so that they might watch over Nana Tumat's soul until she goes to the house of the Great Father.

It was now about nine o'clock and women were arriving from all over dressed in their best molas and wearing all of their jewelry. I went home and decided to change into my best too if that was the custom. I did and returned to Themos' hut.

Two kerosene lights made from old tins were placed at the foot and head of the hammock of the dead woman. The hammock itself had now been sewn up and the behuco vine ropes tied tightly around it. The women were gathered around the hammock sitting on the small benches there talking in low voices of how good the woman had been in life. After an hour's worth of keeping watch with the body, the visitors were put up for the night in various huts around the village and we all went home to our own huts to sleep, leaving the family with their sorrow.

However Wardada came and woke me up and asked if I wouldn't help out the family during the night with the work for the morrow. I got up, got dressed, and followed her back to Themos' hut. I was handed Eta's two-year-old girl and told to rest awhile in a hammock. I fell asleep with the baby in my arms and didn't wake up until the morning when I found Themos standing over me looking at his daughter still fast asleep in my arms. Themos took his child and I went down to the river to wash and prepare myself for the day ahead. The body would remain in the hut all day long and there was to be a big ceremony tonight. I went into my own family cooking hut and Wardada announced that there would be no fire lighted today in her cooking hut as she had to help Themos' family with their cooking and preparations.

"No fire, no meals," I thought and knew that I'd fare badly that day.

I no sooner walked down the river path when a family swooped down upon me and literally carried me off to their kitchen where I was given a heaping meal of bananas, fish, and cocoa drink. I walked out stuffed to the ear lobes. Suddenly an identical situation occured and soon I was being offered food right and left. Evidently the villagers were convinced that if someone as "big" as I was didn't eat, I would die by five p.m. By the time the morning was over, I hoped that death came infrequently to Cangandi or I'd explode all over the river path.

I went into Themos' hut and found additional preparations being carried out. A small boat, complete with paddles, two tiny poles, seats, and a tiny rope tied to its bow had been made. Three large medicine dolls had been placed beside the dead woman's hammock and were keeping watch there. Periodic mourning sessions went on all day long and the sorrowful chanting filled the air.

At twilight Wardada told me to go get my hammock and bring it back to the hut and I did. Tonight the whole village would spend this last night with their friend, remembering her, chanting to the soul, keeping the lonely soul company until dawn. We had to stay awake the whole night through to keep watch and those who slept first were the ones who would die first, so everybody remained awake as long as possible, listening to the Kantule, who had been awake for more than a day singing the Death Chant of the Cuna peoples.

If the woman had been a good woman, her journey to the house of the Great Father would be an easy one. If she had been bad in some way or another it would not be an easy one, but either way she got to the house of the Great Father and lived happily ever after. It does the Cuna peoples credit to know that there is no hell in their religion, although the interim 48-hour trip to the house of the Great Father was not unlike purgatory in some ways. I certainly hope that they keep this part of their religion intact and never forsake it for the belief that the Great Father is not a good God, but one of anger who throws people into eternal fires for the slightest reason—like following one's human urges or for laughing too much and not crying enough. Sometimes I stop and have serious thought sessions on the evolution of our conception of God. Our heaven is the most absurd creation of imagination we could have thought of—flying around, doing nothing all day but singing and praying when those two things are the things nobody in his right mind would want to go around doing for eternity. We omit sex, and in heaven there will be none of the joy this act gives us on earth. Our God, even though he's plagued us time after time with disease, death, sorrow (after all, he *does* permit this) is called the Benevolent God and the Good God. And if we go about desiring or doing any of the acts we're made to perform (after all, God *did* design us) he flies into a rage and sends floods and fires and death and destruction or what have you. He is called the Just God and punishes for all eternity the children of Adam and Eve who commited the first sin (how could they know what sin was when there wasn't any, and this free will—why, then did God give them free will when he must have KNOWN what it was going to lead to). Then the innocent children of these people merit destruction, death, plagues, disease and all kinds of miserable treatment when they didn't even have anything to do with whatever happened in the first place. I wonder about our own sanity in not examining facts concerning the Holy Divine Order which is called God and tagging right, right, and wrong, wrong, as we do in almost every minute thing that happens. The biggest thing, God, we avoid even discussing for fear that a fire will leap from the very heavens and destroy us all! We would do well to re-examine the primitive cultures and their religions and glean a bit of truth from these. Even then, there are several cultures which did concoct a vicious God placated by only human sacrifice and death ,but what could God placated by only human sacrifice and death, but what could brought to them! Perhaps this subject is best left to itself for fear of offending too many peoples who fear this book is going to jump out of their very hands and turn into a ball of fire on the bedroom floor.

Regardless, the Cuna do have a very sensible religion in which evil is punished reasonably on the trip to the house of the Great Father, and not by eternal suffering and damnation, fire, devils, or what have you. *Everybody,* even the worst murderer, eventually gets to the house of the Great Father.

If a woman has mistreated her children, it is believed that she would have to cross a very high mountain covered with thorny bushes to reach her destination. If she has so much as mistreated a dog, she will have to walk over very hot and sharp rocks. For other evils in life, other punishments have been laid out for the soul: biting by red ants, swimming through a lake of blood, running through a gateway made of fire, but then she, the woman's soul, reaches the eternal happiness of the house of the Great Father.

I fell asleep in Themos' hut among the Indians gathered there at a very late hour.

The next morning we were all up rather early. I was still rather sleepy when I put my legs over the side of the hammock and looked at the scene around me. All of these people had kept watch with their loved one. I was promptly carried off and fed royally once again, even before my morning swim in the river.

Late in the afternoon the final ceremony of the burial would take place and I was anxious to watch this as it promised to be most interesting from all of the preparations I had witnessed.

All day long periodic chantings continued around the dead body until about four in the afternoon. Two men untied Old One's hammock from the rafters and carried it out to the village graveyard near Querpepe's hut. A new hole had been dug there and palm fronds lay nearby, ready to be placed on the framework of a tiny protective hut over the grave when the burial had taken place. Two posts had been set into this hole and with all the villagers gathered and the visitors watching, the body was placed in the hole and the hammock slung from the two posts. The head of the body faced east. Immediately, a high-pitched chant broke out from all present. Everybody was crying unashamedly including myself at the loss we had suffered by the woman's death. A piece of cloth was placed over the entire grave and staked into place then banana leaves covered this, then came a thin layer of dirt. The chanting went on until the grave had been covered and the ceremony was half-over.

The entire mass of us went to the river to take a communal bath. This was to wash the woman's soul from our bodies in case it decided to try to stay with one of us and remain in the village. This would be horrible since it was now very vunerable to devils and could be stolen or even worse—it could haunt Themos' hut. But adequate protection had already been made for this.

While I was bathing at the river, Themos came down the path and spoke to me:

"Sipu," he asked, "You have medicine for this?" He held up his left elbow. I told him that I had thought of this and was going to the islands to get some. I would bring him back some and perhaps a stronger medicine man of my own people soon. He smiled and looked much relieved.*

After the bath we all gathered at the grave once again. Themos watched until we were all assembled, then spoke first at the grave:

"Tage Malo!" he said cheerfully. "We'll see you later." Then each and every one of us spoke these words to our friend whose soul was still lurking near the grave.

A long piece of behuco vine was tied from the head stake of the grave to the river and a man was dispatched into the river holding the tiny carved boat in his hands. Bits of plantain and fish had been placed in it. The boat was tied to this vine and all of us looked avidly toward the grave, then followed the string to the river. The soul was now on its way to the house of the Great Father.

* This promise was kept in December, 1963.

The entire gathering went back to Themos' house and began the ceremony for sending the soul on its way in case it was too lonely or sorrowful to go the way on its own. Each of us in turn before entering the hut stepped over a pot of green pepper incense to make sure Old One's soul wasn't still on any of our bodies. Then Themos threw a huge rock all around the area in which Old One's hammock had been lying, and new medicine dolls replaced the others, these were to keep Old One's soul away from the hut and send it toward the river and her boat which awaited her.

New dirt was brought in and laid over the floor where Old One's hammock had been, and Themos brought his and his wife's hammock to the spot and hung them there. The old was gone and the new life now ruled. Eta was the Nana Tumat, or the great mother in her house.

That night, tired and sad, I lay awake thinking in my hammock all that happened. Soon, within four days, I would make my way to the coast and back toward Porvenir and Wichub-Huala again. But the lives I had touched here, the memory of the people I loved I would carry with me. Then there was Junior; he was asleep in his tiny house in the rafters. I was very sad at the thought of leaving this village of Cangandi above all the other places I'd been in and lived in. The jungle Indians are very special, very wonderful human beings.

19

THE GREAT COCONUT WAR

Junior and I arrived safely and soundly on Wichub-Huala at the beginning of December 1963, and life again fell into the safe, secure, laziness of the islands. I planned to leave for New York around the first of January after spending these few last weeks "vacationing" in the area. The secretary to the governor of San Blas had left the area, and had been replaced by an Indian secretary who had been educated in Panama City itself.

Around this time, New York photographer Roy Pinny came to Porvenir and Jim was in the city at the time. He asked if I wouldn't show Mr. Pinny around a bit to the nearby islands so that he could take some pictures and I agreed a bit reluctantly. I don't like tourists. I don't like them because I have found not only from this trip, but others around the world, that they generally are a demanding bunch of people who are prone to make fools of themselves in most situations with native populations. It was with a great deal of pleasure that I found Mr. Pinny a joy to accompany. He just wanted to be introduced into situations where he could get some pictures of the Indians from an "in" standpoint and I brought him to the places in which I thought he would have the most photographic interest. He was most appreciative of my efforts on his behalf and was as pleasant and undemanding a person as I could have wished for. If only all tourists were as pleasant as Mr. Pinny there would be no reason for the present attitude of many foreign populations toward the beloved American tourists in their countries.

Christmas was less than a week off and I looked forward to spending it in the islands. It would be a Christmas unlike any other I had known and I was curious to see if the Indians near Wichub-Huala would do anything to celebrate this outsider's feast. Mr. Pinny would be going on his way by this time back to Panama City and on out to the Bayano River area to photograph the Cuna here and a little further up, the Choco Indians.

A young couple arrived one morning with a note from Jim. He asked me to make sure they got well settled on the island for they would be spending their Christmas holidays camping out on Porvenir. Their names were Michael and Wendy Baring-Gould, a perfectly lovely and wonderful couple and a total joy to have around for the holidays. They were students from the ILCA in Costa Rica. This was to be a delayed honeymoon for them. At the same time Jim gave me permission to spend the holidays on Porvenir Island in the hotel if I wished. I quickly replied that I would be delighted to do so and thanked him for his very gracious offer. I also told him that the young folks were doing fine, and had set up camp on the tip of Porvenir Island near Meditation Point.

I took Michael and Wendy over to Wichub-Huala Island and their reception by the Indians was warm and one of mutual infatuation. The Wichub-Hualans loved the couple and promptly took them under their communal village wing, taking them to all the surrounding islands and explaining local customs and ways to them.

Three days before Christmas I woke to find a very excited Alfredo at my door telling me to look out at the bay. When I did I was quite surprised. There was a huge white cruise ship chugchugging its way toward Carti Island. Jim had mentioned that the season for the cruise ships was coming up and I was delighted to find one in the bay. I was curious about where they went and how they conducted business with the local Indians. Michael, Wendy, and I went out to the cruise ship on a motor boat from Wichub-Huala Island to get a good look at the huge white ship and perhaps get a close look at the passengers on the islands, trading with the Indians. The huge ship dropped anchor off Carti in a deep porpoise filled area there and the porpoise themselves were having a field day with the huge craft swimming all around her and enjoying her bulky presence.

Several motor boats had already been lowered into the sea and passengers were already in Carti when we landed there in our own craft. One very well-appointed woman wearing a Chanel style suit and smelling of Joy was listening avidly to a cruise director with a thick Italian accent explain the Cuna peoples.

"They were head-hunters just ten years ago!" he finished.

We couldn't help overhearing the conversation and Michael, Wendy and I started to laugh uproariously, much to the consternation of the cruise director. He had evidently been instructing all of his charges that they were visiting dangerous and primitive lands and were therefore living dangerously and adventurously.

The lady turned to us and greeted us quite warmly, then asked why we had laughed. I explained that the nearest head-hunters were hundreds of miles from us across the Colombian mountains and she herself replied by laughing at the information. The cruise director drifted away.

"I should have known that they'd try to hoodwink us. Nevertheless these people are very colorful and interesting."

The lady went on her way down the street and Michael, Wendy, and I went over toward the schoolhouse on the island, wanting to spend a few minutes talking with the teacher about his island while we were here. On the way we were cornered by the cruise director who asked us what we were doing here. We told him and were about to continue on our way to the schoolhouse when he made a rather cutting remark about our presence. He asked us to refrain from any further contact with his passengers and leave the island immediately. None of us took too kindly to the remark and the Indian we were with replied in English that we had as much right, if not more, to be on the island as he did. I personally apologized though for interferring with his immediate business on the island, that of conducting a tour and told him that we would most assuredly not speak with any more of his passengers. He did have the right to request this, although our Indian friend was all for going right up to the nearest group and starting a conversation.

The cruise director, strengthened in his own belief that we were common riffraff, continued to speak quite out of turn to us and I became more than slightly upset with this man, who obviously didn't pay too much attention to the rules of common courtesy. He still wanted us to leave the island immediately.

"Do the government authorities know you are here?" he demanded.

I replied markedly that they not only did, but that we were here with their written permission and by the authority of the government itself. I further stated that I thought his language to be quite out of place and that if he insisted on detaining us or employing any further force to inhibit our free passage on an open island, I would take the matter up with his captain. He turned around and walked away in a complete huff.

Michael and Wendy and our Indian charge were also a bit upset with the man. Unknown to us, his white-suited charge had overheard the entire conversation and came over to speak with us immediately after the director had left. She said that she had been listening and would complain bitterly to the captain herself when she returned to her ship about the man's conduct. He was obviously out of turn.

"Upsetting the indigenous population is a serious charge!" she finished laughingly. The lady, whose name shall be withheld here, then asked if we wouldn't show her around a bit. I replied that the gentleman had requested that we not do so, and that I thought he had the right to ask. She asked then that we do this as a special favor to her, stating that she was a very good friend of the captain and if any difficulty ensued she would assume full responsibility for it. We laughed and the lady went off with us to the hut of the chief. The woman talked through our Indian from Wichub-Huala to the chief asking some of the most intelligent questions I had heard a tourist ask yet about the Cuna. We spent a full hour there. The chief was quite fascinated with the woman and gave her three eggs as a symbol of offering friendship. I explained the significance of the gift and she promptly replied by giving the chief a little gold charm she had picked up in Colon. The chief was overwhelmed by the expensive gift, and the woman replied that she hadn't had so much fun in months. We returned to the streets and the woman was given a grand tour of the village and explained the significance of everything she asked about. She was a delightful and intelligent person who took more than an average interest in what was happening around her. Meeting her that morning was a distinct pleasure for all of us. We took her back to the dock and then went about our business in the village of Carti.

The cruise ship left the next morning and soon Mandinga Bay was back to normal. I did however, have a dark memory of the cruise director. All in good fun, it was his kind that caused a good deal of misunderstanding between peoples, and eventually, this could lead to trouble, trouble such as the Tigre incident still vivid in the minds of everyone in San Blas.

Michael, Wendy, and myself spent the rest of the afternoon on Porvenir Island fishing from the dock. Wendy was causing all kinds of a commotion among the government authorities with her bikini.

Well, as it turned out we ran out of liquid gas for the stove in the hotel and had to construct a kind of stove in the front yard of the hotel with driftwood and three cement blocks. We cooked our fish supper that evening, which was delicious fried red snapper, and after supper Wendy and Michael went on over to Wichub-Huala Island with Alfredo and Machi. I decided to spend the night on Porvenir reading a book and perhaps doing a bit of half-hearted fishing.

I went out to the side porch and dock and threw in my lines baited with a fresh chunk of red snapper and sat with line in hand reading by my kerosene lamp light. I had reached page ten of the Ian Fleming thriller, starring James Bond, *The Spy Who Loved Me,* when my line pulled taut and Junior, who was sitting on my shoulder, gave a squawk of warning. The line, a 60 pound test line with a metal leader, snapped and I looked out curiously over the water, lit by the light of the almost full moon to find out what kind of a monster had done it. By the moonlight I found myself staring at the shape of a four foot long shark on the clear sand bottom. I stood up shocked and Junior jumped down off my shoulder and waddled into the hotel. I had always thought this section of water to be the most impenetrable section of water around Porvenir. It was almost totally surrounded by coral reefs and I had swum here many times without the benefit of either a face mask or snorkel tube. I had a good healthy righteous fit of anger at the nerve of that damned fish to come into the bay of water and went into the house and got three 100 pound test lines and three metal leaders and a piece of rope. The lines I made fast to the rope and tied the rope to the dock post set in cement. The leaders and a fresh huge chunk of red snapper were added to this and I threw my line in the water once more. Junior watched curiously from the side door of the inn as I began once again to read. Well, on page 41 of the book the battle was on. The lines quickly whizzed from the dock and I caught sight of a shark's fin careening for the reefs. When he reached these, he still had plenty of slack on the line. I got up and pulled back on the line to dig the large hook deeper into whatever part of his mouth it was in, then the fish went crazy running this way and that. Evidently it forgot where it had come in. The fin zig-zagged about the reefs in a complete panic, then came back to the right and sank under water. I had felt by the pressure on the line that the hook was well placed. I pulled it taut and waited. For two hours I watched and pulled occasionally and watched and pulled. Several times he charged right by the dock and I would pull the line in quickly. Then he charged out toward the reefs again. I felt if I wrapped the lines around the dock post, they would have broken. He might get loose at that. An hour later, the zig-zaggings had become less numerous, then he passed by the dock again. I hit him in the back of the head with a Choco Indian spear, breaking the spear in the process, but when the fin again lunged for the reefs the spear point was visible in the back of its head. He spent several minutes out at the reefs trying to get the spear out of his body, then he suddenly went into a panic and came back by the dock area, swimming about there, looking for an opening to get through. I couldn't understand this action at all. It looked more afraid of the reef waters than of whatever had it by the mouth near the dock. Then I saw why. Another fin came swiftly across the cove followed by another. They came in and lunged at the first shark and began feeding on him. They were much larger than the first shark and I was in a state of complete bafflement as to how they had entered the bay. There must have been an underwater hole in the reefs. My hate for sharks, however, did not go so far as to let this one be eaten alive while he was on a line without a chance to fight or run. I ran in and found my machete and ran back to the dock and cut the lines. The small shark didn't even have a chance. A feeding frenzy was on and even though I was shocked and horrified by the macabre scene before me, I watched it. When the water finally quieted down, I went to bed and slept uneasily.

I didn't get up until after Alfredo and Machi with Michael and Wendy arrived on Porvenir. Alfredo found the cut lines, machete, kerosene lamp and book with the broken spear and came running into the hotel to find out if I were alright. He thought I might have fallen in and been done away with by something during the night. I was fine and told him what happened. He too was upset by the occurrence and promised to look at the reefs and find out where the break in them was situated.

On the 24th of December, the day before Christmas, a private plane flew into Porvenir and I was very ceremoniously handed a huge shopping bag full of food compliments of Jungle Jim from the El Panama Hilton. There were chocolates and a huge Christmas dinner of cornish hen, cranberry sauce, potatoes, vegetables, soups, and all kinds of delights. I was so excited and ecstatic over the gift that someone might have thought I'd just been handed the Hope Diamond. I sent a very grateful note back to Jim for his thoughtfulness. I promptly invited Michael and Wendy to share Christmas dinner with me on the morrow, and they accepted.

A little bit later on that afternoon, I was walking down the beach on Porvenir toward Meditation Point when I spotted two floating coconuts in the water. Since they could buy two loaves of Indian bread and since we didn't have any for Christmas Day, I thought I'd trade a bit and acquire some for the meal on the next day by salvaging these. Otherwise they would simply float out to sea and be lost. I was walking the beach with these under each arm when I met the new Indian secretary to the governor walking toward the point. I greeted him and wished him a Merry Christmas and he shouted for me to unhand the coconuts, in no uncertain terms. I started to explain that I didn't pick them up on the island, but in the water, but he wouldn't listen to me. He once again ordered me to drop the coconuts and of course I did. I returned to the hotel and let the matter drop. He was probably in a bad mood and that was that. He probably wanted to be in the city for the holidays and resented being on the island, miles away from civilization. The governor was away in the city at the time and wouldn't be returning for a couple of weeks. He probably thought I picked the coconuts up on the island, which of course, I wouldn't have done. The coconuts falling on Porvenir Island were government property, but those in the water and floating out to sea were certainly not.

That night, Christmas Eve, Marine, the Negro handyman on the island and a very good friend of mine, Michael, Wendy, and myself went over to Wichub-Huala Island to have a few drinks at Juan's store. Marine had his guitar and the evening promised to be musical and happy. On the way over, Marine tapped me on the shoulder and said:

"You know Sipu, the new secretary has been asking alot of questions about you. He can't understand what an American woman is doing living down here. He ask me about you and I tell him that you here to look at the Indians and that you are my friend. You help that woman that I ask you to help when she was sick on the plane and I tell him this. Still, he asks alot of questions."

I listened in silence and thanked Marine for this news. He was obviously curious as I would be, he being brand new and not knowing anything about me. Marine had been referring to a Negro woman who had been taken sick on a plane and was running a bad temperature from a cyst she had in a very inaccessible spot. I had given her an injection of penicillin and spent the night with her until she could be removed, with a much lower temperature, to Panama City on the morning plane. Marine was still grateful for my having come over from Wichub-Huala to stay with her. There were no other non-Indian woman in the area at the time. In return now, he had done me the favor of keeping me informed of what was happening concerning me.

The whole evening was one of song and laughter and good cheer. The night was happy and we were all content to be there on a Christmas Eve. Marine played the guitar into the night and when we finally got back to Porvenir he played even more songs for us. I thought of all the coconut trees on the island as my own private Christmas trees and of the fruits as my "decorations" and felt very fortunate indeed and went to sleep.

The next day was one I shall not soon forget. Everybody went around hugging everybody else wishing them a Merry Christmas. Michael, Wendy, and myself had a very delicious dinner on the porch of the Cuna Inn with our own Christmas tree. We went out and hacked down a branch of a palm tree and had draped cigarette package silver all over it and topped it with a bright shiny silver star. It sat on the porch all day and Panamanians and Indians alike came up to look at our Christmas tree, bush style. All in all it was a wonderful day spent in peace and good companionship in the beauty of Porvenir.

Since it looked as though it might rain, the three of us spent the night in the inn, they taking the porch hammocks and I relegating myself to the bedroom with Junior. I slept peacefully all that night. Little did I know what was in store for the morning, or of the ridiculous situation that would ensue.

I was awakened the next morning by a pounding at the front door of the inn. I quickly got up and found one of the Indian National Guardsmen from the government installation across the way. Michael and Wendy were awake and making coffee out on our "stove" off the porch.

"Sipu," began the guardsman looking very ill at ease, for what I didn't know, "the Secretary wants to see you immediately with all of your documentation and papers. He told me," he added apologetically looking at the ground then up again, "to arrest you."

I stood there for a moment looking at the man, then bellowed: "What?"

Michael and Wendy had overheard the conversation and came up on the porch to listen.

The guardsman repeated himself and told me that he had orders not to let me out of his sight because I'd probably try to get away and go back into the jungle and then it would take days to find me.

"That's absurd!" I bellowed once again. "Why?" I asked beginning to take stock of everything I'd done since I had been in San Blas. Michael and Wendy looked amused by the whole thing but I didn't think it a bit funny at all. Furthermore, all of my papers were in Panama City. I had given my passport with the papers to Jim so that he could cash a check for me.

I went padding off behind the guardsman, who incidentally was wearing a side arm, a weapon they never wear unless they plan to use the gun. I was secretly frightened by the whole thing and wondered what great law I had inadvertently disobeyed to merit such treatment. Soon, though, I'd know because the secretary would certainly tell me. I was also angry. Why couldn't the guard tell me why I'd been arrested.

I sat down in the secretary's office, and Junior my parrot came scuttling in the door. With a squawk he demanded to be picked up. I picked him up, put him in my lap, and started to scratch the back of his head to quiet him.

"Where are your papers, Sipu?" started the short, very serious looking man right off. I told him that most of them were in Panama City and told him why.

"You don't have any papers?" he summed up.

"Of course I do! How do you think I arrived in your country?" I quietly asked.

"But your papers are not here?" he asked, spreading his arms in the question why.

"I can send for them immediately on the morning plane," I stated.

"You had better," he stated as though if they weren't here on the morrow I'd be shot or hanged from the gallows.

"What is this about, sir?" I asked.

"We'll tell you when we see your papers."

"But I understand that I am under arrest?" I further questioned becoming angrier by the second. This man was obviously out to have my neck and he wasn't going to tell me why.

"Yes, that is correct."

"Then I think you'd better tell me why . . . NOW!" I spoke in a louder voice.

"I would advise you to keep yourself calm. This is a very serious matter."

"Then before I'm put under arrest or before I allow myself to be put under arrest, I have a right to know what the charge is," I stated.

"When your papers come in, then we'll tell you."

"That's ridiculous. By your own law you are supposed to give a charge when arresting." I saw his eyes flashed and knew I'd have to use tact. "Listen," I began in a low friendly voice, "I know that whatever it is it can't be that serious. Let's talk as two people, not two people from different countries. If you were in my place, and particularly a woman, you would be frightened to find yourself in a strange land under arrest for an unknown reason. If your charge is just, then I certainly deserve to be jailed, but if it isn't then I can explain things right now and not have to go through either my embassy or through your own government." I had slightly hinted at a threat and hoped this would be sufficient to at least find out what I was here for. I smiled, he didn't, but shifted in his chair and put the eraser end of his pencil in his mouth.

"It will be necessary for you to send a message into Panama City at once for your papers. When they come, then we will talk further about the situation." I noticed that Marine entered the room and sat down on a bench to listen to what the secretary was saying. He looked very upset. "In the meantime, I have instructed a guard to clean out the cell below the guardhouse for you. You are under arrest until your papers come."

I lost my temper fully and irrevocably for the first time in San Blas.

I told the Secretary in no uncertain and loudly protesting terms what I thought of that rat-house of a cell, him, and his whole bloody office on Porvenir Island. I also told them that they would have to shoot me in order to get me into that cell and he'd better let me know what I had been arrested for by the end of the day or there was going to be a war on, a huge one between myself and him. With this I rose and stalked past a stunned guard at the door and an equally stunned Marine and stalked across the island angrier than I have ever been in all of my years of living. Junior ran after me. I went storming up onto the steps of the Cuna Inn, threatening to throw Molotov Cocktails at the first person who tried to lay an unlawful, unjust hand on me and instructed Machi to tell me when the first man showed his nose on the porch from the other side of the island. Then I calmed down for a moment and told them all of what had happened. Michael and Wendy went off into uncontrollable laughter and the Indians at the inn thought the whole thing equally funny. I still could see little matter for laughter in the fact that a brand new secretary wanted to arrest me and put me in a cell for what, he wouldn't tell me. I sat still raging for 15 minutes before Machi asked me if I wanted some breakfast. I thanked him and sat down to eat. During breakfast, I started to laugh uncontrollably at what had taken place at the secretary's office. I felt rather shocked at myself, but nonetheless righteous at the effect of my stalking out and refusing to be arrested until I knew the charge. But if one person came over and told me that they were taking me into a cell, I would still be in a rage. The whole situation was ridiculous. The thought of people whom I had befriended and tried to help at every turn of the way sticking me in a barred cell was even more absurd. I knew that none of them would even think of shooting me in order to do this, and that, I knew, was the only way they were going to get me in a cell. One way or the other this was going to come to a head before the end of the day. I also knew that they knew I was furious and also knew that I would most probably have to be carried off bodily to the cell. I knew that they wouldn't do this either. They had no way now to back up their demands on me and I could further state my position—I decided to, merely for show, go in and get my machete and wear the thing. That would put a stop even to the thought of carrying me off bodily to a cell. I knew they wouldn't know whether I intended to use it or not, my having been living with the jungle Indians, who in a similar situation wouldn't have hesitated to wield the weapon.

I went in and got the machete and writing paper. I quickly penciled a note off to Jim telling him what had happened and telling him that I feared I was to be jailed before the night came. The plane came in and the note went off safely enough. At least now somebody knew of my plight. Machi spotted my machete and started to laugh. I told him why I was wearing it and he found this even more amusing.

Not soon after this, Machi came bouncing onto the porch to inform me that Marine and a guardsman with a rifle were on their way from the other side of the island. I took the machete from its case, actually somewhat frightened at having it on my person at that moment, but nevertheless decided in going through with my plan.

I sat back in my hammock and waited until Marine peeked his head around the corner of the stairs and requested permission to come onto the porch and speak with me a minute. I told him he could provided the guardsman stayed on the steps. I was hereby declaring the Cuna Inn off bounds to any and all persons with guns or any other weapons on their person. Marine's eyes found the machete and looked into my own questioningly.

"Oh good grief Marine," I started in English knowing that the guardsman didn't speak any, "do you seriously think I'd attack you with a machete?"

"No Sipu," he stated laughing, "but the people over there know you're wearing one now and they're sure frightened that you will." He hesitated then said "Can I speak with you for a minute?"

I replied that he most certainly could and asked Machi if he'd get us coffee.

Marine sat down on a small carved seat on the porch.

I asked him why I had been arrested and what crime I had supposedly commited to warrant such drastic measures as sticking me in a cell. What had I done—incited a riot, murdered someone, smuggled thousands of dollars worth of coffee across the border. What was it? You'd think I robbed the national bank or worse still, the National Lottery Office.

"No Sipu," he began. Then he looked up at me shyly and watched Junior climbing up the hammock strings of my seat. "It has all to do with coconuts, but don't tell anybody I tell you this."

"What in the way of coconuts?" I asked fearing that the authorities had gotten wind of my trip aboard the *Matilda*, but even that was not a crime . I did not help or abet the smugglers in any way. I had been an observer, that was all.

"Well, a few days ago, the secretary says he caught you stealing coco . . ."

"Is he out of his bloody mind?" I asked finally realizing what the whole thing was about and doubly infuriated with it. It was the two coconuts I had taken from the water.

"No Sipu, that's what he says. He caught you stealing coconuts and because he catches you doing this, he arrests you!"

"That is the most absurd, ridiculous, asinine thing I have ever heard in my whole life. The man is a complete lunatic. Go back and tell him that and you might further tell him the following!" I preceeded to tell Marine what had happened with the coconuts. I couldn't believe that the Panamanian authorities on Porvenir had nothing better to do with their time than arrest a girl for picking up two coconuts out of the water. "Good God, Marine, if they really wanted to get technical tell him I claim salvage on the coconuts and that I'll give him three and a half cents as his one-third share of the booty!"

Machi and Alfredo were in the kitchen near hysterics once again.

I had a headache. I was already fed up with this nonsense of the two coconuts and truly believed that the whole thing just wasn't happening. I was silent for a while trying to figure out why this was happening. I decided that the new secretary didn't know me from Eve, and he was after all *new*. He also wanted to make his authority felt immediately. He knew that I was quite friendly with the Indians in the area and wanted respect from them. Maybe this was his play for power and to replace Pacheco in the Indian minds. All of the Indians had loved Pacheco, he had been a wonderful person to them. But even knowing this and sympathizing with the purpose, I couldn't let him get away with a preposterous thing like arresting me for stealing coconuts I hadn't even stolen.

"Marine," I asked thoughtfully, "what is the secretary going to do?"

"He says that he wants me to talk with you to make you go into jail peacefully with no fighting."

"Tell your secretary to go to hell, Marine," I calmly and bluntly stated.

I told him what I thought his whole situation was *really* all about and he reserved his judgment.

"O.K. Sipu, I just work for the man."

Then I thought of the man Marine had living at his house. He had been arrested on a charge of murder in self-defense. Even this man was on his honor to go to the surrounding islands and wasn't placed in a cell. He returned every night to Marine's house and was permitted to go about as he pleased.

"That man you've got in your house Marine. He's on his honor not to leave the area isn't he?"

Marine nodded his head.

"Then go tell your secretary that I give him my word of honor that I won't leave the area. Tell him I won't go back into the river, and wouldn't even dream of it. Tell him that I'm staying right here regardless, just to find out what this situation is all about. When my papers come in we can talk more. O.K.?"

"I see what he says, Sipu," replied Marine who got up and left with the Guardia man tagging behind him.

He returned ten minutes later to tell me that the secretary agreed, but that I would be placed under island arrest, not being permitted to go over to the other islands and stay there until the papers came.

At least now the first battle had been won. I wasn't going into a cell. But I had to get my belongings from Wichub-Huala to Porvenir and told Machi that I was taking a dug-out for this purpose.

Machi looked at me sorrowfully and told me he had orders to not let me take any boats or he'd be thrown in jail in my place.

I stalked fitfully to the government part of the island and bellowed for Marine. I told him to go in and tell his secretary that if I couldn't get a boat to go to Wichub-Huala Island to fetch my clothes, I was going to swim, sharks or no sharks. He relayed this message to the secretary and came back and told me that the man refused my request. I went back to the Cuna Inn once again in a towering rage and telling everybody in listening distance what I thought of the new secretary, then marched over to the government part of the island in my bathing suit. In plain sight of everyone, I walked onto the dock and dove into the water and started to slowly swim my way toward Wichub-Huala Island, and would have gone the whole way had not Marine come out to pick me up and take me over personally with a swiftly written request by the secretary to Machi. He had changed his mind knowing that I probably would swim.

I picked up my clothes and came back to the island. Before I left Wichub-Huala, however, one of the dignitaries of the island told me that they had heard what had happened aand would be sending a dug-out to pick me up that night and take me into the river. The Indians were angry with the entire affair.

I returned to Porvenir Island and spent the rest of the afternoon relaxing and reading on the porch. This was certainly a most interesting arrest at any rate and my first. May I always be so fortunate as to have a resort hotel as my cell if anything similar happens again. (May it please Fate no!)

That evening while I was having supper, a National Guardsman came right into the inn without knocking or calling out to check to see that I was there. I gave him a monumental tongue lashing for such liberties and further stated that I considered this part of the island off limits for the duration of the time I would remain under arrest to any *armed* individual. After all, when no guests were here this was a private home.

I further stated that one never knew when thieves would come in the night to steal things from around the hotel. I told him that I'd keep a good watch from then on and if I saw any shadows that didn't look right around the hotel, I just might have to shoot them. I hoped that I wouldn't mistake any well-meaning people for thieves.

Of course he understood that I would shoot any person caught lurking near this hotel at night and that went for Guardia too. They didn't know whether I had a gun or not, so they could only keep away. I was left in peace for the remainder of the time I was held under arrest at night and during the day.

The canoe came from Wichub-Huala Island and I had been thinking all afternoon about the possibility of going back into the river. But I had given my word, and as ridiculous as the whole situation was, leaving might be an outward admission that I *did* in fact run off with two government coconuts. The whole situation was illogical, but that was beside the point. I told the Indians to go home and that I would handle it. They did.

Junior and I slept fitfully that night.

The first thing I heard the next morning was the sound of Jungle Jim's voice demanding:

"*Where is she?*"

Jim came charging into my room and I sat up in bed holding the sheets to me.

"Now what in the hell is this all about?"

I explained all that had happened since dawn the previous morning and Jungle Jim stood quietly listening. When I finished he bellowed:

"That is the damndest, most ridiculous, nonsensical situation I've ever heard of. You get dressed and stay over here, Joanne, I'm going over to talk to the secretary myself."

Jim returned in a rage. He said that he really didn't think that the coconuts had caused the situation, as I had thought, but after talking to the secretary he found out that it was true. He would fly right back into Panama City and talk to the necessary government officials that knew of my presence in San Blas and obtain my release. He didn't think it necessary to contact the embassy,

"They'd never believe it anyhow!" he stated.

He told me that he'd also dropped a few minor bombs into the secretary's lap after the latter finished telling him of the situation. He said that my father was an Admiral in the U.S. Navy in Washington (a total lie) and that he had been told yesterday of my arrest and was in a towering rage. He was some kind of political big-wig and would raise all sorts of hell if I weren't released immediately.

"You know these rich gringo families!" he finished.

I laughed uproariously. That was enough to frighten the tin god and now there were a few panicked mice in Porvenir's cellars.

Jim finished by asking "How did you manage to get yourself into a situation like this? I've never met anyone in my whole life who could cause so much trouble with two coconuts as you have."

With this parting shot he was off to his waiting plane and into the air again.

Sure enough, ten minutes after the plane had left Marine came padding fearfully toward the Cuna Inn. I invited him up and asked if he wouldn't like some coffee.

"Sipu," began Marine, "you should have told us who your father was."

I decided to play this God-given card from Jim to the best advantage. I replied that I had my own life to lead and didn't want to stand on the merits of my Admiral father. I preferred that the fact that my family was politically strong, rich, and in the military (practically bossing it) in the States was not known to my friends lest they should take advantage of this knowledge to befriend me. Marine was visibly upset.

"Why didn't you tell the secretary that you have permission from the government to come in here"

"I did, but he wouldn't listen to me. Maybe the next time he does this he'll listen to what is being said to him!"

He left and I was in peace for the remainder of the day.

The next morning I was handed a note as soon as the plane got in. It was a letter from the governor telling the secretary to hold me on Porvenir Island and to watch me carefully. A note from Jim told me that the situation was now completely out of hand and that I had become the pawn in an argument between two political factions. Enclosed, however, was a note from the government demanding my immediate release. I gave it to the secretary who looked visibly sick.

"Why didn't you tell me that you had permission to come here?"

"Why didn't you ask instead of acting like the National Security Office?"

He told me to get out of the office, and if he ever set eyes on another redhead in his whole lifetime that it would be one too many. I was still under arrest, however, so I went over to Jim's hotel, lounged on the porch, sun bathed, and continued to read my Ian Fleming novel for the rest of the afternoon.

The next morning I got a note from Jim telling me that all was well and that I was no longer under arrest. However the governor of San Blas was in Chiriqui Province and couldn't be reached for the formality of ordering my release personally which was still necessary. So I remained on Porvenir Island until he finished his vacation and I finally was released on January 7th.

All in all, the entire affair was looked upon as one of the funniest things which had happened in San Blas in many a moon by the local population.

I was, however, much overdue in my return to the States, and decided to leave the next morning, January 8th. Little did I know how difficult it would be to leave the Republic of Panama itself. Unknown to me, a situation had already arisen in the city which would later flare up into an unfortunate and horrible riot situation—the flag raising incident at Balboa High School. I had no inkling of what was to happen in the days ahead. If I had, I would have remained in San Blas until it was all over, and an unrepairable loss to me would have been avoided.

That night when I was sleeping I heard a guitar playing on the steps of the inn's back porch. I went out to see who it was and found Marine, slightly drunk and in a highly talkative mood. I decided to sit with him awhile and listen since I couldn't get back to sleep anyway, having already spent the night sadly thinking about leaving this place I loved.

Marine spoke of his life there, and how peaceful it was with his wife who was a good woman. She would be coming back on the plane in the morning. He told me of a Cuban invasion which had taken place two years ago on Colorado Beach across the point. Ninety-nine men had landed. He said that they entered a Panamanian village and the women kept the Cubans there, laughing and drinking and dancing until the men got help to round up the bunch and send them on their way.

We talked a moment about the wreck of a landing craft out on the reefs. Pacheco, former secretary to the governor, had put it there.

"Alot of things happen in this my country Sipu," Marine told me after each tale of San Blas.

One night a smuggling boat, the one out there on the reefs, had come right by Porvenir Bay and Pacheco had gone out to find out what kind of nuts in the smuggling business would be so daring as to take a smuggling craft right by Porvenir Island.

"That boat Sipu," he continued, "she have much much Colombian coffee on her and Pacheco say to the men 'you bring that boat to the dock.' They did. Later that night the men ask Pacheco, who not put them in jail, if they can go aboard their boat and cook something to eat. He was young then, he say yes. Then there was only me and Pacheco on the island. We hear the motors starting up and the canoa she pull away from the dock. Pacheco holler: 'Marine, get the boat' and we go after her. There was eleven of them all shooting and one of him shooting at them. He scare them so much they go right up on the reef. Pacheco, he was mad, mad. He take all the men back to the island and tie them to coconut trees and beat them up for shooting at him. Then the governor comes back and sees what happened. He calls for a gun and says to the smugglers 'If you've hurt Pacheco in any way, if there is one scratch on him, I will kill you!' Pacheco was as his own son, but he's alright, nobody gets killed.

"Then they go away and the coffee it gets locked in my storeroom. Then one night a boat comes with men from the government. They say 'Give us the coffee.' Nobody tells me to give anybody the coffee. They have guns. I go upstairs and tell the Guardia to radio the police in Panama. Then we fight with guns, all of us, but nobody gets hurt, they don't get the coffee that's all. These men were government people who wanted to sell the coffee in Panama. They were bad people these men. The police come and take them away and they take the coffee too. Lotta things happen in this my country Sipu."

The sound of motors came from offshore and Marine raised his head. I recognized the sleek form of the *Minet-Marcella* and ran over to the dock to say hello to Israel and Fernando. We spent an hour conversing in all. I was invited to join them for another trip down the coast, but sadly refused telling them that I would be leaving early in the morning for Panama City. They said that they too would leave early for the San Blas coast. I went back to Marine but he soon fell asleep saying:

"Lotta things happen in this my country, lotta things happen."

I was by now tired and went to bed and slept soundly for the rest of the night.

The plane arrived early and I had to rush my packing. I looked at the dock wanting to say a last goodbye to Israel and Fernando, but the *Minet-Marcella* had already pulled out. I hugged Machi and Alfredo and we all exchanged a sad "tage malo." I didn't want to leave at all, but I knew that I had to get back to the States. I sadly climbed aboard the plane with Junior, my beautiful cassanga parrot, snuggling in my lap and uttering fearful cries at being swallowed whole by this large silver bird. We taxied to the end of the runway and then rushed the full length of Porvenir Island. As we went by, Machi, Alfredo, Marine, and a bunch of my Indian friends waved us goodbye. I sat back in my seat and felt the plane pull us into the air and up from the island. Looking down into the bay, I remembered the flight here when each island had been a dot, unknown to me. Now each was a precious place full of memories and people I respected and liked. Then I caught sight of a trading boat and asked the pilot to bank us and take us down a bit so that I might look at her. Yes, it was the *Minet-Marcella* and the pilot tipped his wings to her in a farewell from his passenger to the sleek trader. Our shadow crossed her, then we were swiftly over the jungle. I traced the course of the Mandinga River below us and found the Cangandi. I saw the village, very faintly for a moment, then we were in the clouds and heading over the mountains.

Suddenly, I felt the pang of leaving. I sat back in my seat, clutching a still alarmed Junior to me. He was with me and would accompany me back to New York to be the unofficial head of the Kelly household from that day on, if I knew this bird. I had much work to do in the city if I were going to get back to New York on the 10th. I spent the rest of the flight thinking of what lay ahead—the work, the city, making notes in my mind for doing this and that—and knowing that soon I was going home.

20
GOING HOME

Junior and I arrived in Panama City around 7:30 in the morning on January 8th, 1964. While on the plane I made a most amusing discovery—I forgot my shoes which were still on the porch at Jim's. I was so used to not wearing them that I hadn't even given them a thought, however I couldn't possibly check into a hotel in a shoeless condition so Junior and I deposited ourselves into a cab and told the driver to stop at the nearest shoestore on Avenida Central so that I could purchase a pair immediately. Junior clung to me with a tenacity not seen to date. He had no idea what civilization was all about from his first sight of it. He decided if he were to survive at all he had to keep with me and hold on for dear life. The result was that my left shoulder was pretty sore for days.

My driver pulled up to a shoestore and I went in as fast as I could and sat down feeling more than slightly embarrassed by my shoeless condition. My heels were at the Hotel Roosevelt, but I couldn't go there without at least a pair of sandals to fetch my belongings. I sat down and a salesman came over to serve me. It is to his credit that the sight of Junior on my shoulder, sounding his alarm about this whole place in general, and my shoeless condition seemed to not phase him in the least. He waited on me with the utmost courtesy and I soon had myself an inexpensive pair of sandals so that I might check into the hotel in somewhat of a civilized condition. I thanked the man sincerely for his courtesy and service and left to collect my cab once again. We drove downtown to the Hotel Central, an inexpensive but pleasant hotel in the area of the Plaza Francia, Mercardo, or market place, and the sea wall, my favorite places in the city. I was shown to my room and proceeded to unpack.

It took Junior fifteen minutes to work enough courage to decide that this was indeed a temporary camping site, after so many numerous dangers had been met and dealt with successfully. He dislodged himself from my person and proceeded to make a preliminary inspection of the place and finally sing his acceptance by perching on top of the bureau and demanding a banana. I gave him this. It was certain that he thought we had been through no little amount of horror by this time. First of all, there was that huge silver bird that swallowed his mistress and himself and took off into the air—then there were the two huge crawling beasts which swallowed us the moment we landed and after we had encountered the place where all the shoes were. Lastly, there had been the hut that went up and down in the hotel, namely the elevator, which finally brought us to this spot and temporary peace. He must have felt as though he'd been to hell and back by now. At least now he knew that his mistress wasn't going to surrender him to face all of these perils alone. I picked him up, bellowing his protest of such mushy affection and hugged him, then proceeded to scratch his royal blue neck, an act he found a great deal of pleasure in. He was the single most beautiful creature which I have ever been owned by and I am not meaning to say the reverse. Junior owned me lock, stock, and barrel and I wasn't resisting in the least.

When I left the hotel room to go about collecting my belongings and arranging for both his and my passage and exit papers, he ran to the door thinking that I was leaving him there with only one banana to his name. I laughed and told him in dialect that I would be back.

Of the whole day's activities, my exit visa was the most difficult thing to arrange. I had to give a full explanation of all my activities since the day I landed and of what I had been doing in San Blas for half a year's time. A quick call to my friends in the government office hurried my paper through and I was on my way once again to arrange transportation for shipping several articles back which were a bit too heavy to carry with me on the plane. I also made arrangements to send Junior back to the States on a pressurized carrier plane. I would collect him in New York when I landed. I went back to the hotel and collected a happy-to-see-me Junior and brought him to a veterinarian to get a certificate stating that he was free from parrot fever. All went fine. I was anxious to get Junior safely into my New York apartment. I knew he'd like the place. There was plenty of room to wander about in and he'd soon get used to the kitchen being the cooking hut and my bedroom as the sleeping hut and all the other rooms, being just incidental streets on the way to each primary place. All of Wednesday was spent getting ourselves in order and we were ready to leave on a plane Saturday morning. Now I could spend the rest of the time shopping around for various articles in the city to bring back to New York, and also go roaming around at will, without the worry of not having this reservation, paper, or visa.

I was very tired that night, and hadn't had time to speak to a single friend of mine in the city. I went to bed early and didn't wake up until nine a.m. the next morning. I was hungry and Junior only had half a banana left which would last him for about the day, so I went out thinking to have breakfast over at the Napoli. I wanted a jelly donut if they had any. The walk was a long one, but I was anxious to simply walk around at my leisure and enjoy the city. Before I left, Junior sat on the dresser surveying me sadly, and crying out at the injustice of being left behind *again*. When I left, he mumbled his disapproval of my having left him in there alone with no one to sing to. I laughed and went down to the lobby.

I was rather surprised to find no one down there—not a single person in all of the lobby. It was generally crowded; I knew from previous visits. I thought not too much of this though and went out to the street and started to walk up toward Avenida Central. The first inkling I had that something was not quite right was the lack of traffic on the generally crowded street. A car went by loaded with men, and they were flying the Panamanian flag on their fender, an action not generally done. Then as I reached the first line of small shops at the far end of the street I *knew* that something was wrong. They were not only closed and locked, but many of the windows were boarded up. Just from a premonition, I took my camera from my shoulder and put it in my large straw purse so that I would look less like a tourist. I also removed my dark glasses and put them in my purse. With my braids, I now looked rather Spanish, more of a Madrid Spanish than anything else. I continued to walk slowly with a feeling in my stomach that I knew well by now—something was very wrong, and not just on this street but in the whole city. I wondered if a revolution couldn't be underway. It was not only possible, but very probable in this city. Election time was not too far away and that was generally when a revolution occurred if there was to be one that year. When I reached the First National Bank building I knew that whatever was happening, it was not a bloodless and non-violent brand of it. The entire building looked as though some kind of huge mob had overrun the place. The interior was burned out, glass was all over the street with bricks and stones. The doors had been torn down. It looked as though a riot had taken place. I began to seriously think of heading back to the hotel and sitting there until I knew what was afoot. Very few people were walking on the street. And even these were only men, no women. Several of these looked at me questioningly, then went on their way. As I continued to walk down the street, I found more shops burned out and now knew that I couldn't stop to ask anyone what was happening for fear of giving myself away as an American. Only the American owned and run businesses had been wrecked. This was clearly an Anti-American brand of something—what I had no idea. A dull roar was sounding from the plaza 5ᵉ Mayo and as I approached that place I found more and more people surging toward it. I stayed with the crowd fearing to turn and leave at this point knowing that someone would question me.

The first sign that caught my eye in the plaza was a sign saying in Spanish "Drive Out the American Murderers." I felt my heart sink into my stomach. The whole square was full of thousands and thousands of people, and by the looks of the throng in the center it was a student demonstration. National Guardsmen with riot helmets and rifles were trying to contain the demonstrators with no success whatsoever. They would not fire on their own. The roaring in the air from thousands of voices was deafening. Cars were overturned and were burning—all those with Canal Zone license plates. Students jumped atop all kinds of things to stand on and screamed for the death of every gringo in the Zone. I looked at the Hotel International and had to turn away. The Chase Manhattan Bank was still burning and there were fires all over the place. The Pepsi Cola sign was being pulled down across the square. Out in the plaza there was a car burning and dark blood still visible near it. Whoever had been hurt, had been hurt very badly. I turned to look in back of me toward the Canal Zone. The Pan American Building was still smoldering, lines of black soot going from all sides of it, straight up to almost the top. "My God," I thought, "what's happening here. Why are these things happening." In the distance I could hear sirens and the sound of definite gunfire from both machine guns and rifles. Then an explosion rocked the ground in the square and I turned quickly to see what was happening. A car was burning over near the railroad station across the square. A blond haired man was running toward the station; then he was caught, trying to climb clear up a lamp post there. National Guardsmen were fighting with a group of students and they could not get to him. Flames leaped from the burning car. A cab tried to get through flying the Panamanian flag. The only vehicles getting through, and these with not much success were those flying Panamanian flags. The man clung one desperate moment more to the lamp post then was torn from it and was engulfed in a crowd of students. The Guardia fought. The students were beating the man unmercifully. I watched in horror. Then the cab got through, with two Guardia on the side. They got to the man, put him in a cab, having to carry him there. Then the students attacked the Guardia and took over the cab. A student climbed into the back seat with a knife in his hand. I saw the knife go up then down with full force and the student climbed out and the cab was permitted to go on. The knife was bloody and the student raised it for his comrades to see. They cheered. I felt sick and tried to remain calm. Now I knew I had to get out of here. They had killed him, whoever he was.

"Jesus," I whispered.

A woman beside me caught my eyes and all kinds of panic must have been coming out of them.

"You are a gringa?" she asked. I looked at her, then nodded my head.

"Madre Mio, get out of here before they kill you too." She took my arm and whispered hurriedly. "Your American soldiers are firing on us from the Canal Zone. They have already killed more than a dozen people including a small child. You must get out of here. Now that the child is dead, there is no honor in being a woman. If they get you they will hurt you."

No, that was impossible. The Americans firing on the Panamanians from the Canal Zone? A child dead? I thought of my friends here in the city and in San Blas. Marine, Pacheco, and the rest. They would be with their country and I had to be with mine. What happened to cause this?

No sooner had the disbelief and thought registered itself than gunfire broke out from all sides and the crowd ran into doorways or dropped to the ground. Two men were laying on the ground in the plaza when the crowd cleared. One man had two bullet marks right across his shirt, the other was crawling toward us, dragging his leg behind him. I ducked into the hallway of an apartment building with the Panamanian woman with whom I'd been speaking.

I had my camera. I wondered if I couldn't get off a quick shot of this scene for later use in the States. I left the protection of the hallway, having already set my camera and ran quickly into the Plaza, dropping to my knees and snapping away as fast as I could.

The next thing happened so quickly that I didn't even have time to turn or see it. A rock hit my arm and the camera, knocking it out of my hands to the pavement smashing it. I stood up. A group of sudents were advancing toward me. I turned and ran for all I was worth toward the Kansas City Bar on the corner of a red-light district street off Avenida Central. I turned up this street and ran down it, then took a left at the Pan American Building. They were still behind me. I heard a bullet whizz by and it hit the first story window over a small gold shop on the corner of one of the Streets just off Avenida Kennedy, which had formerly been Avenida 4 de Julio. I knew one apartment building had a double doorway, and ran through it to the courtyard and back out into an adjoining street, leaving the students to think I'd taken refuge in the building. Still some followed, just in case I hadn't.

I ran into another doorway and stood there feeling as though my lungs or heart were going to burst in my chest. I couldn't run anymore. If they found me now, I didn't even have enough strength left to fight. I turned, hearing a sound in the hall and found a woman standing there with a bag in her hands. She had just come out of an apartment on the right hand side. Her eyes were red-rimmed and I knew she'd been crying. I could hear the heavy running foot falls of the students in the street. I knew she was going to scream for them now realizing why I was there. She evidently had a bone to pick with someone, but one thing was certain to me, I hadn't caused any of this. I grabbed her pushing her back to the hall floor and put my hand on her mouth. She bit it and kicked furiously and feverishly at me. Still I couldn't take the hand away. All she'd have to do is scream and I'd had it. I held her on the floor fighting with all of the strength left within me until I was certain that the students had passed, then she calmed down and just looked up at me terrified. I told her as quickly as I could that I was truly sorry that I had done this, but that I had no choice. I was in no way responsible for anything that was happening and I certainly wasn't going to be killed for somebody else's mistakes, whoever they belonged to. I got her to her feet and took her to the doorway, my hand still over her mouth. The street was clear. I let go of her and ran back down another street to the right of the gold shop and into another doorway there. I could hear the woman screaming in back of me as I ran, but at least now she couldn't have me harmed or hurt with her screams.

I noted with some relief that during this whole thing I had somehow kept my pocketbook on my right arm. I hadn't noticed it before, but now I was grateful to have it. My left arm hurt from the rock, my right palm was bitten into and bleeding, my clothes were marked with both the woman's shoes and the dirt in the hall.

I proceeded to get myself somewhat in order, taking the marks off my skirt as best I could and putting bandaids which I had been carrying in my pocketbook in case my feet, unused to shoes, developed blisters and tended to my hand and one skinned elbow. Fortunately, none of my blood got on my clothes. I got out my makeup and proceeded on the bottom step of the apartment building to make myself look as Spanish as I possibly could. I wrapped a scarf around my hair to hide the color, tying it in a typically Panamanian fashion, then put on much eye make-up and gold earrings. I examined the results in a small compact mirror and was relatively pleased with them. I then took out a cigarette, lit it, and tried to calm down. I was still shaking. I knew now that the only way I was going to be safe in the city was to get to the Canal Zone or back to my hotel. The Canal Zone was the closest, but that was completely surrounded by a high fence and no doubt people would be watching it. I would hate to be shot by my own poeple, them thinking that some irate Panamanian woman was climbing the fence to throw a grenade or Molotov Cocktail at them. I couldn't go back to the hotel, because the riots were in the way. I couldn't stay here, because somebody was sure to come along and question my being there and my accent would give me away for sure. The only thing I could do then was to risk a run to the Zone, hoping that I could identify myself as American before they started to shoot. Another incident like the one that just happened and the students wouldn't have to touch me, I'd die of fright! The only dangers in an attempt to climb the fence were (1) the fact that I might be shot by the Americans, and (2) the fact that I might be caught and held on the Panamanian side by students who were no doubt watching the street and probably had stationed personnel along the avenue for such a purpose. Then I'd have given myself away and would be subject to them and their mercy. The third danger was in stray bullets or snipers stationed along the Panamanian side of Avenida Kennedy. A rather strange and somewhat funny thought went through my mind—I wished I had a pair of wire cutters—but even then, it would take too long to cut the fence. I'd have to climb over the top and it was about ten to twelve feet high. I didn't relish the thought of doing this at all, but if that was the only thing which was going to give me peace and security I'd have to do it. I am very surprised now at my own coldness of thought at that time. I measured the distance to the fence, searched my mind to remember every obstacle before it, told myself at which point I would identify myself as American in as loud a voice as I could muster, then measured how long it would take me to climb over the fence. My only weapon was a small hunting knife I was carrying in my straw bag. It was about as useful as a toothpick at this point, but I couldn't tell when I might need it. I told myself what I must do when I reached the top of the fence–jump, then stay flat on the ground until my own people could hear me hollering enough to identify me as an American, and let me crawl to a point of safety. I also searched my mind to find the location of the houses of every friend in Panama City in relation to this point. The nearest was a good two miles away, by the American Embassy Building. I certainly couldn't make it out there. Then the only thing to do was try the fence. I left the hallway and walked slowly toward Avenida Kennedy and the Zone. On the corner of the street were a bunch of men and women looking right down at the point where the Zone road to Balboa met with that of Avenida Kennedy and the city. There were cars burning there and all kinds of gun shots emitting from the area. The people standing on the corner were muttering all kinds of obscenities against every living gringo and gringa on the face of the earth, and I joined in in as low a voice as I could cursing my whole civilization in self defense. Suddenly someone touched me on the shoulder. I turned my heart already in my throat and my body ready to run the distance to the fence and found the gentleman who had issued me a visa the previous afternoon for exiting the Republic. He flashed me a warning look and walked away and I walked after him. When we were away from the crowd he turned and said:

"You are not safe here, Miss Kelly. I cannot answer for the actions of a group of rioters should they come by here. Come with me."

I walked beside him slowly. A man ran by and asked if I weren't a gringa. The gentleman, whose name shall be withheld here, told the rioter that I was not a gringa, but a friend. The rioter looked from the gentleman to me then back to him, nodded his head and continued to run down the street in the direction of Plaza 5e Mayo.

When we reached the doorway of an apartment building on the same street, my companion turned and spoke with me.

"The situation," he commenced, "is most dangerous. I advise you to go back to your hotel and remain there."

"My hotel is 20 blocks from here and the riot is going on right in the middle of it."

He winced visibly and shook his head.

"Do you have any friends living nearby?" he asked.

I told him that I didn't and that I had been seriously gleaning my mind minutes ago to find out where I could seek shelter in the city. There was no place but the Zone for me.

"I am certain that you will be hurt if you try to get back to the hotel or to the Zone. I have a friend in this building, but I cannot say if he would be willing to keep you in his apartment under the present circumstances." He looked up at me apologetically, then added, "Come, we will try." I followed him up the stairs to the first floor of the apartment building. All of the apartments in the building led to a small balcony in the back yard overlooking a courtyard below.

We stopped here and my companion was about to knock on the door.

"Wait," I asked.

"What is it—you remember a friend's house nearby?" he asked hopefully.

"No, I can't go on not knowing how this happened or how it began or started. I have no idea what's going on except that everybody is out to shoot the gringos and the Americans are shooting at the Panamanians."

"The American students in the Canal Zone at Balboa High School refused to raise the Panamanian flag along with the American flag."

"Students not raising a flag?" I asked stupidly, not seeing how not raising a flag had caused this.

"*Our* flag," he stated, then proceeded to knock on the door. A viewer was swung open and the door opened. A tall thin man came out into the hall and looked from me to my companion. I went to sit on the stairs while they talked in hushed hurried whispers. The man shook his head and my heart sank briefly. I'd have to muster up enough courage to go over the fence now. Now I knew how an East Berliner felt before he went over to the Western Sector, via the wall. The conversation continued, then my companion motioned me to come quickly into the apartment. The door was closed and I found myself in a small neat kitchen. Air vents were closed on all the windows on that side of the apartment and the conversation continued. I sat dejectedly in a chair. Suddenly a knock came to the door. Both men looked around at me in panic, and motioned me to go under the table. I did. It was a round table and the table cloth hung almost to the floor, it would give me ample temporary cover until they could see who it was. The viewer was opened and the door opened. I could see a man's shoes in the doorway. A conversation took place and the visitor left. I was told to come out. I did and sat back in the chair again.

Finally the Panamanian government official turned to me and spoke hurriedly:

"You can stay here for a few hours until I make arrangements to get you out of the city with your embassy and our Guardia. We have telephone contact with the embassy and our Guardia are evacuating as many Americans from the city as possible. Most of the Americans left the city when the fighting broke out last night."

I thanked the man and was introduced to my new guardian, Mr. G. The official opened the door while I was under the table and left. I got up and Mr. G. looked at me for a full minute in silence, then deciding that I was harmless after all, offered me something to drink. I sat down and said that there was nothing I'd like better and thanked him profusely for his help to a perfect stranger. He made no comment, but showed me a can of coffee. I nodded my head. When the coffee was made, he handed me a cup and left me in the kitchen to drink it in silence, going into the next room. When I finished the coffee I went into the livingroom where Mr. G. was seated. Outside in the street, a mob could be heard running past and screaming. Suddenly an explosion rocked the whole building followed by a rock coming right through the window and landing on the floor after hitting a wall. Then the smell of tear gas started to fill the air and Mr. G and I dropped to the floor. The street blessedly quieted down but the tear gas remained and filled the air. I crawled into the kitchen, took two dish cloths, wet them, and crawled into the livingroom and gave one to Mr. G. He accepted it and put it up to cover his nose and mouth; our eyes were watering, but I for one would wait until I was sure no one was still out on the street to stand up and go into the bathroom and wash my eyes with water.

At this moment the door opened fully, and a wild eyed youth came into the apartment. He stopped short and stared at me angrily. Then I left the livingroom and went into the kitchen. An argument ensued in the other room between the youth and Mr. G. I knew that I wasn't going to be safe here long. The boy came out to the kitchen, sat down in a chair across from me and stared at me, his eyes full of anger. He stayed there for a full ten minutes, just staring at me until I couldn't stand it another minute.

"I am not from the Zone," I stated.

"You're American," he said vehemently and went into the next room with Mr. G. I found out later that the boy was Mr. G's younger brother, and a student at the university.

The door opened again and two women, a young woman and an older one, came in and looked at me startled. Both of them dropped their bags and went into the livingroom. I felt certain I would be asked to leave within minutes and got together my belongings.

The younger woman came into the kitchen and looked at me. She then looked at my elbow. I looked down at it, the blood from the scraping and cut I got there had come through and stained my blouse. She told me to come to the table, where she took off my inadequate bandaids and redressed the wound for me. She then asked if I'd like to take a shower and wash up a bit, then have something to eat. I thanked her with all my heart for her gracious help to not only a stranger now, but an obvious enemy of at least part of the family and went in to take a shower. The younger Mr. G., it is to be noted, was ordered by his elder brother not to divulge my presence to the students, and he never addressed another word to me while I remained in the apartment. We all ate in silence a delicious meal of lama beans and lamb. I helped the women with the dishes and sat down again in the kitchen. The waiting is the worst part of any crisis. I still didn't know if I were going to get to the Zone in relatively good physical condition or not. Even here, the safety was temporary.

The older woman, Mr. G.'s mother-in-law, the younger woman being his wife, came in and asked me if I wouldn't like to change into some other clothes so that I could see to the stain at the elbow of my blouse and I readily agreed. I washed the blouse out and hung it up in the bathroom. Outside in the streets the sound of shooting and rioting continued, breaking glass shattered shrilly and occasional nearby screams pierced the air. The whole city was as though in a state of war.

Afterwards, I returned to the kitchen once again. All of a sudden a horrible thought seized me—Junior—he was sitting all alone with a half a banana to his name in the hotel room probably in a panic wondering where his food and friends were. He was in the present riot area as the rioting had moved down near the Presidential Palace. I had to get him out of there, even if I didn't get one other thing from my room. I told the family that I was going out to get my bird and that I'd be back shortly. The reaction to my words was one of mass disbelief on the part of everyone in the room. Mr. G. raised his arms toward the ceiling and told everyone present what he thought of all gringos in general and me in particular then addressed me in low, pleading tones "La vida, la vida para una pajaro?" "Life, the life for a bird?"

I tried to explain that this was a special bird which only convinced everyone that I *was* indeed out of my head and that there was nothing they could do for me. I was told by Mr. G. that if I stepped foot out of the apartment for any reason, that I could not return. If someone saw me coming into the apartment, then perhaps his apartment would be burned out or his wife or family injured. He was right. There would be no use in rescuing Junior, then having both the bird and myself without a safe place to go. I could not and would not endanger the family by returning. The only thing to do then, was hope that Junior would be safe in the hotel room. I had also left a bag of cookies on the bureau. If he got hungry, he'd chew through the bag and eat them. At least he wouldn't starve to death. He could get onto the bed and to the bureau with relative ease. No, if nobody went into my room, then he would be safe. I stayed, the risk would not justify the end.

A plane flew overhead in the late afternoon and a loud speaker system announced from it in Spanish:

"There are snipers in the trees. There are snipers in the trees. This is a request from your government—return to your homes and stay there. Return to your homes and stay there to await a new report on the situation from your president on radio and television media. Stop these demonstrations and return to your homes immediately and stay there."

The television set was turned on and at last I got the full story from the Panamanian side of what had taken place to cause all of this. It seemed that on Tuesday, the 6th of September, the students of Balboa High School in the Canal Zone had violated an agreement between the Republic and the Zone, by raising an American flag outside of their school building and not raising a Panamanian flag along side it. American flags flew alone over all military installations, but in the Zone itself, the American flag was to fly with the Panamanian flag. The students disobeyed this law. Governor Fleming of the Canal Zone was away at the time. The Panamanians, of course, took immediate note of the absence of their flag and the presence of the American banner and soon word got to the university in Panama City.

The students there dispatched a delegation to the Zone to request the American students to raise the Panamanian flag. Their peaceful request, according to the Panamanian station, was denied. The students returned to their university and delivered an ultimatum which was published in every single paper in Panama City—raise the flag of the Republic with your own or take down the American flag from in front of the Balboa High School. The next morning, the American students raised another flag, the first being confiscated by Canal Zone officials in an attempt to avert trouble, as I later discovered. Wednesday morning the American flag again flew without the Panamanian flag. Again a delegation was dispatched to the Zone from the university. This time, reported the T.V. commentator, their request for a meeting was denied. The students returned to the university in ugly spirits.

Thursday, and the day that I arrived and went to bed early, unaware of the controversy in the city, students from the university marched on the Canal Zone carrying their own flag with every intention of raising it alongside of the American flag in the Zone. When they stated as much to assembled Balboa High School students, the latter group shouted from the balcony of their school, "No! No! No!" There ensued a battle between the university students and the Canal Zone police during which time several people were seriously injured. Immediately, full scale rioting broke out in the city, and four Americans were killed to date. One American had been killed while waiting in the Canal Zone for a train near the Hotel Tivoli to take him to Colon. In the bloody battling which ensued in the city, more than 200 Panamanians had been seriously injured and 15 had been killed. (When the total figures were in at the end of the rioting, 26 Panamanians had been killed, 236 wounded, 150 Americans had been injured and four were killed.)

Pictures of supposed American tanks guarding the border between the Zone and Panama City were shown. I later found these "tanks" to be troop carriers, and I found out from an American colonel who shall remain nameless here the following information "Tanks! We don't have any around we can use!" I further checked and discovered that not a single tank or anything like it had been brought into action during the rioting. The T.V. showed photographs of victims of the rioting being taken to the hospital, and an urgent request went out over T.V. media for blood. There wasn't enough on hand to handle the casualties. Regardless of whose fault this whole thing was, the Leftists were making political hay out of it, that was for sure. It was one of their best tricks.

I was offered the couch in the livingroom as a bed that night and lay down to rest. One thing was sure: if there was any truth to the Panamanian claim that the Balboa High School students had started the riots by not raising the Panamanian flag with their own then I had a bone, a huge one, to pick with them. They had almost cost me my life, and because of that I was going to find out the truth before I left the Republic, that was, if I left the Republic. I'd know who was to blame and I'd blame them with every bit of anger inside of me, remembering a woman in a hall, the horror of Plaza 5e Mayo, and two men had most certainly died there, and my own nightmarish run through the streets.

Saturday passed with more of the same: gun shots, tear gas, explosions, rioting, and what have you. Late in the afternoon a most unfortunate thing occurred. A young girl was shot and killed by a sniper in an apartment upstairs in the building. The family was in tears, both families being close to each other. A heated discussion ensued as to whether I could stay or not. The grandmother of the family had the last word. It seems that 15 years ago her sister had made a trip to New York and had lost her wallet containing all of her money in a city where she knew no one. An American man gave her enough money to wire home for funds and got a hotel room until she could receive a reply without making any demands on her. He hadn't even given her his name.

"Because of this you stay! But now we are even, my people and yours!" She spoke these words pointing an angry finger at me, then started to cry again. Whoever you were, kind man on a cold night in New York City, I thank you from the bottom of my heart for your kindness and the later result of your having saved me from possible harm or death, 15 years later in Panama City.

By this time I was so exhausted with the tension and continual threat of something's happening, that I went to bed and slept. In the middle of the night I was shaken awake to find a man standing in front of me with a machine gun. I thought I was about to be dispatched from this world, but found he was a Panamanian National Guardsman sent to take me to the Zone. I hurriedly got dressed, not having time to fully button my blouse before I was pushed into the kitchen with whispers of "Hurry, Hurry." I noted with some alarm the presence of yet another Guardia man with a similar weapon guarding the door. Evidently they were afraid sombody was going to try to kill me before they could get me to the Zone. With a Guardia man before and after me I ran down the stairs, still buttoning my blouse, and out into the cool silent night. I didn't even have time to thank the family in the rush. An armored car was waiting at the door of the apartment building. I was quickly shoved into the front seat and told to get down on the floor. I did, and with one of my arms wrapped around the gearshift, we started up. Almost immediately with the roar of the motor came the sound of two bullets being fired nearby. "Oh Lord," I thought, remembering the man in the plaza who had been pulled back from the Guardia. One man, the one on my right, was going to get out and find out who had fired the shots or where they came from but the driver stopped him and he hit the gas pedal as though we were in an airplane, not a car. The trip to the Corundu gate of the Canal Zone was the fastest trip I have ever taken in all my life. We were rounding corners on two wheels most of the way. No further incidents happened. The car stopped and I raised my head to find a line of G.I.'s before me, all with rifles pointed toward the Guardia car. I got out, thanked the Guardia and walked toward the line, feeling nothing at all, not even relief at being here, I was too numb for anything in the way of feeling.

"Halt," I raised my eyes from the ground and looked at the soldier.

"Yes?" I asked.

"Are you an American citizen?"

"Yes."

"Do you have your documentation with you?"

I replied that I had only the clothes on my back and my pocketbook and that I was American, but without my passport which was still in my hotel room in the city.

"Where are you from?"

"Listen, I'm from New York. What in the hell do you think I am, a damned Martian!"

"Alright don't get mad at me, there've been hundreds of people through here today and we all ask the same question."

I walked in through the gate and was directed to a bus that would take me to the evacuation center at Ft. Clayton. I boarded it and soon we were there.

I was given a tag declaring me evacuee No. 104 and directed to the U.S.O. center across the way where I was given sandwiches and smoked the first cigarette I had in days. I sat back in a comfortable seat and looked around me. There were nurses, all kinds of high school age children tending to this and that. I was left completely alone and couldn't have been happier at that point. Suddenly the realization that I hadn't been shot, beaten up, or injured in any way came over me. The relief was almost overwhelming but with it also came the realization that Junior was still in that hotel room and I had to get to him and the rest of my belongings. Only half the battle had been won. I looked at the clock. It was 4 a.m., January 11, 1964. I was exhausted and I needed a bath and change of clothes. I sat back in the seat and closed my eyes enjoying the fact that I was now secure at last.

Somebody called my name and I looked up to find a tall blond boy in front of me. He had heard that I spent half a year in the bush living with the Indians. Wouldn't I tell them a bit about it? He sat down with five of his friends. Personally, the last thing I wanted to do was talk about anything vaguely related to the entire Republic of Panama at that moment and was about to tell them so when a thought hit me. I asked the boys where they went to school. Balboa High School, said they. Now I was awake, awake and vengeful. Now I'd get the story. Nobody was going anywhere until I did. I began a harmless enough conversation with the boys telling them about San Blas, then steered off into the flag raising incident. All of the six boys authenticated what I'd heard over the T.V. station in the city. When Canal Zone officials had taken down their flag on Tuesday, furthermore, the boys stated that members of the American Legion of Balboa had *given* them a new one. I couldn't believe my ears. I asked each boy in turn to verify this statement. Each did, all six of them. I listened while the students continued their story, something akin to a white hot rage boiling inside of me to such a degree, that I feared for the very existence of the American Legion Building there when the boys finished their story. That morning I would have blown the edifice off the face of the earth, had I thought it would change anything which had happened.

On Wednesday, the boys told me of the other delegation coming from the university in town. Then they got around to Thursday and the opening rioting and cries of "No! No! No!."

"How do you feel now about what has taken place?" I asked one upper classman, trying to control the rage inside of me.

"I just wish I had a gun," he replied.

"You really think that, after so many people have died and so many others have been hurt or have come as close to getting hurt as anyone could?"

"Yes," he stated. "Nobody's going to tell us we have to fly our flag with anybody else's flag. I'll fight first."

"Don't you think you've done enough?" I asked, feeling all the anger released by the tension and waiting waiting of two days and nights full of fear.

The boy finished by hurling a curse at every student in Panama City across the table and I quickly got up and left the U.S.O., walking out into the cool morning air. I had to or I was going to murder that boy with my own hands. I walked around for almost two hours before I felt I could control myself enough to not slap that misled, unfortunate human being right in the face when I next saw him. I'd heard enough—enough to let me know what had happened and fix the blame.

It is my belief that the members of the Balboa American Legion, who openly helped and abetted the disobedience to American law by handing over another flag to the students of Balboa High School, should be found out and driven from that otherwise worth-while organization. Their actions in saying "Here, here's another flag to put on your pole kids, we're with you all the way," should be condemned in the strongest language and with the strongest action possible. It served to show the students that they had adult approval for their actions and further nudged them on into direct disobedience to their own law. Why in the world the parents of these children didn't say "O.K. dear heart, that's enough," I'll never know. All I can say is that the whole matter is beyond my power to understand, when the parents of high school students let their children for *three days* disobey American law and cause an international incident. Are there no *men* and *women* in Balboa? If anybody tries to tell me that the matter was beyond their control, then I can't see why. Balboa is possessed of a very efficient police force, fully equipped to handle the local high school children. I sum the whole affair up as the following:

The riots which took place on January 9th, 10th, and 11th were caused by, in my own estimation, the inability of a group of parents and an entire police force to control the students of Balboa High School and force them to respect and obey American law.

They were openly helped and spurred on by the American Legion of Balboa in the Canal Zone, and I do not mean this as a condemnation of that branch of the organization. I do state that whichever men in that branch who did encourage these children should be sought out and punished most severely for their actions. The actual rioting in Panama City I blame upon Leftists elements, but I'm afraid that the students of Balboa gave them their bone to pick. That was all that was needed. If Governor Fleming had been present in the Zone during the affair, the whole incident might have been averted. He is a very capable administrator and an intelligent man. I for one place the blame for the deaths and property destruction in the city on Leftist elements for the following reasons. It's an old trained terrorist trick to take advantage of any bad situation and make the most political hay out of it. They did here. They led most of the rioting students, and, it is my belief, caused most of the deaths. It is a fact that most of the deaths in Panama City were caused by bullet wounds from high powered rifles or machine guns. No machine guns were used at all by any American personnel, military or otherwise, during the whole affair from beginning to end. It is to be noted, too, that before the rioting got too much out of hand, the soldiers at the Hotel Tivol were using shotguns loaded with bird shot. Tear gas was used i place of actual shooting on many occasions. The deaths caused o Thurday night, when the soldiers were not using rifles and jus tear gas and the shotguns, were many. The tactic of killing a few t convert many to the cause is not new in the annals of terrorism. think many of the deaths were out and out murders on the part c the Leftists, many of whom were Cuban trained, to cause chac and confusion, hate and further rioting. I sincerely hope tha someday the Panamanians realize this fact before it is too late an remove these undesirable elements from both their society an governmental structure. Much death and property destructio will be averted in the future.

When I returned to the U.S.O. center on Sunday morning, was taken into the home of Captain and Mrs. William Thacher i Ft. Clayton. Their kindness and warmth shown to me in a time trial shall not soon be forgotten. There were many like this coup